The Death of "Why?"

The Death of "Why?"

The Decline of Questioning and the Future of Democracy

Andrea Batista Schlesinger

BK

Berrett–Koehler Publishers, Inc.
San Francisco
a BK Currents book

Berrett-Koehler Publishers, Inc.
235 Montgomery Street, Suite 650, San Francisco, CA 94104-2916
Tel: (415) 288-0260   Fax: (415) 362-2512   www.bkconnection.com

ORDERING INFORMATION

QUANTITY SALES. Special discounts are available on quantity purchases by corporations, associations, and others. For details, contact the "Special Sales Department" at the Berrett-Koehler address above.

INDIVIDUAL SALES. Berrett-Koehler publications are available through most bookstores. They can also be ordered directly from Berrett-Koehler:
Tel: (800) 929-2929; Fax: (802) 864-7626; www.bkconnection.com

ORDERS FOR COLLEGE TEXTBOOK/COURSE ADOPTION USE. Please contact Berrett-Koehler: Tel: (800) 929-2929; Fax: (802) 864-7626.

ORDERS BY U.S. TRADE BOOKSTORES AND WHOLESALERS. Please contact Ingram Publisher Services, Tel: (800) 509-4887; Fax: (800) 838-1149; E-mail: customer.service@ingrampublisherservices.com; or visit www.ingrampublisherservices.com/Ordering for details about electronic ordering.

Berrett-Koehler and the BK logo are registered trademarks of Berrett-Koehler Publishers, Inc.

Printed in the United States of America

Berrett-Koehler books are printed on long-lasting acid-free paper. When it is available, we choose paper that has been manufactured by environmentally responsible processes. These may include using trees grown in sustainable forests, incorporating recycled paper, minimizing chlorine in bleaching, or recycling the energy produced at the paper mill.

LIBRARY OF CONGRESS CATALOGING-IN-PUBLICATION DATA

Schlesinger, Andrea Batista.
The death of why?: the decline of questioning and the future of democracy / Andrea Batista Schlesinger. — 1st ed.
    p.   cm.
Includes bibliographical references and index.
ISBN 978-1-57675-585-3 (hardcover: alk. paper)
1. Youth — United States — Political activity. 2. Civics — Study and teaching — United States. 3. Political participation — United States. I. Title.
HQ799.2.P6S354 2009
306.43'20973 — dc22

                                                        2009011268

First Edition
13 12 11 10 09   10 9 8 7 6 5 4 3 2 1

Project management and design by Valerie Brewster, Scribe Typography. Copyediting by Todd Manza. Proofreading by Don Roberts. Index by Stephanie Maher Palenque.

For my parents, who have suffered the most
from my love of questions.

Contents

Introduction

Questions and Power

WHY?

Why is the first question most children ask. With this question we express, to the delight and the chagrin of our parents, our power.

In my life, questions have always been power. Asking them enabled me to overcome the challenges I faced as a young woman sitting at tables where I didn't automatically belong.

The link between questions and power in our democracy is at the heart of this book. As the market reaches ever deeper into every aspect of our lives, as consumerism grows and as globalization shrinks the distance between countries and people, where will our power as citizens in a democracy come from?

I think it will come from our ability and willingness to ask *why*. To question our government, our schools, our communities, and ourselves. Inquiry is more than asking simple questions that come with yes or no answers. It is a process of discovery, asking, re-asking, synthesizing, and evaluating until we can get close to something that approximates truth.

Inquiry is more than an act; it is a value deeply embedded in our notions of democracy. Democracy — which in this book I use to mean not only our representational form of government but also a system that values equality, justice, and the idea that each member of the group has something worthy to offer the whole — requires citizens who pay attention, who synthesize and analyze, who evaluate the information they

1

have uncovered, and who are discerning about its source. Democracy needs citizens who can inquire.

When I look at contemporary culture, however, I see an obsession with answers, not questions. I see an environment that prizes projections of certainty over the wisdom gained from questioning, and questioning again. I see us asking our media, our politicians, our self-help gurus for the answer, any answer, to help us understand the world around us. We live in a country where *The Secret,* a self-help phenomenon, was on the *Publishers Weekly* best-seller list for one hundred weeks.[1] We want the answer to making money, the answer to the proper way to raise our children, the answer to understanding in simple terms this complicated world of ours.

The Internet makes our addiction to answers even easier; all we have to do is plug a few words into the search engine and, like Columbus, discover what was already out there and pretend that it is ours. Our very definitions of curiosity are changing as Google becomes the lightning-speed mediator of our inquiries. We are less concerned with interpreting what we find online because we believe that the Internet understands what we want and will deliver it to us. We are less committed to discovering truths than to locating them.

Our schools send the message to children that the answer is all that counts. We test students to death, conveying the idea that correctly filling in the bubbles is the same as learning. Our classrooms become dedicated to the cause of test preparation, as science and its guiding philosophy—that we must discover, ask questions, accumulate evidence, make determinations—become optional. Although we proclaim ourselves a model of democracy, justifying our international aggression, we do not trust that young people can question the way their communities work, so we underinvest in civics. Instead, we look to financial literacy education and teach our children to navigate the market, not to question it—so that they will choose better, not so that they will participate in the creation of those choices.

This addiction to answers affects our democracy, too. We have the mistaken belief that even the most pressing challenges facing our country—climate change, globalization, health care, poverty—are problems to be "fixed" once and for all, if only we can find the right solution and the right person to implement them.

What we need to acknowledge, now more than ever, is that we do not know everything. We cannot know everything. Knowledge changes. Absorbing and acting on today's answers is simply not enough. The future is a moving target, and the ground beneath us will never be still. The only thing we can count on to see us through an uncertain future is our ability to ask questions.

I'll admit right now that I spend my days trying to change the world and have been doing so since I was a young person, when I represented the voice of over a million of my fellow students on New York City's Board of Education. I have come to understand, however, that no matter how hard I try, I cannot fix things today for forever. We cannot "solve" the debate between globalization and national interest. We cannot "solve" the debate over the appropriate role of government. There is no one answer to settle the ongoing conversation about the social contract that each generation has had with its successors since the beginning of our nation. No matter how hard I try, I cannot fix any of those things so that my grandchildren won't have to. What I can do is ensure that the generations to come are prepared to ask the questions that will force the constant reexamination that is at the heart of America's democracy.

Good educators understand the limits of absolute knowledge; they don't try to teach everything there is to know. The best they can do for their students is to teach them how to inquire so they can navigate whatever course they encounter throughout their lives. Yes, young Americans must know the difference between fact and fiction, between what is real and what is unreal. But the best way for them to learn and internalize these distinctions is by discovering them for themselves. We can cultivate in them the habits of mind of inquiring, critical thinkers. They won't get critical thinking skills through memorization, ideology, or groupthink, no matter how Web savvy they are. They won't get there if we send them the message that the answer is out there and Google has it. Answers cannot simply be retrieved; they must be constructed.

Are we teaching our children to question? Are they growing up believing that inquiry should be valued?

I don't know the answer definitively. Nor can I offer a how-to for emphasizing inquiry where it currently goes undervalued, for encouraging questions where intellectual and technological shortcuts prevail. In fact, to do so would be contrary to the values that have driven my investigation. This book is not an answer; it is my question.

It seems fitting, therefore, that questions would guide the exploration in *The Death of "Why?"*. In part I, I ask, Does our society value questions or answers? I discover that all too often the latter takes precedence, and I offer quick snapshots of the ways in which our obsession with answers manifests itself in contemporary culture. Our increased ideological rigidity, reflected even in Americans' growing preference for living only among those with whom they agree, offers protection from the risks of inquiry, disguised in a collective cloak of self-righteousness. Why question when you just know — and everyone in your town, everyone in your social network, really knows — that something is true? We encourage the media to do more opining and less reporting because we want to be told how to interpret events as they unfold — preferably if that interpretation squares with our political ideology.

The Internet is as much a part of our culture as it is a tool. More than a medium such as television or radio, the Internet is a place where young people live. It may seem strange to wonder whether the Internet, where so much knowledge resides, encourages inquiry. It may seem counterintuitive to wonder whether the Internet, where we can become "friends" with someone on another continent, leads young people to ask more questions about their world.

Yet these are questions that we must ask, because what I have heard, read, and observed challenges conventional wisdom. Young people are substituting search engines for an inquiry process. They plug in their terms and press Enter, print the first three articles that come up, rinse, and repeat. This automated search cycle is not inquiry. They do not think carefully about the question they are asking; they do not refine that question based on preliminary exploration; they do not consider the credibility of the sources they encounter; they do not synthesize what they read. The coping mechanism for unlimited information is superficial exploration and expedited searches for certainty.

If Google took the day off, would we have any idea how to find information? It is a profound irony that, just when so much information is available to us, we are raising children who are so poorly equipped to critically engage with it. If they only learn to retrieve, and not to interpret, when and where will they think new thoughts?

It is in our schools, however, that the lack of questioning should trigger the greatest alarms about the future of our democracy, and this is where I spend the most time in this book. In part II, I ask, Are our schools aspiring to prepare citizens or consumers? I argue that the focus on answers rather than questions demonstrates a changing understanding of the purpose of the public school system, that schools have moved from preparing young people who can question their democracy to preparing workers for our economy. The spokespeople for the latter approach say that it is in our nation's best interest. The evidence suggests otherwise.

America's employers aren't interested in test scores; they are interested in people who can think, question, adapt, and perform. On these scores, in survey after survey, employers register disappointment with the talent pool. We have created an educational environment devoid of curiosity, creativity, and inquiry, all in the name of coping with changed times that, in actuality, would be best served by graduates with those criteria in abundance.

Finally, in part III, I ask, When it comes to our political process, are we teaching our young people to be connected or engaged? I explore whether young people are learning enough about the world around to them to participate effectively in their democracy. They are constantly connected to one another and to the latest breaking news, but they do not read the newspaper. The youth who seek out the news online are snackers, grazers. They skim headlines on online news sites or get updates via text message. They are constantly in the know, but they are not more aware. They zero in on the news that already interests them.

As is true of the American appetite, excess does not mean fulfillment. Technology has certainly allowed young people to tell their own stories as a way of challenging the limitations of our corporatized and consolidated mainstream media. But without a shared knowledge about current affairs, without rigorous attention to the credibility of our sources, without the ability to read for meaning and not just consumption, how can we ask the questions that form the basis of collective decision making for our democracy?

I look at our presidential debates, powerful vehicles that are so important to our decision making but that are too scripted to demonstrate any kind of genuine questioning. I worry about the message that these closed, elite, and heavily negotiated sessions send to our young people. The current structure of our political debates doesn't give any citizen much hope that their questions remain central to our politics.

In some places across our country, such as in Hampton, Virginia, we see the promise of engaging young people in local politics. With the support of adults who realize that their best hope for a healthy community is the involvement of young people in deciding their own fate, Hampton's young people learn to ask questions. They have a role in the decision-making processes of their town. They experience the relationship between smart questions and effective public policy, and as they experiment with democracy, their community becomes a better place for everyone to live.

Hampton is not the only positive note. Much in *The Death of "Why?"* inspires even this naturally cynical New Yorker, such as the community discussion and decision making facilitated by America*Speaks,* or New York City's School for Democracy and Leadership, where every student is required to participate in a "change project" in their local community and where over 90 percent of the senior class graduates.

When I encounter college students who proclaim themselves activists despite only a vague awareness of what is going on in the world, I ask them, How can you change the world when what you know of it comes from content provided in text messages, headlines skimmed on the Internet, and updates to Facebook pages? I teach them how to read the newspaper critically, how to ask questions about what they read, and how to identify and locate the information that would enable them to act. I see them awaken and transform. They have the potential for effective citizenship, a characteristic that places them ahead of the one out of three of their peers who have no connection with the news on any given day. And they have fun in the process. I know, because I have seen it firsthand.

Unfortunately, however, these examples are exceptions.

Abundant in our culture, intrinsic to our education policy, predominant on the Internet, are incentives, expectations, and penalties that favor answers, not questioning.

One note to guide the reader: The research on "inquiry" as such is limited. Therefore, this book offers few psychological or educational theories about inquiry or how it is developed. In addition, although there is contemporary research on the effects of civics education, there are few definitive reviews of its role in history. Neutral, nonindustry research on financial literacy is limited as well. When there was no formal research, I interviewed practitioners and psychologists. I visited schools and talked to educators. I did my best to synthesize the available research on a topic that is remarkably unexplored — but perhaps that is precisely the point.

Fundamentally, this book tells stories about how current conditions do or do not inspire children to learn the value of asking questions. Naturally, I hope that these stories will inspire further questions.

Societies rightly fear that inquiry challenges the established order of things. Questions beget change. And despite its political utility during election years, change is a scary idea. I see a country mitigating the risk of inquiry. We numb inquisitiveness with consumerism. We fool ourselves into devaluing it in our public schools. We escape it through technology. Questions are a risky business. There's a reason Socrates was sentenced to death, after all.

A colleague of mine asked why I would write a book about inquiry and children. Why not write about one of the issues on which I've focused directly in my work — urban policy, the economic health of the current and aspiring middle class, education, or the preservation of access to the courts so that regular Americans may hold corporations accountable?

Yes, those are all issues that intrigue me. Addressing them has motivated my work, from my beginnings as a student activist, to directing a campaign to engage college students in the conversation about Social Security reform, to working as an education policy analyst for a New York City public official and mayoral candidate, to my current position as the executive director of the Drum Major Institute for Public Policy (DMI), a progressive think tank, where I've been since 2002.

But the issue that is the focus of this book underlies them all. If we do not have a populace prepared to question, a populace that is engaged through the very process of questioning, the issues that concern me have no future. How easy will it be to concretize legal obstacles that tilt the scales of justice in favor of corporations if no one is asking questions? What kinds of public schools will we have if the vast majority of Americans are disconnected and disengaged from their local institutions?

Whether young people are prepared to question events as they unfold, to question their democracy and the status quo — all of the issues I care about depend on this.

I've read countless books that claim to know the right answer or to explain how other people got the wrong answer; to demonstrate why some people don't get the right answer, no matter how hard we try to convince them, or how we used to get the answer right but now don't because of where we live, who we are, what we eat, who we love; to tell me which words are used to describe the answer, which impulses these words trigger, and whether we vote with this answer in mind. Underlying the "correct answer" approach is the mistaken idea that the health of our democracy depends on our ability to know the answers and to act on those answers, rather than on our ability to ask questions.

Inquiry is natural for us; infants inquire even before they have language. But they will only engage in it if they have the safety of attachment to at least one person. A child's explorations are cued by this person. Approving looks mean "explore more," whereas disapproving looks mean "danger." Children trust their caregivers unconditionally and, as a result, they feel safe to begin a life of inquiry. Trust and inquiry go hand in hand.

If we want our children to grow up inquiring, we will need to restore trust in one another and in the institutions of our democracy. It is surreal to live in a time when citizens who question their democracy are considered unpatriotic, whereas those who wish to slowly unravel the civic purpose of our public institutions in favor of the commercial purposes of our private institutions are said to have our best interests in mind. It stretches the imagination that teachers who encourage young people to question their local institutions would be attacked on editorial pages as propagandists, even while we trust commercial search engines to understand and deliver what we want to know.

Our democracy can handle inquiry. It can handle a citizenry asking complicated questions. In fact, such questioning is essential. It is entrenched power, feeding off ignorance and resignation, that our democracy cannot abide.

My question is not, Do we inquire more or less than we used to? The question I ask is, Are we teaching our children to inquire as much as the times demand?

Part I

Culture:
Questions or Answers?

"Stop searching. Start questioning."

GEERT LOVINK[1]

t was October 2008 and the stock market was crashing. I sat on the New York subway, immersed in my newspaper. Capitol Hill was contemplating a historic bailout, something to the tune of $700 billion. Companies whose Manhattan headquarters I had walked by just a few days before were now out of existence. People were comparing the coming crisis to the Great Depression.

As New Yorkers often do, I looked over my shoulder to catch a peek at what my neighbor was reading. It looked like a script: double-spaced, bound on the left side, a clear front cover. My eyes were drawn in to these words on the page:

> To attract money, you must focus on wealth. It is impossible to bring more money into your life when you are noticing you do not have enough, because that means you are thinking *thoughts* that you do not have enough . . .
>
> The only reason any person does not have enough money is because they are *blocking* money from coming to them with their thoughts . . . If you do not have enough, it is because you are stopping the flow of money coming to you, and you are doing that with your thoughts.[2]

I looked at the title in the page footer: *The Secret*. Having sold almost 4 million copies in the United States alone,[3] *The Secret* is a self-help phenomenon, but until then I'd never seen it in the flesh (well, a bootlegged version of the flesh). Its basic premise is that what you visualize—including money—shall be yours, a result of what it calls the Law of Attraction. The book is a dressed-up how-to, one that appeals deeply to our desire to "know" the formula for achieving all that we believe the American Dream can offer.

How seductive, on a day such as that one, with a looming economic crisis throwing our collective fiscal futures into chaos, to seek solace in a book that offers some certainty. How comforting to not wonder about what the impending collapse would mean to regular people like the two of us sitting on that train. To not focus on the causes of this crisis or whether a bailout of such epic proportions was the right medicine for the disease. To not wonder about what it means to the American Dream that home ownership had become such a toxic pill, or how our economy, so heavily dependent on Wall Street, could ever recover.

Questions. Questions. Questions. Isn't it easier to find solace in the answer?

Maybe on the train ride that day. But for how long?

There are as many definitions of culture as there are people to define it; as a "sphere," it is both nebulous and ubiquitous. American culture shapes and is shaped by the books we read, the television we watch, the food we eat, the jobs we work, the way we raise our children, the way we think about our country, the way we define success, and a thousand other things. Fundamentally, culture describes the choices we make and the values we hold that influence those choices.

Society offers rewards and incentives, and in today's culture we reward and encourage the sound bite, the high test score, the confidence and volume with which opinion—however ungrounded—is delivered.

Our national obsession with answers is reflected everywhere in our culture. We value solutions and being "right" over thoughtful inquiry; we value outcome over process, and the speed by which those outcomes can be produced. We make decisions, therefore, based on the desire to move as quickly and efficiently as possible toward a quick fix or the "absolute" or "the answer"—even if none of these things exist.

This desire is evident in our approach to public schooling, in the shallowness of our political discourse, and in the increasingly narrow role our media play in informing us. It is evident in America's addiction to self-help, an $11 billion industry, up from $9.73 billion just two years ago. In 2007, Americans generated $1.52 billion in retail sales after watching self-improvement infomercials. They spent $2.45 billion on self-help audiobooks. They spent over $1 billion on motivational speakers.[4] To put this into perspective, $11 billion is how much Americans spent in one year to drink bottled water.[5]

Although I applaud the instinct to better ourselves, I don't believe that true and lasting change will come about by plugging billions of dollars into an industry that has no real incentive to actually solve its target market's problems (who, then, would buy such books?).

We look for answers in ideology, whether religious, political, or cultural. In fact, Americans have become more fervent and more polarized in our ideologies, and this polarization is determining where we pray, for whom we vote, and even where we live. In ideology, we find refuge. Ideological solutions offer the comfort of uniform, predictable answers. And now, as our nation faces incredible challenges domestically and abroad, who wouldn't want a little bit of comfort and predictability? From that perspective, it makes perfect sense to read *The Secret* on the very day that the next Great Depression is forecast.

But our democracy pays a price for this comfort. Despite being citizens of the same nation, we operate increasingly within echo chambers, bubbles of thought and belief that are protected by virtual and geographic gates. In an echo chamber, we hear the same message bouncing back and forth, amplifying its supposed certainty. We spend hours online every day, among people with whom we agree. We listen to the news station that tells the story just as we want it to be told. We retire to homes near neighbors who will not question us, either. By click or by clique, we avoid questioning ourselves, each other, and our democracy.

Traditionally, we have looked to our media to ask questions, especially of the powerful, but today's press increasingly deals us answers and opinions. Media business models are changing, forcing media outlets to work cheaper and faster, an embodiment of the conflict between consumerism and inquiry in our culture. Our appetites are changing as well. We consume opinion; we are addicted to those who give it to us. Investigative journalists are still out there on their beats, trying to uncover what Richard Tofel, general manager of independent newsroom ProPublica, described to me as "stories of moral force," but the role that media plays in our country is changing to resemble the role of entertainment.

Our obsession with answers—and its partner in crime, instant gratification—is perhaps nowhere better evidenced than by the monumental role that Google plays in our daily lives and common culture. The Internet's blessing and curse is the information it puts at our fingertips. The way we interact with that information reveals the priority we place on trivia over investigation, consumption over exploration, speed over reflection.

Yes, the Internet offers abundance. But it also limits our ability to engage with that abundance. In other words, it is not just what we do to the medium; it is what the medium does to us. We must consider the notion that the Internet changes those who read and think within its borders, like children who grow up near power plants and wind up asthmatic. The Internet changes how we read, think, and breathe in other aspects of our lives as well. And the Internet is changing us in ways that profoundly—and, I believe, negatively—affect our ability to ask questions about and participate in our democracy.

Democracy requires us to ask thoughtful questions whose answers must be constructed, not simply retrieved.

We are born curious; we ask questions with our hands before we can speak. But there is no guarantee that our childhood curiosity will turn into a lifelong commitment to asking questions. We have to send the message that this journey—this journey of asking questions, of exploration—is as important as where we end up. The journey is a risk that our children, and our country, must be willing to take.

1: Inquiry Is Risky, Resilience Is the Reward, and Other Lessons from Childhood

"YOU DON'T HAVE TO TEACH BABIES TO ASK QUESTIONS," Dr. Gwenden Dueker told me. "If they could ask *why* at birth, they probably would—and once they can say *why*, they say it all the time. They are constantly exploring and picking up information."

Dueker studies infants and how they learn to categorize the things they encounter. From her post in Grand Valley State University's psychology department, she spends much of her time observing babies and the ways that parents interact with them. When I interviewed her on the telephone, I could hear her eleven-month-old baby in the background. I wondered what it was like to have a newborn when your business is studying newborns. Talk about pressure.

We are naturally inquisitive at birth—this everyone knows—but we don't automatically stay that way. In a safe environment, children are instinctively inclined to explore and inquire. "It's not something that you have to teach children to do," she explained, "but it is something you can prohibit children from doing."

Exploration and discovery, the first steps in an inquiry process, are natural behaviors for infants, but the next steps are not guaranteed, because infants intuitively understand what many adults suppress or only recognize subconsciously: that inquiry is risky. Exploration of the unknown is risky. What will happen if I touch this object I'm unfamiliar with, the infant asks when she looks up to her mother, awaiting the sign that it is okay to proceed. The adult asks, What will happen if I challenge this long-held assumption, this way of life that I've always believed to be right and true—although as we grow older there often is no one to signal that it is okay, or even desirable, to proceed. Inquiry can open us up, broaden our understanding of the world. Inquiry can lead to change. But it is and will always be a frightening concept.

If we avoid the risk of inquiry, however, we undermine our ability to build the resilience necessary to face future challenges. It is enjoyment of the *process* of exploring the unknown, of asking questions, that we want to instill in our infants. I believe it is also what we want to instill in our society.

Wisdom from the Crib

We can encourage inquiry through the environments that we create for our children. First, to feel safe to explore and tackle the unknown, infants need a secure connection to at least one caregiver. The research shows that securely attached children are "more persistent, cooperative, enthusiastic, and effective at solving problems than are insecurely attached kids."[1] This attachment must be physical; it cannot be replaced by technology. This physicality is important to bear in mind as so many of us are working longer and harder, responding to the realities of an increasingly unforgiving economy, and as our young children spend more time alone in front of television shows and video games than they do around family dinner tables.

Second, research shows that inquiry in infants is catalyzed by external contact. "Inquiry is mostly fostered in interaction with other people," Dueker told me. This requirement for interaction has implications for how we raise our children but also for how we think of one another. We cannot be physically isolated from those with whom we disagree, from those who are different from us, because it is these disagreements and differences that could lead us to ask questions. We need to bump up against the unknown in order to question it.

However, even if the unknown is there, ready to be bumped up against, not all children have the motivation to do so as they get older. Just as we can foster inquiry through the environments that we create, so too can we inhibit it. In this country, we care a lot about the self-esteem of young people. We believe that adolescents with higher self-esteem are likely to be more ambitious and more successful, and so we think that if we praise our children for their inherent intelligence and ability we are giving them the confidence to face new challenges. But as Stanford psychology professor Dr. Carol Dweck discovered, there's praise that leads to inquiry and praise that does not, and we have to be careful about which approach we choose to take.

I've heard immigrants to this country remark on the strange parenting behaviors of Americans obsessed with building up the self-esteem of children. It is literally foreign to these immigrants to see children praised so effusively and regularly. Although such praise is intended to give children the confidence to succeed, it can in fact also inhibit the intellectual risk-taking that leads to greater achievement.

Dweck is an expert in the relationship between praise, motivation, and achievement. She has worked for four decades with people of all ages in the United States and abroad, to understand what makes people ambitious. General opinion holds that ambition stems from self-confidence in one's intrinsic talent and intelligence. However, the results of Dweck's studies of young people go against the conventional wisdom and indicate that, rather than inspiring young people by telling them how smart or talented or perfect they are, we would be wise to praise instead their effort.

A 1998 study by Dweck demonstrates the power of praise to affect resilience and achievement.[2] Teaching assistants hired by Dweck offered several hundred fifth graders, divided into two groups, a three-round, nonverbal IQ test. The first round comprised relatively easy questions, and the children did well. In response, they were given two kinds of praise. Group A was told, "Wow, that's a really good score. You must be smart at this." Group B was told, "Wow, that's a really good score. You must have worked very hard."

For the next round of the exam, the children were given a choice: either stay at the same level of difficulty or increase it. Group A, praised for its intelligence, opted for the same level of difficulty. Group B, praised for its effort, opted for a harder exam. The children who were praised for being smart did not want to take a risk that they would fail. When faced with a challenge, they were more worried about losing their standing as "smart" than interested in what they could learn from the exercise to make them even smarter. They wanted to get the answer right. The children praised for their effort, however, looked forward to the challenge. In their view, the process of learning was what counted, and the challenge of learning brought them reward.

Dweck believes that there are two mind-sets when it comes to intelligence. Those with a fixed mind-set (an outgrowth of the messages children are sent about their value) "shun effort in the belief that having to work hard means they are dumb." Those with a growth mind-set, on the other hand, believe that one can work hard and get smarter. They enjoy challenges. According to Dweck's studies, students with a growth mind-set are those most likely to succeed.

Simply by signaling what we think is most important, therefore, we can change a person's motivation. Our children can be *intrinsically* motivated to take action that is rewarding in itself—such as thinking critically about a new and harder task. But our answer-obsessed society is organized to cultivate *extrinsic* motivation—rewards, such as the praise earned from getting the right answer, even on a simpler question.[3]

When we send children the message that they should enjoy the very process of learning, we cultivate in them the kind of motivation that will serve them as they confront the obstacles that are inevitable in life. When we praise their effort, we cultivate in them resilience that leads to achievement.

I believe there is a cautionary note in this for those who lead our nation. Our nation must be resilient if we are to confront the challenges ahead. To create this resilience, our leaders would be wise to worry less about reinforcing our national status — as the smartest, as the best — and more about cultivating in our citizenry the desire to learn, to question, and to confront the unknown.

Inquiry Builds Resilience

Unknowingly, and despite their stated preferences, the students of both group A and group B in Dweck's study were then given the same exam, a harder one. The "smart" group quickly became discouraged, doubting their ability. They "assumed their failure was evidence that they weren't really smart at all," Dweck writes. The hard-working group, on the other hand, remained confident in the face of the harder questions, and their performance improved significantly on subsequent, easier problems. They became more involved, "willing to try every solution to the puzzles . . . Many of them remarked, unprovoked, 'This is my favorite test.'"[4]

A final round of easy tests showed that "[students] who had been praised for their effort significantly improved on their first score — by about 30 percent. Those who'd been told they were smart did worse than they had at the very beginning — by about 20 percent."[5] Enjoyment of the process led to resilience, and resilience led to achievement.

Practitioners that I spoke with across the country echoed this view, without even knowing of Dweck's experiments.

They all linked the cultivation of a love of inquiry in young people to the cultivation of a strong spirit and persistence.

"As individuals, we learn better when we are curious and interested," Lynn Rankin of the Institute for Inquiry at San Francisco's Exploratorium told me. "That self-motivation of wanting to know something and struggling because you're so passionate you want to understand it, it allows you to persevere and cross a lot of barriers." Driven by questions rather than the need to have the right answer, and supported in environments that reward effort rather than status, these young people are better equipped to confront the unknown and the difficult. They are committed not just to the outcome but also to the process.

Our National Motivations Matter

I can't help seeing a parallel between these children who are praised out of their will to question and our own nation. We are a unique nation in our insistence that we are number one. I do believe strongly that we are a special nation. Although our nation has faced monumental challenges from the moment of our founding to today, we have overcome them faster than any other. To paraphrase the Rev. Dr. Martin Luther King Jr., the arc of history is long but it bends toward justice, and I believe that our nation's arc is shorter than any other.

But we are also a prideful nation, more so than most. (One study places us in a tie with Venezuela for first place, based on two measures of national pride,[6] a comparison that has very interesting implications.) Our national self-esteem is intimately connected to our perception of America's status in the world. The risk of this association is that, like the students praised for being smart, we are less willing to engage in the collective risk of questioning ourselves or the world around us.

As Dweck's and Dueker's work shows, the willingness of young people to question depends on the messages we send them. What about our national ethos? Do we cultivate in our citizenry the belief that it is okay to question our country, and that doing so is the way that it can become a better, stronger, fairer nation? Does this rule apply during presidential campaigns, during wars, during times of economic crisis? Do we believe, as a nation, that the exploration of the unknown is a worthwhile process in and of itself, or do we attach to that kind of questioning a value that makes it too risky a proposition for the average citizen to undertake?

Ultimately, our resilience as a nation will depend on our success in struggling with what we don't know, not on our success in maintaining our image to the world. But to struggle with what we don't know, we must first encounter it — and as more Americans sequester themselves in bubbles of sameness and ideological homogeneity, we're giving ourselves fewer and fewer opportunities to do so.

2: Ideological Segregation by Click and by Clique

WHEN WAS THE LAST TIME YOU CHANGED YOUR MIND ON something important? I've changed my mind a few times. One thing I can say for sure is that I've never changed it while surrounded by people who agree with me. But we are insulating ourselves from more and more opposing viewpoints — through the places we live, the way we vote, and who we turn to for news and information — and finding fewer and fewer catalysts to question our beliefs.

Bill Bishop has lived and worked for newspapers in Kentucky and Texas, on both the writing and the publishing sides. Today, he and his wife publish *The Daily Yonder,* an online publication covering rural America, including places that much of the mainstream media has abandoned. Bishop argues that our country has become increasingly segregated by ideology. Americans are moving to towns and cities to live with people like themselves, who believe similar things. We are clustering "in communities of sameness, among people with similar ways of life, beliefs, and, in the end, politics."[1] One way to see this trend in action is to look at our elections.

The increasing incidence of "landslide counties" (counties in which a candidate wins by 20 percentage points or more) exemplifies how Americans are becoming more homogeneous on a community level. Between 1976 and 2004, the number of counties in which the presidential election was a landslide doubled, from a quarter of the population to half. It is conventional wisdom, for example, that the 2004 presidential election was one of the closest presidential campaigns in history. Yet, as Bishop points out, nearly half of American voters lived in places where a single candidate won definitively. On a macro level, America is closely divided. But these elections aren't close calls in our communities, because we've moved to places with neighbors who believe what we believe and vote the same way.

Our changing demography isn't the result of mass migratory patterns such as those we have seen in our nation's history, but of people who are sorting themselves one by one. We are concentrating ourselves by belief, and the result is localities that are becoming "politically monogamous." Bishop calls this phenomenon the Big Sort.[2]

It was in his capacity as a columnist for the *Austin American-Statesman,* while trying to understand how certain cities like his were thriving economically while others remained stagnant, that Bishop came across the Big Sort. Despite an admission that his decision to locate to Austin was based on the same kinds of decisions that Americans are making throughout the country—to be in places that serve the food we like, offer the church services we prefer, and so on—Bishop believes that "democracy was not meant to be operating in an atmosphere where people don't meet or discuss or come across those who disagree with them."[3] If that were the case, would we even have a democracy? When we read the Declaration of Independence and the Constitution, we aren't exactly seeing first drafts. The Founders didn't share the same outlook on all matters, but through debate and discussion they were able to come to consensus.

There is little that will hasten the death of *why* in our country more effectively than raising our children in ideological homogeneity. There just aren't many incentives to question when everyone around us shares our views. And it is in our neighborhoods, where we spend so much time, that we could most easily encounter those with whom we disagree, those whose lives and experiences might lead us to question our values and beliefs.

Ideological segregation in America is perhaps a natural outgrowth of the increasing ideological polarization gripping our nation. Although some dispute the idea that all Americans are more ideological, the evidence is convincing that, at the very least, American voters surely are. Our ideological identification determines how we vote, up and down the ticket, and how we feel about the issues. In a study of the 2006 midterm elections, ideology was identified as a strong predictor of the party a voter would support.[4] If we are more ideological, and our ideology predicts our party, then we vote by party. No need to ask many questions there.

According to a study by Alan Abramowitz and Kyle Saunders, the gap between Democrats and Republicans doubled between 1972 and 2004. The same study reinforces the finding of a dramatically increased correlation between ideological identification, party identification, and positions on issues. On issues such as jobs, living standards, health care, and presidential approval, partisan polarization has grown significantly over time. Some political scientists, such as Morris Fiorina, claim that only political elites — not regular Americans — are more polarized; Abramowitz and Saunders disagree. Their study concludes that "these divisions are not a result of artificial boundaries constructed by political elites in search of electoral security. They reflect fundamental changes in American society and politics that have been developing for decades and are likely to continue for the foreseeable future."[5]

Despite President Barack Obama's impressive 2008 electoral victory, the electorate remained just as divided in 2008, segregated not only by politics but also by income, education, and geography. After the election, Bishop calculated that 48.1 percent of the population lived in landslide counties in 2008, almost exactly the same as the 48.3 percent who lived in them in 2004. In fact, in 2008 there were thirty-six "landslide states" where a candidate won by 10 percentage points or more, an increase from twenty-nine states in 2004 (including Washington, D.C., in both cases). Writing a week after the election, Bishop concluded, "The country is split in much the same way it was divided four and eight years ago. People continue to sort by age and by way of life. As a result, our communities (and states) are growing more like-minded . . . It is easy to ignore people on the other side when they aren't your neighbors. But that doesn't mean the country is less polarized — because it isn't."[6] Obama's election victory might have brought change to Washington, but it certainly did not reflect a less divided electorate.

News We Can Believe (In)

Our ideology even directs how we choose to learn about the world around us. According to a study undertaken by Natali Jomini Stroud, using data from the 2004 National Annenberg Election Survey, people are interested in consuming media that share their ideological bent. After analyzing newspaper, cable television, talk radio, and political Web site consumption habits, Stroud found that almost two-thirds of conservative Republicans consumed at least one conservative media outlet, compared to a quarter of liberal Democrats. On the other side, over three-quarters of liberal Democrats consumed a liberal outlet, compared to about 40 percent of conservative Republicans.[7] It's not a surprise, I suppose, that we, in our ideologically segregated neighborhoods, would invite onto our television sets only those who share our ideology.

The way Americans filter media through an ideological lens can be extreme. One study that tested whether the logo of a news company appearing on a screen would determine the likelihood of a participant clicking on the news headline found that "no matter how we sliced the data — either at the level of individuals or news stories — the results demonstrate that Fox News is the dominant news source for Americans whose political leanings are Republican or conservative." On political subjects, the likelihood of conservatives clicking on the Fox story was understandably high. But here's the kicker: this was also true for soft news. Conservatives were more likely to click on sports and travel stories that came from Fox. Apparently, sports and travel coverage also needs to be mediated through our political ideologies.[8]

This increased polarization in how we live and how we learn about how others live has profound implications for the policies that govern our lives. Because we are increasingly concentrated by ideology, we are increasingly electing people who represent that ideology well, by being either very left or very right. This extremism has led to a paralysis in our national politics.

Congressional districts, reflecting their residents, are overwhelmingly Republican or overwhelmingly Democrat. Bishop sees these landslides as an affront to the vision of the Founding Fathers, who intended that members of Congress would meet in D.C., bringing with them a variety of perspectives and beliefs, to hash out the nation's business.

"Now," Bishop told me, "they fly in on Tuesday, oftentimes they live with members of their own party, in their own dormitories with ideologically similar members, then they fly home on Thursday to their homogeneous districts, and they never have to do the work of politicians, which is to make deals and compromise." And when politics becomes merely an expression of ideologies rather than a process of figuring out how to actually improve the quality of people's lives, we all suffer.

Don't Know, Don't Ask

I agree with Bishop that ideological segregation is destined to have a negative effect on our politics, but not just because our politicians are ill-equipped or unmotivated to do the business of politicking. The environment created by the Big Sort instills in us a sense of complacency. We are less likely to ask questions of those who represent us, because we assume they have our interests in mind.

In 2008, the Drum Major Institute for Public Policy commissioned a poll to find out which policies the current and aspiring middle class think would improve the quality of their lives. We asked a random sample of Americans throughout the country about pieces of legislation that had been voted on by Congress, but not signed into law, during the previous session. For example, we asked about the Employee Free Choice Act, which makes it easier for employees to join unions; an expansion of the State Children's Health Insurance Program to provide health insurance to more middle-class children; and taxing the income of hedge fund managers at the same rate as everyone else's income. When we asked respondents how they would have liked their member of Congress to vote on these bills, the answer was overwhelmingly in favor of a yes vote, among Democrats and Republicans alike. But when we asked, How did your member of Congress vote on this bill?, the overwhelming response was *Don't know.*[9]

We don't know, and we don't ask. We figure that our members of Congress have our back, because we share a spot along the ideological spectrum with them. We agree on some big-picture issues, maybe on cultural values, maybe on the rhetoric about the role that government should play in our lives. So we don't ask what they are up to, and they don't feel obliged to tell us. Despite advanced communications at our fingertips, only one in four of our respondents reported hearing from their member of Congress on a regular basis. We don't ask, and they don't tell. And our problems do not get solved.

If we want to preserve our democracy, we will need to move away from decision making by ideological cues and toward helping American voters to access and understand the policies being debated by our legislators. This may mean that we opt for solutions that emerge from one side of the policymaking spectrum or the other, but no matter. If we are thoughtful, questioning citizens, we have a shot at making our politics — and our politicians — work for us. In the absence of this attention, we can expect them to continue to operate with impunity.

Ideological Polarization Online

If people aren't engaging in robust debate about their democracy in physical town halls — as many New England towns still do on a yearly basis, to set budgets, levy taxes, and buy and sell town property — what about their virtual town halls? Here, too, we find people choosing to locate themselves within circles of agreement. Despite the choices offered to users — or perhaps because of them — the Internet often functions as an intellectual and ideological cul-de-sac, full of places where only residents turn in, while those who accidentally enter may look at the houses but will then circle right back out. Cass Sunstein, Felix Frankfurter Professor of Law at Harvard Law School, argues that "the Internet is serving, for many, as a breeding ground for extremism, precisely because like-minded people are deliberating with greater ease and frequency with one another, and often without hearing contrary views."[10] Sunstein is essentially describing the online version of the Big Sort.

The extension of ideological polarization to the Internet is evident in the rise of political blogs. Top political blogs receive millions of visitors each day.[11] I'm one such visitor. I believe strongly in the power of the blogosphere to provide a voice for those who are otherwise left out of the political and policy formulation processes, and to challenge a mainstream political press (see chapters 3 and 9) that is too often in dereliction of duty when it comes to holding powerful entities accountable. In fact, I've helped to create two policy-focused blogs at the Drum Major Institute (dmiblog.com and tortdeform.com). I visit blogs to stay up to date on events as they unfold, to get perspectives I otherwise wouldn't read, and, I'll admit, to keep current on the latest political gossip.

Blogs have an increasing presence in my daily life and work, and I am not alone. Andrew Lipsman, a senior analyst at comScore, an Internet marketing research firm, has pointed out the increasing significance of the Internet "in shaping the stories of the day that are so crucial in formulating public opinion on issues and candidates."[12] The 2008 presidential campaign cemented the blogosphere's role as the third leg in the opinion-journalism stool.

In September 2008, just before the presidential election, traffic to political blogs and news sites had exploded. According to the comScore analysis, huffingtonpost.com had 4.5 million visitors in September (up 472 percent from the previous year), politico.com attracted 2.4 million visitors (up 344 percent), and drudgereport.com had 2.1 million visitors (up 70 percent). A majority of the sites growing at the most rapid clip occupy spots on the left of the political spectrum.

How are people congregating in these online town halls? Do people engage in healthy debates and discussions with those who hold opposing perspectives? The evidence suggests otherwise, pointing instead to the same trend Bishop sees in our neighborhoods. People are self-segregating on blogs that speak to their political leanings. And because political blogs of one stripe are unlikely to engage with political blogs of the other stripe, there remains little likelihood of encountering something that might provoke a question on the part of the regular visitor.

One study of forty political blogs found that, just as like moves near like, so too does like link to like. The authors found that "12 percent of all outbound links from conservatives is sent to liberal blogs while 16 percent of all outbound links from liberals point to conservative bloggers." Around half of the links from blogs on one side of the spectrum that actually do link to the other side are in posts that offer strawman arguments, meaning, in the words of the authors who read all of these posts and came up with the system to categorize them, arguments "for ideologically like-minded blog readers" that "direct attention to the 'obvious' deficiencies of the ideological opposition."[13] Ah yes, the obvious deficiencies! With such a setup, it is hard to imagine substantive questioning of opposing viewpoints.

Researchers found a similar tendency among political blogs prior to the 2004 presidential election. For two months before that election, which the study cites as the first in which blogging played an important role, the researchers analyzed postings on "forty A-list blogs" to determine how often the blogs referred to one another and to identify any overlap in their topics of discussion. The researchers found a relatively small amount of cross-ideology interaction, with links from liberal blogs to conservative ones and vice versa accounting for only 15 percent of the links. Even discussion of certain political figures was concentrated among either conservatives or liberals, with people such as Dan Rather and Michael Moore cited predominantly by conservatives and Donald Rumsfeld and Colin Powell cited predominantly by liberals. Mainstream media sites such as Fox News and salon.com followed the same pattern, with right-leaning media receiving the overwhelming majority of their links from conservatives and left-leaning media receiving the overwhelming majority of their links from liberals.[14]

Other studies emphasize that a small number of political Web sites dominate Internet traffic. In a study of millions of Web sites, Matthew Hindman, Kostas Tsioutsiouliklis, and Judy Johnson found that "in each of the topical areas studied — from abortion to the U.S. presidency, the U.S. Congress to gun control, general politics to the death penalty — the distribution of inbound hyperlinks follows a power law distribution . . . [meaning that] the information environment is dominated by a few sites at the top." They call this "Google-archy — the rule of the most heavily linked," and consider it the dominant feature of political information online.[15] In articulating a theory of the political blogosphere's influence that situates mainstream journalists as key actors in disseminating information from political blogs, Henry Farrell and Daniel Drezner emphasize this skewed nature of links and traffic.[16] Thus, not only do blogs tend to self-select ideologically, but also users limit themselves to a relatively small number of blogs as sources of political information.

The issue at hand isn't whether bloggers and those who read blogs are thoughtful and intellectually rigorous. Nor is it that people who sit in the same ideological camp, roughly speaking, can't disagree among themselves. The Drum Major Institute's progressive blog, for example, took a stand against the $700 billion Emergency Economic Stabilization Act (better known as the financial bailout) while writers on other progressive blogs disagreed. This happens all the time among thoughtful people, around the dinner table or online. The question is whether the culture of the political blogosphere and Internet news, unique to itself, creates incentives and rewards for people to spend time engaging with others from very different perspectives. My personal experience, and my review of the research, suggests it does not.

Sure, it is pretty easy to offer angry comments on the posts with which you disagree. The anonymity of the Web makes this easier and more frequent. I've been on the receiving end of those kinds of comments many a time, especially when I'm writing about something controversial, such as immigration policy. And, yes, the Internet does make it pretty easy to encounter viewpoints with which you disagree — a lot easier than moving to another town. But good faith consideration and engagement of those on the other side is not rewarded as much as creating or joining a strong community of sameness. And it is incredibly simple to spend all day online, learning about the world through my own ideological lens, without ever being forced to consider a reasoned viewpoint on the other side. But we are bigger than our online communities and our towns, and democracy depends on us having a shared understanding of what is happening in the world around us.

Transcending Ideological Segregation through Deliberation

Whether we are infants, members of Congress, or regular citizens, it is encountering the unfamiliar that prompts us to question. If people are living in their ghettos of belief, where is the catalyst to inquire?

Bringing people together who don't already agree is Carolyn Lukensmeyer's business. I know firsthand, because I worked for Lukensmeyer in my first job out of college. It was the late 1990s, and she was on a mission to engage Americans in a conversation about the future of Social Security. My job was to run the Social Security Challenge, a campaign within the broader campaign, focused on inspiring college students to talk about the seventy-three-year-old program and its future.

At the time, President Clinton wanted to "save Social Security." This effort was controversial. First, there was disagreement about whether Social Security needed to be "saved" at all. Experts lined up on both sides, some arguing that the program would soon go bankrupt and was in need of an overhaul, others projecting that the program would fulfill its commitments into the foreseeable future and attributing claims to the contrary to a political agenda of dismantling entitlement programs. The controversy, however, went beyond the analysis of the program's fiscal future. At the heart of it were questions about what exactly is owed to Americans as they age, whose responsibility it is to fulfill this pledge, and the best way to steward these commitments. Should the United States run a program of social insurance, in which everyone pays in, knowing that only some may need the contributions, or should it become an investment program, in which people can choose to invest their own dollars in the stock market however they wish, and where a higher return on investment was assumed in those days? Should people who make more contribute more of their paychecks to the system?

The idea driving Lukensmeyer's Americans Discuss Social Security campaign was that any discussion that might result in a change in the mission of a universal program such as Social Security couldn't just happen behind closed doors in Washington, D.C. Americans needed to talk. They needed to weigh in on a conversation that was about more than the mechanics of the program, that was about our values and commitments. And if politicians were going to be successful in whatever decisions they made (whether to keep the program or to change it), they would need the support of the American people. Lukensmeyer organized town hall meetings, inviting thousands of Americans to talk about the program, in their own neighborhoods.

The Americans Discuss Social Security effort was massive, spanning all fifty states and Puerto Rico. It involved four teleconferences between citizens in twenty-three states and policymakers in Washington (including Clinton), large-scale citizen forums in an additional seventeen states, and meetings on more than one hundred college campuses. The Social Security Challenge that I ran reached five thousand students.

The forums were far more than sessions designed to make attendees feel they had fulfilled their civic duty. Participants became better educated about the Social Security debate, and consensus emerged about what people expected from the program and desired from its reform. At the forums, diverse participants from diverse communities tackled thorny economic and political issues but were able to engage each other as well as policymakers in developing concrete, plausible proposals for policy action.[17]

Although Clinton's efforts to reach some kind of deal for the program's future collapsed in response to the scandals of the year, Lukensmeyer saw the promise in engaging people directly in conversations about the issues that affect their collective future. So, soon after the conclusion of Americans Discuss Social Security, Lukensmeyer founded America*Speaks*, where she continues to serve as president. This organization is hired by local and state governments, nonprofit organizations, foundations — anyone who wants citizens to come together to deliberate on a particular issue and reach consensus about what needs to happen next. For example, thousands of New Yorkers who lived in the area affected by 9/11 came together to develop their vision for how they wanted their neighborhoods in Lower Manhattan to redevelop. Thousands of California residents came together to decide on the kind of health care they would like to see the state offer. Six hundred students, university presidents, and young activists met as part of the Clinton Global Initiative to develop plans for student action on issues of global importance, such as climate change, health, human rights, and peace.

America*Speaks* calls their events 21st Century Town Meetings, and to look at the forums is to understand why. In person, the sessions resemble a cross between bingo and a trade show. Hundreds or thousands of people are seated at round tables. There is a laptop at each. A facilitator asks questions to help move the group toward accomplishing their goal for the day. As people deliberate, their responses transmit via computer to a central "theme team," which identifies the big picture threads around the various tables. The theme team posts results on the big screen at the front of the room. Participants hold devices that enable them to vote yea or nay with the push of a button as proposals are refined and prioritized. Opinions are constantly evaluated within the small discussion groups and within the larger forum, and feedback is ever present, with participants considering new proposals and variations on old proposals throughout the day.

But it isn't the high-tech tools that make the town halls special; it's the people. There is no Big Sort here. America*Speaks* picks participants through random sampling to represent their broader community. They are sitting next to people they don't know. There are no ideological cliques. They don't possess expertise in the issues they are there to discuss, and they aren't expected to. Their job, no matter what they believe, is to discuss an issue, debate the policy options, and reach consensus. And they do.

The participants are not unlike the residents of the communities that Bishop writes about in *The Big Sort,* but the America*Speaks* experience illustrates that, in the right environment, with the right incentives and support, we can transcend ideological segregation, both as a group and within ourselves.

"Many of [our participants] live in communities like Bishop describes," Lukensmeyer told me. But "even those people who come from very polarized ideological backgrounds, when placed in a context and facing real human beings who are really different than they are, and given the basic information that they need to participate in the discussion, and given questions designed to make them think — they think."

Perhaps the most striking element of the America*Speaks* forums is the capacity and willingness of participants to transcend their personal interests to consider — and to consider acting on — policies that might force them to make trade-offs in their personal lives. In a session to discuss recovery priorities for New Orleans, for instance, one attendee humbly noted to his discussion colleagues that "I am going to vote for [priority] three, but I am personally affected by number two."[18] The America*Speaks* forums are about inspiring participants to think beyond their own policy ideas and political ideologies; at the forums, participants must listen to and engage with other reasonable, respectful people with contrasting ideas, responsibilities, and life experiences. At Governor Schwarzenegger's urging, the California health-care forum concluded by asking, "How willing would you be to share in the responsibility of paying for health-care reform that covers all Californians?" Eighty-four percent of participants expressed some level of willingness.[19]

So it is not that we have lost the capacity to think beyond our frames of reference; it is that we aren't presented with enough opportunities to do so. But when we are presented with such an opportunity, surrounded by people we don't know and who have different experiences and views, talking about an issue that affects the quality of all of our lives, we wind up going in unexpected directions. Proof of this is the frequency with which participants change their minds.

"[The participants] follow lines of inquiry," Lukensmeyer told me. "And . . . they don't necessarily come out with the programmed answer that they would have come in with. Huge numbers, up to 70 percent of participants, change their position."

The experience at the California*Speaks* daylong conversation on health-care reform is typical of other America*Speaks* programs. Though participants represented a more engaged public than the California public at large, the deliberations had a significant effect on attendees' thinking and knowledge. One in two participants altered their views on health-care reform during the meeting[20] and over 93 percent of participants agreed that California*Speaks* had made them more informed.[21]

When we bump up against new perspectives and experiences, when we are asked new questions that force us to think more deeply about our assumptions, we can change our minds. We don't have to — but the fact that we can is most important. This type of interaction, these expressions of deliberative democracy, are the antidote to the inward direction of our daily lives. When we create the right environment for people to come together around a shared goal, and the format and the facilitation to help them expose their own biases but move toward an end, we can arrive at consensus. In that consensus, there is power.

In New Orleans, public input shaped the development of the city's Unified New Orleans Plan, later approved by the city and the state. After the Listening to the City town meetings in New York, which included almost six thousand participants, the initial plans for the World Trade Center redevelopment in Lower Manhattan were scrapped, and the consensus shaped the criteria for the next round of plans. In Washington, D.C., Mayor Anthony Williams's Citizen Summits, facilitated by America*Speaks,* shifted millions of dollars in city spending based on input regarding the city's strategic plans.

When we allow ourselves to question our assumptions and our positions, when we willingly emerge from our ideological isolation, we have more power to affect the decisions that determine the quality of our lives. Those in power are more likely to listen because they cannot use our divisions as an excuse for their inaction.

But when participants exit the town hall meeting, they return to a culture in which deliberation across ideology is not encouraged. In fact, according to Lukensmeyer, it is actively discouraged.

"For the vast majority of people's time," she said, "they are spending their lives and experiences in structures and processes that are not carefully designed to help them inquire and think and discuss; they are sitting in structures and processes that are intentionally designed to get them to think in a way that someone wants them to think."

Perhaps the problem is that we ask too little of ourselves in our democracy today. If we knew that it was up to us to ask the questions that would determine the quality of our lives, if we were given actual assignments to improve our communities (beyond voting every four years), maybe then we would view differently our responsibilities as citizens. Maybe then we would willingly undertake whatever questioning it took to get to consensus, rather than focusing on finding the perfect posture from which to hold our ideological ground. Maybe, if it were up to us to solve the problems of our whole city or state, we would see those with whom we disagree as necessary partners, would engage rather than avoid. But, isolated not only from one another but also from a clear understanding of how our participation matters, the Big Sort remains — until Lukensmeyer and those like her force us to question it, one 21st Century Town Meeting at a time.

3: Consuming Opinion

WELCOME TO THE WORLD OF AMERICAN MEDIA. BELLICOSE anchors opine about the state of world affairs, on cable news channels that don't actually report the state of world affairs. Political blogs and Web sites are visited by millions each day—millions of people who already agree with the points of view expressed there, that is. The *New York Times* television critic is given front-page real estate to analyze political debates between presidential candidates as if they were the season finales of network dramas. Media consolidation has left 90 percent of the top fifty cable stations in the hands of the same parent companies that run the broadcast networks, and the major media conglomerates in control of 75 percent of all prime-time viewing.[1] As Samuel Goldwyn once famously said, "When I want your opinion, I'll give it to you."

A culture shift is clear in the state of American journalism today. It is a transition that speaks to our changing wants and to the vested interest of concentrated, corporatized media in guiding those wants in the direction that best supports their bottom line. And it has led this organ of our democracy to stray further from its most important function: the asking of questions.

Let's start with the explosion of cable news, in which actual investigation is secondary to the cost-effective business model of headline reading, anchor chatter, and the pronouncement of opinion by "journalists." Median prime-time cable news viewership increased steadily in the early 2000s, growing 32 percent from 2000 to 2001 and 41 percent from 2001 to 2002. Growth slowed and then declined in 2005 and 2006 but rebounded in 2007, with the median prime-time audience increasing by 9 percent.[2] The Project for Excellence in Journalism's State of the News Media report identified a change associated with the 2007 spike: "programming built around a cast of hosts, often but not always the edgiest of cable personalities."[3] Personalities had replaced reporting on breaking news.

The more or less steady growth in median audience paid off for the networks that turned their airtime over to personalities. Fox, MSNBC, and CNN reported collective profits of $791.5 million in 2007, up from $133.9 million in 1997, with Fox by far the most profitable.[4] Though more people still watch the network news — it outranks cable by a factor of ten — fewer people are watching it with each passing year. Network news has lost more than 20 percent of its total audience since 2000, during which time the median cable news audience has grown by almost 125 percent.[5]

Cable news, though, doesn't offer much in the way of news; most of what we see isn't actual reporting. Fifty-six percent of the cable news programming studied by the Project for Excellence in Journalism was what they call "live, extemporaneous journalism."[6] We watch anchors interview guests, talk to each other, read headlines, and pontificate about the meaning of those headlines.

With their super high-tech sets and the anchors always at their desks, cable news is intent on "creating the impression that things are being reported as they happen," but they aren't. Only 3 percent of cable news time is spent covering live events. Most importantly, less than a third of their airtime is spent on "correspondent packages," a fancy way of saying "real stories," compared to 82 percent of network nightly newscasts and half of morning news programming.[7] We aren't actually learning about the world on cable news; we're watching current affairs stand-up.

And then there are those whose job is to tell us what they think and, by definition, what we ought to think. If ratings are any indication of affection, we love them for it. A prime example of this is Lou Dobbs, the consummate cable television news personality. Dobbs's questions aren't meant to be illuminating; they are statements wearing question-mark costumes. I can speak to this from personal experience.

"Andrea, this is Lou Dobbs."

True story. I picked up the phone, and it was Lou Dobbs —formerly Lou Dobbs of CNN *Moneyline* and now Lou Dobbs of *Lou Dobbs Tonight,* or more specifically, Lou Dobbs and his million-plus viewers watching tonight.

"I'd like to invite you to come on the show."

Dobbs was calling because I had written him a letter. The Drum Major Institute was very interested in the issue of immigration, so we embarked on a yearlong project to understand the effect of immigrants on middle-class Americans. Our conclusion, based on research conducted by our research director, Amy Traub, was that immigrants — both legal and illegal — make significant contributions to the economy that benefit native-born citizens, and that public policy needs to strengthen the standing of immigrants in the workplace or else the wages and working conditions of all workers will decline.

I felt strongly that Dobbs's portrayal of the immigration debate was incomplete. With the nonstop barrage of images of Mexicans illegally crossing the border and fearmongering about a "NAFTA superhighway" and a North American Union of Mexico, Canada, and the United States, I grew concerned that the viewers of his show weren't being exposed to any real discussion about the positive effects of immigration on our economy.[8] Viewers needed to know that, far from being a burden, immigrants are contributors to our economy — through their tax dollars, their entrepeneurship, and their contributions to systems such as Social Security, from which they will never benefit.

So I sent Dobbs a letter outlining the main points of our report and urging him to spend more time on some accurate discussion about how our immigration and trade policies actually affect the economy. He called me up, and a week and at least three layers of awful makeup later, I was introduced.

"The Drum Major Institute for Public Policy, a liberal think tank, is criticizing my position on illegal immigration and border security," Dobbs said, while I sat there, ready for my debut, too nervous to take umbrage at that characterization of my position.[9] I was on the show to talk about economics; I hadn't said a thing in my letter, or in the Drum Major Institute's work, about border security. We weren't proponents of open borders. Already, before my mic had even been turned on, I was typecast. In Dobbs's world, there are only two kinds of people: those who agree with him and those who don't.

And we're live.

> DOBBS: Let's start with the first issue. I have said for a
> long time now, we can't reform immigration if we
> can't control it. We can't control immigration if we
> cannot secure our ports and our borders. Where does
> that logic fail?

Again, I was confused. First, I wasn't there to talk about border security. I'm not against border security. I was invited on the show to talk about the economic impact of the immigrants already living in the United States, so that we could figure out what to do with them. Second, that wasn't really a question. Was Dobbs asking me for my opinion, so that we could have a conversation, or did he want me to disprove his opinion?

So I did what I was supposed to: I went back on message.

SCHLESINGER: Three quick points. The first is that your viewers need to know that the middle class actually has a vested interest in this debate. They are positively impacted by the role of immigrants in the economy. So that's the first piece. The second thing is, knowing that, the only way that we can create comprehensive remedy to an immigration system that we agree is broken is if we both recognize the critical role that immigrants play in the economy, and then direct our attention toward the private sector that is interested in pitting immigrant versus middle-class worker — for their bottom line, not the bottom line of Americans.

DOBBS: All right, since you won't respond to my syllogism, I'll respond to yours. Is that all right?

It didn't get much better from there. I could make no point without interruption. I was asked no question that either allowed me to express the results of our analysis or forced me to think critically about that analysis. It wasn't an interview, nor was it really a conversation. More than anything, it was two people putting forth opinions that, even if we weren't contributing to a constructive dialogue on the topic, probably made for entertaining television.

As soon as the camera went off, Dobbs was all smiles. "Let's have you back on the show."

The rise of "opinion journalism" is seen in the success of, and investment in, cable news programs such as this. These hosts, with the exception of Dobbs, are usually settled onto networks that share their ideological leanings and are watched by those who share those leanings, as well. (I can attest to this because my e-mail in-box filled with hundreds of messages criticizing my views — and my shirt, my glasses, my name — just as soon as I turned on my BlackBerry post-interview.)

The questions asked on shows such as these are rhetorical, but such shows aren't exclusively the province of cable. The crazy uncle of cable news opinion journalism is talk radio. The number of stations with talk programming exploded to 1,400 in 2006, up from 400 in 1990.[10] In yet another popular and potentially important medium, meaningful investigation of the news is simply not a priority. Talk radio feeds off of the big stories that lend themselves to ratings. As the 2008 State of the News Media report concludes, "Whatever one's view, talk radio tends to amplify the handful of stories best suited to debate and division." A case in point was the week between May 13 and May 18, 2007, during which several important stories were breaking. Just three events, however — the debate over Iraq policy, the presidential campaign, and immigration — "consumed 50 percent of the airtime. Many of the other stories of the week got short shrift."[11]

Talk radio, along with most other mainstream media, is in the business of magnification, not illumination. We don't need to ask questions about what is happening in the world; we are awash in a sea of pontification, bobbing along as though we know something, when we are really just being carried further adrift. This narrowing of the mainstream media is ironic, considering that we seem to have so many more choices — but perhaps that's the explanation. As others have theorized before me, there is so much information available that people need to find some way to get through it, so they turn to those who will offer a clear perspective on the issue (or three) of the day. We want the answers to understanding our world. And with every answer delivered, so, too, is a profit delivered to the sponsoring media corporation, which had to invest a whole lot less in opinion than in actual reporting. Not a bad deal.

A Different Kind of Talk Show Host

After hearing a neighbor say that he would rather be shot than be caught listening to President Franklin Delano Roosevelt's fireside radio chats, George V. Denny Jr. was inspired to take action against what he thought was a danger to America. How could democracy function if citizens didn't want to listen to those with whom they disagreed? Without listening, what potential was there to change our minds? In 1935, using the model of a New England town meeting as his guide, Denny hosted his first episode of *America's Town Meeting of the Air.*[12]

Each week, a voice would shout, "Town meeting tonight! Town meeting tonight! Bring your questions to the old town hall!," and listeners would know it was time to turn up the volume on their radios and gather around. From 1935 to 1956, up to 3 million listeners a week tuned in the NBC Blue and ABC networks to hear Denny moderate.[13] People formed discussion clubs — more than one thousand of them — to debate the broadcast's topics among themselves.[14]

Denny invited into the studio knowledgeable people with different takes on the issues of the day and let them have it out. The first broadcast of *America's Town Meeting of the Air* asked the question "Which Way America? Communism, Fascism, Socialism, or Democracy?," and included a communist, a fascist, a socialist, and a democrat as speakers.

"Having it out" was a slightly more civilized proposition on Denny's show than anything we would see today. Before introducing his program "Should We Plan for Social Security," one of the few of which an original recording survives, Denny defined the parameters of the program: "This is not a debate. It is a joint discussion in which two qualified authorities, approaching the problem from two widely different viewpoints, discuss the subject . . . These meetings are conducted in the interest of the welfare of the whole American people, and in presenting two or more conflicting views at the same time during the same hour we believe a highly useful and constructive purpose is served."[15]

As David Goodman notes in the definitive compilation *NBC: America's Network,* the program featured between two and four speakers with different perspectives who read from prepared scripts. There were no shouting matches, no fight to get in the thirty-second sound bite before being interrupted by the aggressive host ready for the next question.[16] The guests on the Social Security program, Secretary of Labor Frances Perkins and George E. Sokolsky, author of *Labor's Fight for Power,* each spoke for fifteen minutes, laying out their positions, interrupted only by applause.

It's difficult to imagine that kind of respect for the capacity of the audience to listen in today's media environment. But then again, it's hard to imagine Denny as a host in today's media environment. He had little in common with his counterparts in today's business. Whereas Denny wanted his listeners to be open to questioning their positions after hearing different views hashed out on the show, Dobbs and his kind want their listeners to agree with them. In fact, today's hosts just assume their audience does agree with them — and they are probably right, as I discussed in chapter 2.

The restraint of the format was not an indicator, however, of a lack of passion about the discussion. The show was known for the active involvement of its audience; the approximately 1,500 people gathered at New York's Town Hall were called "spectator-hecklers."[17] According to a 1938 *Time* magazine profile, "What makes [the programs] exciting is uninhibited heckling. The speakers heckle each other and the audience heckles everybody. The auditors boo and cheer, are made up of the rich and poor, the well informed and the ignorant."[18] But most importantly, no matter who they were, the audience could ask questions. This live audience questioning was considered "a significant innovation in American broadcasting." The questions were to be written down, to be fewer than twenty-five words, and were approved by a committee.[19] The best question earned the questioner a prize from Denny.[20]

In fact, self-described "intelligent listeners" of *America's Town Meeting of the Air* "prided themselves on . . . their openness." As Goodman tells it, "They understood themselves as receptive to new information and open to reasoned persuasion." Indeed, research supported these assertions: Half of the show's listeners "usually" continued discussion after the program's conclusion, and "34 percent reported having changed their opinions as a result of listening." One in two of the listeners in the survey preferred that no definite solution to problems be arrived at in the show. "*ATMA* sought to persuade Americans that the truth was complex and might not be grasped immediately," writes Goodman.[21] And how could it be otherwise, when addressing topics such as "How Should the Democracies Deal with the Dictatorships?" and "What System of Medical Care Should We Have?".

Denny believed that his program's emphasis on openness would have political implications. "We'll educate the independents — those voters who hold allegiance to no party — so that political parties will have to produce candidates that appeal to them," he said of his program. "This will tend to counteract malicious pressure groups, sickening political campaigns and, above all, the dangers of dictatorship."[22] Discussion and questions — these were the things that would counteract dictatorship and narrow, ideologically rigid politics. Open minds characterized patriotism, not the profession of loyalty to the democratic system. Denny's job was to catalyze, not to proselytize.

Of course, *America's Town Meeting of the Air* was only possible because the NBC Blue network made it possible. There was no advertising, no commercial sponsorship. The show was considered a public service, produced after the debates surrounding the passage of the Communications Act of 1934. Though the act did little to ease the commercialization of radio that had taken place in the late 1920s and early 1930s, public discussion about the act did prompt media companies to take public service programming more seriously. According to Goodman, "The NBC hierarchy had a clear sense among themselves of the worth of the program in political capital, even as they wished to produce it as cheaply and uncontroversially as they decently could."[23]

Today, political capital is a lot less important than the bottom line. And dialogue is a lot less important to that bottom line than is a formula of strong opinion on one side or the other, which guarantees an audience. I wonder if Denny would make it as a radio talk show host today. I wonder if we would let him.

A Different Kind of Media Today

Of course, a lot has changed in the world of American media in the time from Denny to Dobbs, but the more things change, the more they stay the same. In Denny's time, NBC and CBS came to dominate commercial broadcasing, even while the former produced a public interest show such as *America's Town Meeting of the Air.*[24] Today, six conglomerates dominate the media environment. General Electric, Time Warner, Walt Disney, News Corporation, CBS, and Viacom rule the television, radio, cable, movie, and print media industries.[25] Name a source of news or entertainment and you can bet that one of these names is behind it. Watching *60 Minutes* or reading *The Secret*? CBS Television and CBS's book publisher Simon & Schuster are behind those. Reading the *Wall Street Journal* or watching *The Simpsons*? That's Rupert Murdoch's News Corporation. Watching *Batman Begins* on digital cable while you surf the Web? There's a good chance the TV and Internet are being brought to you courtesy of Time Warner.

Aided and abetted by government policy, these enormous corporate entities have muscled out small, local, diverse voices and have concentrated media sources in a few very powerful hands. Media programming now skews in favor of the bottom line of these industries, leaving us with soft news, entertainment, and of course, Dobbs. Unless *America's Town Meeting of the Air* included a celebrity dance portion, it is unlikely that it would wind up on anyone's lineup today. The reduction of differing viewpoints in the marketplace, the pressure to make money, the disincentive to take risks in reporting on the industries that share an owner with the news station itself—none of this bodes very well for the role of inquiry in our culture today.

The media environment didn't always look this way. Before passage of the Telecommunications Act of 1996—the first revision of telecommunications law in sixty-two years—regulations prevented concentration of media ownership, restricting mergers and acquisitions and limiting the number of TV and radio stations any one corporation could own. However, the Telecommunications Act and the Federal Communications Commission's subsequent rule making lifted many of these restrictions in the name of lower barriers to entry into the communications business and increased competition. The effect of the legislation, though, was the opposite, resulting in concentrated ownership and media behemoths. Whereas prior to the act a company could own only forty radio stations, the radio giant Clear Channel now owns more than 1,200. Relaxed restriction on TV station ownership had a similar effect, provoking mergers and increased concentration of ownership. Cross-ownership rules that had separated cable and broadcast networks were eased, allowing broadcast stations to gobble up attractive cable networks.[26]

The result has been not only concentration of influence over the media inside a handful of corporate boardrooms but also degradation in the quality, source, and diversity of the information these corporate boardrooms relay. Ben Bagdikian, media critic and author of *The New Media Monopoly,* believes that large media conglomerates have "damaged our democracy." He cites two main causes: the monopolization of media by large companies and the Federal Communications Commission's failure to act in the public interest.[27]

It was this mandate to serve the public interest that allowed Denny to air *America's Town Meeting of the Air* for nine years without commercials, without the need to raise funds through ceaseless pledge drives (which surely wouldn't have yielded much at the time), and without pressure to sanitize the programming so as not to offend advertisers.[28]

The incentive to maximize profits keeps the Dobbses of the world in business, maintains empty chatter as the norm among news anchors, and ensures that talk radio is ever present. We watch and we listen, for sure, but not without some reservation. Americans have grown skeptical of the media, with 55 percent believing that the press is biased.[29]

Indeed, if the perspective of those within the industry itself is to be considered, Americans' suspicions of bias are warranted. A 2004 survey by the Pew Research Center for the People & the Press found that 66 percent of national newspeople and 57 percent of local journalists believed that increased bottom line pressure was "seriously hurting" the quality of news coverage.[30] Studies have found that concentration of local television ownership degrades the quality of news Americans receive, that coverage of negative economic news tends to be more about corporations and investors than about the general workforce, and that a change in ownership from a local entity to a chain reduces coverage of local issues. Conversely, in radio markets with more diversity of station ownership, there is greater variety in programming.[31]

The Consumers Union, the Consumer Federation of America, and Free Press have compiled substantial evidence of the negative effects of media concentration, in filings to the Federal Communications Commission. "Editorial preferences are deeply embedded in commercial mass media not only on the editorial pages but also on the news pages," they argue. "Rather than claim that many outlets owned by a single entity will present a neutral, objective, or balanced picture, public policy should recognize that diversity and antagonism of viewpoints comes from diversity of ownership."[32] Denny's show would not have inspired his viewers to ask questions if he invited only one guest, with one view — his. Similarly, we can't expect that people will ask *why* in a concentrated media environment where the view of the owner determines the views of the news we see, hear, and read.

These changes in the media were not inevitable. Although corporate desire to make money is ever present, it is ultimately up to public policy to oblige them. Generally, this collusion is assisted by the absence of inquiry. The public debate about the Telecommunications Act of 1996 was limited. Most people today have absolutely no idea what it was or how it has affected their lives. But then again, was there much incentive for media to report on the changes that would change how the media was to report?

"The Telecommunications Act was covered (rather extensively) as a business story, not a public policy story," writes media scholar Robert McChesney, who also notes that "the silence of public debate is deafening. A bill with such astonishing impact on all of us is not even being discussed."[33]

We got what we paid for. Thanks to no questioning from the public, we got a media that does less questioning.

Young people today not only must cut through the soft news that has proliferated during the past thirty years[34] but also must carefully evaluate information sources that seem diverse but are in fact owned and controlled by a very few, very powerful corporations. Unfortunately, there isn't much bottom line pressure to develop the skills of discernment in our culture today. Maybe we need some more spectator-hecklers today.

4: In Google We Trust

I THINK IT'S IMPORTANT TO SAY FROM THE OUTSET THAT I love the Internet. Its possibilities are endless. Technology has always been a big part of my life, thanks to my father. He studied computer science in college but had to drop out just prior to finishing his degree to support his widowed mother. Despite this, my dad taught himself how to make a living with computers, and that appreciation for technology put me through college. I run an organization considered by many to be on the leading edge in using technology to disseminate ideas. The point of this chapter isn't to dissect whether the Internet is a good or bad thing — that's beside the point. The Internet just *is*.

But if we care about raising children in a culture that values inquiry, I believe we must pause and investigate our assumptions about what the Internet does and what we do on it. At this moment of immense political challenge and technological opportunity, it is important to ask whether the very structure of the Internet creates rewards and incentives that affect the development of questioning citizens. We must acknowledge its incredible potential while also thinking critically about the default behavior that the Internet inspires. Only through such investigation can we figure out what, if anything, to do about it.

I believe that the Internet, and the role it plays in our culture, is changing us. It's changing how we think about information, how we learn about the world around us, even how we define our notions of truth. But most importantly, the Internet is changing how we think of the meaning of a question, and this matters to the future of democracy.

Discerning citizens, citizens who can process, interpret, and question the credibility of the information they encounter, matter to democratic discourse. Citizens with a shared base of knowledge, who use that base of knowledge to question events as they unfold, matter to our ability to influence social change. Democracy requires an attention span long enough to realize its promise.

We are so awed by the very possibility of all the information available to us on the Internet that the process of formulating our entry into that information is secondary. As long as we're on the information superhighway, who cares where we're going? But navigating the information superhighway is very different from navigating the local library or a print newspaper, and we have adjusted accordingly, if subconsciously. We are developing new habits of mind on the Internet. They are not all bad habits of mind, but they are new. And these habits have profound implications for our democracy.

Marcel Proust writes, "We do not receive wisdom, we must discover it for ourselves, after a journey through the wilderness which no one else can make for us, which no one can spare us, for our wisdom is the point of view from which we come at last to regard the world."[1] I worry that the culture of the Internet is directly at odds with the development of wisdom, because the noise is so constant, the pace so fast, the choices so overwhelming, the openness to discovery supplanted by the skill of retrieval. The echo chambers tell us how to regard the world. We have come to believe that wisdom is accessible somewhere on a Web page, if we only find the right one. The very notion of an intellectual journey through the wilderness becomes irrelevant.

I saw a commercial the other night for a new cell phone

that has a partnership with Google. There were quick cuts between scenes, happy music in the background. Do sharks have eyelids? asks a woman at the beach. Do we have the same fingerprints? ask twins. Can we get this cheaper somewhere else? ask a husband and wife riding a lawn mower in a hardware store. The tagline for this new phone? "Curiosity is everywhere." The Internet certainly makes it easier to find answers to these questions, which then makes us want to ask more questions like them. But what about the deeper questions that democracy requires? Will we grow accustomed to only asking the questions that we know we can answer by using our cell phones?

In meetings with my hyperactive young staff at DMI, I ask them to heed the advice given to me by yoga teacher: to register full. That is, after you've inhaled, take a moment to register that you are full of air. After you have exhaled, take a moment to register that you are empty. As you register full, you absorb. You take in. You reflect. Cruising on the Internet, we do not register full. We simply exhale when our eyes grow tired.

It is a disturbing irony—just when we have acquired all this knowledge at our fingertips we have lost the interest and capacity to truly engage with it.

Some technologists argue that critiques of the changes wrought by advancements in technology—critiques such as mine—miss the bigger picture of what is gained. Clay Shirky, author of *Here Comes Everybody: The Power of Organizing without Organizations,* captures this sentiment, arguing that "our older habits of consumption weren't virtuous, they were just a side effect of living in an environment of impoverished access. Nostalgia for the accidental scarcity we've just emerged from is just a sideshow; the main event is trying to shape the greatest expansion of expressive capability the world has ever known."[2] Thus, according to Shirky, it is silly to mourn the loss of a particular newspaper (which I'll do in more detail in chapter 9), when it is confined to an average of sixty-five pages during the week (with at least a third of its space devoted to advertising) and when you can find newspapers from more than forty countries in at least seventeen languages at the click of the mouse.[3] It is silly to be wistful about the decline in interest in the nineteenth-century Russian novel when the Internet will inevitably widen our definition of who can and will shape our cultural identity. Isn't it?

At the risk of sounding like a Luddite, I argue that such analysis misses the ways in which the Internet is more than a communications technology — it has become a place where people live. I disagree that the hubbub about the Internet is simply the same as what happened when the printing press, radio, and television arrived. The Internet is more than a technology. It's more than a medium. It's an environment. But is it an environment in which inquiry is valued?

Information Drive-by and the Google Generation

"Google is the living (and highly capitalized) proof that the Internet encourages curiosity," Tom Watson told me. Watson is the author of *CauseWired: Plugging In, Getting Involved, Changing the World,* a Drum Major Institute board member, and a friend. He points to graphs and charts of online searches over the past decade as proof that we have become a search-oriented society — "not just unimportant, mundane stuff, either. People search for meaning, for answers in the digital realm."

He is right. We have certainly become a search-oriented society. Between August 2007 and July 2008 there were more than 175 billion searches performed on the top search engines — nearly 100 billion searches on Google alone. According to July 2008 statistics, approximately 550 million searches were performed using the top fifty search engines *every day*.[4]

And there is plenty to search. By 2008, Google's search index had processed around one trillion links, and the number of indexed Web pages increases by several billion pages per day.[5]

Are these searches reflective of our curiosity? Absolutely. The Internet responds to curiosity as much as it creates it. Is our growing use of search engines reflective of a search for meaning, our growing appetite for inquiry? On that, I am not convinced. Unless we believe that searching for answers is the same thing as asking questions.

"It's not necessarily apples and oranges," according to Watson. "I think Google has made people more inquisitive, not less, and that's a good thing. It can be a quick thing—or it can be part of a deep inquiry process. Certainly, we're in far better shape, in terms of tools and ability, for deep inquiry than we used to be."

Are we?

When I survey the search engine landscape, I see conditions that are less than inspiring of "deep inquiry," especially for our youngest. I see the formation of habits of mind characterized by a dangerous lack of discernment. I see young people who casually plug key terms into search boxes instead of taking the time to formulate their questions. I see blind faith in whatever such plugging-in delivers—as if the results weren't produced by commercial, for-profit companies that have their own reasons for ranking things the way they do. The tools may be there; on that, I agree with Watson. But the ability to wield those tools effectively? I'm not so sure.

Three poor habits of mind developed on the Web pose a direct threat to the development of questioning citizens. First, young people search for information online without any intention. They bounce all over the place, hopping and skimming their way through content. When they plug terms into search boxes, they take whatever top three results are given to them and consider that research. Underlying their behavior is the assumption that Google or some other search engine, in its infinite wisdom, understands what they want and will deliver it to them. Young people then print these results out, assuming they have met their teachers' expectations. There is little room in that process for critical thinking, for deciphering the meaning of the information that was retrieved.

Second, young people don't question the sources of the information they find through their searches. Study after study of online research behavior demonstrates little discernment on the part of young people. They take whatever they get from the search engine and don't think about its origin — a habit as bad for their education as it is for our democracy. With more information available, it is all the more important that young people know how to scrutinize and assess.

Third, young people are barely reading what they find anyway — because the Internet is changing the very way they read. As they sit in front of computers for hours a day, and as the computer becomes more a part of their classroom and home environments, we need to think about whether the type of literacy encouraged on the Internet is compatible with a democracy whose history of struggle for fairness and freedom is inextricably linked with the people's use of the written word. Much has been written on the subject of the changing literacy of "digital natives," as they are called,[6] and it is not my intention to explore this further here. But it is worth noting that the changing literacy of our children in a culture dominated by the Internet should be a concern to us all.

The intellectual shortcuts encouraged by the Web are interrelated. If children read carefully, they might question the credibility of what they retrieve. If children think carefully about the question they are trying to answer, they are less likely to accept the first round of results yielded by their searches. In any case, let's start with the reality of where we find ourselves now.

First: the bouncing, lazy search. After a review of the literature and an examination of the tracks left by millions of scholars (both young and old) researching in virtual libraries, in what they called the Google Generation project, researchers at the Centre for Information Behaviour and the Evaluation of Research at University College London compiled a definitive study about how children interact with the Web. They describe the way Internet users search for information as "horizontal, bouncing, checking and viewing in nature."[7] Students demonstrate little concentration, little attempt to actually engage with content. They are doing what the Internet encourages them to do — to get on that information superhighway and see how far it can take them. The downside, for the purpose of developing questioning students and citizens, is that this process begins to change the way they think of the actual search for information.

"Library users demand 24-7 access, instant gratification at a click, and are increasingly looking for 'the answer' rather than for a particular format," the researchers report, "so they scan, flick and 'power browse' their way through digital content, developing new forms of online reading [along] the way that we do not yet fully understand (or, in many cases, even recognize)."[8] Of course they want the "instant gratification" of "the answer" and are willing to jump all over the place until they think they've found it — that's what our culture encourages.

Although the Google Generation study focused on younger adults, researchers found that professors, lecturers, and practitioners in academic communities fall victim to the same bouncing/flicking tendencies. They search "horizontally rather than vertically. Power browsing and viewing is the norm for all." Ultimately, the authors conclude, we as a society are "dumbing down."[9] We are searching left to right, click to click, speeding through whatever our search engine renders.

As our access becomes more complex, our thinking processes simplify.

Professor Ulises Mejias, who studies how information and communications technologies shape social networks, has a perfect laboratory: his own college students at State University of New York, Oswego.

"I do think that the Internet is changing our research habits and our relationship to knowledge, for the worse," he wrote to me. I asked him about his thoughts about an article by Nicholas Carr in *The Atlantic,* "Is Google Making Us Stupid?,"[10] which met with quite a bit of controversy for suggesting that the Internet was reducing the author's attention span for longer-form reading and deeper thinking.

"What's interesting," Mejias wrote, "is that when I discussed the Carr article with my students, they said, 'The Internet is not making us stupid; it's just making us lazy.' That's even worse! We can't help it if we are stupid. But to be lazy suggests that we know there is an alternative, perhaps even a better alternative, but we consciously choose to go with the option that requires the least effort and that places less demands on questioning what we are doing. This is typical mass behavior." Our culture encourages the intellectual race to the bottom, and there are few incentives to be the exception.

Our children are engaged, en masse, in "information drive-by" behavior on the Internet, which speaks to the consumption impulse on the Web — an impulse to plug, click, browse, skim, and watch. Just because a person snacks all the time doesn't mean he is either hungry or eating well. Likewise, incessant searching isn't necessarily a reflection of actual curiosity. It certainly isn't a reflection of our ability to meaningfully inquire, to figure out just what we are asking in the first place, to digest and analyze and synthesize until we have answers — answers that can't simply be printed out and handed in. And if this is mass behavior, as Mejias states, there is popular incentive only to maintain the status quo. Anything else would take more time, more energy, more questioning.

"You Have to Read It"

Emily Drabinski is not what you probably think of when you picture a librarian. She is young and hip and her glasses are on her face, not hanging on a string around her neck. She is the Electronic Resources and Instruction Librarian at Long Island University in New York.

"I want my students to always have the capacity to ask, to know where to get answers to their questions, always with the idea of generating more questions so they can live an intellectually curious life. That's my ethos as a librarian," she told me.

She became a reference librarian five years ago because she "loved books and people, and wanted to work with both." And although she is far from a critic of the Internet and hasn't issued any manifestos calling for all research to be done only within university stacks, she is concerned about the way the young people in her library think about questions and answers.

In my conversation with her, she recalled what she described as a "chilling" encounter with a student the previous year. The student wanted to write a paper about the idea of the courtesan and how it manifests itself in modern society. Drabinski was using one of her favorite tools — Google Book Search — to help the student search by keyword to unearth appropriate sources. At one point the two were looking at a book on the screen, with the keyword *courtesan* highlighted in yellow, as Book Search does, when the student asked, "How do I know if this is about what I need it to be about?"

Drabinski asked, "What do you mean?"

"Well, I see my words highlighted, but does that mean this is relevant?"

After some confusing back and forth, during which Drabinksi was trying to understand the student's question, she finally understood the difficulty. The student didn't realize that, to determine whether the book was relevant to her research topic, "she had to *read* it. You have to read it, and think about it. She didn't seem to know. And I think that that's Internet related. I really do."

The young people that Drabinski encounters—high school and college students, and sometimes even their teachers—don't understand that only *they* can determine the relevance of the information they retrieve, not Google, not Yahoo!, not even their librarian. This discernment requires reading and thinking and evaluating, because there isn't one answer out there to the questions that require analysis. As computer critic Joseph Weizenbaum says, "There is only one way to turn signals into information: through interpretation."[11] And, unless I'm behind on technological developments, interpretation can only be done by the human brain.

What was life like before the Internet? "Before you had the Web, where you could just go to Google and type in 'Should there be a Palestinian state?,' when there was a card catalog, you had to think of your subject," noted Drabinski. "You had to think critically about the kind of words and language you wanted to use, because you had to guess where in the card catalog that information could be found." A researcher would begin by assembling a list of keywords—*Palestine, Israel, diaspora, Israel-Arab relations.* Then the searcher would pursue these avenues of research as each round of effort helped to refine the question. "Now you don't do that. You just type it in and take the top three results on that page and you hit Print."

For several years, Drabinksi worked at the library of a liberal arts university near a public high school in Yonkers,

New York. This school is one of the few public schools to have an International Baccalaureate program, a rigorous educational and assessment program with an international focus. I went to speak with students who had worked with Drabinski, and their teacher, Brigid McMaster, a former nun and now a history teacher, whose classroom is decorated with question marks and handmade posters advertising academic databases.

McMaster decided that, in light of all of the talk about our economy entering its period of greatest challenge since the Great Depression, she would move around the curriculum of her History of the Americas class to talk about that period in U.S. history right away. This kind of switch would be unheard of in a typical class that had to adhere closely to the curriculum, which itself adheres closely to a standardized exam. But so would be a program that requires students to take a class in the theory of knowledge, which relates learning from various disciplines to concepts, historical events, current events, and issues of importance.

I asked Julie, a senior at Yonkers High School, how she would go about searching for information on the Great Depression to prepare for her classroom discussion tomorrow. I was prepared to hear that she'd Google *Great Depression,* go to the Wikipedia page, and take it from there. I was wrong.

"Well, 'Great Depression.' That's kind of broad." She proceeded to explain how she would have to narrow down the question and use keywords, and through a presearch discern a much clearer idea of what she wanted to learn.

With so much gained in terms of access to information, with the advent of online research tools, what's missing now, according to Drabinski, is "a sense of research as work." Previous research methods—including the use of card catalogs—forced people to be more creative and rigorous in the effort to access the information sought. Now, said Drabinski, students think all research will be easy. "The Internet makes research easier until it doesn't, and then students aren't equipped to deal with things not working, or going wrong. [The Internet] de-skills you."

Students can't find what they're looking for unless the Internet does it for them. Sure, it's reasonable to ask why students should have to work so hard to find information if it's not necessary. But then we are forgetting that the purpose of these research exercises is not to produce papers worthy of entry into academic journals—though they might—but to develop habits of mind that will serve these young people throughout their lives.

Drabinksi also worries that students fail to recognize that the way information is structured online—its content, form, presentation, and authority—is "invisible in a way that it wasn't before." It becomes invisible as information is privatized. The algorithms containing the secret of how our search engines give us information are themselves secret. Do we even think about where the information comes from or are we just happy to find the answers we are looking for?

Yahoo!—One Authority Young People Don't Question

"The speed of young people's Web searching indicates that little time is spent in evaluating information, either for relevance, accuracy or authority and children have been observed printing-off and using Internet pages with no more than a perfunctory glance at them," according to the Google Generation report.[12] This phenomenon—the search, print, and run—was familiar to every educator I spoke with across the country.

A 1999 report by Sandra Hirsh found that fifth graders "rarely mentioned" authority as an evaluation criterion and generally "did not question the accuracy or validity of the information they found from any electronic resources."[13] It's not that they couldn't figure whether the source was credible, if they wanted to; it's that they didn't think to question the legitimacy and accuracy of the information they got through their search engines.

Unfortunately, understanding the importance of the credibility of information, and the skills to ascertain that credibility, doesn't come automatically with age. A 2001 report by Michael Lorenzen found that high school students "had given very little thought to how to evaluate what they found on the Web," and they didn't understand whether the information they uncovered was "good." They didn't know how to figure it out.[14] Likewise, a 2000 report by Nathan Bos found that high school students conducting research online would be hampered in their ability to practice the evidence-based reasoning at the heart of science because they couldn't identify biases in the scientific resources they encountered on the Web.[15]

These findings and others led the author of the article "Children, Teenagers, and the Web" to conclude, "Young users encounter problems in selecting appropriate search terms and orienting themselves when browsing. They have a tendency to move from page to page, spending little time reading or digesting information, and have difficulty making relevance judgments about retrieved pages. Information seeking does not appear to be intuitive, and practice alone does not make perfect."[16]

In a culture that prizes finding "the answer," it becomes less important to evaluate the source, the relevance, or the authenticity of that answer. From mindlessly plugging in terms to power browsing through whatever is found, with little attention paid to whether those sources are relevant or credible, young people are determined only to find their answer.

Many recent studies indicate that children are not asking

questions to make judgments about the information they retrieve. They're not asking, Is this information true? Is it relevant? Is it credible? Is it authoritative? Does it withstand scrutiny? How would I go about scrutinizing it? They believe and trust that search engines are neutral actors, simply offering what is most helpful to them in their pursuit of an answer.

This belief in the objectivity of search engines is both inaccurate and dangerous. Even more than the World Book encyclopedias that my parents proudly brought home when I was in fifth grade — a sign that we had indeed arrived in the middle class — search engines are commercial enterprises with their own incentives and rewards. The Google Generation study found that teenagers believed that if a site was indexed by Yahoo! it had to be authoritative and did not need independent verification.[17] But Yahoo! cannot claim objectivity, and it certainly can't be responsible for the truth of the pages it indexes.

Search engines use programs called spiders (or crawlers) to "crawl" the Web, looking for Web pages and storing them in their search databases. These spiders follow the links that appear on every Web page. Search programs then quantify the relevant words and create a data tree or index from these terms. This index connects those terms with specific Web pages. Finally, the engines use a search algorithm to rank search results by relevance. Relevance is determined by many factors, including the number of times a word appears on a page, the title of the page, and where on a page a term appears. The algorithm might also, as in Google's case, rank a Web page higher based on "link analysis," which considers a Web page's association with other Web pages.

Ultimately, search engines don't search each Web page each time a query is submitted — they search the indexes or data trees, which are one step removed from the information itself. The algorithms used to accomplish this search are proprietary, and unlike the library, there is no help desk.

Google, Yahoo!, ask.com — these engines are not unbiased presenters of information. Neither is the mainstream news, of course, and we still watch CNN and read the *New York Times*. Yet, just as we should question the biases of the mainstream news, so too should we train our young people to be savvy, literate, questioning consumers of what they get from search engines. The service that search engines provide is invaluable, as is mainstream media, but only if it is understood in context. Understanding context requires discernment; ascertaining credibility requires inquiry.

As Jay Moonah, a market strategist whose job includes search engine optimization, puts it: "Everything has editorial choices, whether they're made by a human editor who's intentionally making them for a point or they're made for technical reasons. In the cases of search engines, there are editorial decisions made in the . . . way that content gets into those engines."[18] We simply don't understand those decisions, and we certainly aren't teaching our children about their implications.

In an era in which so much misinformation and distrust plagues our political discourse, in which online rumors are not accidents but rather intentional campaign strategies, in which neither expertise nor accuracy is a criterion for publication, it is all the more important that young people think about the credibility of the information they find on the Internet. To find the answers that our democracy requires, we need to think. We need to construct and synthesize our answers, not merely print them out.

Young people will need to be taught these skills of discernment and broken out of their habits of erratic searching and lazy search-term entry. We will have to stop worshipping the power of the Internet for just a moment so that we can see all the work we need to do to enable children to use it wisely.

Leaving Room for Observation

Those of us who aren't digital natives may already feel that, thanks to the Internet, we are living in a science fiction movie, some kind of invasion of the body snatchers. Our minds are working differently. Our appetites are changing. A friend of mine recently lamented that the Internet had given her attention deficit disorder — not an uncommon feeling.

To author Maggie Jackson, the issue is one of distraction. We cannot complete any of our tasks with intention because we are living in an era of distraction.

"The way we live is eroding our capacity for deep, sustained, perceptive attention — the building block of intimacy, wisdom, and cultural progress. Moreover, this disintegration may come at a great cost to ourselves and to society," she writes in her book *Distracted: The Erosion of Attention and the Coming Dark Age.*[19] She details the ways in which we have become distracted, diluted, and divided. We watch television while pretending to care for our children. We type on our BlackBerrys while having dinner with old friends. We have bigger networks and fewer close relations. We multitask incessantly. Even our toddlers learn the skills.

As Jackson recognizes, one of the major forces shaping this new period of distraction is the presence of the Internet. It is both the cause and the perfect manifestation of our inability to focus. People may be online longer, but their attention span decreases. They may plug in more search terms, searching for more information, but they have less interest in meaningful inquiry and less energy to pursue it. The authors of "Googlearchy" write, "Computers may offer us orders of magnitude more information than previous generations enjoyed; but human attention, it seems, is not a scalable resource . . . The Web demonstrates the consequences of a poverty of attention on a massive scale."[20] In the end, having access to an infinite amount of information is meaningless.

What matters is how we use the information that we happen upon, seek out, and are taught.

In this sense, the Internet creates a different kind of focus — a seductive, "just the facts, ma'am" focus. We are so relentless in our pursuit of the answer — so focused — that we forget that the first step in asking a question is observation. As the kids we'll meet later are learning at the Institute for Inquiry, the first step is to encounter some phenomenon with which we are unfamiliar. We forget, in this answer-obsessed world, that the cultivation of our minds isn't about the answer. As librarian Drabinski put it, "There's only questions and reshaping the question and grappling with different ideas."

I was talking about this book with a friend's son — he's about nine years old. He told me about his classroom teacher. When a student says something that prompts her to say, "That's interesting," the student gets a prize. Students are rewarded not for the right answer alone but also for interesting observations. Imagine if this were true in all of our classrooms, if we created space and incentives for original thinking rather than savvy regurgitation!

As they grow up spending so much time on the Internet, are our children learning to be observers of what is interesting? Are they in an environment in which observation is valued? Even efforts to teach children to use the Internet better often focus on their facility with the technology. But what about observation? Sir Isaac Newton discovered the law of gravitation by contemplating the fall of an apple. Galileo Galilei challenged centuries of scientific "fact" that the earth is the center of the universe, upending science and religion by observation — not by learning more of what was already known. It is often serendipity and the blank state of mind that lead to the discovery of new truths.

The Internet can provide access to an overwhelming number of facts, if properly searched, but we also have to send the message to our children that all of the information isn't out there — otherwise, what is the incentive to create new truths through our observations of the world around us?

Geert Lovink, in analyzing computer critic Weizenbaum's work, writes, "The Internet is not a vending machine in which you throw a coin and then get what you want. The key, here, is the acquisition of a proper education in order to formulate the right query. It's all about how one gets to pose the right question."[21]

If we don't want our children to see the Internet as a vending machine, we have to empower them to focus on the question. I believe that inquiry can be the antidote to the distraction that the Internet offers us. I believe we wouldn't become distracted so easily if we investigated rather than viewed, if we questioned more than we consume. We must reclaim the attainment of wisdom as a goal that supersedes our need to know. We must view questioning as a form of liberation that is necessary if we are to be truly connected to one another. Communication among us cannot take the place of our personal journeys through the wilderness.

As Professor Mejias so eloquently told me, "We've come to believe that Google has all the answers, without realizing that what is changing is our ability to formulate questions Google can't answer."

Yes, what about the questions Google can't answer?

We cannot raise our children to measure their lives by their ability to navigate what *is;* we must encourage them to imagine what *can be.* This requires a recommitment to the art of the question. It requires taking a step back from marveling at the technical prowess of our young people and ensuring that they are developing the habits of mind that will prepare them to engage effectively throughout their lives.

Part II

Schools:
Citizens or Consumers?

"The essence of mathematics resides in its freedom."

"To ask the right question is harder than to answer it."

GEORG CANTOR

n 1912, Romiett Stevens studied classroom questions and found that two-thirds of the questions required repeating exactly what was in the textbook. In 1956, Benjamin Bloom looked at classrooms and found that 95 percent of test questions required recalling information — not processing or synthesizing, just recalling. In 1970, Meredith Gall repeated Stevens's experiment and found that "60 percent of the questions students hear require factual answers, 20 percent concern procedures, and only 20 percent require inference, transfer, or reflection."[1] Nearly forty years later, in the era of No Child Left Behind, we can pretty much guarantee that the numbers haven't shifted dramatically. We test a lot, but not all questions are created equal.

Motivated to unearth and categorize these different sorts of questions, Bloom came up with what educators refer to as Bloom's Taxonomy. It's a pyramid representing the goals of education, on a scale organized by levels; each level represents what one can do with what one knows. The bottom level is Knowledge, the most basic level of cognition. If you know something, you can define, duplicate, label, list, and memorize it. The pyramid works its way up to levels that require more critical thinking, from Comprehension (you can explain it), to Application (you can illustrate it), to Analysis (you can outline it and distinguish between it and something else), to Synthesis (you can organize A and B and come up with C), to the highest level, Evaluation. At the level of

Evaluation, you can make arguments or predictions, place a value on information, and make tough decisions among competing positions.[2]

Questions are the tools of educators, but what kinds of questions are best to ask? It depends on what we expect children to be able to do. Most questions asked and tested over the past hundred years simply force students to recall information: who, what, where, when, how. It is, as one educator put it, an exercise akin to the game Trivial Pursuit. Naturally, it's important to know such things as multiplication or who represents you in Congress. But is this really our highest expectation of students, that they can remember what they have learned and repeat it back?

It's all in the question. The type of question we pose will determine the quality of the answer we get. Our questions are the manifestation of our goals and expectations for young people and for our public discourse. If we organize our entire educational system around asking students to recall information, let's not be surprised when they have not developed the skills to formulate opinions on complicated matters. And if they don't develop the skills to formulate opinions on complicated matters, let's not be surprised if they grow up disengaged from our democracy, overly reliant on the charisma of politicians rather than the substance of their positions.

Questions are so important because our ability to teach answers is limited. The answers change. Information changes. This is the essence of inquiry-based learning.

"Allowing kids to be inquirers gives them the opportunity to learn how to learn," the Institute for Inquiry's Lynn Rankin told me. "Yes, you have to have a certain set of skills, but a lot of what we focus on is outdated by the time kids can use it. In the end, you want people who can find their way through whatever it is they have to deal with in life, whether it be career or family or society." When inquiry drives the educational process, we define success as providing young people with the ability to grasp the moving target that is the future.

Elana Karopkin, founding principal of the Urban Assembly School for Law and Justice, a New York City public school that graduated 93 percent of its first class and sent 80 percent to college (compared to citywide averages of 56 percent and 60.5 percent, respectively),[3] is quite clear on her goal. She told me, "We're not just teaching content. We're not even just teaching skills. We're teaching what is known as habits of mind." It is these habits of mind that will enable graduates to succeed as they encounter the unpredictable. Today's high school graduates are likely to have eleven jobs and move nine times over the course of their lives.[4] Good educators want their students to practice the habit of probing deeply so that they can navigate whatever they encounter; they enforce this habit through their questions.

What are the habits of mind of our culture? Do we question? Do we teach our children to question? Or are we too busy imparting the message that it is possible to know all that there is to know? Are we teaching children to value the process of questioning and thinking critically, or are we encouraging getting the right answer at any cost?

Our public school system, like our culture more broadly, is increasingly focused much more on the answer than on the question. This shift is disguised as necessary in order to prepare young people to succeed in our economy. The ethos driving today's public school system is a departure from its historic mission of preparing citizens who question their democracy, which I describe in chapter 5, to preparing consumers and workers trained only to navigate things as they are. This shift is dangerous. And unnecessary.

We see this shift evidenced in the movement toward teaching by standardized exam, in which the habit of mind of the critical thinker is less important than attaining the highest possible score. We see it in the structure of our public schooling, in which science, civics, art, and every other subject in which questioning and discovery are most important get pushed aside in favor of subjects that are quantifiable.

President George W. Bush's education legacy is the transformation of the role of public schools, not only in policy but also in our collective imagination. Absent even in the 2008 campaign to succeed him were mentions of the role of our public school system in preparing citizens—despite our collective national embarrassment at the low voter turnout in national elections, and the constant meme of low civic participation in our communities. It is no coincidence that civics is less on our minds at a time when No Child Left Behind and education-reform-by-testing have set the terms of any debate about public education. Our entire school system is driven by student performance on standardized exams. The question today is not how will a given lesson help children but how will it help children pass their exams?

The proponents of standardized testing do not acknowledge what gets lost in favor of an unrelenting focus on test performance. Every educator I spoke to across the country has limited his or her curriculum in order to "teach to the test." The hard data confirm this trend. Supporters of standardized testing make the case that a curriculum of test preparation is somehow an adequate substitute for civics and history instruction, that learning "the basics" will somehow turn a child who has never been encouraged to question into a thoughtful and engaged citizen.

On May 16, 2007, U.S. Secretary of Education Margaret Spellings heralded the results of a national civics exam on which eighth graders showed a slight improvement but on which only one in four high school students exhibited proficiency. "These results are a testament to what works," Spellings said. "While critics may argue that [No Child Left Behind] leads educators to narrow their curriculum focus, the fact is, when students know how to read and comprehend, they apply these skills to other subjects, like history and civics."[5]

In fact, the results of the exam were so poor that it required spectacular hubris to declare "mission accomplished." In addition, the reasoning fails. When would children perform this application of reading and comprehension skills if they are too busy preparing for reading and comprehension exams to take civics or history classes?

Children do need the basics, as the proponents of No Child Left Behind argue. But they also need to know why the basics matter. We used to send the message that better citizenship was the reason. We don't any longer—a missed opportunity to meet even the goals of the standards movement, because children who take civics and are involved in the local democracies of their schools achieve at higher levels than those who do not. The *why* matters. But I don't hear a lot about it.

Financial Literacy in the Schools

What I do hear a lot about, though, is an emerging movement to bring financial literacy to our nation's schools. As the foreclosure crisis began to lead to the implosion of our housing bubble in January 2008, Bush convened the President's Advisory Council on Financial Literacy.[6] On today's editorial pages, I read more and more columns calling for mandatory financial literacy training in our schools: "Financial Literacy: A Tough Teachable Moment—The credit, housing meltdown has shown that lessons in money management must start as soon as kids can count"; "Financial Illiteracy Plagues America"; "We Teach Teens Trigonometry, Why Not Money 101?"[7] During the same week that Congress voted for a historic rescue of Wall Street, supposedly designed to prevent an economic catastrophe provoked by the excess, fraud, and greed of financial institutions, I listened to a news anchor for CNN Business tell a group of educators that if she had "one wish, just one wish," it would be that every child would take a financial literacy class in high school.

I'm sure that a financial literacy training class would have prevented the massive deregulation that led to our economic crisis — if it had been offered to bank presidents and members of Congress. It was the financial literates who got us into this mess, after all.

Young people, particularly those most likely to live on the margins of our economy, should know the basics of personal finance. But the growth of the financial literacy industry — particularly when it focuses on the classroom as the appropriate place to impart these lessons — tells us something about this moment in time. Formal civics, where inquiry is valued, encouraged, and understood to be integral to effective citizenship, is on the decline. Standardized testing, where the only thing that matters is filling in the right bubble, is on the rise. And financial literacy is increasingly considered to be an important purpose of public education.

Our economy functions in a framework with limitations dictated by our democracy. The shape our economy takes is not inevitable; it never has been. Yet, financial literacy curricula foster acceptance of the market's status quo rather than the skills to question — and potentially to change — that status quo. Financial literacy education prepares students to be better consumers of products provided by established financial institutions. Civics, by contrast, educates students to understand their government and to question the nature and behavior of institutions in a democratic society. The latter is a more appropriate purpose for public schooling, not just because it is romantic but also because it will more effectively serve our democracy.

I believe that America's economic crisis is the perfect illustration of the absence of civics, not of an absence of financial literacy. It did not result from too much interference with the inner workings of the market but from too *little*. Some parties—business, the administration of the former president—would have us believe otherwise. And in that case, we need to question the source.

In most schools, individual teachers don't have to choose between teaching financial literacy and teaching civics. But in the bigger picture, that is our choice. Do our schools prepare young people to be citizens or consumers? Do our schools prepare young people to ask questions or to get the right answer? What do we value? And which value really best prepares our young people, and our nation, to succeed?

Our democracy will suffer if the youngest among us grow up thinking that today's society and the economy that sustains it are working just as they should. Our hopes of becoming a fairer and more just nation will suffer if our young grow up without knowing how to navigate their own democracy, without the experience of creating change in their communities, without the sense of empowerment that comes from the very asking of questions. The stakes are higher than the educational experience of any individual child. It's about whether our youngest are prepared to assert their collective citizenship at a time when democracy is skewed toward the powerful few.

These experiences in citizenship can be created in our schools. In fact, there are educators trying to do this in schools throughout the country. But, until we accept such a thing as a purpose of public schooling, their efforts will be viewed as peripheral, distracting, and, by some who fear that democracy itself can't handle questioning, unpatriotic.

I'm not naive. I don't argue for a return to the "good old days" when children learned how bills become law and returned home to manicured lawns, fathers reading the daily paper, and healthy snacks. Those who say that we live in a new age are absolutely correct. Our economy has changed dramatically since the time when children went home with civics grades on their report cards. The contours of our democracy are changing as well, leaving most of us with less power to influence decisions as regular people than is possessed by the multinational corporations that have emerged from the ashes of our twentieth-century social contract. My argument, however, is that young people who know how to question, think about the world around them, and ask *why* are those most likely to succeed in this new world. It is up to our public schools to prepare them to do so. Our democracy depends on it.

5: **The Three Rs and a Why**

Civics: n. the study of civic affairs and the duties and rights of citizenship

I WAS NOT A VERY GOOD SCIENCE STUDENT. IN FACT, I don't think much about science in my daily work, beyond fretting about those who don't want to teach it in our public schools, the deep sadness that comes with knowing that access to the laboratories and equipment of teaching are dependent upon privilege, and of course, the regular unease about what unchecked globalization has done to our ever-warming environment. But beyond that, not much. Thus, it was somewhat surprising that my investigation into the relationship between inquiry and democracy took me to the Exploratorium.

Founded in 1969 by Frank Oppenheimer, nuclear physicist, Manhattan Project alumnus, and former high school science teacher (after being targeted by the House Un-American Activities Committee), the Exploratorium is an incredible sight to behold. It sits in the three-acre hall that formerly housed San Francisco's Palace of Fine Arts. It's a science museum with hundreds of interactive exhibits designed to allow anyone, of any age, to interact with the natural phenomena of the world.

Oppenheimer described his rationale for wanting to connect people to the forces shaping much of their daily lives: "The fruits of science and the products of technology continue to shape the nature of our society and to influence events which have a worldwide significance. Yet the gulf between the daily lives and experience of most people and the complexity of science and technology is widening."[1] Rather than taking these questions on by offering an authoritative analysis of just how we interact with science, the Exploratorium is an environment where people can figure out how things work, where they can observe, touch, and play, and in the process, "nurture their curiosity about the world around them."

The Exploratorium is visited by 550,000 people each year. One sunny day in September 2008, I was one of them. I wasn't there to play but to visit the Exploratorium's Institute for Inquiry and its director, Lynn Rankin. Based in a bay-side bungalow across the street from the Exploratorium, the Institute teaches inquiry, or rather, demonstrates how teachers can use inquiry as the basis from which children should learn. Rankin was an elementary school teacher for seven years before coming to the Exploratorium in 1975. Her career here started with a visit, when she was "captivated" by the possibilities of this environment where kids were given an opportunity to pursue whatever provoked their curiosity.

The Institute trains teachers and professional developers from across the country—thousands from thirty-nine states, at last count. It invites teachers and professional developers of elementary school children to experience inquiry for themselves—a necessity before they can teach it to anyone else. The Institute's trainings are designed to offer a transformative experience for teachers who, as Rankin told me, "might already think they're doing inquiry, and after they have the experience [here], they might say, 'I'm not really giving my kids the opportunity to ask a lot of questions.'"

I asked Rankin about what it means to "do inquiry," a phrase she repeated a few times. According to Rankin, doing inquiry boils down to who is in charge. Inquiry-based teaching allows children to "have some ownership and responsibility for the question . . . You are guiding rather than giving them all the information. You're guiding the learner to help them understand as much as they possibly can on their own." In other words, doing inquiry means that the question steers the conversation.

The Institute's work is a direct challenge to some of the ways in which our school system, ever obsessed with the answer, has subverted science. Karen Wilkinson, a science educator at the Institute, pointed out to me that "we were taught from the scientific method that you develop a hypothesis first. But when you really talk to scientists, that's not where they start. We are teaching kids to go about science by coming up with the answer, and then asking them to state it in the form of a question." The school system manages to subvert the scientific process from open-ended inquiry to something that we can package neatly around answers. The Institute's work is to help teachers flip this script. First we observe, and then we question. Only then can we try to answer.

In the No Child Left Behind era, science is less of a priority than the subjects evaluated through high-stakes testing. This decline would surely be regrettable to Oppenheimer, who would likely be unable to reconcile the growing presence of technology in our lives with the decreasing presence of science in our schooling. Others lament science's low spot on the totem pole, viewing it as an indictment of our national priorities. They ask, How will we be competitive, technologically, economically, if we don't produce more engineers, scientists, and entrepreneurs?

But I think of the de-emphasis of science as speaking to something else that isn't important to us in the realm of public education today: the exploration of our democracy.

What if we encouraged our citizens to approach democracy just as the students at the Exploratorium approach science? If we let them go out there and observe it, as children at the Exploratorium do when they explore their self-consciousness in the Mind exhibit or stumble through the Tactile Dome with only their sense of touch to guide them? There is no doubt in my mind that if we cultivated a hands-on approach to democracy among our youth, we would develop citizens who think more critically and acquire the resilience of the scientist, who regularly pursues one path only to realize that she must start over.

Like science, democracy is a messy business. We try one hypothesis and it doesn't work, so we try another. It's through the *exploration* of democracy that we can uncover its properties and understand our relationship to it. The kids at the Exploratorium fall in love with science because they can touch, feel, see, and ask questions about what otherwise seems so remote; we can do the same with democracy if we let children in. As with science, democracy is all around us. But we need to experience it firsthand. There's a name for that: civics.

The Civic Function of Schools

It seems bizarre to have to make the case that the public school system should prepare citizens for democracy. This is, after all, why our public school system was founded in the first place.

The Civic Mission of Schools — a landmark report released in 2003 — explained that, in his farewell address as president in 1796, "George Washington recommended 'as an object of primary importance' the creation of 'institutions for the general diffusion of knowledge.' He gave a democratic argument for investing in education: 'In proportion as the structure of a government gives force to public opinion,' he said, 'it is essential that public opinion should be enlightened.'"[2] In other words, if we've gone through all of this effort to make the United States a democracy out of the belief that we the people should decide our own fates, we the people should be as informed as possible in order to make good decisions.

It was Thomas Jefferson, though, who made explicit the case for creating a public school system, from the early grades through university, and for that public school system to function with a civic purpose in mind. He expressed his view on civics in the context of his view of "the essential principles of our government" at his March 4, 1800, inaugural address, stating that the principles of justice, freedom of religion, freedom of the press, and the "anchor of peace" should be "the creed of our political faith, *the text of civic instruction,* the touchstone by which to try the services of those we trust."[3]

One hundred years later, the American Political Science Association appointed the Committee of Five to examine how schools were, or were not, preparing high school students for citizenship. They asked, somewhat rhetorically, "Is it not a curious fact that though our schools are largely instituted, supported, and operated by the government, the study of American government in the schools and colleges is the last subject to receive adequate attention?" The committee wasn't pining for history classes but for classes that would offer "practical education to enable people to meet their civic duties."[4]

This practical education in our duties and responsibilities as citizens is civics. History is the study of that which has happened. Civics is about preparing each and every one of us to make our own history, by giving us the skills to navigate our democracy.

In practice, "civics" means different things to different people. I sat with a lawyer in her forties who told me that she listened to jingles in school that told her to look both ways before she crossed the street and to be nice to strangers; to her, this was civics. To others, civics is how a bill becomes a law. A colleague who grew up in a conservative town described how her civics teacher assigned readings from Adam Smith and Karl Marx and asked the students to debate whether capitalism or Marxism was a better system for

America. In Hampton, Virginia, civics means engaging young people in discussions about school policy. At the School for Democracy and Leadership in Brooklyn, New York, civic engagement happens when young people identify something in their community that they want to change and then learn about it. When I facilitate a discussion with college students about what they've read in the newspaper each morning, challenging them to read carefully and critically but inspiring in them the desire to learn more about current affairs, I am giving them a civics education (more on this in chapter 9).

I don't ever remember taking a civics class that was labeled as such. But Mrs. Lorraine Wachtel observed my interest in her American government class, encouraged me to participate in student government, and in doing so, began my lifelong commitment to public policy, thereby dashing my parents' hopes of corporate lawyerdom.

There is no formula for best preparing citizens. We've done it different ways throughout our nation's history. We've emphasized history education — teaching a limited history, at that — to facilitate the assimilation and acculturation of immigrants. We've required children to take classes such as Problems in Democracy, in which they engaged with the debates of the day.

Until the 1960s, we offered civics classes that served as "indoctrination in Americanism, patriotism, and so forth. Sort of a mindless George Washington and the cherry tree," according to Charles Quigley, executive director of the Center for Civic Education, who has been in this business for over forty years. And though the corresponding "correction," as the market would call it, led to an improved and more accurate treatment of history, "the history books then left out American government or the history of American government. You would have a seven hundred–page textbook, which would have twelve pages on the Constitution," Quigley told me. This form of history, too, was inadequate for the preparation of citizens.

In times past, it has been a priority to figure out how to prepare citizens through our public education system. Since the early times of our nation, the question wasn't *if* the public schools should prepare effective citizens, but *how*. That is the question we need to be asking today. Less important than the shape that civics education takes is a commitment to the goal it sets out to accomplish.

The *Civic Mission of Schools* report is a helpful guide. The product of a year of meetings and collaborations among fifty-nine practitioners and prominent Americans from across the political and ideological spectrum, the report offered an indictment of our system's preparation of young citizens. It defined the goals of civic education as the following:

> Civic education should help young people acquire and learn to use the skills, knowledge, and attitudes that will prepare them to be competent and responsible citizens throughout their lives. Competent and responsible citizens:
>
> 1. are informed and thoughtful; have a grasp and an appreciation of history and the fundamental processes of American democracy; have an understanding and awareness of public and community issues; and have the ability to obtain information, think critically, and enter into dialogue among others with different perspectives.
>
> 2. participate in their communities through membership in or contributions to organizations working to address an array of cultural, social, political, and religious interests and beliefs.
>
> 3. act politically by having the skills, knowledge, and

commitment needed to accomplish public purposes, such as group problem solving, public speaking, petitioning and protesting, and voting.

4. have moral and civic virtues such as concern for the rights and welfare of others, social responsibility, tolerance and respect, and belief in the capacity to make a difference.[5]

Civics education in schools creates young people who turn into the citizens that our democracy requires. And, most importantly, civics in schools works. Young people who study civics talk more frequently about political affairs with their parents, peers, and teachers.[6] Young people who have taken a civics course are often "two or three times more likely to say they have engaged in political activities than those who have not."[7]

This civic engagement — and the sense of responsibility it creates — leads to greater commitment not only to democracy but also to one's education. Young people who participate in civic engagement activities will do better in high school reading, math, science, and history, and are more likely to graduate from college.[8] They learn the three Rs but they also learn the *why*. The *why* makes all the difference.

The State of Civics Knowledge

In 1906, the Committee of Five "linked poor preparation at the early levels to the plethora of bad politicians and weak public servants its members believed dominated turn-of-the-century American government." According to Hindy Lauer Schachter's analysis, the debate about civics was more than academic. The success of our participatory democracy was viewed as being directly related to the preparation of its youngest citizens.[9]

If you believe that this is true today, then you must also worry that our democracy is in sorry shape.

Since 1969, the federal government has tested young people on their civic knowledge — that is, their understanding of the inner workings of government and their rights and responsibilities as citizens. These exams are part of a larger battery of tests in all subjects, called the National Assessment of Education Progress. Unlike the other exams, however, NAEP civics is tested only every four years. By comparison, math and reading are tested at least every two years, as required by No Child Left Behind.[10]

The abysmal performance of American children on these civics exams tells the story of how we are failing to educate our children about their critical role as citizens. According to the NAEP's *Report Card*, proficient students "should be able to describe similarities and differences among constitutional systems of government, and they should be able to explain fundamental American democratic values, their applications, and their contribution to expanding political participation. They should understand the structure of American government and be able to evaluate activities of political parties, interest groups, and media in public affairs. They should be able to explain the importance of political participation, public service, and political leadership. They should be able to describe major elements of American foreign policy and the performance of major international organizations."

On the 2006 exam, only one in four American twelfth graders was found to be "proficient." Five percent of twelfth graders tested could explain three ways in which the president can be checked by the legislative or judicial branches. One in two could explain the outcome when state and national laws conflict. Twenty-eight percent of eighth graders could articulate the historical purpose of the Declaration of Independence. Only one in four could, when presented with a photograph of Martin Luther King Jr.'s 1963 March on Washington, explain "two specific ways in which marches and demonstrations such as the one illustrated can achieve political goals."[11]

Although exams mostly test knowledge of facts rather than understanding, there are some questions that explore young people's ideas about citizenship. In a question that would require the skill of "evaluating, taking, and defending a position," as the test lingo describes it, fourth graders were asked to use their understanding of what it means to be a good citizen to talk about how the following actions would affect other people in their community: not returning library books, volunteering to help senior citizens with chores, and littering. Only 18 percent completed the question. Among students who had supposedly demonstrated a "basic" civics knowledge, only 15 percent were able to offer a response to this question at all.[12]

The civic ignorance of our young people, as evidenced by these scores, is a long-term threat. The decision to vote — and then the basis on which people make their decisions in the voting booth — can be traced to our civic knowledge. According to Samuel Popkin and Michael Dimock, "Nonvoting results from a lack of knowledge about what government is doing and where parties and candidates stand, not from a knowledgeable rejection of government or parties or a lack of trust in government."[13] That was George Washington's point all along: active citizens are integral to democracy, and schools are the training grounds for those citizens.

If I were writing a script for a Hollywood movie in which democracy is threatened, I wouldn't start with weird creatures, lots of flashing lights, and pummeling, robotic arms. Instead, my opening scene would be an American classroom in which children aren't learning to ask questions because they are drilling for an upcoming standardized test, in which they don't talk about current events because they are being taught by bank executives how to open checking accounts, in which they don't know what the Supreme Court is or the role of political protest or how they as citizens can change the policies that govern their lives.

Though I might still cast Tom Cruise.

The Decline of Civics as a Priority

Whenever I talk to people across dinner tables or boardroom tables about the importance of civic education, I encounter vigorous head nodding. It's a guaranteed applause line from both sides of the aisle — similar to "energy independence" and "high standards." It seems like motherhood and apple pie. Teaching kids to be good citizens — I mean, that's just American!

Our elected leaders do give it lip service. As Republican Senator Lamar Alexander put it in 2003, when he hosted hearings on teaching civics and American history, "It is time to put the teaching of American history and civics back in its rightful place in our schools so our children can grow up learning what it means to be an American."[14] On September 17, 2002, just over a year after 9/11, Bush summoned historian David McCullough to the Rose Garden to launch a new effort to connect America's young people to our nation's history.

"American children are not born knowing what they should cherish — are not born knowing why they should cherish American values. A love of democratic principles must be taught," Bush said.[15]

But when to teach it? Where? In financial literacy class? Between drills for the upcoming math exam? Civics was not a priority in the Bush administration.

Indeed, Bush's willingness to back up the statement made in the Rose Garden was inconsistent at best. After budget proposals in fiscal years 2002 and 2003 that recommended elimination of funding for the Center for Civic Education's signature We the People program, Bush did make room in his 2004 and 2005 budgets for the initiative. But his fiscal year 2006, 2007, 2008, and 2009 budgets all recommended defunding We the People. In his budgetary justifications for elimination, Bush suggested the programs should either be cut completely from the Department of Education budget or should be funded through broader department initiatives. Referring specifically to We the People, Bush's justification read, "Request is consistent with the Administration's policy of terminating small categorical programs that have limited impact, and for which there is little or no evidence of effectiveness, to fund higher priority programs."[16]

Rather than strengthening We the People and the Center for Civic Education, Bush set his priorities elsewhere and was willing to abandon the program completely. Although he created a separate (and completely different) We the People program at the National Endowment for the Humanities, the Bush administration attempted to push civics programs away from specific spending authorizations and into broad programs where funding was anything but certain.[17] In effect, the administration tried to get rid of the Center for Civic Education.

When civics was more important in the schools, children brought home civics grades on their report cards. In fact, students took three civics classes, including Problems in Democracy, in which they talked about current affairs and challenges facing American government.

"We know that a substantial percentage of kids in the mid-twentieth century took that Problems in Democracy course," lamented Peter Levine, director of the Center for Information & Research on Civic Learning and Engagement. Today, that course is gone, with nothing to replace it. "I really do think that [coursework] probably can't be found in the intricacies of today's curriculum," Levine told me. "It's not like they're doing that somewhere else."

Educators had something special in mind when they devised the Problems of Democracy course. A 1930 article in *The School Review* describes how the ideal Problems of Democracy course would be taught:

> After having become familiar with the fundamental political, social, and economic problems contained in the various syllabuses, the teacher will select problems according to their timeliness. The approach should always be concerned with a current issue, either local or national. In order to present the subject properly, it is absolutely essential to devote one day a week to current events. The systematic study of newspapers and periodicals will stimulate interest and will make it possible to bring the material in the textbook up to date . . . Definite current problems should be presented . . . Should our city adopt the city-manager plan of government? Is American family life deteriorating or is it merely in a state of transition? Should the tariff commission be given a greater share in tariff-making?[18]

There was a place in the classroom not only for current events and newspapers but also for challenging and timely questions.

Even Quigley's Project Citizen, part of the Center for Civic Education and one of the most popular civics programs, which he described to me as "actively engag[ing] kids in going into their communities, interviewing people, doing survey research, identifying public policy problems, developing their own proposed solutions and political action plans, and trying to have an impact on City Hall," only reaches about 500,000 students each year — 1 percent of the nation's school-age population in 2006.[19] No wonder America's children know so little about how their democracy operates.

Quigley was an elementary school teacher before entering

the civics business, and he attributes to the 1960s the decline in civics as a formal part of schooling.

"Vietnam and then Watergate brought disenchantment, rebellion, experimentation, a loss of faith in traditional institutions and traditional leaders, the breakup of consensus, the weakening of the core culture," he told me.[20] Why learn about democracy at a time when people saw government as inherently corrupt? Is it even safe to engage people in conversations about current affairs when ideological divisions are so strong? Were young people — those out on the streets — to be trusted to become more involved in their democracy rather than less? Perhaps it was best just to focus on reading, writing, and math.

Civics programs in the 1960s were not very effective at imparting knowledge or excitement about political history or contemporary events. Or, as Quigley puts it simply: the courses were boring. "More attention was paid to the memorization of facts, important as that may be, than to inquiry, discussion, and debate." Effective civic education programs now use case studies to bring "reality and relevance into the classroom as well as the excitement of discussion and debate." Other simulations, such town meetings, hearings, and lobbying exercises, develop participatory skills.[21] But although Quigley calls this movement effective, he readily acknowledges that it is severely limited in scope.

In recent history, the priority given to civics has changed as our notion of what needs to take place in schools has changed. Schools have become places where children learn the basics so that they can succeed in the workplace. Americans are torn on the question of which is more important, work or citizenship. In a 2000 Gallup poll, 59 percent of Americans thought it was more important for the schools to prepare students for college or work, compared to 34 percent who thought it was more important to prepare students for effective citizenship. However, when the question was asked differently, respondents rated "preparing people to become responsible citizens" a nine on a ten-point scale of importance. Helping people become economically self-sufficient received an average score of 8.6.[22]

Similarly, in a 2004 poll sponsored by the Campaign for the Civic Mission of Schools and the Alliance for Representative Democracy, 71 percent of adults said it was important to prepare students "to be competent and responsible citizens who participate in our democratic society."[23] There may not be perfect consensus across every poll on which comes first and which comes second, but there is consensus that the schools need to prepare responsible citizens.

Uninterested in these debates about the role of public schooling, Bush's education policy centered on the No Child Left Behind initiative he championed. Created to impose accountability on a system functioning poorly for low-income students, its primary offerings are the standardized reading and math tests that expose students' achievement levels. Although this clarity is a critical development in a system known to hide the poor achievement of low-income kids and children of color by jumbling them up into the mix with white middle-class kids, the punishment doled out for failure has resulted in a system obsessed with reading and math test scores and little else. According to Deborah Meier, a teacher and principal who has successfully educated students of color for forty years, somewhere along the line we have come to believe "that's the new idea: testing as reform, not for reform."[24] Tests are the measure, but what content are we measuring?

In his address to the joint session of Congress in 2001, Bush addressed critics of standardized testing by saying, "They talk about 'teaching to the test.' But let's put that logic to the test. If you test a child on basic math and reading skills, and you're 'teaching to the test,' you're teaching math and reading. And that's the whole idea."[25] The fact that teaching to the test is viewed as "the whole idea" is precisely the problem.

The victim of this emphasis on testing is instruction in history and civics. Bush and his second secretary of education, Spellings, believed that concentration on the basics that get tested will "trickle down" into students' understanding of history and civics. Spellings assured those who were worried about the absence of classes in history, civics, arts, and so forth that "job one is to do reading right and well, and some of the rest of this stuff I think will take care of itself."[26]

But there has been little progress in the performance of America's young people on civics exams since the introduction of No Child Left Behind. The civics knowledge of eighth graders has not changed since 1998, the last time the exam was offered. Twelfth graders, too, performed the same in 2006 as they did in 1998. Although there was an increase in performance in the fourth-grade pool, fewer than one in two could identify the role of the Supreme Court. Seventy-five percent of students knew that one has to be a U.S. citizen in order to vote in a presidential election; the others thought one must be a citizen to drive a car, own a business, or write a letter to a newspaper editor. Only 14 percent recognized that defendants have the right to a lawyer. The average score for fourth graders was 154 out of a possible 300.[27]

Trickle-down theories — whether in economics or in education — didn't work out too well for the Bushes, and they don't work out well for the future of our democracy. Students don't automatically learn history just because they learned reading. They don't acquire the skills transmitted through civics class just because they can do math. Children cannot apply their reading and comprehension skills to history or civics if there is no forum for the application. And with teachers and schools making dramatic shifts in their educational programming to emphasize the subjects that are being tested, to the point of excluding everything else, Spellings's argument about the ripple effects of emphasizing the basics becomes impossible to prove.

It's true that students who read and write better would be more likely to thrive in a history class, and would bring a stronger base from which to engage in a conversation about how to understand and participate in their government. But how would we know? Spellings's argument is circular: these tests increase reading skills, and — when applied — reading skills improve history, so let's keep up the tests and take time away from history. Not to worry; students will continue to have the skills to apply to something that they will never learn.

Civics, on the other hand, teaches young people not just how to absorb information but also how to question. They ask how their democracy works and why. They ask how it could work better, and what we can do to make it work better.

"One of the things about this movement in civic education," Quigley told me, "is that it does foster an inquiry method. It's like case studies, examination, analysis, discussion, debate, role playing, simulations."[28] As Levine puts it, "Civic education that teaches people to admire a flawed system is mere propaganda. Instead, we should reform major institutions."[29] The reform of institutions — whether the local school board or Washington lobbies — begins with asking questions.

Asking questions is not innate among our young people anymore, not in a culture in which what matters most is doing well on standardized exams. We have managed a Herculean effort — stifling the natural curiosity of our young in the name of education "reform" and college and workplace preparation.

"As people, we're all naturally curious," Allyson Graul, director of the Youth Civic Engagement Center at Alternatives Inc. in Hampton, Virginia, told me. "But in so many ways our society has shut down our curiosity and replaced it with these right-wrong answers. Our school system has created young people who are just about getting the 'right' answer without really looking beyond that." This direction is not inevitable. It is the result of how we think about the central purpose of education.

In Graul's city, young people are learning how to ask questions again. Their canvas is the democracy of their schools and city. Hampton youth are learning how their government and systems work and are learning that questions are key to their ability to express their own power. High school students are decision makers. They sit on a youth commission, are hired to work in the planning department, advise superintendents, and even give away city funds to endeavors they view as worthwhile. The town created this system of youth civic engagement not because it was cute or because they were particularly motivated by Thomas Jefferson (though it was supposedly in Hampton that Jefferson's mentor, George Wythe, was born). They did it because they saw the disaffection of their young and they knew that the only way to change direction was to let young people ask questions and have the power to deal with the answers.

In Hampton, where we'll return in chapter 10, we can see the promise of civics. Four hundred miles away, in an East Harlem schoolroom, we see the perils of its absence. There, a well-dressed bank executive takes over a math class every week to lecture fourth graders on the importance of saving. The program that sends him and thousands of other financial-sector volunteers into city schools was announced with a fancy press release. The children's eyes are glazed over for most of the forty-minute period. They do not ask any questions when he is done.

6: No Piggy Bank Left Behind

IN THE BUSINESS OF POLITICS WE HAVE SOMETHING called a "push poll." Maybe you have been an unwitting victim of it. You get one of these in-the-middle-of-dinner phone calls from an innocent-sounding voice that asks for just a few moments of your time. She says she is from some kind of official polling outfit and then asks you questions that go a little like this: "Did you know that City Councilman Smith voted three times against increases in salaries for our police officers? Did you know that City Councilman Smith voted to raise taxes on families just like yours? Did you know that City Councilman Smith is a bad child who doesn't love his mother? Do you intend to vote to reelect City Councilman Smith?"

We call this a push poll because it isn't a neutral survey like those conducted by Harris or Nielsen or an academic institution, in which respondents tell pollsters what they think about what they watched on television last week or read in today's papers. This poll is designed to push people one way or another — that's why the sponsors pay for it in the first place.

The growing movement toward financial literacy education in schools works in much the same way. Consider the following question from materials distributed to fourth graders to test their "financial literacy":

> Don and Bill work together in the finance department of the same company and earn the same pay.

Bill spends his free time taking work-related classes to improve his computer skills, while Don spends his free time socializing with friends and working out at a fitness center. After five years, what is likely to be true?

(a) Don will make more because he is more social.

(b) Don will make more because Bill is likely to be laid off.

(c) Bill will make more money because he is more valuable to his company.

(d) Don and Bill will continue to make the same money.

If you answered (c) Bill will make more money because he is more valuable to his company, you are correct. You join the 67.9 percent of high school seniors surveyed by the Jump$tart coalition as part of its biennial survey of our nation's youth.[1] If you answered (a), (b), or (d), you need to go back to financial literacy school.

In our nation's education system, what is tested gets taught. So, as I hold the Jump$tart survey in my hands, I am aware that it exists to do more than satisfy the curiosity of its sponsors. It's an instrument designed to convey a message. Each question corresponds to knowledge that Jump$tart would like young people to possess, and that it would therefore like the schools to teach. Dara Duguay, former executive director of Jump$tart, testified before Congress, "If it is not in the standards, if it is not tested, you can have the best curricula in the world and it will never, ever get into the classroom."[2] And Jump$tart wants financial literacy in the classroom.

Although the answer to the question about Don and Bill speaks to our shared vision of the United States as a meritocracy, there is no guarantee that hard work means upward mobility. To answer this question correctly is not to be literate but to misunderstand the fundamentals of the present economy.

The complicated question of mobility is certainly worthy of exploration in a classroom. Students could absolutely benefit from examining the changing nature of the workplace, which has resulted in shorter tenure at companies with fewer avenues of upward mobility; the decline in protections that would facilitate advancement for most workers; outsourcing and offshoring; and the increasing presence of jobs in this country that require either a lot of education or not much at all.

Such exploration, however, is not the intention of this test question, or of the test in general, or of the lessons that Jump$tart believes should be taught in schools. So what is the intention?

To explore this question, we must turn to the goals of those who seek to make financial literacy a more integral part of our educational system. We must look at why corporate America is funding this movement and why those of us who are interested in preparing young people to be effective citizens — not just effective consumers — should be paying attention.

A Dream of Financial Literacy — Who's Behind It?

Founded in 1995, Jump$tart is a national coalition of organizations dedicated to improving the financial literacy of kindergarten- through college-age youth by providing advocacy, research, standards, and educational resources. Jump$tart strives to prepare youth for successful, lifelong financial decision making.

"A Dream of Financial Literacy," published in *Credit Union Magazine* and written by Lewis Mandell and Maykala Hariharan, explains how the operation came to be:

> In 1996, a group gathered in Washington, D.C., to try to understand two powerful but seemingly opposite

trends. On one hand, it was the best of economic times, with increasing affluence for people of every income. On the other hand, it was the worst of times, with personal bankruptcies threatening to wipe out the assets of a million families in a single year. How could so many people be doing so poorly at a time when the growing economy was doing so well?

We concluded that much of the problem was due to a newly deregulated but very innovative financial system that demands of its users a high level of financial sophistication. Our suspicion was that many Americans lacked the basic financial literacy to make decisions in their own best interest.[3]

The group thus decided to focus on improving the financial literacy skills of young people. Today, Jump$tart is a big player in a growing financial literacy movement — a term that appeared on the scene in a big way only fifteen years ago — but it is by no means alone. Financial literacy curriculum has increasingly shown up in classrooms across the country. According to a survey by the National Council on Economic Education (now called the Council for Economic Education), the number of states that included personal finance in their education standards increased from twenty-one in 1998 to forty in 2007; seven states currently require students to take a personal finance course as a high school graduation requirement, up from just a single state in 1998; and nine states require the testing of student knowledge in personal finance, whereas only a single state did in 1998.[4]

As further evidence, the Working in Support of Education (w!se) Financial Literacy Certification Program, headquartered in New York City, has grown from 2,208 participating students, seven participating schools, and one participating state in 2003 to 22,511 participating students, two hundred participating schools, and twenty participating states in 2008.[5]

The Consumer Bankers Association's 2003 survey of financial literacy recognized that "despite varying opinions on how and where students should learn about personal finance, the push to have financial education integrated in public schools continues to gain momentum." Its 2004 survey found that 89 percent of banks surveyed had a public school financial literacy program, compared to 73 percent in 2003, with the average bank-sponsored public school program reaching 142,967 students.[6]

Financial literacy has become a political favorite, as well. Congressional resolutions recognize April as Financial Literacy Month, including celebrations on Capitol Hill and events organized by financial institutions and nonprofit organizations across the country. At least nine committee hearings on financial literacy were held between 2002 and 2007. Furthermore, federal legislation has increasingly supported financial literacy education. For example, a bill "to promote youth financial education" was first introduced in 1999 and has been introduced in every congressional session since.[7] The Excellence in Economic Education Act, which seeks "to promote economic and financial literacy among all students in kindergarten through grade twelve," was included in No Child Left Behind.[8]

In May 2002, the Office of Financial Education was created in the Treasury Department "to promote access to the financial education tools that can help all Americans make wiser choices in all areas of personal financial management, with a special emphasis on saving, credit management, home ownership, and retirement planning."[9] A Treasury Department white paper on integrating education concepts into school curricula helped lead to the inclusion of the Financial Literacy and Education Improvement Act in the Fair and Accurate Transactions Act.[10] The former created the Financial Literacy and Education Commission to develop a national strategy to improve financial literacy and education. By 2004,

Congress appropriated $1.5 million to the National Council on Economic Education under the Excellence in Economic Education Act, an appropriation that would be repeated in 2005, 2006, 2007, and 2008.[11] Finally, on January 21, 2008, Bush established his Advisory Council on Financial Literacy by executive order.[12]

Daily papers rarely used the term *financial literacy* before 1995 (*economic literacy* was used more frequently, to refer to knowledge of economics as well as money sense and personal finance). In 1981, the *Christian Science Monitor* described a California requirement for schools to teach economics, a mandate that led to the development of an economics curriculum in consultation with a California bank. This meeting represented "the first time district offices [have] handed out anything other than material that has been developed in-house."[13] A 1989 *Washington Post* article cited a financial literacy program for small businesses.[14] A 1992 piece in *The Guardian* (UK) noted the growing necessity for financial literacy in the context of a critique of widespread privatization:

> But the business of money is different. Fifteen years ago, its place in the public consciousness was confined to pay packets and a particularly awful song by ABBA. Now, anyone who seriously aspires to be part of the chattering classes has to be financially literate. The ugly argot of economists — PSBR, ERM, DM — has, as it were, become common currency. The change within no more than a generation is astonishing. One has a vague recollection from the 1960s: one's parents were shocked to learn that the couple up the road were borrowing a huge amount of a money (a thousand or so) to buy a house. This bordered on delinquency . . . And running parallel to our progression came a series of books, fiction dressed up as futurology, which reflected our growing financial literacy.[15]

Financial literacy was more apparent in the 1990s, making appearances in the *New York Times, Philadelphia Inquirer, St. Petersburg Times,* and *Washington Post.* All called for education to improve financial literacy. The increased coverage corresponded to a 1994 study conducted by Merrill Lynch (which funded Jump$tart's surveys before going under in the crash of 2008, thanks to its own financial illiteracy) that showed that four out of five Americans flunked a "financial literacy" quiz.[16]

After 1996, the usage of *financial literacy* in print media skyrocketed, with references frequently linked to surveys of Americans' poor financial management skills. In 1996, the *Boston Globe* stated blithely, "There is no qualifying education level that makes a person financially savvy, but the truth is that 'financial literacy' lies somewhere between knowing how to balance a checkbook and the know-how to manage a mutual fund."[17] As a financial crisis took hold in the fall of 2008, financial literacy was mentioned more and more frequently in the press, in articles describing sessions for homeowners at risk of foreclosure, college students racking up student loans, and how to use the financial disaster as a "teaching moment."[18]

The sponsors of financial literacy programs are drawn from the ranks of our largest financial institutions. Jump$tart receives money from Visa, American Express, and Capital One, among others, to serve as the national advocacy arm of 48 affiliated state coalitions throughout the country. It is only one among many organizations whose function is either to raise awareness of or to directly provide financial literacy education, and whose activities are underwritten primarily by industry contributions.

Why the corporate interest in funding financial literacy? As David Dieterle, president of the Michigan Council on Economic Education, put it, "[Businesses have] seen the correlation between people who are economically and financially literate. They make better workers, they make for smarter consumers."[19] And what better place to prepare these workers and consumers than in the schools? John Hope Bryant, founder of Operation HOPE (another big player in the financial literacy movement) told me of his wish: "Right now, people say 'reading, writing, and 'rithmetic.' Well, I believe in 'reading, writing, 'rithmetic, and financial literacy.' It should be a common core building block for our culture."

The American public agrees. According to a 2007 survey undertaken by credit card company Visa, nine out of ten people believe financial literacy should be taught in every American high school.[20] As the economic crisis we find ourselves in worsens, the numbers will surely grow.

During his presidency, George W. Bush was a staunch proponent of financial literacy, establishing the President's Advisory Council on Financial Literacy. The Council brings together businesspeople, faith-based workers, and nonprofit activists to develop recommendations for better educating people about financial matters. The Council has created several committees to address various aspects of financial literacy, including a Youth Committee, and has launched a National Financial Literacy Challenge to test American high school students on personal finance issues.

On Bush's watch, Congress appropriated grants worth nearly $6 million between 2004 and 2007, and another $1.5 million in 2008, for the National Council on Economic Education, under the Excellence in Economic Education Act. That act was included in No Child Left Behind; other financial literacy initiatives were included in major housing and higher education legislation passed in the summer of 2008.[21] Financial literacy work took on special urgency for Bush's administration as the fallout from the home mortgage crisis continued throughout 2008; it was easier to talk about the financial illiteracy of borrowers than about the collapse of our regulatory framework.

The enticements for the sponsoring companies, beyond the ability to influence how young people think about the economy, is, well, financial. As early as 2001, the Bush administration linked the cause of financial literacy to the bottom line of banks. In an advisory, the Office of the Comptroller of the Currency issued a regulation clarifying that national banks can undertake school banking programs without having to go through the formal process that they usually do in starting a branch. The advisory encouraged banks to use financial literacy programs as a means to reach the "unbanked": "Bank involvement in school-age programs not only provides education, but also promotes name recognition for the bank. In addition, when students participating in these programs come from unbanked households, they may share their knowledge of products and services promoted by the bank with family members who have a need for them."[22]

There is almost no subtlety about the motives of the banks that are encouraged to participate. Teach financial literacy, promote your products, and you could very well wind up with more customers. Surely, more of the unbanked should become the banked, but should this happen through a message delivered by children and their homework?

I don't oppose financial literacy education. Young people should be prepared to make good financial choices. Those working in the trenches to improve students' financial management skills are motivated by real concern that young people are accruing debt from which they will never recover. This debt is especially dangerous for youth already living outside of the economic mainstream, with low-paying jobs, in neighborhoods where payday loan outfits outnumber banks.

But what does it say that we have opened up America's public school classrooms for banks to hock their wares — supposedly in the name of our children's advancement? What does it say about us that we are embracing financial literacy in the schools—and what does it say about the members of corporate America that are underwriting it?

What do the banks want to teach our children?

One Person's Test Question Is Another Person's Push Poll

Here's another question from Jump$tart's 2008 survey of 6,856 high school students:

> Matt has a good job on the production line of a factory in his hometown. During the past year or two, the state in which Matt lives has been raising taxes on its businesses to the point where they are much higher than in neighboring states. What effect is this likely to have on Matt's job?
>
> (a) Higher business taxes will cause more businesses to move into Matt's state, raising wages.
>
> (b) Higher business taxes can't have any effect on Matt's job.
>
> (c) Matt's company may consider moving to a lower-tax state, threatening Matt's job.
>
> (d) He is likely to get a large raise to offset the effect of higher taxes.[23]

Can you guess the correct answer? Yes! It's (c). Matt's state is raising business taxes and Matt's plant may consider moving to another state; therefore, Matt might lose his job. Sounds reasonable enough, which is the least we can ask of a test question. But let's consider the likelihood of such a scenario.

First, the fact that Matt works in the production line of a factory in the United States makes him a rare breed. Approximately 50 percent of all U.S.-owned manufacturing production is located in foreign countries.[24] Production isn't moving from one state to another these days, but from one country to another. In fact, only four states have gained manufacturing jobs since 1998 (Nevada, North Dakota, Utah, and Wyoming); the rest have lost them. To put an even finer point on it, these four states have gained 18,000 jobs since 1998, while the United States as a whole has lost 3,718,000 jobs since 1998.[25] In other words, manufacturing jobs aren't going from state to state in response to tax rates. They are going south of the border and to Asia.

In addition, the test question implies that Matt's factory job would be protected if state taxes stay low or decrease — an implication that doesn't hold up to close scrutiny. No one likes to pay taxes, of course. But one of the biggest shifts in our country over the past several decades is the effort to identify taxes as the root cause of evil. This campaign was funded by a conservative coalition intent on selling the idea that government is inherently bad. And because taxes are the fuel that keeps our government going, and are the subject of regular debate and decision making at all levels of government, it is possible to use your attitude toward taxes (tangible) as the litmus test for your thoughts on government itself (abstract). The terms *small government* and *low taxes* became inextricably, if erroneously, linked.

"We're going to continue to trust the American people with their own money," Bush said as he signed the Tax Increase Prevention and Reconciliation Act of 2005, otherwise known as the millionaire's tax cut.[26] This kind of language is used repeatedly by those who subscribe to the philosophy captured by Americans for Tax Reform strategist Grover Norquist when he said that he wanted to shrink government "down to the size where you could drown it in a bathtub." When Bush said that we would "trust" the American people with "their own money," rather than giving it to the government, he was saying this: that government is a distinct entity, one whose priorities are not shared by the people; that once money goes into government, it no longer belongs to the people; and finally, that if government is a big beast, it is best to starve it. Lost in this equation is the notion that government is *us*. It belongs to the people. And what we put in — in the form of taxes — we surely get out in the paved roads we cross, the police officers and firefighters who protect us, a military that defends us, and the teachers who educate our children.

Rhetorically, though, the argument is powerful. For those who feel that the White House promotes an agenda based on values they do not share, it is easy to view government as a bully that needs to be reined in. For those who feel they have yet to achieve the promise of the American Dream, it is easy to resent contributing precious dollars out of a stagnant paycheck to a public sector whose benefits do not seem to translate into individual benefit. And for those in power, who opt to favor the few instead of creating public policy that could benefit the masses, it is easier to blame the institution of government for being greedy and dysfunctional than to take on those labels themselves.

This collective aversion to taxes is captured perfectly by Bush's talk of trusting people more than government — at a press conference called to announce a tax cut that, in conjunction with his previously enacted cuts, would provide 70 percent of its benefits to the top 20 percent of earners in 2006 (people making more than $97,030), draining our national coffers and contributing to the economic crisis in which we find ourselves today.[27]

It becomes clear that any discussion about taxes — particularly in the form of a test question — is loaded. The way we present that discussion in schools has profound implications for how our children learn to view government. Do we perpetuate a notion that taxes feed the beast that is government, in order to pursue a policy agenda that rhetorically serves the interests of the few, or do we restore taxes to their proper place in the equation that is deeply wound up in our democracy, as the vehicle by which we invest in the things that collectively benefit us and that represent our values? Subscribers to the former school of thought may be less willing, for example, to support a progressive income tax increase that would provide much-needed revenue to a state system of public education. The stakes are high.

If the point of teaching financial literacy in the schools is to explore the depth of this debate, here are some questions that could kick-start a conversation: Why did Matt's state government raise taxes? State governments generally raise taxes when they have no revenue coming in from the federal government to pay for the things that states are obligated to pay for, such as police officers, firefighters, public schools, roads, parks, and playgrounds—things we tend to take for granted. And why would there be less revenue coming in from the federal government, forcing state governments to raise revenues? Well, state revenues generally suffer when the federal government cuts taxes on its wealthiest citizens, a phenomenon we saw play out over the course of the George W. Bush presidency.[28]

If students were really going to get into it, they might ask why the number of manufacturing jobs has declined so significantly over the past thirty years, whether this shift has been good for the country, and how policy can best address the root of this shift as well as its effects. But the financial literacy curricula and standards promoted by groups such as Jump$tart don't include room for these questions. They imply that the issue has a correct answer, rather than encouraging students to examine its complexity through questions. End of discussion.

So, Who Gains?

Who gains from the unrealistic and unexamined nature of the Matt question scenario? Who gains from young people believing that state taxes need to be low or factories will up and move to another state? It's hard not to conclude that the funders of Jump$tart are the same entities that want tax rates to be as low as possible. And now they are building a group of future voters who share their view. Not a bad strategy. But a questionable use of school time.

Still, Jump$tart is not alone. The National Council on Economic Education also advocates the financial literacy of young people. Their primary funders have been Merrill Lynch, the Mortgage Bankers Association, the Vanguard Group, Wells Fargo, Bank of America, and HSBC—all contributed more than $100,000 or more to the NCEE's Campaign for Economic Literacy.[29]

In 2005, the NCEE surveyed young people and adults and issued its findings in the report *What American Teens & Adults Know about Economics*. Eight in ten adults understand, according to the report, that "investing in more research and development in the computer industry" and not taxing inventions in or "increasing government regulation over the computer industry," would most likely "accelerate innovation."[30] Regrettably (for the NCEE), only 61 percent of students agree.

But not all hope is lost. Nine in ten adults and three-quarters of students answered correctly a question about limiting trade.[31] When a similar result occurred in the 1999 version of the survey (when students performed even "worse" on the innovation question), the NCEE wrote, "A larger proportion of students than adults understand that when countries engage in voluntary trade, all parties involved benefit. Adults, however, are more likely to understand that trade sanctions benefit producers and not consumers."[32]

I have to wonder just what these students and adults do or do not "understand." Trade is a complicated topic, and even many Americans who support limiting trade barriers may dispute the assertion that "all parties involved benefit." Indeed, because American trade agreements have undoubtedly led to the exportation of jobs to places with lower wages and poorer working conditions, many people like Matt have wondered why they lost their jobs while their former employers and other American firms are doing just fine.

Prominent American leaders from across the ideological spectrum have agreed that a reexamination of our trade policy is in order if we want to protect American workers. Some of that protection may look like something less than the unfettered access that supposedly aids consumers (although I guess the NCEE view doesn't consider those consumers as workers). So, who gains from this narrow view? Who gains from young people growing up to believe that simplistic, anti-tax, and pro-trade assertions are truth?

This type of financial literacy education reminds me of an episode of *The Twilight Zone* I saw many years after its original airing in 1962, "To Serve Man." Huge aliens land on earth, head straight to the United Nations, and proclaim that they are here with the best of intentions, a stance seemingly supported by the translation of the title of one of their guiding books, *To Serve Man*. They teach the humans their advanced agricultural methods, solve famine, eliminate disease, and advance world peace. Eventually, the aliens allow humans to visit their home planet (the spaceflight was free, and therefore not limited to Russian oil magnates and Google founders). Too late, however, some industrious translators realize that *To Serve Man* is, in fact, not a treatise but a cookbook.

The financial institutions say they're doing us a favor by educating our young to understand how to navigate the market. But when students are taught to believe that all is well in the American workplace, that they can move up with just hard work, that taxes are bad and best kept low, that free trade is good for everyone, who really benefits? Such thinking creates complacency at best and delusion at worst. Is it really in the interests of our children to learn, in the hour after geometry, the agenda of the corporate lobby?

You might think I'm suspecting a bit too much conspiracy — that I'm attributing to financial and economic literacy harmful motives instead of accepting its simple goal of wanting to educate and empower our young people. Although I am from New York and, therefore, a little paranoia does come naturally to me, it's not conspiracy theory in this case. John Morton, of the Arizona Council on Economic Education, and formerly the vice president for program development at the National Council on Economic Education, explains the motivation for his efforts this way: "Until economic literacy is widespread, don't hold your breath waiting for voters to defeat referendums that increase the minimum wage, build new sports stadiums, or mandate health coverage."[33]

Yes, maybe one day we will all be financially and economically literate enough to oppose the minimum wage and health-care coverage for our fellow citizens, no questions asked. I wonder what Matt, Don, and Bill will think about that, after losing their jobs on a shrinking assembly line and being forced to rely on the wages of a spouse who earns the minimum wage, while trying to provide a healthy diet for their children who have no health coverage.

7: Questioning the System, or Beating It?

JOHN HOPE BRYANT FOUNDED OPERATION HOPE IN THE aftermath of the 1992 Los Angeles riots that followed the acquittal of the police officers who beat Rodney King. Financial literacy is not Bryant's passion. As he told me, he cares about "justice and not just us. I'm interested in history and not his story. I'm interested in empowerment and giving people a hand up and not just a handout. I think that dignity comes from knowing what you can do for yourself." Photos on his Web site show him next to former presidents George W. Bush and Bill Clinton, Chairman of the Federal Reserve Ben Bernanke, and Oprah Winfrey. His mentor is Andrew Young, Martin Luther King Jr.'s chief of staff and a former mayor, congressman, and ambassador to the United Nations. Bryant is a long way from a childhood during which his father fell victim to a predatory lending scheme and lost his home, when his family spent fourteen months homeless.

Bryant got to where he is by understanding how the market works — or doesn't work. That's why he believes that financial literacy is the means by which marginalized inner-city African-Americans will attain the knowledge to become successful, to break the cycle of economic disenfranchisement that is impoverishing them. In his mind, communities of color are in a new phase of the struggle for equality, and so, as he told me, we need to move from the civil rights movement to the "silver rights movement."

Operation HOPE brings financial literacy to inner-city schools to accomplish two goals: to give urban youth the tools to create the wealth that the civil rights movement did not, despite the movement's many advances in creating racial equality; and to use the acquisition of wealth as motivation to stay in school, given that dropout rates in inner cities (40 to 75 percent) are much higher than the national average (which is about 30 percent).[1] Bryant believes that young people will want to stay in school if they believe it can make them rich.

"Most people don't want an education for education's sake, unless you're an academic," he told me. "You want what education can give you. It's aspirational. And we have disconnected the aspiration from the education. So how do you make education relevant to [young people's] future? Show them how to get rich legally. That's financial literacy. That's free enterprise and capitalism. That's ownership. That's silver rights. Entrepreneurship."

Operation HOPE is impressive in its accomplishments. It's a testament to Bryant's leadership and hustle, and its success reflects the resonance of financial illiteracy in our post–mortgage meltown period. Bryant operates by establishing relationships with financial institutions and engaging their executives as volunteers to teach financial literacy, using the Operation HOPE curriculum, in inner-city schools. Over the past 10 years, some four thousand HOPE Corps volunteers have educated more than 280,000 youth in the United States and South Africa.

Bryant has several high-profile partners, about whom he regularly issues press releases. For example, over four hundred Citigroup employees have taught financial literacy to more than ten thousand children since their partnership with Operation HOPE began in 2002.[2] Bryant has a healthy skepticism about the role of big financial institutions in this movement, however, and is quick to say that his marketing is meant as much to inspire as it is to thank. "There are more press releases than there are dollars going to financial literacy," he told me.

Although Bryant is one of many leaders in this movement, he is one of the few who feels the issues so personally. Ultimately, I think Bryant wishes that he himself could mentor all of the children he encounters, imparting to them the lessons he has learned on his own path to success. Perhaps his personal desire to mentor explains why he chooses to send into classrooms volunteers who have found success in the outside world, rather than teaching teachers how to incorporate the basics of financial literacy into their own lesson plans. In fact, Operation HOPE's latest campaign is to "make smart sexy" by ensuring that at least 5 percent of every community consists of role models. Bryant noted that Malcolm Gladwell has found that communities reach stability at 5 percent, whereas at 3.7 percent and below, teen pregnancy, crime, and high school dropout rates skyrocket. Operation HOPE's campaign is a "five percent movement to stabilize communities with role models so kids have an image of who they can be," said Bryant.

But as I spoke to Bryant, I wondered: Although the prospect of becoming rich might be enough to motivate children to stay in school, is it enough to motivate young people to question a world that has to advance a silver rights movement in the first place? What are the long-term implications of a generation taught to navigate the existing economy but not given the skills to question the economic policies that disenfranchise them?

I am uncomfortable with the notion that our public schools are the setting for an infomercial about how to get rich in America. I am not convinced that the prospect of riches is enough to keep children in school; it's already no secret that those who stay in school are more successful than those who do not (entertainers and athletes aside). I'm not even sure that financial literacy training is actually going to prepare young people to thrive financially as adults.[3] The rules of the game by which people could become rich today won't necessarily be the rules in three years.

To help young people succeed in today's economy and attain silver rights, we must concern ourselves with developing their creativity, their capacity for inquiry, and their critical thinking skills. In a survey of nearly one thousand U.S. chief executive officers, sponsored by the Conference Board, "the challenge of stimulating creativity, innovation, and entrepreneurship" ranked among their top ten concerns.[4] A follow-up study of four hundred employers, *Are They Really Ready to Work?*, found that "creativity and innovation, and the applied skills that support innovation such as critical thinking, communications, and problem-solving, were considered more important than the traditional skills of basic reading, writing, and math. And these companies further stated that the importance of creativity and innovation would only increase in the future."[5]

But those skills are becoming more difficult to find in potential employees. Eighty-five percent of employers concerned with hiring creative employees "can't find the applicants they seek." More than one in two employers report high school graduates to be "deficient" in the applied skills of creativity and innovation, and only one in five employers rates employees with a four-year college degree as "excellent" on the same metric.[6] The shortcomings of our education system are clear: we aren't raising questioning, curious, creative young people.

This failure is not of concern to Bryant and his colleagues, who believe that education should primarily be concerned with offering young people a shortcut to financial success. But even if Bryant's prescription can indeed do good, it can never realize his underlying goal of creating a more just world for the communities he serves and the community from which he comes.

Bryant founded his organization in a time of violence, in the midst of the 1992 Los Angeles riots. Research indicates that "political violence by citizens is also tightly linked to feelings of disaffection and alienation."[7] The violence in L.A., committed primarily by African-Americans, stemmed from a profound sense of powerlessness in our public sphere — no voice, no power, no recourse, and no way of holding accountable those who would perpetrate injustice. Those profound frustrations weren't just about a market that African-Americans could not figure out how to beat. It was about a system that catered to and was directed by the interests of the privileged.

Young African-Americans in the inner cities that Bryant's program serves will not rise above these obstacles by learning how to get rich legally. Financial success will not bind them together. Being rich does not inoculate society against the failure of institutions to ensure equity and justice. Bryant emphasized that the subprime mortgage debacle, a crisis he attributes in great part to the financial illiteracy of buyers, was a middle-class phenomenon, because it was the middle class that could afford to purchase homes in the first place. Even in Bryant's mind it is clear that arrival in the middle class did not automatically give African-American homeowners the social capital, strength, or capacity to question the authority figures before them. Nor did having a record number of minority millionaires give the American public the social capital, strength, or capacity to question the authorities who deregulated our institutions while we sat idly by, convinced that it was in our own best interest.

Martin Luther King Jr.'s Poor People's Campaign, which he conceived just months before his death, was not about the acquisition of financial literacy skills and the corresponding wealth. It was about transforming our institutions so that they would be more just. Institutions fail. They fail to promote justice. They fail to educate. They fail to promote social equality; in fact, they often exacerbate social inequality. They police marginalized communities differently, which furthers the marginalization. To change the lives of the disenfranchised, we must change the institutions that contribute to that disenfranchisement. Unfortunately, that is not where Bryant and his financial literacy movement are focused.

Toward the end of our discussion, Bryant mentioned his admiration of King's desire to "transform the Jericho Road," a metaphor for the journey of marginalized people throughout America's social and economic landscape: "One day we must come to see that the whole Jericho Road must be transformed," said King, "so that men and women will not be constantly beaten and robbed as they make their journey on life's highway. True compassion is more than flinging a coin to a beggar. It comes to see that an edifice which produces beggars needs restructuring."[8]

I understand why the statement resonates with Bryant; it does with me, too. Ultimately, however, transforming the Jericho Road takes place when we transform the system that created such danger and neglect. That transformation does not start with putting more money in the pockets of its travelers. It starts by empowering young people to question, and creating a public school system that values inquiry, so that young people are empowered to transform that road and the institutions that leave them marginalized.

Anything less than institutional change is bound to fail our democracy. Young people must be educated to question things as they are, so that they themselves can do the transforming. Simply teaching them to navigate what we have created undermines all they have to offer.

Does It Even Work?

Lewis Mandell, a professor at the University of Buffalo and an expert on financial literacy, was present at the formation of the Jump$tart coalition. He is the author of the Jump$tart surveys. He brings to his work a long background in both academia and the private sector and doesn't seem wedded to any one ideology. As an accounting professor, he is far from a firebrand. Most importantly, he genuinely wants young people to learn how to take care of themselves and their most basic financial needs. And what does he think about financial literacy?

That it isn't working.

Despite the 350,000 students per year that JPMorgan Chase says it has assisted through its $3.9 million in grants for financial literacy programs between 2006 and 2008, despite the $15 million that Visa has invested in financial literacy education, despite the $3.2 million that Bank of America provided to the National Council on Economic Education in the early 2000s, children aren't learning more.[9] They aren't becoming more financially literate. They don't know better how to use a debit card or balance a checkbook. They don't better understand inflation, pensions, or insurance.

Only 16.8 percent of high school seniors know that stocks tend to have the highest longer-term growth; only 36.2 percent of high schoolers know that retirement income paid by a company is called a pension; only 40.4 percent know that their health insurance coverage may stop if they receive health insurance through their parents and their parents are laid off.[10] High school seniors answered only 48.3 percent of Jump$tart's 2008 financial survey correctly, a decline from 57.3 percent in 1997.[11] After more than ten years of testing — after the implementation of personal finance standards in nineteen more states, congressional hearings, federal legislation, investments of millions by banks — the financial literacy of high school seniors *declined* by 9 percent.

Although a 2005 survey by the National Council on Economic Education found that economic knowledge was increasing, fully 60 percent of high school students received an F on the NCEE economics quiz and only 9 percent received an A or a B.[12] Charles Schwab's 2007 survey of teens found that only 51 percent of teens are very or somewhat knowledgeable about how to write a check, 47 percent about how to use a debit card, and 34 percent about how to balance a checkbook or check the accuracy of a bank statement, all declines from 2006.[13]

After visiting one financial literacy program, I can't say I'm surprised by these findings.

I sat in on a sixth-grade financial literacy lesson at a public middle school in East Harlem, whose student population can be described as approximately 30 percent African-American, 48 percent Hispanic or Latino, 15 percent White, and 6 percent Asian or Native Hawaiian/Other Pacific Islander.[14] The financial literacy volunteer — Mr. Smith, we'll call him — is the director of catering and special events at a large financial institution. Before stepping into this classroom, he went through standard training: two hours.[15]

In his navy blue suit, yellow tie, and white handkerchief perfectly placed in his pocket, Mr. Smith was well prepared to explain to the twelve-year-olds present why it was important to save and how they should go about it. The children sat at clustered tables, as they do every day in their sixth-grade math class, organized by their "corporations," with names like Math Divas and Wall Street.

The blackboard gave clues to the lesson ahead: "How to make your money grow," "Short-term goals," "Long-term goals," "Savings account," "Certificate of deposit," "Savings bonds." And, tucked away in the upper right-hand corner, bankrate.com, betterinvesting.org, and the Web address of his own company.

Mr. Smith began with vocabulary, including abstract terms such as *responsibility* and *priority*. He asked the students to define short-term goals, almost all of which had something to do with some kind of consumption, such as buying a new computer or television. Long-term goals were bigger versions of the short-term goals — save to buy a house, start a business, and, inserted helpfully by Mr. Smith, save up to go to college.

"Don't your parents do that?" Mr. Smith asked the kids. "Don't they set a long-term goal so you can have a future? So you can go to school, so you can get a good education, so you can get a job, so you can afford all the things that we discussed before?" While he distributed a handout entitled *How Your Money Can Grow,* along with the most recent stock table, I wondered if any part of Mr. Smith's training focused on the economic realities facing the parents of this middle school's students.

Mr. Smith asked the students how many of their parents had started savings accounts for them. Almost a third. He asked some of the students whether they were allowed to see the money and how their parents earned the money, and he provided encouraging words to those who walked the family dog and answered the phones at their parents' jobs.

He then moved to the heart of the lesson: how to increase the frequency with which children save. He explained to the students where one can get a savings account. Though he said, "It can be from any banking institution," he underlined the name of his employer on the blackboard and said, "I work for them."

So much for no product placement.

"You want to choose the bank that's going to give you the best interest and the best return on your money for little fees."

Interest? Return on your money? Fees?

"Check out www.bankrate.com. Look at all the multiple banks that are out there that offer their services with free checks, no monthly fees, 3.75 interest—some out there are 4.75 even. Write that down. Check it out and we'll talk about it next week."

From savings accounts we moved on to higher yields.

"Let's talk about certificate of deposit. Does anyone know what that is? No? The bank has certain rates that they offer for $5,000 or $10,000, and it is in the bank, which you can't touch for about six months or nine months. It varies. A lot of banks right now are trying to gather that information so that they can make money off of your money. The profit they earn, they give it to you. A CD is basically a higher rate than a savings account. If you were making 3.75 on your savings account, the rate of return—a good term to write down—is higher than your savings account. You don't have immediate access to it. So, therefore, without immediate access, [it differs from] the savings account, [from] which you can take out twenty dollars here, twenty dollars there. The CD allows you to reach your long-term goal."

The children were getting restless, maybe the result of hearing too many terms with which they were entirely unfamiliar, or maybe because it was a sunny June morning and the end of the school year was just weeks away.

We moved on to talk about stocks. "Which stock did you pick?" asked Mr. Smith of the first student corporation.

"Target."

"Don't say that. Say 'mid-end retailer' so other people won't know your stocks."

The kids looked at each other and shrugged.

"Why did you pick it?"

"It was going up."

"Are all of your stocks in the retail industry?"

Blank stares. One boy offered what he correctly assumed was a departure from that industry: blacksmithing.

"Blacksmithing? Sounds like you are diversified. You spread your money across the board for earnings that could potentially rise, but because there are always fluctuations in the market, it will go up and down. Retail stock may go up and the labor stock may go down."

Diversified? Labor stock?

On to the second group, Wall Street. They'd decided to invest in McDonald's.

"How is that food service provider stock working for you?" Mr. Smith asked. The students didn't understand why he wouldn't allow them to explain how they came to their decision. Neither did I. Wasn't that the point of the exercise? Were we training them to become financially literate or financially cunning?

On to the next. Mr. Smith was pleased with their choice of a pharmaceutical retailer. "[It's] a constant, and everybody needs that. As you get older, you'll realize what the market is and where it is going." And with a mention of compound interest–related platitudes — "The more you save, the more you earn, the more your money will grow" — Mr. Smith asked his students again how many of them were saving. A few hands went up. Mr. Smith asked, "Is your money growing? Are you happy with what you are seeing? Does it make you want to put more into it?" The students said yes.

Are you happy with what you are seeing? I'm not.

After an introduction to the concept of budgeting, Mr. Smith looked at his sleepy class and said of a student with an allowance, "So, if she spends forty dollars, she's got twenty dollars left over. What does she do with that twenty dollars? Is she going to spend or in . . ." He trailed off.

The class, in chorus, completed the fill-in-the-blank: "Invest it."

The push pollsters would have been pleased.

"I have five minutes left, and I'm actually done," Mr. Smith said. Done with what? What had begun here?

After the class ended and the students filed out for recess, I tried to identify what I found so troubling about those forty minutes. It wasn't the intention of imparting to these children the value of saving. That intention was good, and Mr. Smith was sincere in his hope that the young people before him might fulfill their parents' dreams and buy all that their hearts desired. It wasn't even the chalky corporate product placement, which I'm sure is a departure for the class and (I hope) for the program.

What bothered me the most was that no child learned a thing. You know how I know? Not one of them asked a question. Not a clarifying question, not a *what-did-that-mean* question, not a *how* question, and certainly not a *why*.

I left understanding why Mandell is so certain that financial literacy education isn't working, despite its increasing popularity. And worse than the failure of the financial literacy movement is the fact that Mr. Smith's lesson takes place every Friday morning for four weeks, from 9:00 a.m. to 9:40 a.m. in this classroom on 100th Street, consuming approximately 20 percent of the class's available instructional time for mathematics for a month.

Other classes around the country may be better. If the dynamic Bryant had been at the head of the classroom, the children likely would have learned more, or at the very least might have seen his successful rise out of poverty as a model for their own potential futures.

But that's precisely the point, isn't it? The model of recruiting volunteers from among professionals in the sector provides few screens for quality. There is no screening for dynamism, personal success, entrepreneurship. With results that are inconsistent at best, one wonders why they continue in this way.

Ask the financial institution sending in the volunteer.

Other Models: Different Approach, Same Flaw

Other models represent strides forward. Educator Phyllis Frankfort's Working in Support of Education focuses on training teachers to incorporate financial literacy into their curriculum. Unlike the other programs out there, this one includes some actual measurement of progress and, therefore, accountability. Teachers and schools are rewarded for success — effective teachers can become Master Financial Educators and join a network of such teachers who are now helping to "educate the educator" in the best practices of teaching financial literacy. As Frankfort told me, "This is not about spin — it's about education."

Since 2003, the w!se Financial Literacy Certification Program has reached more than 60,000 students in two hundred schools across twenty states.[16] On average, Frankfort told me, those students demonstrate a 25 percent improvement in their personal financial literacy after completing the curriculum.

When I explained to Frankfort that I was interested in the relationship between civics and financial literacy, and the current role of each in our schools, she talked not of her work on the latter but about the Quality of Life program she began, which helps young people identify problems in their communities and formulate a feasible recommendation for change. Unlike her financial literacy programs — which are funded by Citigroup, the McGraw-Hill Companies, and Allstate — Quality of Life was on its last legs due to lack of funding. We were both saddened, though not altogether surprised, that w!se had an easier time finding funding for financial literacy education than a program in which young people learn how to navigate their local institutions and actually work to get problems addressed.

Most leaders in the financial literacy effort, by contrast, are not thinking about how to develop in their young people the capacity for inquiry or broader engagement. Perhaps this limited vision is the reason for their limited success. As Jump$tart itself noted, after another year of disappointing results in its surveys of high school seniors, "It is clear that students don't appear to be learning or retaining those things that are needed for making important financial decisions in their own interest."[17] They aren't retaining it because, in most programs, such as the one at the middle school in East Harlem, they aren't actually learning. They are sitting through advertisements for financial products.

When school administrators say there is no room for civics education because of standardized tests, and no time for science because of math, please tell me why a financial literacy program such as the one in East Harlem is allowed to take up the time of more than 75,000 students each year.[18] Tell me it doesn't say something about our priorities as a nation. And then tell me it doesn't have something to do with that corporate name on the blackboard.

What keeps this movement for financial literacy rolling on, flush with dough? It's a good question. Surely the attraction of financial literacy education has something to do with the increasing fragility of our nation's economy and the necessity for people to understand things such as debt in an era when the personal savings rate hovers just above zero, revolving debt (mostly on credit cards) rose to over $900 billion in 2007, and more than three out of four families have some type of debt.[19] Even so, those funding the financial literacy movement are motivated by something far different from a desire to provide a community service.

In his conversation with me, Mandell acknowledged that financial literacy education "may be a way of fending off re-regulation. Rather than taking away all of this choice, which has given us some degree of wealth, let's do the best thing—which is, let's equip people to be able to handle the wonderful set of choices." In other words, it's not only about choosing; it's about choosing better. Don't ask why these options and not others; don't question the market or the government, which have done all they can do for you.

But have we ever been a country whose motto was "Don't question, just choose better" from among the approved choices? Don't we all want a country that demands newer and better choices for each generation?

Mandell insists that financial service firms have never directed or edited his research, but, "on the other hand, you have to say, Why are they so interested in funding this?" Then he promptly answered his own question: "The reason is, they would really like to come up with a market-based solution, based on education, that would not really limit their ability to offer product."

I don't begrudge the financial sector's desire to reach its future customers while building a base of like-minded people, which would then allow financial companies to continue reaching more and more customers in a friendly environment. I just wish democracy did the same.

Ironically, John Hope Bryant *does* want people to ask questions. Questions about payments and interest rates. Questions of banks and brokers. Questions of themselves. But Bryant doesn't realize that, in order for our children to grow up into adults who question as a matter of course, they need to start learning at a young age how to question, in an environment that values inquiry. And that can't be accomplished by dispatching several hundred Citigroup, JPMorgan Chase, and PNC employees to preach the importance of savings and to get kids to remember the difference between a CD and a 401(k).[20]

Cultivating the kind of inquiry that will ultimately benefit young people in the way Bryant hopes requires something deeper — something that may even run contrary to the express purposes of its patrons. The growing financial literacy movement reflects our shift toward caring more about preparing our young people to be consumers than about preparing them to be citizens. Sadly, this shift is to its champions' per-il, because both the financial literacy movement and our democracy are destined to fail unless our children know how to ask *why*.

Bryant and the financial literacy movement argue that we should operate within a broken system by putting our heads down and learning the rules of the game. But what we really need are more people to behave like Bryant himself. He questioned the game instead of playing along with it, a move that took him from Atlanta to meetings in the White House.

I agree with Mandell when he wonders whether the answer to getting young people to be more financially savvy isn't . . . more civics education. Perhaps engaging young people in the world around them would lead them down the path to accepting more responsibility—for themselves and their financial futures, for their communities, for our democracy.

8: The Marxist, Anti-American Conspiracy to Convert Young People to Engaged Citizenship

NANCY GANNON IS NOT AN IDEOLOGUE, AN AMERICA HATER, or an activist determined to recruit revolutionaries to her cause. She's just a high school principal.

She's a principal in one of the toughest places to be a principal: the New York City public school system. Yet, despite the enormous challenges of educating children in a city where only slightly more than half of all ninth graders graduate high school, Nancy's mission goes beyond securing as many diplomas as possible. She told me she wants to help prepare citizens who are equipped with "voice, power, and responsibility."

This is probably why the very first schoolwide activity Gannon oversaw as principal at the School for Democracy and Leadership was the registering of eligible students to vote, instilling in them the value of this most fundamental responsibility of American citizenship.

The Crown Heights–based school was motivated by "change" even before it became the motif of the 2008 presidential campaign. Although the focus of the teachers and staff at SDL is to prepare their students for college, they are also, in Gannon's words, "incredibly steeped in activism. We encourage the students to pick something in the world or the community they want to change and then act on it together."

Like the children of Hampton, Virginia, participating in Project Citizen as part of their civics curriculum, the students of SDL are encouraged to put their citizenship into action on a local level. They are required to complete a "change project" of their own choosing each year. These change projects have included writing a proposal for a school library where there was none, working with junior high school students on a project to teach safe-sex education, and building more community through joint poetry readings among the schools that share SDL's campus.

In Gannon's mind, these small efforts at SDL are both preparation for and a microcosm of effective citizenship in our democracy. "To be a good citizen means that you have to be always thinking about your responsibility in the world," Gannon told me. "I think that every school, whatever they call it, should be talking about each of our responsibility to maintain and build responsible community, to look out for those who do not have power and who don't have voice. Those are the reasons I love my country, because I believe that in its best moment that's what it strives to be."

In a time in which the apathy of young people is lamented far and wide, and in which the disaffection of young people in poor, urban communities is apparent, efforts such as SDL's to both educate and engage its student body in strengthening their communities would seem likely to earn universal praise. But, although the word *civics* inspires wistfulness for a bygone era, there is some controversy today about how schools should express that commitment to preparing effective citizens. Not everyone wants to encourage students to question how democracy is functioning — in their schools, in their communities, or in their country — and to figure out how to make it work better. Some believe that such an exercise is inherently unpatriotic. And because the people making that argument have power — and a megaphone — it is important to understand their resistance.

Social Justice in the Schools

On the editorial page of the *New York Daily News,* and in the journal of the Manhattan Institute, the think tank for which he works, Sol Stern put the School for Democracy and Leadership, along with two other small New York City schools, on his "dishonor roll." Why?

According to Stern, "New York City's ideal of public schooling as a means of assimilating all children into a common civic culture is under assault—not by teachers who care too little, but by those who, in a perverse way, care too much."[1]

He is talking about SDL's affiliation with a movement of practitioners who believe in "social justice" education, of which Stern and other fellows at conservative, right-wing think tanks have been critical. Educators who subscribe to social justice teaching (also known as critical pedagogy) believe that real-world issues should be brought into the classroom, in any subject from social studies to math, to spark students' questioning of that world and of the systems that govern it.

"It's about seeing yourself not just as a consumer [of information], but as an actor-critic," says the curriculum editor for an educational publisher motivated by the idea "that public education is central to the creation of a humane, caring, multiracial democracy."[2] Social justice teaching "considers how education can provide individuals with the tools to better themselves and strengthen democracy," in the words of one proponent,[3] and has its roots in the work of John Dewey, who encouraged teachers to connect students with the world around them so that they could learn more effectively and be better prepared to exercise effective citizenship. Simply put, educators who teach social justice want their students to question power.

There are two specific thrusts to Stern's critique of social justice education as it is embodied by the School for Democracy and Leadership. Underlying both of his arguments, in my view, is a resistance to the notion that schools are a place to prepare young people for their democracy. The first critique is that efforts such as SDL's change project, evidence of the school's commitment to social justice, take time away from what Stern considers to be the appropriate role of public education: teaching the basics.

"Social justice teaching is a frivolous waste of precious school hours, grievously harmful to poor children, who start out with a disadvantage," Stern writes. "School is the only place where they are likely to obtain the academic knowledge that could make up for the educational deprivation they suffer in their homes. The last thing they need is a wild-eyed experiment in education through social action."[4] This emphasis on the basics is consistent with the education policy of the Bush administration, in which the civic purpose of schooling was de-prioritized, as I discussed in chapter 5.

I don't think anyone would dispute Stern's characterization of the urgency of Gannon's mission as an educator. But critics of social justice education, such as Stern, David Horowitz, Phyllis Schlafly, and others, overlook two critical points. First, this "wild-eyed experiment" is in fact a historic function of public schooling, supported by parents who view the schools as institutions to prepare students not only for college and work but also for effective citizenship, as indicated by the polls cited in chapter 5. Second, there is a mutually reinforcing relationship between civic involvement and academic performance. Students who are more engaged in their communities are also known to have higher levels of academic achievement.[5] Engagement in their communities provides students with a context for the importance of a basic education: we must read and write if we are to vote, participate, and effectively advocate for ourselves and our communities.

Involvement in change projects also cultivates a sense of agency in the students who participate. "The skills you need to do a change project are the same set of skills you need to fill out a college application or follow up on scholarships or get into college and do well there," Gannon told me. "I definitely think that there is a correlation between developing their sense of personal agency and making sure that they feel able and ready to go to college."

And Gannon ought to know. Despite its placement on the Stern dishonor roll, SDL graduated over 90 percent of its first graduating class, in a building where the former occupant, serving the same community, graduated only 43 percent.[6] All but two or three of the graduates will immediately go on to college, including some who will attend institutions such as Brown, Williams, Union, and Sarah Lawrence. SDL received high marks on its most recent New York City Progress Report, signaling its strong academic performance and student progress.[7] The change project creates in the students of SDL the sense that they have a role in determining their future and the future of their communities. They show up to school because they want to learn how.

Matthew Spalding and David Bobb, fellows at the Heritage Foundation, an organization closely aligned with the Manhattan Institute, share Stern's critique of the thinking behind the change projects. In 2005, they wrote in support of Bush's proposal to eliminate funding for the Center for Civic Education, the organization that sponsors Project Citizen and offers 3 million children across the country education about the Declaration of Independence. They saw the Center for Civic Education as "an important shift away from civics education as *knowledge* toward civics as an *activity*."[8] It is fair to make the distinction, but the assertion is incorrect. Civics was never intended to be just knowledge but to be a practice for young people learning to navigate their democracy. What the children at the Exploratorium have discovered about learning science is also true of learning about democracy: it is more exciting to learn by actually observing it up close.

The second thrust of the critique is that efforts to connect what students are learning and doing at school to the broader questions facing our democracy are inherently propagandistic. Or, as Stern puts it, that the teachers of schools like SDL are "a group of radical teachers . . . who advocate the use of public school classrooms to indoctrinate students in left-wing, anti-American ideology."[9] As an example, he cites one group of students whose change project was to investigate why the science equipment in their school was so woefully outdated. In the process, they learned how the New York City school system is funded, analyzed the tax policy of New York State, and then decided to take action. The students raised money for an advocacy organization working to secure additional state dollars for city schools, beginning by writing a brochure expressing their "commit[ment] to fighting against the injustice and inequality within our education system."[10]

The students' position on inequality in the New York City public school system is not a radical view. In fact, the historic decision in *Campaign for Fiscal Equity, Inc. v. State of New York* found that New York State's funding system was inequitable, with disastrous effects for New York City, and required the state to send more money to city schools so that students like those at SDL wouldn't have to learn with antiquated science laboratory equipment.[11]

Such a project is certainly not "anti-American." In fact, I can't think of any better experiment in democracy than to support students in writing a pamphlet declaring their support for equality. Sound familiar?

As I noted in chapter 5, it was commonplace in the middle of the twentieth century for high school students to take classes such as Problems in Democracy, in which they discussed current affairs. The idea was to get young people interested in the world around them, to hook them into wanting to learn more about history and social studies by engaging them in contemporary debates. We know from research that students who talk about current events with their families are more likely to be engaged citizens and that engaged citizens who participate in civic activities are better students.[12] When we are invested in the world around us, we want the education that is required to participate actively as a citizen. We need to support more current affairs conversation in today's classrooms, in the absence of its formal place in the curriculum.

But current events, too, strike Stern and others as inappropriate in the context of public schooling. As further evidence of left-wing, anti-American indoctrination, Stern writes about Jhumki Basu, a ninth-grade science teacher at the Urban Assembly School for Democracy and Leadership before her passing in 2008, and the "three-week project in her physics class on the international controversy over Iran's nuclear program."[13] He doesn't offer any specific illustrations of how such an idea is "anti-American," likely not because of limited space — his City Journal article is nearly six thousand words — but because there wasn't a case to be made.

What Stern also fails to mention is that, in a nationwide system in which less than 30 percent of high school students take physics,[14] every single student at the School for Democracy and Leadership is required to take physics — a reflection of the school's commitment to high expectations for academic rigor.

When we teach Project Citizen or encourage change projects, when we talk about current events in the classroom, we encourage young people's curiosity about their world. We empower them to solve problems. We offer inspiration for their academic pursuits. The results speak for themselves.

The arguments of Stern, Spalding, and Bobb reflect attitudes that have led us to where we are now, with a radically different notion of the civic purpose of schools. Preparing students to understand the world around them is neither a distraction nor anti-American; it's as American as can be.

Trusting Young People to Question

What's the difference between education and indoctrination? In our popular usage of the term, *indoctrination* assumes that the consumer of information will not question it. It takes two to tango, and the young people in this school dance are not capable of questioning the information they receive.

Proponents of social justice education, followers of the education theorist Paolo Freire, want to talk to students specifically about the issues that confront our democracy — poverty, homelessness, inequality, racism — and how power structures in our country create and perpetuate these ills. We don't have to be card-carrying Marxists to imagine that such topics will come up in an American classroom today, without prompting, particularly in a school located in a neighborhood like Crown Heights, Brooklyn, where the surrounding community is 76 percent African-American, 11 percent Hispanic, 11 percent White, and 1 percent Asian, and where 32 percent of children under eighteen live below the poverty line, 23 percent of households get by on less than $15,000 a year, and the median household income is $34,000 a year.[15] Seventy-three percent of the students at the School for Democracy and Leadership qualified for free or reduced-price lunch based on their low socioeconomic status in 2006–07. Some students live in shelters and foster homes.[16]

Yet, to critics such as Stern or David Horowitz of the David Horowitz Freedom Center, discussions of poverty and oppression have an ulterior motive: to indoctrinate students in anti-American views. According to Horowitz, social justice educators are working to convey the message that "American

society is an inherently 'oppressive' society that is 'systemati-
cally' racist, 'sexist,' and 'classist' and thus discriminates insti-
tutionally against women, nonwhites, working Americans,
and the poor."[17] Stern speaks similarly of social justice educators: "In their ideologically induced paranoia about America, the radical education theorists, like most ideologues,
cannot see what is right in front of their eyes — that America and democratic capitalism are actually doing very well,
thank you."[18]

As our nation confronts the greatest financial crisis since
the Great Depression, in which joblessness will continue to
soar and more of the parents of SDL children will find themselves in food banks instead of school supply stores, we can
be assured that seeds of doubt about our system of democratic capitalism need not be planted by teachers. So just who is
out of touch?

Students will always bring their experiences to bear when
questioning the system around them. That is natural and,
frankly, it should be encouraged. But we should not be so
quick to assume that facilitating those conversations results
in the creation of unpatriotic, anticapitalist leftists. The young
people at SDL — as is true anywhere — identify with a variety
of perspectives across the political spectrum. There are students who may join the Peace Corps one day and those who
are already signing up for the Marine Corps. They can talk
about poverty while still believing in our system of democratic capitalism; I do it all the time. Ultimately, we must trust
that young people can question what they see around them
and still fall in love with their democracy.

In fact, there is no evidence that conversations with young
people about challenges to democracy are necessarily liberal. It could just as likely be the opposite. Peter Levine, an
expert in the field of civics education, told me that "the only
evidence we've ever had was asking kids what themes they

remembered in their own high school [civics] classes, and the themes they remember are highly conservative."

We just can't make assumptions about what we think young people will say or think. Levine, who conducted an intensive project with children from Northwestern High School in Hyattsville, Maryland, found that "if you get a bunch of kids together and they start talking about what should be done about school systems, they don't talk about more teacher salaries and stuff like that. They talk about [how] the schools have gone to hell because there is no discipline. They talk about more school choice. I don't think you get necessarily lefty solutions out of kids. Maybe you should, but you don't." We need to trust that young people can formulate their own opinions. They may surprise us.

We also need to trust their teachers — including those who want to encourage young people to question their democracy and to follow those questions into creating concrete change in their communities. When we call Gannon and the teachers at the School for Democracy and Leadership — all of whom are desperate to engage students in the learning that represents their only chance of surpassing the expectations for their neighborhood — "radical teachers using the classroom to trash the American system,"[19] we not only mischaracterize their motives but also create the perception that what they are doing is unpatriotic. No one wants to be labeled an ideologue, and certainly not in the pages of the *New York Daily News*. The intention is to silence teachers, and it's the oldest game in the book.

It is a troubling irony that this lack of faith in students and teachers emanates from think tanks on the conservative right, whose principal message is that we ought to trust people to make their own decisions.[20]

An even more painful irony is that a writer such as Stern heralds the "democratic optimism of the Founding Fathers, Abraham Lincoln, and Martin Luther King Jr.,"[21] wishing that it was they who inspired people such as Gannon, while failing to acknowledge that, in their time, these people, too, were considered radical and antiestablishment for their questioning of the status quo. The Founding Fathers questioned why they could not live in a democracy; King questioned why our democracy would not let him live as the Founding Fathers had envisioned.

We need more SDLs today. We need more innovative small schools that will restore the connection between young people and their communities and cultivate the skills of inquiry, problem solving, and creative thinking that our democracy and our economy desperately need. Such efforts should be encouraged, not censured, and such teachers should be supported, not labeled. Those who are most powerless in our system today—the children of the School for Democracy and Leadership—are the children we must engage the most. When we enable them to talk about what they see, to learn that they can improve their communities, we cultivate their faith in their democracy and in themselves.

To rebuild our civic fabric, we'll need to resist the temptation to fear inquiry. We'll need to trust in the power of our democracy to weather all of the questions we have. Democracy is, after all, always the answer.

Part III

Politics:
Engaged or Connected?

"He seems to me to be the only one in politics to approach the subject correctly, because it's quite right to make young men and their future excellence your first concern—just as a good farmer is likely to concern himself first with the young plants, and only then with the others."

SOCRATES TO EUTHYPHRO IN *EUTHYPHRO*[1]

During the fall of 2008, as the presidential campaign was roaring to a close, I spoke to a group of undergraduates majoring in political science at the City College of New York. After I encouraged the students to become more involved in politics and to think more about the questions they have about their democracy, a young African-American student in the back raised her hand.

"So let's say I follow the news, and I think about it, and I have my questions for the presidential candidates. How do I ask them? Is Senator Obama going to answer my question?"

Uncharacteristically, I stumbled. I said some things about contacting her local officials, writing letters to the editor, joining discussions on campaign Web sites. The truth is that I had no idea how this young woman would get her question answered. I just wanted her to keep asking questions.

As we stood there in that classroom, I thought of all the ways in which inquiry is devalued in what she sees every day. From the classroom to the newsroom to the Internet, it is answers that we prize, that we expect, that we seek. That's why I felt in that moment the great challenge of our time. We need to encourage young people to ask more of their democracy and equip them to participate in the decision making that affects their lives, but at the same time we must recognize that the broader structure of our politics does not facilitate their involvement and does not leave much room for their questions. We need them to read the newspaper every day, even though the news coverage so often disappoints us. We need them to want to be involved in the politics of their local communities, even as the world seems smaller, our issues more interconnected, our countries more interdependent. We need them to want to think about their role as citizens, even though our schools send the message that young people are thought of primarily as consumers and workers.

Much was made of the involvement of young people in the 2008 presidential election campaign, and rightly so. Voter turnout among young people under the age of thirty rose to approximately 52 percent, an increase of 4 percentage points over 2004 and of at least 11 percentage points over 2000. It equalled the 1992 turnout, which was the highest since 1972.[2]

Yet, despite this impressive turnout, I believe we are confronting a paradox when it comes to assessing the political engagement of young citizens. Technological advancements make it easier for young people to participate in politics in some form. They can voice support for a political candidate, register their call for action in Darfur at the touch of a button, and raise money for the causes that move them. They are connected to one another and to their networks. This connection presents a tremendous opportunity for youth to find their individual voices and to collectively question those in power.

With these technological advancements, however, come obstacles to meaningful engagement. Young people can learn about current affairs via Facebook updates, but within networks that are only good at bringing similar people together —just like the ideologically segregated communities of the Big Sort. Young people can customize their news consumption, screening out what they aren't interested in (or think they aren't interested in), which leaves little room for serendipity and the questions that serendipity catalyzes. The newspaper has been widely replaced by the "always on, always updated" news available online, and most of the young people I encounter don't read news in print. Nor do they really learn about the world around us by using the Internet, contrary to conventional wisdom. They are online news headline skimmers. They are constantly updated but inadequately informed. They do not really know what is happening in the world. But they sure do get a lot of text messages about it.

The millennials—young people born in the 1980s and 1990s, and even in the early 2000s (more or less anyone under the age of thirty in 2009)—have already been sliced and diced as a generation. Consider the titles of books published in the past couple of years alone: *Millennial Makeover: MySpace, YouTube & the Future of American Politics; Millennials Rising: The Next Great Generation; Generation We: How Millennial Youth Are Taking Over America and Changing Our World Forever;* and *Youth to Power: How Today's Young Voters Are Building Tomorrow's Progressive Majority.* I don't want to repeat that exercise here, because I'm less interested in this particular generation than I am in the conditions that will affect generations to come.

Mark Bauerlein, a liberal arts professor and author of *The Dumbest Generation,* certainly has strong opinions. These are captured, as is true of most books these days, in his subtitle: *How the Digital Age Stupefies Young Americans and Jeopardizes Our Future.*[3] Through 200-plus pages methodically recounting research, Bauerlein laments the changes that characterize younger generations today. He argues, persuasively, that America's children perform poorly academically, despite an abundance of information at their fingertips, that they are uninformed about the basis of our democracy, that they read less and play more, that they are addicted to their screens, and that the grown-ups fascinated by these dramatic shifts in communications style and technological savvy are complicit in the millennials' rejection of the fundamentals of informed citizenship.

In the opposite corner we have Neil Howe, William Strauss, Michael Connery, and a growing movement of young activists who believe that today's young people are the most engaged generation in history. They argue, also persuasively, that today's young people — they speak of a slightly older generation than does Bauerlein — have developed unprecedented communications vehicles, connecting their suburban bedrooms with the movement for peace in Darfur and with hundreds of thousands of their peers throughout the country. Our youth weren't so civically disengaged when they helped elect a president, were they? They may not read the newspaper, but they create their own media to fill in the gaps not addressed by the mainstream.

Who has it right? Answering that question is less important than the implications of the truths in each of the arguments. Despite the assertions of young activists, there are some seriously dangerous signs about our youth's capacity to hold forth the torch of democracy. We've talked about their deficient civic knowledge. We cannot be satisfied when only half of today's college seniors can tell you the opening line of the Declaration of Independence. And when only 5 percent of our nation's high school seniors can name three ways that the power of the president can be checked by the legislative or judicial branches,[4] we need to worry about whether future administrations will be held accountable.

But it's not just the civic knowledge; it's also the predisposition to make good use of that knowledge. The Joan Shorenstein Center on the Press, Politics and Public Policy at Harvard's Kennedy School of Government reports that fewer of today's young people engage with daily news than was true two or three decades ago.[5] A recent study on the civic health of the nation revealed that, among all age groups, young people are the least attentive to the news across all types of media, including online news sites.[6] No matter how interested young people are in picking up their video cameras to share their own perspectives, there is no substitute for understanding what is going on in the world today. And although one can and should be awed by the power of today's twenty-somethings to network nationally and even globally, it isn't clear that they are equally interested in, or capable of, harnessing the power of their local school board or city council — though those institutions are vitally important to the rights and opportunities available to us all. Maybe it's that the young don't seem very interested in institutions at all.

It is positive for our democracy that the millennials do not feel limited to changing government policy through party politics — especially because political parties long ago stopped investing in involving young people, instigating a self-fulfilling prophecy about youth engagement. Young people want to move the market by leveraging their buying power. They concern themselves with the national and the global. But, ultimately, we need young people to do more than vote and buy and click; we need them to question the systems that govern their lives — starting in their local communities.

There are millions of young people like that student at City College, who have questions about how their democracy works and want to get those questions answered. There are young people sitting on planning boards in Hampton, Virginia, interviewing candidates for local office. There are organizations such as Mobilize that use technology to help young people all across the country get the tools to create change in their local communities.

Ultimately, it is up to our larger society to show young people that there is a role for questioning in our politics. If we do value it, if we want to raise young people who believe that they have agency to improve not only their lives but also their communities, we'll think a lot more expansively about our political processes and whether they leave room for us to ask questions of politicians or to ensure that politicians ask questions of themselves. We must not settle for politics as performance.

Tomorrow's young people will undoubtedly be connected to politics. But the future of our democracy requires them to be engaged. You know how a teacher knows when her students are engaged? They ask questions.

9: Black and White and Dead All Over

THE CONFERENCE TABLE IS LITTERED WITH BAGELS, JUICE, and newspapers. Newspapers everywhere. Some are neatly folded, as I taught my students to do in our first lesson, the way I learned to do it so I could read the paper on the subway to high school. Even during rush hour, there I was, one hand with ink-stained fingertips and the other resting coolly on the metal railing overhead.

Each morning during the Drum Major Institute's Summer Scholars program, I find these fourteen college students from community colleges and Ivy League schools and everywhere in between across the country hunched over their papers, desperately trying to finish reading in the thirty seconds it takes me to get my coffee, sit down, and begin the interrogation. This is my favorite part of the day. It is a symphony of newspaper crinkling and crackling.

This symphony isn't exactly high up on the collective playlist of today's youth. Most young people don't read the newspaper anymore. In fact, today's young people read the newspaper less than any previous generation since experts begun studying such things. Only 16 percent of Americans aged eighteen to thirty read the paper on a daily basis, compared to 35 percent of those over thirty. The younger generation fares even worse, with fewer than one in ten twelve- to seventeen-year-olds experiencing the feel of newsprint in their hands every day. According to *Young People and News,* the definitive 2007 study from the Joan Shorenstein Center on the

Press, Politics and Public Policy, "Half of all teens and young adults said they rarely if ever read a newspaper."[1]

I remember a joke from my childhood. You had to say it aloud to get it. Question: what's black and white and re(a)d all over? Answer: the newspaper! I loved it. I repeated it to as many people as I could. That was only twenty years ago. Today the newspaper is dying. Maybe it should have stayed in black and white.

It may seem anachronistic, in the Internet age, for me to mourn the newspaper's demise. It may even seem ironic, given that I am in my early thirties. Why am I worried? I know as well as my younger peers that the Web is here to stay. It has all that we need to know about what's happening in the world at any given nanosecond. Today's young people — digital natives — don't need to bother with paper. They are online in so many other aspects of their lives, it makes sense that they get their news online. The medium has changed, but the practice has not. Right?

Although it is true that the young people who want to learn what is happening in the world on a regular basis are going to the Web to do so, their numbers are too few. According to the latest Pew Research Center Biennial News Consumption Survey, one in three people between the ages of eighteen and twenty-four does not follow the news on any given day.[2] Anywhere. Not in the newspaper. Not on the radio. Not on the television. Not even on the Internet.

In looking at the relative level of consumption across newspaper, radio, and the Internet, the Shorenstein Center was forced to conclude that "an absolute majority of teens and young adults are non-users." After scoring participants of all ages based on the intensity of their exposure to the media, they gave 28 percent of teens and 24 percent of young adults a score of zero — meaning, in their words, that those teens and young adults "paid almost no attention to news, whatever the source." Another 24 percent of young adults and 32 percent of teens scored a one: "They paid little or no attention to three of the mediums and made only moderate use of the fourth."[3] These are our future leaders, future teachers and politicians, future journalists, policymakers, business executives, artists, and parents — and one-third of them don't follow the news.

As access to technology increases, the young people who do read the news on the Internet may be connected to the headlines but aren't engaged with the content. The tendency to skim headlines and graze on the news rises. Serendipity is lost as young people look only for what they already know interests them. Studies confirm this, and we have all witnessed it firsthand. We cannot blame the technology alone — this technology is built and utilized in a culture that has clearly sent children the message that it is okay not to engage with the world — but the technology does matter.

Ultimately, the question for us is what such inattention to the news means for the future of our democracy, a future driven increasingly by the power of multinational corporations, in which secrecy and distortion already characterize too much of our policymaking process. Ignorance is the most powerful accomplice of the status quo, and the less our young people engage with the news, the more ignorant they will become.

Through the DMI Scholars program, where we train young activists to pursue careers in public policy, I have seen the power of the news as a platform to cultivate inquiry among young people. I've played matchmaker between young people and the newspaper for a long time. I do so because I think it's important for young people to know what is going on in the world and because I think that reading the print newspaper in particular creates in young people the habits of mind of an engaged, critically thinking person.

Kat Barr, political outreach director of Rock the Vote, an organization that uses popular culture to register young voters, said on a panel that I facilitated last year that today's college-aged young people are "the most engaged generation in three decades."[4] It is fair to say that young people, as a demographic group, were critical to electing President Obama. But policy isn't made through elections alone, and engagement cannot be measured solely through voter turnout. Sustained social change requires an informed populace.

Some believe that the generational rejection of the news is harmless and even, in light of the bias of the mainstream media, to be encouraged. Old-school news-reading habits, they argue, will be replaced by young people learning the new tools of the journalism trade and using them to tell their own stories. We are all journalists now. And as more and more media outlets become part of national conglomerates like News Corporation, of which I wrote in chapter 3, it becomes more and more important that we raise a generation skeptical of those sources. So maybe I shouldn't worry too much.

But then I flip the pages of today's newspaper to learn something new that I otherwise would not have uncovered, some new challenge to the fulfillment of democracy's promise. I dig deeply into an article that I never would have read based on its headline on a Web site alone, and I am left with questions that I otherwise would not have asked. I think about the one-third of today's young people, and likely half of the subsequent generation, who do not follow the news, and I think I'm worried just the right amount.

Snacking on the News

I enjoy food metaphors almost as much as I enjoy food. During my review of the literature on the news habits of young people, a theme emerged. Today, young people are "snacking" or "grazing" on the news. The young participants in one study were described as "consuming a steady diet of bite-size pieces of news."[5]

The situation reminds me of the paradox of childhood obesity in America today: our children become obese not from too many big and well-rounded meals but from too much snacking, too much garbage filling an emptiness that can never be filled with such light fare. With excess can come deprivation. This is true of food and the body, and it is true of the climate of today's "information age" and the mind. When it comes to knowing what is going on in the world, technology does not automatically improve our diets.

But it's not just about the newspaper; young people aren't intentionally connecting to the news via *any* route. They watch television news significantly less often — 30 percent of teens and young adults watch on a daily basis, compared to 60 percent of those thirty and over. When young people do watch television news, they watch for less time. They listen to radio news significantly less often as well. And about as many of them as older adults access the Internet for news on a daily basis — 20 percent.[6]

Although 55 percent of adults in the Shorenstein Center study sought out the news each day on the Internet, two-thirds of the teenagers "who get at least some news from the Internet said it typically occurs when they 'just happen to come across it.'" On the Internet, 64 percent of young people (between eighteen and twenty-five) "say they more often follow links to news stories, rather than go directly to the home pages of news organizations themselves." This is compared to 48 percent of adults between twenty-five and twenty-nine who go directly to home pages.[7] Today's young people are a generation of accidental users.

The Associated Press recently commissioned an ethnographic study of young people and how they interact with the news. They observed young people from around the world who consumed the headlines — "above the fold," in newspaper parlance — that were delivered to them through their technology of choice (e.g., PDA, e-mail in-box, or cell phone). In a world of technology-facilitated multitasking, these young people typically read the news while doing something else, such as watching television, driving, or working. They had an ingrained "habit for e-mail/news checking," and news updates and headlines were cited as ways to "pass time and break boredom." The end result was that "participants were checking news more frequently but not exploring stories in any depth."[8]

This behavior — consuming the news while doing a million other things, just checking the news without actually reading it — comes at a cost. In the Shorenstein Center study of more than 1,500 teens, young adults, and adults, young people couldn't recall the facts of major news stories taking place at the time of the survey. After being quizzed on both soft and hard news — stories ranging from Anna Nicole Smith's death to Britain's decision to remove troops from Iraq — young people not only were less likely to know about the stories but also were less likely to identify a key fact about the story that would demonstrate their knowledge. In the case of the hard news stories about the war, policy, and the stock market, only one in three young adults knew about a given story at all. And of those, only 40 percent could identify the factual element, proving knowledge.[9]

After observing the young people in their natural habitat, the Associated Press concluded that "Stories 'below the fold' seemed in danger of becoming vestigial news organs,"[10] of ceasing to have any significant function. Of course, calling such stories — the meat of the news, that is — vestigial also implies that an evolution has occurred. But is this direction in news consumption — in which young people do not connect with the news, do so only when also engaged in other tasks, and are unable to remember a thing about the news when asked — in the best interest of our democracy? Are we casting off that which we no longer need?

I just don't think so. Not in a time when so much is at stake, when we are determining how our country will relate to the world on issues of globalization, war and peace, our financial system. When people are quiet, when they do not know, they end up following the path chosen by entrenched power. Only when people know, and ask, is there a chance that the voices of regular people will be heard.

The implications of younger generations' news consumption are great not only for the young people involved but also for the press as an arm of our democracy. "If the news industry continues to support this habitual response," the Associated Press reports, "a cycle of 'above-the-fold' scanning for headlines and updates will likely be perpetuated, limiting demand for—and ultimately the supply of—more in-depth news coverage."[11] In other words, if young people stop coming, the press will stop building. What then? How then will we find out that there were no weapons of mass destruction in the country we attacked because it supposedly had weapons of mass destruction? How will we find out about corrupt politicians violating the public trust? Through their own press departments? Through our favorite blogs? Blogs are important, and represent some of the most cutting-edge investigative reporting today, but if they represent our exclusive source of news, how will we all have access to a shared set of information and facts? Without the information below the fold, how will we understand what our government budgets really contain, how people in countries around the world really think, live, work, and are affected by our policies, or how our own lives are affected by the decisions made by our local governments?

My father taught me that if you do something for thirty days, it becomes a habit. When you start the day with the newspaper, you start with the recognition that you are a person in the world, with a need and responsibility to engage. This habit is good for our democracy.

Most people who develop a news habit do so because, to hark back to the public service announcements of my youth, they "learned it by watching you." An international study of young people and their news consumption revealed as much, finding that "most respondents said they had vivid memories of having a newspaper in the home when they were growing up; fathers, in particular, were most often cited in participants' recollections of newspaper reading."[12] I know that, in my case, newspapers were rarely ever seen when I was growing up—maybe on the weekends, when you found the sales circulars and coupons. But the evening news was a fixture. Hours of evening news. Evening news while dinner was cooking. Evening news while we ate dinner, all of us staring at the television set on our kitchen table (yes, on the table). To this day, "Did you hear about . . ." is a regular beginning to a conversation with my parents. It's no wonder that I fell in love with the news.

It is harder to create a news ritual in the present era. "Even the on-demand feature of Internet news can work against the formation of an online news habit because it breaks the link between ritual and habit," concludes the Shorenstein Center report. "Research has found that online news exposure is less fixed by time, place, and routine—elements that reinforce, almost define, a habit."[13] Newspapers help to develop habits of mind that are lost through the random but unrelenting force of headline updates via technological devices.

What will the children of the millennials remember about how their parents interact with the news? A parent snatching glances at a BlackBerry to read the CNN headlines or to open up a Google alert en route to a playdate? Are these habits—headline reading and skimming, reading articles triggered only by an expression of prior interest in the topic—the ones we wish them to take with them for *their* lives?

The Limitations of Do-It-Yourself News

I felt hopelessly old school. I was talking to Lance Bennett, who has probably at least a decade on me, and I felt quaint. A professor of communication and political science at the University of Washington, Bennett also founded and directs the Center for Communication and Civic Engagement, whose mission is to understand "communication processes and media technologies that facilitate positive citizen involvement in politics and social life."[14] According to Bennett, the future of young people's interaction with the news isn't around a table at something like the DMI Scholars program; it centers around them making their own news.

"News audiences are, as you know, declining," Bennett told me. "I think that participatory news is where people are going. That involves simple participation, such as setting up an iGoogle page and deciding what you want on it, to actually participating in creating news accounts — going to a political rally and shooting your own video and posting it on YouTube." He sees it as an issue of authenticity, which our current news lacks. "News events are staged, dramatized, scripted," very little of it is spontaneous, and too much of it looks like "bad reality TV." Participatory media, where people tell their own stories, "brings motivation and credibility . . . Young people are beginning to experiment with their own news formats. We'll see where that goes."

I find the idea of participatory media incredibly exciting. It means that young people are engaged enough to want to tell their own stories, to attend a political rally and upload their video to a blog where everyone can see it. It means that they aren't reliant on the "official" reporting of these events when those official reports don't sync with their own experiences. In fact, the Drum Major Institute supports participatory media by teaching community activists to blog. I want those activists to tell the stories of the community residents who have to live with the consequences of good and bad public policy, perspectives that are rarely heard in the mainstream dialogue. In my opinion, doing so makes for more authentic news, and it makes for a policymaking environment that is based on reality.

Bennett is certainly correct that a conscientious consumer of the media has good reason to question the authenticity of information channeled through an increasingly concentrated and profit-driven sector. We cannot accept the press as a neutral actor. If we want to teach young people to inquire, we must teach them to be skeptical.

However, there is potential danger if participatory media *supplants* mainstream media in the lives of young people. Participation is my interest as well; it's the driving force behind my work and, certainly, behind this book. But let's look at just one of Bennett's suggestions, that setting up Google alerts is a way to participate in media. It's simple enough to set up alerts on the keywords that interest you the most — *affordable housing, Yankees, estate tax, Brangelina*. When a new article including any of those keywords appears on the Web — on anything from a neighborhood blog to a major newspaper — you get an e-mail with a link. You click, and you read whatever is up and new. I do this. I find it a helpful tool to track things I really care about.

But how engaged with the news can we be when we're setting up iGoogle pages so that only the news we know we're interested in is coming our way? How can we ask questions if the scope of our inquiry is limited to the interests we have already identified? A Google alert can't replace the experience of flipping the pages of a newspaper to learn about things that we otherwise wouldn't have known to seek out. As DMI Scholar Samantha Contreras, discussing her experience at the Summer Institute, put it: "Reading the newspaper has widened my perspective immensely. I am now more aware what is happening with other important issues, rather than just my issue, immigration. Reading my local newspaper has helped me to be on top of what is happening with housing, new antigang laws that are being debated, the environment, and so on." If her interaction with the news revolved around receiving Google news alerts for stories about immigration, she would be far less likely to gain exposure to issues outside her central sphere of interest.

It leaves me to wonder whether technology and the "choice" that it brings too easily allow us to limit our scope of reference to that with which we are already familiar and comfortable. For infants in the crib, students learning science at the Exploratorium, or high school students learning civics, inquiry is prompted by the discovery of new phenomena. Serendipity leads us to ask questions. How will we learn to inquire about our world if the boundaries of our exploration are predetermined? As technology writer Geert Lovink observes, "Our techno-cultural default is one of temporal intolerance . . . Serendipity requires a lot of time."[15] The culture of the Internet does not reward the taking of time.

When I pick up today's paper, I see front-page stories on the hoarding of food driving up costs, the shape of new milk jugs that will require less fuel to transport to stores, the United States secretly advising Iraq on oil deals, and the expansion of al-Qaida into Pakistan. In these four cover stories I see one big picture, one narrative about the state of the world today that connects our foreign policy, its relationship to oil, the innovative steps we can and must take to minimize our footprint at a time when our natural world is increasingly fragile. It's one story. A story that can only be understood by engaging with the newspaper — all parts of it. It's a story that I never would have learned through iGoogle or by picking up a video camera. It required me to turn the pages.

On the Britannica Blog, "where ideas matter," a lively debate followed the publication of Nicholas Carr's "Is Google

Making Us Stupid?"[16] One response in particular struck me. Commentor Dan Miller characterized the critiques of Carr and his lamentation of the demise of "old media" — such as general interest newspapers, read by everyone — as arguments that "the individual knows best which cultural products he or she should consume. You hear this particularly with regard to the demise of newspapers. How much better, we're told, when we'll all create our own customized news feeds from around the Net, so we can get just the information we want to get, and nothing else."

But Miller, and all of us, can already see the damage that such a course of endless customization does to our collective ability to understand the world around us: "For a preview of the consequences," he continues, "see today's political climate. When some of us get our news from Fox and others from Keith Olbermann, there's no common set of facts from which political discourse can proceed. There's no need to wrestle with contradictory facts or opinions. Indeed, we don't really need facts at all: I have my opinion, and that's just as valid as yours, whatever the facts may say."[17]

What is at risk here is that our vista will become more limited rather than more expansive. Our worlds are narrowing, not broadening. In the absence of a shared knowledge of what is happening in the world, how can we make informed choices? A culture change is under way, and it is not inherently positive simply because it is interesting.

In the name of choice — which, by the way, is not the same thing as participation — we cannot remove ourselves from the discourse about what is happening in our world. We cannot simply reject a newspaper trade that has been refined since the seventeenth century. We have to push the press. We have to make it more honest. But we cannot have democracy without it.

If we abandon the news, we will continue heading down the current path: entertainment passing as current affairs;

anchors yelling at people and pretending they are journalists. We must continue to care about exposing young people to the importance of the news so that they will become advocates for its improvement.

The issue here isn't whether a young person picks up a video camera or a newspaper. Ideally, those options are not mutually exclusive. But we cannot stop conveying the importance of engaging with the news in substantive, inquiring ways. We must instill the value of digging deeply into the news as a way of increasing knowledge and context, and as critical practice in developing the habit of asking questions. We can encourage their skepticism but we must not encourage their isolation. We can encourage them to tell their own stories but we cannot enable their ignorance by saying it is progress.

Bennett is correct that young people want more of a say when it comes to the news. In 2006, citing the results of a multinational poll of ten thousand people, the BBC suggested that mainstream media outlets are threatened with marginalization by "a generation who want the news they want, when they want and in whatever shape they want."[18] They've grown up in a consumer environment that gives them every indication that they can have it their way. It makes sense that they would think of the news as another commodity.

But what if the shape they want it in is insubstantial? What if the news they want is news on the subjects that they were already interested in? What are the prospects for social change in a democracy in which there is limited shared understanding of what is happening in the world, in which everyone is pursuing what they want, when they want it, in whatever shape they want it?

If today's young people were engaged with the news in a meaningful way beyond newspapers, I would rejoice. But they are not. If I could observe a way of using technology that would result in young people learning to read as carefully and critically as they do while sitting around a bunch of newspapers at the DMI Scholars Summer Institute, I would rejoice. But I have not. The good news is that it's not hard to change people's habits, if we try.

Using Newspapers as a Tool for Inquiry

Frustrated by the small number of young activists from diverse communities in public policy careers, I created a program to train young people in the skills required to pursue these jobs and to understand why this work is important. Through the Scholars program, led by its founding program director, Tsedey Betru, DMI offers college sophomores and juniors the training and networking to become the legislative aids, policy analysts, and researchers who will change the world in the not-so-distant future.

Our time with the students is limited. We cannot teach them every fact it would be good to know. Information changes, anyway, as the world changes, and their lens depends upon their particular field and experience.

Instead, we train them to think critically and to ask questions. At every possible opportunity, I encourage them to identify the core question at the heart of the discussion they are having, the news article they are reading, the policy proposal they are evaluating, the expert lecture they have just heard. They begin to employ the refrain like it was the punch line to a joke. (What time is it? Is that the core question?) I don't care if they are laughing at me, as long as they are asking questions. That skill, once learned and turned into a habit, will be their ticket to success as professionals and as engaged citizens.

The programming for the two-week Summer Institute that introduces Scholars to the policy world is rich, but I have the enviable role of starting each day with them, reading the newspaper. Being in New York City, they are expected to have read the *New York Times* and one other paper before arriving for our one-hour "newspaper breakfasts." I know that if the Scholars are to succeed in their possible career paths, working to make the world a better place, they cannot be disconnected from what's going on in the world. So I grill them.

"What's news?" I ask them each morning. They tell me about the articles that sparked their interest. I ask them questions. Lots of questions.

What is the issue at stake in this article? Is there a conflict? What are the positions of both sides?

Who are the "experts" in this piece? What is the source of their expertise? Which voices are missing?

Why were the front-page stories selected to be on the front page? What does that signify? Are these stories more important than other stories? How do we determine which news is important?

What does the selection of images in today's paper tell you?

What's the function of the editorial page? Who reads it and why? What role do editorials play in shaping policy and politics? What is their agenda today?

Is there a relationship between news coverage and what's in the op-eds today?

What's a letter to the editor? If you were writing a letter to the editor today based on some article in the paper, which article would it be? What would you say?

And so on. Each day during the summer session, the Scholars and I digest and then deconstruct the paper, trying to better understand what is happening in the world and to better understand the role of news in interpreting and shaping those events. We don't accept that the newspaper in our hands is an unquestionable arbiter of truth. Instead, we consider it to be a vehicle to learn about the world, to question what is happening in the world, to learn how to distinguish between reporting and opinion while also understanding the often fuzzy lines between the two. I want them to think, not just read; to process, not just look.

The Scholars' feedback suggests that this kind of rigorous attention to questioning works. "The exercise forced me to look past the words written in the paper for the underlying purpose and meaning of the article," said Quiana McKenzie, a 2008 graduate of Washington and Lee whose first job after graduation was as a fellow to the chief of staff of the governor of Illinois. "I definitely think that I am a smarter and more observant reader of the news now."

And, of course, I want them to ask questions, too. I regularly ask the Scholars to imagine that they are researchers for the Drum Major Institute. I encourage them to dig deeper into the issues addressed in a given article. "What questions would you ask to determine if this is an issue that the Drum Major Institute should tackle?"

In the beginning, they are uncomfortable with this version of newspaper Jeopardy. I ask them for questions and they give me opinions. I ask them for questions and they give me answers. They are uncomfortable asking questions, despite the fact that they are politically active, overachieving, Web-savvy college students. They must not be asked to think of questions very often.

I find this significant. If you cannot formulate a question to learn more about what you have read, you aren't really paying attention. Sure, you can click more. You can find an embedded link in an online newspaper article and then click to another article, and find an embedded link in that newspaper article and click on that one. But when do you stop to ask a question?

So I push. I know their lack of questioning is not because they lack intellect; all of them are quite bright. They simply have not developed the habit. But during the two weeks that the Scholars begin their days with me, they evolve. Their natural curiosity is unleashed. Despite the fact that we start our days at an ungodly hour, there are no quiet pauses. They are engaged. Learning. Asking questions.

The habit sticks. Or so they tell me.

"Hi, Andrea. Guess what? I read the newspaper early in the morning now and I think of what are the policy implications of that particular article. Thanks for the opportunity," wrote Mario Lopez, a 2008 Scholar, on my Facebook wall.

Nana Duffour, a 2007 Scholar from Doylestown, Pennsylvania, wrote, "I take my time more with the newspaper in print. I also don't avoid as many stories with headlines that don't immediately pique my interest. With the Internet I'm often reading stories about things I already know or am interested in, so the paper in print exposes me to more."

"Usually I read the paper as a form of getting updated with current affairs, like Oh, that's interesting or Oh, that's messed up. This taught me to read the article and think of the implications," said Jason Walker, a student at the University of Louisville. "Now I think of possible solutions, then think from an organizing perspective about who has to be influenced. It gave me a critical framework of how to think about things."

Lauren Silverman said, "The most obvious change is evident in the questions I ask myself after finishing an article. I generally ask myself questions such as 'How does this affect policy?,' 'What are the implications for the progressive movement?,' 'What questions do I still have, and where might I go to find out more?'"

"I think reading online is a lot easier, but I feel that reading the newspaper requires that you are more attentive and really paying attention," wrote Christian Plummer. Exactly. And that's not a bad thing.

The Scholars were a special group before they even got to us, for sure — but not when it came to their news habits. In the first session of each program, when I ask for hands of who reads the newspapers on a regular basis, almost no hands go up. They prove the studies are accurate: they look at Web sites, scan headlines, and read what they want to read.

They become newspaper readers because we teach them how. They stay newspaper readers because the practice ignites their minds. They learn about things they never would have learned about without these new habits. They pause to ask questions where they otherwise would have just clicked to the next link.

It is never too late to change anyone's habits. Ask the DMI Scholars.

10: Who's Afraid of Virginia Youth?

THE ANSWER WAS NO.

The proposal was for a trade high school in the city of Hampton, Virginia. Proponents argued that such a school would decrease the dropout rate in Hampton, where 73 percent of students graduate.[1] It was January 2007. The mayor felt one way; the young people present felt another way. The pressure was intense.

After careful questioning it became clear that the trade school, however compelling a proposal in its own right, would not actually solve the problem it was intended to solve. Young people were dropping out for reasons that could not be addressed by the presence of a trade school. Therefore, a trade school was not a viable solution. The answer was no.

No to the mayor, that is.

You see, in Hampton, things are a bit reversed. When Mayor Ross A. Kearney II came up with the idea of starting a trade high school, in October 2006, he knew that the endorsement of the Hampton Youth Commission would be critical to its chances of becoming reality, so he went to them with his proposal. These twenty-four young people were drawn from a community whose school-age population is 63 percent African-American, 31 percent White, 3 percent Hispanic, and 2 percent Asian.[2] They didn't prepare for the meeting by rehearsing compelling speeches or preparing in-depth PowerPoint presentations. Instead, they learned how to ask questions. They learned the direct relationship between asking questions and having the power to improve their communities. And they learned all of this using their local democracy as their textbook.

Much has been said and written of late about the new ways that young people are expressing their commitment to changing the world: they are using the Internet, organizing their friends through online social networks, raising money for causes through Facebook. However, speaking as someone who started as a student school board member and has advised two candidates for mayor of New York, I know there is no substitute for involvement in politics at the local level. That is where we truly learn how to ask questions of those in power, develop the habits of mind of engaged citizens, and assume the posture of agents who have the power to make a difference — because we already have.

When the Answers Aren't in the Room

When I awoke in Hampton, it was the kind of hot, muggy day that made it clear to me that sweet tea is one of the most important inventions of the nineteenth century. I left my hotel overlooking the Chesapeake Bay and walked to city hall. It was easy to recognize, being only one of two multistory office buildings in the city. I was on my way to meet Cindy Carlson, who for fifteen years has championed the cause of youth engagement in Hampton as the director of the Hampton Youth Commission.

Carlson is in her mid-forties, with sandy hair and glasses. She came to Hampton to follow a then-boyfriend and pursue a career as a therapist; she met her husband, Richard, and chose a new career path soon thereafter. She is passionate about the work of empowering young people in the city of Hampton, though wistful when I ask about the photos of Washington State that adorn her walls. Maybe one day there will be time to kayak and hike with Richard, with whom she has made this strange journey, from social work to receiving Harvard's 2005 Innovations in American Government award to speaking at a conference on engaging youth in civic participation in Dubai. But, for now, there are young people to organize, a teen center to build, and visitors like me to show around.

The unique experiment of the Hampton Youth Commission began with the aim of creating a "competitive workforce to spur economic development" driven by "a citizenry that would contribute to the community rather than drain its resources."[3] A high priority was to figure out what to do about the dropout rate and disaffection of the city's youth. The mayor and the city manager brought together youth and community leaders and the heads of social service agencies and told them to come up with a plan.

"It was a very traditional group," Carlson told me. What they wound up with, however, was pretty untraditional: a plan not just to serve youth but also to engage them.

With the "traditional" group assembled, Carlson's husband looked around the table and said, "The answers to our questions are not in this room. We have to go out and find them.'" He recognized that if they stayed in the room, literally and metaphorically, by consulting only with the directors of social services, committees on homelessness, and so on, they would be stuck within those boundaries. They would wind up addressing the same problems with the same programs.

Thus, Richard and some of his staff went into the community to gather a diverse group of young people who had faced and overcome tremendous challenges. The adults invited those youth to work with them to make recommendations about overcoming barriers in their community.

"Some of the community leaders were very uncomfortable, very resistant to that whole process," Carlson said. But the insight the young people brought to their collective problem-solving efforts quickly demonstrated the value of their presence. "The adults were absolutely blown away," Carlson told me. "It was incredible."

From there, Hampton realized that it needed new voices around the table permanently if it wanted more than the same old task force report. After a meeting of city leaders in 1990 recognized the importance of treating young people as community resources and began devising ways to involve young people in community decision making, the Hampton director of planning hired two "youth planners" in 1997. They served in the city's Department of Planning and, along with other youth and adults, developed a plan for addressing issues important to young people. A year later, Hampton acted on its realization that the city needed a robust group of young people to inform the community plan and advise the youth planners. The planners advocated an entire system of youth civic engagement that involved young people at all levels of power. The Hampton Youth Commission was born.[4]

The Hampton Youth Commission comprises twenty-four youth commissioners, young people of high school age who are selected by youth and adult commission members and are charged with representing their peers in the city decision-making process. These youth commissioners have, as they put it, four "power plays": policy, programs, partnerships, and philanthropy. With the youth planners, they set policy by owning a piece of Hampton's Community Plan, a comprehensive planning document that sets short- and long-term priorities for the city. They recommend and start new programs, from neighborhood service and diversity promotion to youth-friendly spaces. They form partnerships with organizations throughout the city. They even have a small pot of money ($40,000) that they can give away each year to support local efforts of their peers.

Hampton is only one city, of course, with a population of only 150,000 people. But its model demonstrates the power of youth engagement not only to affect the quality of the lives of the young people involved but also to improve the community. Everyone I interviewed during my visit affirmed how different Hampton is since these efforts to engage young people began. People from across the country come to learn from Hampton, and for good reason. All of our communities can benefit from the engagement of our young citizens. And all young citizens would benefit from this firsthand opportunity to make a difference.

The Community Plan is an important vehicle for the youth planners. "One of their goals is that young people would be prepared for a career," Carlson told me. "So they have played around with some ideas about working with the school division on what's required, what's available to young people in the area of careers outside of the career and technical education program." The youth commissioners have worked on cell phone policy, requirements for participation in extracurricular activities and sports, and the school calendar. Their schools are not only the place where they learn the three Rs but also the setting for their experience in democratic participation.

Although many of today's young people see government institutions as remote and inaccessible, Hampton's youth actively engage in them. The Hampton Youth Commission organizes mock city council and mayoral elections to coincide with citywide elections.

"It's like a game show," explained Troy, a youth commissioner. "We ask [the candidates] questions that youth want to know the answer to and see who is youth friendly and who would be good to work with the Hampton Youth Commission, because we do work with the city council. We actually have a mock election—and for the past three times we've done it, it came out to how the actual election came out. It's considered a good omen of who is going to win. They actually take it very seriously and so do we. Every two years we do it, and this past year it was pretty successful. A lot of youth came out — we had a full house and actually had to put more seats out."

The adults have to sit in the back and are not allowed to say a word. The Youth Commission screens the questions. Troy said the bottom line about whether a question gets asked is if the city council has something to do with it. "Someone may have a question about the schools, but the city council doesn't have anything to do with schools," so that question is a no go.

"It's a really good way to get students interested in politics and involved locally. If you're over eighteen you can register to vote. It's a good way to get young people interested in voting," Troy said of the forums. Maybe that's one reason that the turnout of young Hampton voters in the 2004 elections was 29 percent higher than the national average.[5]

Like the students at the School for Democracy and Leadership, Hampton's youth are learning that involvement in local politics not only improves their community but also gives them a sense of agency, which comes from seeing how their engagement can directly change public policy. They are more confident in themselves and more confident about their role and responsibilities in their democracy. There is nothing abstract about their involvement; they are like the kids at the Exploratorium, digging their hands into local issues and institutions. They have power, and with it they are making sure that they ask the right questions.

"Cause" and Effect

The political activity of the students of Hampton may seem positively antiquated when compared with how we think about the political activity of young people today. Much has been said and written about the millennials' savvy in creating and taking advantage of online social networks to work for social and political change, particularly during the 2008 election. Yes, young people went door to door to turn out voters to the polls, but impressive levels of activity also took place online. For example, on Election Day 2008, the Causes feature of the Facebook Web site allowed users to "donate" their status—the part of a user's profile that informs other users about what one is doing—to encourage voting. This didn't involve a monetary donation, just a decision to replace whatever update the user would normally have made with a message reminding others to vote. As of 3:30 p.m. on November 4, 1.6 million people had donated their status and a total of 4.7 million status messages had been posted. Millions of people couldn't help but be reminded to vote.[6]

Today's young people are the first generation to have at their fingertips such incredible technology for political organizing. They also are the first generation that has so deliberately linked their consumption to their activism, using the power of their purse to pursue change.

In *Social Citizens Beta,* a thoughtful report for the Case Foundation, Allison Fine examines the activism of the millennials. She draws a portrait of a generation that is "fascinating and important for what they are growing up with (digital technology); how they work (collaboratively); what they believe (that they can make the world a better place to live); and how they are living their lives (green, connected, passionately, idealistically)."[7] She describes a generation that is committed to social change but is expressing it in unique ways, taking advantage of communications technology to share information and organize, and notes their value as a highly sought-after demographic group in the marketplace.

The report, based on reviews of the research and interviews across the country, is helpful to understanding the generation. And although Fine, like many others who write about the millennial generation, is clearly enchanted with them, the report asks tough questions about the depth of their involvement even as it praises their savvy. While examining young people's motivations for activism, however, Fine identifies what I see as an unhelpful dichotomy that has lasting implications for the engagement of young people in questioning their democracy: "By and large, millennials are not interested in or focused on the creation of new government policies as solutions for the issues they care about. They are focused primarily on taking action and seeing results."[8]

Why is working to affect government policy different from "taking action and seeing results"? The dichotomy that Fine captures here, one that I think is increasingly popular in the narrative about today's generation, would be unrecognizable to the young people of Hampton, whose involvement in government policy is directly related to obtaining results and taking action to improve their city for the young people who live there.

How does Fine describe the millennial vision of taking action and seeing results? Sure, there is community organizing, such as using social networking to turn out hundreds of thousands of young people to protest the failure of Congress to pass comprehensive immigration reform, or volunteering in record numbers (though the post-9/11 increase in youth volunteering has subsequently declined).[9] But Fine also broadens the definition of engagement from the types of democratic participation we see in places such as Hampton, to reflect millennials' interest in market-based action to change corporate decision making in the areas that matter to them. This "activism through capitalism" idea is illustrated by the preference of eighteen- to thirty-year-olds for brands that give back to the community, are environmentally safe, or are connected to a cause. As Fine puts it:

> They are more than purchasers of goods, however.
> They are shapers of corporate behavior. They are drawn

to brands with strong socially responsible cultures, such as Patagonia, Nau, Trader Joe's, Whole Foods, and Ben & Jerry's. They are attracted not just by the products these companies sell, but by the activist campaigns they spearhead. One result of corporate benevolence, and the government's perceived failures during events such as Hurricane Katrina, is that young people report a higher degree of confidence in corporations than in government institutions. They want and expect to see direct, concrete actions taken by corporations to address social ills.[10]

I agree that young people should view the corporate sector as a target and a channel for their activism. It is possible for corporations to improve their labor practices, their investment practices, their philanthropic practices — if they think that it is in their best interest. Plus, not all problems of injustice and inequality can be solved by government. Nor should they be.

Nonetheless, the notion that, armed with technology and credit cards, today's youth are able to transcend the messy, long-term business of trying to change the policies that govern our democracy strikes me as deeply unsatisfying. Similarly superficial is the notion that the immediacy of an online protest, a new Facebook cause, volunteering, or the satisfaction that comes from buying this brand of ice cream rather than another is "taking action and seeing results." Changing government policy *is* taking action, action that questions the very system by which our lives are governed. Buying differently within that system does not. We cannot purchase our way to a world without global warming. No one brand will guarantee that our mayor makes the right decision about whether to spend our city's resources on a vocational school.

My argument is not with Fine, who simply articulates the conventional wisdom that the millennial generation is practical and pragmatic and therefore not much interested in government policy. But conventional wisdom, and the narrative it implies, matters. We need to challenge young people's acceptance of this dichotomy if we want to set them on the path to meaningful citizenship as they mature.

The young people of Hampton are trying to change the policy of their local government, and thanks to their increasing efficacy as questioning and critically thinking leaders, they are doing so. They are acting locally and, in the process, are gaining confidence that they can shape government if they learn how. They are learning the habits of mind of engaged citizens. Those lessons require hands-on practice, sitting around tables and learning how to question the mayor. This is every bit as practical as supporting socially responsible businesses, but I think it is ultimately more important for adults to encourage.

Learning about power in politics means interacting with power in politics. This is nonnegotiable if we want to change the systems that force us to send messages to corporations only by refusing to buy their products. Any problems created by the outsized role of consumption and corporate power in our society will not be solved by consuming differently. We need to make this clear to young people today. We need to say to them that failure of our public policy will not be resolved by online organizing unless they also know how to change public policy. Young people need to keep using technology, and linking their purchases with their values, but they also need to learn how to change public policy from the ground up.

Power Precedes Policy

Harry Pozycki founded the Center for Civic Responsibility about ten years ago to help people see action and results in their communities through their engagement with local politics. He told me he agrees that the Internet is a potentially powerful tool for young people's civic engagement, "but the same missing element that was absent in the pre-Web world is still missing — the education in practical politics and the power structure and where the levers of power are available to regular citizens. I think that if people understand the power, they'll more readily actualize." We can't change the machine if we don't know how it works. And, notwithstanding progressive consumerism, that machine directly governs our lives.

The Center for Civic Responsibility has a high school curriculum that has been adopted as part of the New Jersey social studies curriculum. They have an Academy for Citizen Empowerment that "teaches a path to constructive leadership power for any citizen who has, on average, two hours a week of time and a commitment to the common good." These are people without money or political connections, Pozycki emphasizes, people who are taught how the system works and how to make the system work for them.

Although Pozycki laments the formal loss of civics from the classroom over the past two or three decades, he distinguishes between what he sees as "observer civics" and "participation civics." The latter is his specialty. He wants those who participate in his program to actually go out and navigate the system. Observer civics "doesn't say to you, Well, here are your legal rights to engage with the mayor and council, the planning board, the local political parties, and the school board," he said. With the knowledge of participation civics, on the other hand, comes the chance to attain power and, as the Center's organizational motto puts it, "power precedes policy."

Pozycki told me the story of a high school in Plainfield, New Jersey, where the Center presented. This group wanted the town to include in its master plan a requirement to clean up contaminated brownfields in the community. After participating in Center for Civic Responsibility training, the students did their research, took their findings to the planning board, and, according to Pozycki, "got laughed out."

The students weren't happy. They had followed the rules of participation civics. They figured out who was in charge and then showed up to get them to do the right thing.

"Well, you didn't look at all of the pieces of the power structure that we taught you," Pozycki told them.

They realized that they had missed a critical piece of the puzzle: the local Democratic Party committee. So they took their plan to the committee, explained that the contaminated sites were in their districts, and told them it was time to take action. The committee did, but not before another demonstration in participation civics was necessary.

"One of the committeewomen told one of the young women, who was from the high school class, that she should go mind her books and leave the politics to her. And the young woman said, 'Well, one of the things that we learned in Empowerment Civics was that, because I'm going to turn eighteen by the next election, I can file this form' — and she had a copy of it, with just ten names on it — 'and I can run for your seat.' And that committeewoman became the greatest advocate of the environmental plan."

The Center for Civic Responsibility's focus is entirely local. It is at the ground level that we can teach young people and adults to question their democracy and then go out there and get results. Pozycki wants them all to run for local office, and he has the stories — of all the people who never thought they would but currently occupy such offices — to demonstrate that it is possible. His fear is that the enthusiasm of some of the young people currently mobilized on the Internet will dissipate if they don't learn how to translate it into action.

"If you don't know where the levers of power are, and you don't know where to enter and take real leadership positions that have real power within them, then getting excited about Darfur or climate change or whatever is the issue of the day will perhaps even seed more cynicism," he told me.

The process of approaching a town planning board is a lot less glamorous than organizing two thousand online friends to support a cause. But what can and should define this generation, and the generations that follow, is the ability to do both. That thought gives me great hope for our democracy.

Training, Creativity, and Youth Civic Engagement

Inextricably wound up with the young people of Hampton learning how their local government works, and asserting their role as citizens in the decision-making process, is the discovery of how to ask questions. Without this ability, their power would be for naught.

During my time in Hampton, I joined visitors from Morgantown, West Virginia—three young students and their chaperone, a recovering political operative who now runs youth programming for the Department of Parks and Recreation—on a tour of Alternatives Inc. Alternatives, founded in 1973, was one of the early pioneers of "youth development," looking at young people as assets who can and should be actors in the systems that affect their lives. Their brochure reads, "Let young people see they have a meaningful role in today's world." Their storefront looked like the kind of place where children come for fun. Pictures and posters lined the walls. A table was cluttered with candy bars and snacks for sale, the proceeds going to the organization. With only a woven basket to capture the dollars, this effort operated on the honor system.

For the visitors' benefit, Andrea Sealey, a former teacher and a mother from a nearby town, drew on butcher paper a pyramid with the three elements of Alternatives' organizational mission: training, creativity, and youth civic engagement. To accomplish this mission, Alternatives teaches teachers how to develop young people's civic capacity. They work with the city of Hampton on all of their youth civic engagement programs. And they teach children how to paint.

To what?

"We emphasize creativity and problem solving. Have you seen *The Apprentice*?" Sealey asked us. "It's all about new ideas and creativity. Creativity leads to resilience."

Teaching children to paint is connected to teaching them how to identify and solve problems in their community. It's about observing, about making a space in which young people can think creatively about how to capture what they see, about helping them learn to ask the questions that will change what needs to be changed.

The youth commissioners were trained by Sealey's colleague Allyson Graul to question the mayor about the trade school. Graul began her career as a drug counselor at Alternatives, twenty-three years ago. At that time, Alternatives was a national award–winning drug prevention agency. But it shifted its mission, thanks to the input of the very people they were trying to serve.

"They told us that they weren't problems waiting to be fixed—they wanted to be part of the solution to community problems," Graul told me. "People thought we were out of our minds, but we thought it was the right thing to do. If more people felt empowered in their communities and in their own lives, we would have far less of any kind of problem." Alternatives and the city government of Hampton decided that cultivating in young people a sense of agency would be far more important to their health and success than just serving them and treating their ills.

Helping young people ask questions—trying to "build critical problem solvers," as she puts it—is now Graul's life's work. Young people aren't the only ones, however, who could benefit from some attention paid to questioning.

"I don't think this is just for young people," she told me. "We see it all the time in Washington and everywhere in our world. We're not asking the right questions; therefore, we're getting at the wrong solutions." In Graul's view, raising questioning, critically thinking young people is an investment not only in the process but also in developing the "leadership skills that are actually going to make a difference in our communities."

Before the big meeting with the mayor about the trade school, a couple of the youth commissioners had spoken with him privately and were compelled by his arguments. Graul used the situation as a teaching moment. She encouraged the youth commissioners to think like much-younger kids, like children full of curiosity.

"What if we were to be open to finding out everything about this proposal? What are all of the possible questions that can be asked? I even talked about the different kinds of questions—a conceptual *what,* a comparative *which,* a procedural *how,* a suppositional *what if,* an evaluative *why.* We talked about all of the different kinds of questions, and I just let them go." Graul's approach didn't require teaching the youth commissioners anything they didn't already know innately—she simply reminded them of the curiosity that already existed within them.

"Some of the questions were really brilliant," Graul told me with pride. "They asked things like, 'If the current technical center we have isn't working, rather than operating a new one, why don't you just change the courses?'" The mayor wasn't prepared for this kind of questioning, so he responded with the sound bites that he had prepared. Emboldened, the young people persisted, and eventually the mayor left empty-handed. There would be no trade school for Hampton—at least not without a better rationale and a way to measure its success.

The young people of Hampton are always looking at public policy. They do so because public policy is inherently about asking questions and figuring out how to allocate resources and solve problems. We have to ask questions to make public policy, or else we wind up with policies that do not solve the problem. Alternatives helps Hampton's young people learn the difference between Band-Aid policies and policies that create real, lasting change.

I was moved by my day in Hampton in a way that I rarely am. I was moved as I saw the self-possessed and confident young people around a fancy boardroom table in the Department of City Planning introduce the visitors from Morgantown to their efforts. I was moved by Cindy Carlson, who has spent the past twenty-eight years of her career shepherding these young people through a process of self-discovery and leadership, bumping up against those adults who would rather things operate as they always have. I was moved to learn that a group of former youth commissioners who left Hampton to attend college a couple of hours away have decided to try to create such a system there, to involve their local youth. If civics is the study of civic affairs and the duties and rights of citizenship, then Hampton's young people embody the power of civics to connect young people to their democracy. Engagement such as that of Hampton's youth shows the possibilities of creating a culture of inquiry.

What would our country look like if all of its towns and cities operated like Hampton? If children were learning to identify problems in their communities and to ask questions about those problems? If young people's creativity was understood to be intimately related to their ability to solve problems? If we all agreed that understanding the causes of problems, and learning how to come up with solutions to them, is critical to our ability to contribute effectively to our economy and to our democracy?

Of course, when it comes to politics, young people have to deal with the system they are given. Pozycki quoted Caroline, his wife and his partner in their Center for Civic Responsibility: "Young people need example."

What example do our politics offer to today's young people? Unfortunately, when it comes to valuing questions in our politics, our most public displays of democracy leave much to be desired. Perhaps the Commission on Presidential Debates should take its lead from the young people at the Hampton Youth Commission. I'm sure Alternatives Inc. would be more than happy to train them.

11: **Lights, Camera, Debate!**

OCTOBER 15, 1992: ROBBINS FIELD HOUSE AT VIRGINIA'S
University of Richmond. Two hundred and nine uncommit-
ted voters sit in the audience, 69.9 million people sit in front
of their televisions at home, and President George H. W.
Bush, Governor Bill Clinton, and Ross Perot sit on stools.
This is the "town hall" format presidential debate. The questioner from the audience is an African-American woman who
looks to be in her thirties, dressed in a pink business suit and
large-rimmed glasses that fit the time. The moderator is journalist Carole Simpson of ABC.

> QUESTIONER: How has the national debt personally
> affected each of your lives? And if it hasn't, how can
> you honestly find a cure for the economic problems
> of the common people, if you have no experience in
> what's ailing them?

> [*Perot's response.*]

> GEORGE H. W. BUSH: Well, I think the national debt
> affects everybody.

> QUESTIONER: You, personally.

> BUSH: Obviously it has a lot to do with interest rates —

> MODERATOR: She's saying, "you, personally."

> QUESTIONER: You, on a personal basis — how has it
> affected you?

MODERATOR: Has it affected you personally?

BUSH: I'm sure it has. I love my grandchildren—

QUESTIONER: How?

BUSH: I want to think they're going to be able to afford an education. I think that that's an important part of being a parent. If the question—maybe I [am getting] it wrong. Are you suggesting that if somebody has means that the national debt doesn't affect them?

QUESTIONER: What I'm saying is—

BUSH: I'm not sure I get it. Help me with the question and I'll try to answer it.

QUESTIONER: Well, I've had friends that have been laid off from jobs.

BUSH: Yeah.

QUESTIONER: I know people who cannot afford to pay the mortgage on their homes, their car payment. I have personal problems with the national debt. But how has it affected you, and if you have no experience in it, how can you help us? If you don't know what we're feeling?

MODERATOR: I think she means more the recession—the economic problems today the country faces, rather than the deficit.

BUSH: Well, listen, you ought to be in the White House for a day and hear what I hear and see what I see and read the mail I read and touch the people that I touch from time to time . . . [1]

The scene is incredible to watch unfold, and not just because Bush so badly mangles the answer. It is striking to see the interaction between the questioner in the audience, who insists that her question be answered, and the president of the United States, who genuinely wants to answer it, even if he wasn't well equipped to do so. The exchange is powerful, as Bush attempts not just to answer but also to address the underlying assumption of the question: that in order to make policy, one must have firsthand experience with policy failure. It was not to his benefit to make clear this assumption, but it does show a respect for the questioner that today seems quaint by comparison.

Contrast this with the 2008 town hall debate between Senator Obama and Senator John McCain. There was no back and forth between questioners and candidates. No clarification of intent, no opportunity for accountability. The questioners weren't human beings — they were props. The rules made sure of this.

Yes, there were a lot of rules — thirty-one pages of them. These rules covered everything from the trivial, such as the type of chair and the camera angles, to the more substantive. The exchange that took place in 1992 would not have been possible in 2008 because audience members were not allowed to ask follow-up questions. In fact, the microphones of all audience questioners were turned off immediately after they asked their question. Nor was the moderator allowed to ask a follow-up or clarifying question. As the final nail in the coffin, cameras were allowed to show a person asking his or her question but not the questioner's reaction to the answer.[2] This was no town hall debate — it was a performance, carefully controlled to create an illusion of conversation where none existed.

Is this how we ask questions and respond to the answers of our prospective leaders in a democracy?

Some people want to be president when they grow up; I've always wanted to moderate a presidential debate. Even if my preferred candidate isn't performing as strongly as I would like, even if the topics I would like to see addressed aren't, I love watching the debates. As PBS *NewsHour* anchor Jim Lehrer, a regular moderator of the presidential debates, put it, "I have a very simplistic, old-fashioned view of this. It doesn't matter what the format is, it doesn't matter who the moderator is; anytime you get the candidates for president of the United States on the same stage, at the same time, talking about the same things, it's good for democracy."[3]

Indeed, open, thoughtful, constructive debate is a critical component of democracy, both as an opportunity for citizens to get their questions asked and their voices heard and as an opportunity for our leaders to demonstrate their capacity for real dialogue. Our country could not have been founded, or survived its early challenges, without that kind of dialogue.

At the same time, however, I see today's debates as emblematic of our democracy's mixed relationship to the question. Although the debates are important to developing our political consciousness, and although they do inform and sometimes even inspire, they aren't really about inquiry. Despite a format that purports to make questions central, the debates are actually characterized more by the frequency with which questions go unanswered and answers go unquestioned. I believe the backseat that questions take in our highest-profile political event sends the message that inquiry is not valued in our democratic process. But I don't believe it has to stay that way.

The Role of the Presidential Debates

The presidential debates in their current form are a relatively recent invention — they have only taken place continually since 1976 — although they are now a permanent part of our electoral process. Unlike just forty years ago, it would be completely unacceptable today to conduct a presidential election without several opportunities to hear and see the candidates standing next to each other on television. That says something about our impulse to bring questions into the picture. It also says something that an average of 57.4 million people watched each presidential debate in 2008 and that 69.9 million watched the vice presidential debates.[4] The United States ranks 139th in the world in voter turnout,[5] which is a regular measure of political and civic involvement, but the fact that the debates are such major events indicates that our citizens still view politics as important to their lives.

What purpose do the presidential debates serve? According to Newton Minow, one of the architects of the modern presidential debate apparatus (which he began as an aide to Adlai Stevenson in the 1960s) and a member of the board of directors of the Commission on Presidential Debates, the debates are meant to give a sense of the personality of the candidate.

"The debates give us a chance to see how presidential candidates handle pressure, how well they think on their feet. We do not want to know who is the best debater or the better policy wonk. In presidential debates we want the candidates to demonstrate something of their general education, leadership ability, character, and personality. There will always be scripted lines and canned speeches, but always, always there are moments of authenticity that we would otherwise miss, moments that inevitably seem to capture the essence of the candidate and the campaign."[6]

John Del Cecato, a key strategist for Obama's 2008 presidential campaign, agrees with Minow's characterization that the debates give the viewers a sense of the personality of the candidates — which is why he believes the debates were "pivotal" to his candidate's victory. The debates showed "Barack's even temperament," he told me, and although the vice presidential debate "reassured voters that [Alaska Governor Sarah] Palin could get through a debate, [it] didn't convince them that she was ready to be president." According to Del Cecato, the debates "gave voters a window into how the candidates made decisions under pressure, the depth of their knowledge, and their ability to focus. No matter how much preparation you do, a presidential candidate can't fluke their way through a debate."

People look to the debates to help them make a decision about who they want to lead our country. This was especially so in 2008. As of September 25 of that year, almost 30 percent of registered voters said the debates would help them make up their minds about which way to vote.[7] When we went looking for the information to help us make up our minds, we got a sense of the policy positions of the candidates. We knew that Obama wanted to give a tax cut to the 95 percent of Americans earning less than $250,000 per year. We knew that McCain did not want to withdraw troops from Iraq on any kind of predetermined timetable. We would not have learned how it was that such a tax credit would make sense in terms of stimulating economic growth, or how Obama intended to measure its success. We would not have known the indicators McCain intended to use to know when the war in Iraq was officially over. But we'd get the broad strokes of the policy and, in rarer moments, a glimpse of the ideology that informs those positions.

The debates can even, according to some research, reduce young people's cynicism about the political process at a formative time in their development. Researchers Mitchell McKinney and Sumana Chattopadhyay measured the effect on thirty-two undergraduate students of watching the 2004 debates and found that they were "significantly more cynical before watching the debate." The participants also recorded greater "information efficacy" after watching the debate, an indicator of an increase in the kind of political confidence that can determine whether one votes.[8]

As much as I appreciated the 2008 presidential debates as

an exercise in democracy, I was also disappointed by them. I was struck by the rigid time constraints that prevented meaningful conversation, by the rarity of any spontaneous exchange, and by the lack of authenticity in the formats. The questions served mainly as pivot points that allowed the candidates to deliver the talking points they had already prepared. Moderators intervened infrequently, hamstrung by the official rules negotiated by the candidates, even as candidates avoided responding to the direct question being posed or offered answers that were logically inconsistent.

The "town hall" debate was nothing like the town hall tradition in America introduced in part 1 of the book. Questioners were unable to follow up, to insist that their questions be answered, or to ask for clarification where it was warranted. This left me with the impression that the questioners were merely props — not a great message to send to those we want to participate in the democratic process. Because the debates are "the only televised political event capable of attracting the attention of 'marginally attentive' citizens,"[9] because they are the principal occasion when the majority of Americans have the opportunity to see our candidates on the same stage at the same time, we need to do better.

The Role of the Questioner

The role of the debate moderator is decided upon by each campaign during elaborate negotiations and is captured in a "memorandum of understanding." I've read one such memorandum, and it is quite a sight to behold. It's hard to imagine what Lincoln and Douglas would have done with rules such as "Each candidate must submit to the staff of the Commission prior to the debate all such paper and any pens or pencils with which a candidate may wish to take notes during the debate" or "The chairs shall be swivel chairs that can be locked in place, and shall be of equal heights." For the 2004 debate between George W. Bush and Senator John Kerry, the memorandum stated that "the candidates may not ask each other direct questions, but may ask rhetorical questions."[10] (Reading this recently, I could almost picture Kerry saying to Bush, "What on earth would make you think you deserved another term in office?" but then clarifying, in response to a moderator rebuke, that this was a rhetorical question.)

In the September 26, 2008, debate moderated by Jim Lehrer, the rules were loosened significantly. For each topic, there was a five-minute period in which candidates were encouraged to talk to each other. They had trouble doing it, much to Lehrer's chagrin, and directed most of their responses to the camera, the audience, and most especially to Lehrer. Perhaps they were just unaccustomed to such behavior being encouraged.

The limited role of the moderator was most evident during the 2008 vice presidential debate, during which journalist Gwen Ifill asked the following question of Senator Joseph Biden Jr. and Alaska governor Sarah Palin:

> IFILL: Let's talk conventional wisdom for a moment.
> The conventional wisdom, Governor Palin, with you,
> is that your Achilles heel is that you lack experience.
> The conventional wisdom against you is that you lack
> discipline, Senator Biden. What is it really for you,
> Governor Palin? What is it really for you, Senator
> Biden? Start with you, Governor.

It is a fair question—a twist on the old "What are your weaknesses" question that anyone who has ever interviewed anyone for a job has asked. Palin went first:

> PALIN: My experience as an executive will be put to
> good use as a mayor and business owner and oil and
> gas regulator and then as governor of a huge state,

a huge energy-producing state that is accounting for
much progress towards getting our nation energy
independence and that's extremely important.

But it wasn't just that experience tapped into, it
was my connection to the heartland of America . . .

You combine all that with being a team with the
only track record of making a really, a difference in
where we've been and reforming, and that's a good
team, it's a good ticket.[11]

In no way did this resemble an actual response to the question. It is possible that Palin did not understand what "Achilles heel" meant. Ifill could have pushed Palin: What are your
weaknesses? That is my question. Some say it is experience.
What really is your Achilles heel? But there was no follow-
up to clarify.

This happened repeatedly throughout the debate, as a
question was posed and Palin's response had almost nothing
to do with the actual question. Questions in this debate were
merely devices that enabled the candidate to pivot to her pre-
scribed talking points.

Candidates will always want to evade and avoid. It is practically impossible to get them off of their raps, which is understandable — they spend a lot of time developing those raps.
The only way to stand a chance is to actually empower the
questioner to ask questions. Otherwise, the debate is simply
a performance.

Ifill was clearly not encouraged to ask follow-up questions. Although the 2008 memorandum of understanding has
yet to be released, and likely won't be (as I will discuss in a
moment), it is impossible to imagine that follow-up questions
were permitted; otherwise, they likely would have been asked
at least once during the conversation.

In the absence of such questioning, however, why ask Ifill,

a respected journalist, to participate? Why not Alex Trebek or another television personality accustomed to reading from cue cards?

Lehrer says of his moderator role that it is "to be a catalyst, really. It's about the candidates. It isn't about the moderator. It isn't about pressing the candidates. It's to make it possible for the people who are running for president to exchange their ideas rather than to bounce off mine."[12]

His reserve is wise. There is a difference, however, between making the debate about the moderator and insisting that each candidate actually respond to the questions that have been thoughtfully prepared by a respected journalist who has been specifically asked to prepare such questions. In the absence of such attention to the answer, it sends the message to those watching that, in politics, the question is a device.

This is particularly damaging as increasing numbers of citizens, and especially younger generations, question whether the mainstream media are truly capable of holding our nation's leadership accountable. Do we want to convey the message that with more power comes less responsibility to answer the questions posed? Do we want young people to know that those participating at the highest level of our political process can structure these conversations so that they are not forced to answer the questions asked? That, even worse, their political performances are to some extent measured by their ability to *not* answer the question?

Control of the Process

It is understandable that candidates would want to mitigate the risk that questioning brings. But the fact that they are allowed to do so in such a brazen manner speaks to the insularity of the process. Critics of the current debate format point to the Commission on Presidential Debates as the epitome of this insularity. A nonprofit, bipartisan group established "to ensure that debates . . . provide the best possible information to viewers and listeners," the Commission took over the official role of organizing and executing the debates in 1987. (The League of Women Voters had organized debates in federal, state, and local elections for the previous eleven years.)[13]

Some criticize the Commission for being a vehicle of the two major political parties, evidenced by how extremely difficult it is for third-party candidates to join the debates. For instance, the Commission excluded Ross Perot in 1996, even though he had won almost 20 million votes (19 percent of the popular vote) in 1992.[14] Critics also lambaste the Commission for being too beholden to the parties' desires when it comes to the structure of the debates. Although the Commission determines the format, dates, moderators, and locations of the debates, and tells the campaigns that such details are nonnegotiable (a very recent development), they do work closely with the candidates of the major parties on everything else. The memoranda of understanding, for example, are not made publicly available as a matter of course.

As I write this, we still do not know the exact details of the rules of the 2008 presidential debates as agreed to by the candidates, because the memorandum of understanding has not been released. The campaigns did not want to release it and the Commission did not insist. Nor could I watch the footage of the debates on the Commission's Web site. I have to buy it through C-SPAN. It worries me that our presidential debates aren't considered public property.

In 2008, a group called the Open Debate Coalition sprang up to call for changes in the debates. Spearheaded by Lawrence Lessig, professor of law at Stanford Law School and founder of Creative Commons, the Coalition runs the gamut on the ideological spectrum, from Newt Gingrich to Eli

Pariser, the executive director of MoveOn.org. The Coalition's platform comprised four planks, requesting:

1. that the debate moderator be given broad discretion to ask follow-up questions after a candidate's answers, so the public can be fully informed about specific positions.

2. that the moderator ask some online questions that have been voted on by the public through technology such as Google Moderator.

3. that the media release all debate footage into the public domain and allow the public to reuse the video material without fear of breaking the law.

4. that the Commission on Presidential Debates be reformed or an alternative to the Commission be created so that the debate process is transparent and accountable to the public.[15]

The Open Debate Coalition is asking important questions: Why should the questioning of presidential candidates be such a tightly controlled affair that regular people can't even use the videotape? Why can't the moderators insist that candidates answer the questions posed? Why are TV networks and the two major parties colluding to make debate rules that are kept secret from the public?

Ultimately, however, they are asking one essential question that we should all ask: who should own the debates?

If we, the American people, own the debates, it makes sense that we should participate in the formulation and selection of the questions asked. Lehrer says that the debates aren't "a journalism exercise"; they are debates.[16] In that case, why should only the journalists get to decide the questions?

Lessig's proposal is to open up to the masses the process of questioning the candidates. The town hall debate during the

2008 general election did a faint imitation of this, enabling regular Americans to submit their suggested questions to moderator and respected journalist Tom Brokaw, who chose among them. The YouTube debates of the 2008 primary campaign, in which regular people submitted questions via video, also moved in this direction, while signaling the Commission's commitment to new technology. Ultimately, however, this format still "put too much discretion in the hands of gatekeepers," Lessig says. And what was the result of this gatekeeping? "Many of the questions chosen by TV producers were considered gimmicky and not hard-hitting enough, and never would have bubbled up on their own."[17]

Lessig and the Open Debate Coalition want the questions selected for the debates to result from a bubbling-up process. We pose questions and then we vote on the questions that we want to see asked. Now, one can easily argue about whether such a process will produce the best or most appropriate questions. But then again, who is to decide which questions are best or most appropriate? If, in our democracy, we do not even have control over the question, what is there to have control over?

Lessig believes that if we engage regular people, "the best ideas rise to the top, and the wisdom of crowds prevails."[18] I do not know whether it is wisdom that will rise to the top. It is more likely that we will hear questions about the concerns that are most pressing to the American people. We may not hear about every topic, but nor do we now. In none of the presidential general election debates did I hear a question about immigration or the criminal justice system. In the twenty-two primary debates, there were just three questions (out of several thousand) about conservation and renewable energy.[19] Who, then, is above reproach when it comes to deciding on questions?

Candidates Shouldn't Fear Questioning

Yes, we need to change the rules to make the process more transparent and to ensure that the debates can actually raise and then answer the most pressing questions of the American people. But, although it may seem counterintuitive, I think one of the best actions is to organize more debates. There were thirty-five debates between the primary candidates in 2008.[20] These debates were good for the American people, but they were also good for the candidates, who were able to articulate and refine their arguments and their positions.

With more general election debates, we also could experiment with different formats: debates before young people (what a message to send, that the questions of young people merit their own debate!), debates moderated by experts and not just journalists, debates on specific issues, debates before Congress, and so on. We must allow, too, for debates in which the questions bubble up based on the priorities of the American people, and to allow the questioners to interact with the candidates so that their questions are actually answered. There is an endless number of ways to find a formula that truly demonstrates our commitment to questioning our nation's leaders. We just have to be willing to experiment.

The debates should not be viewed as just ninety-minute television events. They are the last occasion when our nation's leader is required to be questioned. Sure, elected officials hold press conferences. But the president can decide how many of those to have and, of course, which reporter to call on while at the podium. As David Sirota, author of *The Uprising,* said to me, "I think the whole frame of 'presidential debates' is merely one tiny piece . . . Our presidents should be subjected to ongoing rigorous questioning." The prime minister of Britain, for example, has to come before the House of Commons each Wednesday to answer questions from the people's representatives. Our debates do allow us to size up the candidates and learn a little bit more about them and their personalities, but as the principal occasion on which our leaders are questioned, they dangerously disappoint.

Without some other major restructuring of our political process, however, the debates will continue to be the biggest and most important opportunity not only to question our leaders but also to demonstrate to the world that we believe such a process is important in a democracy. The irony is that the candidates need not fear questioning. In fact, response to questioning can resuscitate a flagging campaign, or kill one that is perceived as closed. When McCain's campaign was flagging in 2008, he did town meeting after town meeting and took question after question and his campaign rebounded. When Senator Clinton was criticized for not being available enough, she said she would "take questions at every stop. And in New Hampshire she did it, and she won the New Hampshire primary," Howard Wolfson, communications director for Senator Hillary Clinton's presidential campaign, recounted.

Despite the many criticisms of our electoral calendar, some of which I certainly share (for example, its favoring of the rural and homogeneous white communities), our electoral process begins with the asking of questions in towns throughout New Hampshire and Iowa. As Wolfson, who was there with Clinton, described it to me, "Primaries do foster and inculcate an ethos of inquiry. You cannot run for president in this country without going through Iowa and New Hampshire, and you cannot go through Iowa and New Hampshire without really submitting yourself to their questions." Those states may not be representative of our entire country, but their culture of questioning represents the best of what our campaign process can be, before it gets swept up in cross-country travel, endless amounts of money spent on campaign commercials that educate no one, and, of course, impotent debates.

"I started the process with some degree of skepticism about the role that these two states play, and I came to actually realize and respect and admire the dedication that people in those states brought to this. They take this very seriously. And they are out there asking informed questions," said Wolfson. Of course, they are motivated to do so because they know those questions will be answered. Candidates are motivated to answer the questions because they know that is the only way they have a chance at becoming their party's nominee.

Questions and power. As interrelated in the town halls of New Hampshire as in the meetings of the Hampton Youth Commission in Virginia.

Conclusion

A Call for Slow Democracy

WHEN SOCRATES WAS PRONOUNCED THE WISEST MAN IN the world by the oracle at Delphi, he wasn't overjoyed; he was puzzled. *How could I possibly be the wisest man in the world?* he must have asked himself. *I am a humble and penniless philosopher.* Socrates decided that he would simply go out and find a wiser man, thus proving the oracle wrong.

Socrates went first to a politician who had a reputation for wisdom, but the goal of the interview was not accomplished. "Well, I am certainly wiser than this man," Socrates said afterward. "It is only too likely that neither of us has any knowledge to boast of; but he *thinks* that he knows something which he does not know, whereas I am quite conscious of my ignorance . . . I am wiser than he is to this small extent, that *I do not think that I know what I do not know*"[1] (emphasis added).

This obsession with knowing continues to afflict our politicians today, but they are not alone; none of us is immune. We are constantly connected, looking for the latest headline. We rely on Google to provide the trivia of our daily lives. We power browse the Internet. We demand that our politicians know things — or at least that they pretend that they do. At the same time, however, we aren't too choosy about where we get what we know. We'll take it from talk radio because we believe the host shares our values. We'll take it from a search engine because we think that must mean it's true. As our impatience to know more increases, our patience for discernment decreases. Our endurance for inquiry — for taking a moment to observe, decipher, synthesize, evaluate — is changing.

Perhaps it is time for us to slow down.

It is my habit to use food metaphors and I won't stop now. The "slow food" movement blossomed in the late 1980s to "counteract fast food and fast life, the disappearance of local food traditions and people's dwindling interest in the food they eat, where it comes from, how it tastes, and how our food choices affect the rest of the world."[2] Our democracy, too, suffers when we do not slow down enough to question it. It suffers when we are superficially connected to one another, because we get our information from the same information wholesalers, but are disconnected from our own local politics; when we choose to live in isolated ideological homogeneity, learning about the world solely through the lens of that ideology; and when we accept the systems that deliver our democracy and our capitalism to us, rather than questioning those systems to determine whether there is a better, healthier, more respectful way.

"When I was chief of staff in the office of the governor, in 1990," my former boss, Carolyn Lukensmeyer, told me of her time in Ohio, "the river flooded. We had to make some statements in the first hour. But before the governor had to do any assessment or blame, we had plenty of time to get on the ground, talk to the relevant players, and come up with a wise statement about how what had happened could be mitigated in the future."

Today, such a process is impossible, thanks to the 24-7 news cycle, the Internet, the need for instant answers. "Today," Lukensmeyer continued, "when [Hurricane] Katrina happens, one hundred fifty outlets have a microphone in every official's face and they expect them to say something at that moment. That has profoundly distorted our elected officials' capacity to analyze, to connect with the right number of people before they are on the record and then held to what they say on the record—and later castigated for changing their minds after getting more data." We want instant gratification, even if the information we get in that instant isn't ultimately what is going to serve us well.

We need a slow democracy movement. A movement that recognizes that we cannot expect our leaders to have all of the answers and that we should instead measure their wisdom by the process by which they determine how our nation will face its challenges. A movement that allows time to ask questions of our leaders and to deliberate with our neighbors. A movement that assumes that we will do better as a people if we do not simply accept the terms of the market and figure out how to best it, but rather question that market and figure out how to shape it. A movement that takes a break from the test scores and the desperate need to show whether one idea is "working" and instead asks fundamental questions about whether our schools are serving their intended purpose and whether they are best serving our democracy.

A slow democracy movement prizes civics classes, where young people experiment with democracy, one change project at a time. Despite everyone's impatience with a never-ending presidential campaign, we need to slow down and demand better debates between our prospective leaders, marrying the spirit of the primary season's Iowa and New Hampshire town hall meetings with the technology that will invite more Americans into the process of asking questions and witnessing the value of those questions to the democratic process.

This slow democracy movement is about changing systems, but it is also about our values. We can take the time to read the newspaper in front of our children. We can encourage young people to get involved with their local governments, even as we encourage their technology-facilitated participation in the causes of the world. We can make sure that our children know who sits on their school board. We can pull them away from their search engines.

Just as slow food creates healthier individuals and healthier agricultural systems, so too does slow democracy create healthier citizens and a healthier political system.

Slow democracy doesn't mean we can't respond and react to politics in real time — blogs aren't going away, and neither will entertainment news, practically speaking. But we can recognize these things for what they are — fast politics — and see that they must be weighed along with a wealth of other sources when it comes time to take real action. We can begin to define transparency as openness rather than immediacy. We can demand that we build in time for questions.

Socrates' designation as a wise man, one that has lasted for centuries, was not about how much he knew and how quickly he could learn it. It was about his ability to ask questions. People came to him fully confident in their definition of justice or their conception of right and wrong. Through his questions, they often realized the flaws in their reasoning. They came to consider that perhaps there were other definitions of justice. Perhaps the self-righteousness with which they pronounced certain behaviors good or evil was unfounded.

Socrates' young students appreciated this talent. They loved this process. They loved the questioning. The older generation did not. The government thought he was sowing the seeds of disloyalty against the state, even though he had never preached such a thing. They tried him for treason.

Questions are powerful devices because inquiry has the potential to challenge the status quo. The United States was founded out of one such disruption. In fact, I see the history of this country as one big question that has led to many disruptions to the status quo over time; that question, I humbly submit, is *Why can't I be free?*

We first asked this question of the British monarchy, which

led us to become a nation in which questions were critical to our nascent democracy. The documents that captured this spirit at our founding were unique in the world. The founders built in the right to question our government and to question ourselves. Underlying the freedoms of press and assembly is essentially the right to ask *why*. When we do not ask questions, we jeopardize our freedom.

I learned the value of questions early on in my career. As a teenager at Edward R. Murrow High School, I was elected by my peers to represent their interests on New York City's Board of Education, at that time the decision-making body for the school system. The role earned me interviews with the press. I had access to the chancellor and his staff and could visit schools, meet with student governments, and learn a lot about how education worked around the city.

There was only one problem. Unlike the seven grown-up members of the board, who were all appointed by elected officials, I didn't have a vote.

I was a token, and I knew it. But because I was sixteen, and because I was born in Brooklyn, I was undeterred. I would figure out how to assert myself and get the voices of students into the education decision-making process, vote or no vote.

That was when I discovered the power of the question.

It may seem to be an oversimplification, and perhaps it has become so as sixteen years have passed and my memory has faded. But it changed my life when I realized that, in the absence of equal standing, the best way that I could assert myself was by asking questions.

I organized press conferences with high school student newspaper reporters and senior Board of Education officials. I still remember one press conference with the head of school safety. The students grilled him. I had never seen someone sweat like that. They asked him questions such as, "If students consistently report that they feel most in danger on the way to and from school, why is our school safety strategy confined to safety officers and metal detectors in schools?" By asking him a question, rather than simply making a statement, they forced him to respond.

Emboldened by my mission and assisted by an underdeveloped sense of tact, I continued to ask the questions that got to the heart of the matter. In the fall of 1993, inspectors realized that many school buildings were filled with asbestos. The school system had to delay the opening of school by three weeks. The Board of Education was forced by state law to keep schools open a certain number of days, so they canceled some holiday observations to make up for lost time. When the chancellor suggested keeping schools open on Columbus Day, Italian-American groups throughout the city raised a protest. I found their objections objectionable. I asked, "If we really want students to learn about Columbus, why not keep school open and organize schoolwide assemblies?" My question earned me praise on the *New York Daily News* editorial page but glares from the more politically motivated voting members of the board.

Today, I ask questions for a living. I invite policymakers and experts in from around the country and ask them about their work, about their motivations, about their impact. I play devil's advocate. I ask proponents of a policy that would guarantee paid sick leave to all workers in a city whether it is fair to dismiss the arguments of small businesses that such a requirement would harm their bottom line. I believe in the policy, but I think it is important to question ourselves.

I also try to question the paradigms that I believe limit our discourse. I recently debated a scholar from a conservative, right-wing think tank who insisted that the critical question to ask about a tax policy is whether it supports fairness or economic growth. His dichotomy was misleading. But rather than simply advance my policy goal — one in which those who have more pay more — I questioned the terms. In our country, fair policies have always led to more economic growth; why should we assume that one precludes the other?

My passion for questioning does not mean that I am ambivalent about the outcome. Nothing could be further from the truth. My passion for questioning results directly from my firm belief that America is meant to be, and must be, a progressive nation. I believe that we need a vigorous government that uses its power to advocate for those who do not have power. I believe that our democracy will function only when people have a fair shot against the interests of powerful entities. I believe that our economic system must reflect our democratic values, and not the other way around. I believe that we should err on the side of equality. I believe that no one becomes wealthy solely because of their innate talent, but because they benefited from a public infrastructure of streets, schools, hospitals, and safety in which we have all collectively invested. I support the policies that express these beliefs, and I want other people to support those policies, too.

But I recognize that, although public policy has the potential to immediately and significantly affect lives, it is ultimately a short-term expression. Public policy is the result of negotiation and circumstance. Circumstances change. Negotiations change as the power of those participating in them changes. As a progressive, it is not enough for me to win a policy victory at this particular moment. I want to know that the beliefs that drive this victory are held. And the only way that those beliefs can be held is if they are questioned.

Some people benefit when citizens do not question. The status quo benefits. The market benefits. Entrenched interests benefit. Big banks that pay for financial literacy education for young people so that young people think that government regulation is bad benefit. The wealthy few who want to privatize Social Security benefit, counting on the fact that young people don't know why Social Security was founded in the first place and don't understand the concept of social insurance because it was never discussed in a Problems of Democracy class.

Incumbents benefit when young people are sufficiently disconnected from politics and the news that they do not vote. And even when they do vote—on what are they basing their decisions? What is their agenda? The market benefits when young people use consumer-oriented products to "talk" to each other, selling charity as just a click away, without enabling any of the clickers to understand the source of the crisis that required the charity in the first place.

I want young people today to question because it is our best hope for an enduring progressive America. The forces against a progressive America are quite strong. Our politicians act with corporate-purchased impunity while our media consolidates itself into corporations concerned only with their bottom line. Newspapers around the country are withdrawing their reporters from Washington, D.C.,[3] while our papers of record cover politics as a horse race. There are few opportunities to question our leaders as they run for office, and even fewer after they win. The system isn't built for progressive outcomes. That's why we must question.

I believe all progressive policy victories in our system of democratic capitalism are momentary rearrangements of power, and that the people in our nation who have power to engage in these rearrangements are generally members of government or industry. I have tried to offer stories in this book that show the conflict between industry and questioning—the consolidation of media that results in more opinion journalism and less investigation, for example, and the corporate-funded education that aspires to align students' views of the economy with those of the people sitting in boardrooms. Government is equally wary of questioning, which has led to—among other things—the decline of civics education and an electoral process that cloaks questioning in so many layers of performativeness that it becomes impossible to tease out the difference. We need to be skeptical of the powerful institutions that govern our lives. We learn how to be when we learn how to inquire.

It takes time to inquire, of course, and everything in our lives moves so quickly. The only way to cope with so much more information is to explore each piece less deeply. In modern society, everything is about more, more, more, so we go less, less, less deeply. I believe we suffer personally from these habits, but I believe our democracy suffers, too. We need a slow democracy to counteract this tendency toward superficial engagement.

In a telling experiment conducted by Dr. Susan Engel, teachers were presented with a list of twenty-five goals for their teaching and asked to circle the top five. "Curiosity" was circled by a majority. But when teachers were asked to name the top educational goals without reference to such a list, there was almost no mention of curiosity. Engel concluded that "teachers may passively endorse curiosity, but we have evidence that they do little to actively promote it."[4]

If we were presented with a list of qualities that we'd want to cultivate for effective citizenship, I'm sure we'd circle "questioning." But if we had to come up with that list on our own, I wonder if we'd include inquiry at all. If this book can accomplish anything, I hope it is that we will begin to think more about the asking of questions as a necessary component of a healthy democracy.

Those committed to change in our country are rejoicing at the election of a new generation of leadership in the 2008 elections. As am I. I rejoice at the record voter turnout in the elections, the highest since 1968.[5] I rejoice at the new technologies that are connecting people in unprecedented and potentially powerful ways. I am optimistic.

But though my years are (relatively) short, my memory is long. Waves of optimism fade if we do not challenge the political framework that tells us that our leaders will solve our problems for us; they never can, and they always disappoint. This human fallibility doesn't mean that we should believe in government or politicians any less. It means we need to ask more questions of them. It means we should encourage them to ask questions of themselves. We need deliberation where we have been seduced by false wisdom. We want to ask more of our own participation than voting. We need to ask more questions of ourselves and our neighbors. Questioning is a habit, not a solution, but it is a necessary habit for democracy.

Now, more than ever, as "knowledge" multiples before our eyes on several billion new Web sites each day, as even the means by which we can know new things evolves at lightning speed, we need to worry less about knowing everything. We need to concern ourselves more with asking questions, with the process of critical thinking, with personal and community deliberation. We need a little bit more Socratic wisdom in our lives and a little less faux certainty. We need a little more *why*.

Notes

INTRODUCTION: QUESTIONS AND POWER

1. "Latest Bestsellers of Hardcover Nonfiction," *Publishers Weekly*, week of November 24, 2008, http://www.publishersweekly.com/bestsellerslist/ 1.html?listdate=11%2F24%2F2008&channel=bestSellers&q=week+of+ november+24%2C+2008.

Part I

INTRODUCTION

1. Geert Lovink, "The Society of the Query and the Googlization of Our Lives: A Tribute to Joseph Weizenbaum," *Eurozine*, September 5, 2008, 6, http://www.eurozine.com/pdf/2008-09-05-lovink-en.pdf (accessed December 25, 2008).

2. Rhonda Byrne, *The Secret* (New York: Atria Books, 2007), 98–99.

3. Nielsen BookScan reported sales of 3,888,301 near the end of 2008. Because only 80 percent of outlets report to BookScan, the number is likely 20 percent greater: approximately 4.7 million.

4. According to Marketdata Enterprises, as cited in "Self-Improvement Market Growth Slows as Recession Takes Toll," *PRWeb*, press release newswire, http://www.prweb.com/releases/2008/10/prweb1466054.htm (accessed December 25, 2008).

5. Anita Soni, *Allergic Rhinitis: Trends in Use and Expenditures, 2000 and 2005*, Medical Expenditure Panel Survey Statistical Brief #204 (Rockville, MD: Agency for Healthcare Research and Quality, U.S. Department of Health and Human Services, May 2008), http://www.meps .ahrq.gov/mepsweb/data_files/publications/st204/stat204.pdf; and David Lazarus, "Spin the (Water) Bottle: With $11 Billion in U.S. Sales, the Beverage's Marketers Have Become Clear Winners," *San Francisco Chronicle*, January 17, 2007.

CHAPTER 1. INQUIRY IS RISKY, RESILIENCE IS THE REWARD, AND OTHER LESSONS FROM CHILDHOOD

1. E. Mavis Hetherington and Ross D. Parke. *Child Psychology: A Contemporary Viewpoint*, 5th ed. (Boston: McGraw-Hill, 2003).

2. Carol S. Dweck, "The Secret to Raising Smart Kids," *Scientific American,* November 28, 2007, http://www.sciam.com/article.cfm ?id=the-secret-to-raising-smart-kids.

3. David L. Schachter, Daniel T. Gilbert, and Daniel M. Wegner, *Psychology* (New York: Worth Publishers, 2009), 397.

4. Dweck, "Raising Smart Kids." See also Po Benson, "How Not to Talk to Your Kids: The Inverse Power of Praise," *New York Magazine,* February 12, 2007, http://nymag.com/news/features/27840.

5. Benson, "How Not to Talk."

6. Tom W. Smith and Seokho Kim, "World Opinion: National Pride in Comparative Perspective: 1995/96 and 2003/04," *International Journal of Public Opinion Research* 18 (2006): 129–30. The study included two measures of national pride. The "domain-specific" measure assessed "positive feelings towards national accomplishments in specific areas, but is not overtly nationalistic, imperialistic, nor chauvinistic." The general national pride measure, in contrast, assessed feelings about superiority and assertions of national allegiance over moral judgment. The United States ranked first on the domain-specific pride measure and second on the general national pride measure. Venezuela ranked first on the general national pride measure and second on the domain-specific pride measure. Australia ranks third on both measures. The authors note that research shows a sustained increase in domain-specific pride in the United States since the September 11, 2001, terrorist attacks. They also point out that "general national pride is strongly and positively associated with having a demanding sense of what is important for someone to be considered a true member of a country and with opposition to multi-lateralism and internationalism . . . Domain-specific pride is moderately associated with having a restricted view on citizenship."

CHAPTER 2. IDEOLOGICAL SEGREGATION BY CLICK AND BY CLIQUE

1. Bill Bishop, *The Big Sort: Why the Clustering of Like-Minded America Is Tearing Us Apart* (Boston: Houghton Mifflin, 2008), 5.

2. Ibid., 5–6, 29–30. One argument against the phenomenon of the Big Sort is that districts have been gerrymandered by political parties through years of redistricting to create safe districts for incumbents. Bishop argues that the gerrymandering thesis is incomplete. Political parties "aren't in the business of building supermajorities for incumbents," he writes, but instead are intent on ensuring that they have a comfortable enough lead in as many districts as possible. That is, it is not in their best interest to build a few lopsided districts, but to build more districts in which they have a lead. Sometimes this effort can leave incumbents less protected, rather than more. Bishop cites Alexander Abramowitz, Brad Alexander, and Matthew Gunning, who

write, "Partisan redistricting often has the effect of reducing the safety of incumbents." "Don't Blame Redistricting for Uncompetitive Elections," *PS: Political Science and Politics* 39, no. 1 (2006): 88. Bishop (*Big Sort*, 30) argues that, after the redistricting of 1980, 1990, and 2000, "there were no immediate jumps in lopsided districts."

3. Bill Bishop, interview with *Democracy in America*, in "Bill Bishop on Political Clustering," *The Economist*, June 19, 2008, http://audiovideo. economist.com/?fr_story=a036ce1986e0bac50364de82322783a55c66 c3b1&rf=bm.

4. Alan Abramowitz, "Constraint, Ideology, and Polarization in the American Electorate: Evidence from the 2006 Cooperative Congressional Election Study" (paper presented at the annual meeting of the American Political Science Association, Chicago, August 30, 2007), 9, http://web.mit.edu/polisci/portl/cces/material/Abramowitz-CCES .pdf.

5. Alan Abramowitz and Kyle Saunders, "Why Can't We All Just Get Along? The Reality of a Polarized America," *The Forum* 3 (2005): 5, 9–10, 19.

6. Bill Bishop, "No, We Didn't: America Hasn't Changed as Much as Tuesday's Results Would Indicate," *Slate*, weblog entry posted November 10, 2008, http://www.slate.com/blogs/blogs/bigsort/ archive/2008/11/10/no-we-didn-t-america-didn-t-change-as-much-as -tuesday-s-results-would-indicate.aspx (accessed December 26, 2008). See also Bill Bishop and Robert Cushing, "Income, College Degrees Greater in Rural Obama Counties," *Daily Yonder*, weblog entry posted December 10, 2008, http://www.dailyyonder.com/incomes-college -degrees-greater-rural-obama-counties/2008/12/10/1795 (accessed December 26, 2008).

7. Natali Jomini Stroud, "Media Use and Political Predispositions: Revisiting the Concept of Selective Exposure," *Political Behavior* 30 (2008).

8. Shanto Iyengar and Richard Morin, "Red Media, Blue Media: Evidence for a Political Litmus Test in Online News Readership," *Washington Post,* May 3, 2006, http://www.washingtonpost.com/wp-dyn/ content/article/2006/05/03/AR2006050300865.html (accessed December 25, 2008).

9. Drum Major Institute for Public Policy, "DMI's First Annual Survey on the Middle Class and Public Policy Finds Broad Policy Agreement among Fearful Families," August 19, 2008, http://www .drummajorinstitute.org/library/report.php?ID=73. The Employee Free Choice Act requires recognition of a union after a majority of employees sign cards affirming their support for union representation, and strengthens penalties for violations of labor law. Legislation to expand the State Children's Health Insurance Program, which provides health coverage to 7 million children of low- and middle-income families,

would increase the number of children enrolled in the program and likely would encourage states, which fund the program along with the federal government, to enroll more of the lowest-income uninsured children in Medicaid. Carried interest, which is the fee that hedge fund and private equity managers earn for managing investments, is currently taxed as capital gains at a rate of 15 percent, rather than as earned income at a rate of 35 percent (the income tax rate that high-income managers would be subject to). Tax legislation would alter the tax code to close this loophole.

10. Cass R. Sunstein, *Republic.com* (Princeton, NJ: Princeton University Press, 2001), 71.

11. Josef Graf, "The Audience for Political Blogs: New Research on Blog Readership" (2006), 3, http://www.ipdi.org/uploadedfiles/Blog%20Readership%20-%20October%202006.pdf.

12. comScore, "Huffington Post and Politico Lead Wave of Explosive Growth at Independent Political Blogs and News Sites This Election Season," October 22, 2008, http://www.comscore.com/press/release.asp?press=2525 (accessed December 25, 2008).

13. Ezter Hargittai, Jason Gallo, and Matthew Kane, "Cross-Ideological Discussion among Conservative and Liberal Bloggers," *Public Choice* 134 (2008): 78, 81.

14. Lada A. Adamic and Natalie Glance, "The Political Blogosphere and the 2004 U.S. Election: Divided They Blog" (paper presented at the International Conference on Knowledge Discovery and Data Mining, Chicago, August 21–25, 2005).

15. Matthew Hindman, Kostas Tsioutsiouliklis, and Judy A. Johnson, "'Googlearchy': How a Few Heavily-Linked Sites Dominate Politics on the Web" (paper presented at the annual meeting of the Midwest Political Science Association, Chicago, April 3–6, 2003): 27–28, http://www.cs.princeton.edu/~kt/mpsa03.pdf. To highlight this point, the authors write, "Any site which is more than three clicks away from *any* of the top 200 Google or Yahoo! results on a given topic is definitely off the beaten track, and not likely to have any substantial impact on mass politics."

16. Henry Farrell and Daniel W. Drezner, "The Power and Politics of Blogs," *Public Choice* 134 (2008): 16, http://www.danieldrezner.com/research/blogpaperfinal.pdf.

17. America*Speaks, Americans Discuss Social Security: Report to Congress* (Washington, DC: America*Speaks,* 1998).

18. America*Speaks, Unified New Orleans Plan Community Congress II High-lights* (Washington, DC: America*Speaks*), January 22, 2007, http://www.americaspeaks.org/index.cfm?fuseaction=page.viewPage&PageID=665&d:\CFusionMX7\verity\Data\dummy.txt (accessed February 13, 2009).

19. "Nearly 3,500 Californians Gather at Eight Sites across the State to Discuss Health Care: 82% Believe the System Needs Major Change," *PR Newswire,* August 12, 2007; and America*Speaks, Public Impacts.*

20. Interestingly, this shift was true at the individual level, while at the group level, little shift in opinion was evident.

21. Archon Fung and Taeku Lee, *The Difference Deliberation Makes: A Report on the CaliforniaSpeaks Statewide Conversations on Health Care Reform* (Washington, DC: America*Speaks,* 2008): iii, 8–15.

CHAPTER 3. CONSUMING OPINION

1. Common Cause, *The Fallout from the Telecommunications Act of 1996: Unintended Consequences and Lessons Learned* (Washington, DC: Common Cause Education Fund, May 9, 2005): 5, http://www.commoncause.org/atf/cf/%7B8A2D1D15-C65A-46D4-8CBB-2073440751B5%7D/FALLOUT_FROM_THE_TELECOMM_ACT_5-9-05.PDF.

2. The Project for Excellence in Journalism, "Cable TV: Cable News Prime Time Median Audience" in *The State of the News Media 2008: An Annual Report on American Journalism* (Washington, DC: Project for Excellence in Journalism, 2008), http://www.stateofthenewsmedia.com/2008/chartland.php?id=604&ct=line&dir=&sort=&c1=0&c2=1&c3=1&c4=1&c5=0&c6=0&c7=0&c8=0&c9=0&c10=0&d3=0&dd3=1 (accessed December 25, 2008).

3. The Project for Excellence in Journalism, "Overview: Audience" in *State of the News Media,* http://www.stateofthenewsmedia.org/2008/narrative_overview_audience.php?cat=3&media=1 (accessed December 25, 2008).

4. The Project for Excellence in Journalism, "Cable TV: Cable News Profitability" in *State of the News Media,* http://www.stateofthenewsmedia.org/2008/chartland.php?id=607&ct=line&dir=&sort=&c1=1&c2=1&c3=1&c4=0&c5=0&c6=0&c7=0&c8=0&c9=0&c10=0&d3=0&dd3=1 (accessed December 25, 2008).

5. The Project for Excellence in Journalism, "Cable News vs. Network News Viewership," March 12, 2007, http://www.journalism.org/node/1363 (accessed December 25, 2008); idem, "Network TV: Evening News Viewership, All Networks" in *State of the News Media,* http://www.stateofthenewsmedia.org/2008/chartland.php?id=745&ct=line&dir=&sort=&col1_box=1 (accessed December 25, 2008); and idem, "Cable News Prime Time Median Audience."

6. The Project for Excellence in Journalism, "Cable TV: Content Analysis" in *State of the News Media,* http://www.stateofthenewsmedia.org/2008/narrative_cabletv_contentanalysis.php?cat=1&media=7 (accessed December 25, 2008).

7. Ibid.

8. See Media Matters Action Network, *Fear & Loathing in Prime Time: Immigration Myths and Cable News* (Washington, DC: Media Matters Action Network, May 21, 2008), http://mediamattersaction.org/static/pdfs/fear-and-loathing.pdf.

9. Author interview by Lou Dobbs, *Lou Dobbs Tonight,* CNN, May 30, 2006, http://transcripts.cnn.com/TRANSCRIPTS/0605/30/ldt.01.html (accessed December 25, 2008).

10. The Project for Excellence in Journalism, "Radio: Talk Radio" in *State of the News Media*, http://www.stateofthenewsmedia.org/2008/narrative_radio_talk_radio.php?cat=6&media=10 (accessed December 25, 2008).

11. The Project for Excellence in Journalism, "Radio: Content Analysis" in *State of the News Media*, http://www.stateofthenewsmedia.org/2008/narrative_radio_contentanalysis.php?cat=1&media=10 (accessed December 25, 2008).

12. See David Goodman, "Programming in the Public Interest" in *NBC: America's Network* (Berkeley: University of California Press, 2007), 48; James S. Fishkin, *The Voice of the People: Public Opinion and Democracy* (New Haven, CT: Yale University Press, 1995), 136; and John Dunning, *On the Air: The Encyclopedia of Old-Time Radio* (New York: Oxford University Press, 1998), 30–31.

13. See Goodman, "Programming in the Public Interest," 44. For audio of *America's Town Meeting of the Air*, see "America's Town Meeting of the Air in the Great Depression," American Studies at the University of Virginia, http://xroads.virginia.edu/~1930s/Radio/TownMeeting/TownMeeting.html (accessed December 27, 2008).

14. Dunning, *On the Air.*

15. "Should We Plan for Social Security?" *America's Town Meeting of the Air*, NBC, December 19, 1935.

16. Goodman, "Programming in the Public Interest," 48. See also James S. Fishkin, *The Voice of the People: Public Opinion and Democracy* (New Haven, CT: Yale University Press, 1995), 136.

17. Goodman, "Programming in the Public Interest," 48.

18. "Town Meetings," *Time,* January 17, 1938.

19. Goodman, "Programming in the Public Interest," 48.

20. Newton N. Minow and Craig L. LaMay, *Inside the Presidential Debates: Their Improbable Past and Promising Future* (Chicago: University of Chicago Press, 2008), 10.

21. Goodman, "Programming in the Public Interest," 49, 52.

22. "What's Your Opinion?" *Current History* 50 (1939): 39.

23. Goodman, "Programming in the Public Interest," 50. The Communications Act of 1934 created the Federal Communications Commission to regulate radio, previously overseen by the Federal Radio Commission, and telephone services. The act reinforced provisions of the Radio Act

of 1927 that had authorized the Federal Radio Commission to grant radio licenses if "public interest, necessity, or convenience would be served." After an explosion in radio ad sales in the 1920s and 1930s, which heralded the commercialization of a radio system that had previously been operated to a significant degree by nonprofit organizations, reformers attempted to use the 1934 act to ensure adequate public access to broadcasting. Worried about the bias of corporate-controlled broadcasting, reformers sought to lock in a nonprofit broadcast system. The reformers, however, were rebuffed by Congress, and commercialization and consolidation in the media industry ensued throughout the twentieth century, though with certain restrictions, such as ownership caps, in place until the 1996 Telecommunications Act. Still, debate about public interest in broadcasting stirred reforms by some media companies.

24. As the media scholar Robert McChesney put it, "By 1928 . . . U.S. capitalists began to sense the extraordinary commercial potential of broadcasting. With the support of the newly established Federal Radio Commission, the U.S. airwaves were effectively turned over to NBC and CBS and their advertisers." "Graham Spry and the Future of Public Broadcasting," the 1997 Spry Memorial Lecture, *Canadian Journal of Communication* 24 (1999), http://www.cjc-online.ca/index.php/journal/article/view/1081/987.

25. StopBigMedia.com Coalition, "Super-Concentrated: Who Owns the Media?" http://www.stopbigmedia.com/chart.php (accessed December 23, 2008).

26. Common Cause, *Telecommunications Act of 1996.*

27. Ben Bagdikian, "Grand Theft: The Conglomeratization of Media and the Degradation of Culture," *Multinational Monitor* 26 (2005), http://www.multinationalmonitor.org/mm2005/012005/bagdikian.html (accessed December 25, 2008).

28. Goodman, "Programming in the Public Interest," 50–51.

29. Pew Research Center for the People & the Press, *Internet News Audiences Highly Critical of News Organizations: Views of Press Values and Performance: 1985–2007* (Washington, DC: Pew Research Center), 8, http://people-press.org/reports/pdf/348.pdf.

30. Pew Research Center for the People & the Press, *How Journalists See Journalists in 2004: Views on Profits, Performance and Politics* (Washington, DC: Pew Research Center, 2004): 1, http://people-press.org/reports/pdf/214.pdf.

31. See the Project for Excellence in Journalism, *Does Ownership Matter in Local Television News: A Five-Year Study of Ownership and Quality* (Washington, DC: Project for Excellence in Journalism, 2003), http://www.journalism.org/files/ownership.pdf; Christopher J. Kollmeyer, "Corporate Interests: How the News Media Portray the Economy," *Social*

Problems 51 (2004): 432–52; Consumers Union, Consumer Federation of America, and Free Press, *The Case against Big Media: Compendium of Public Interest Research on Media Ownership, Diversity and Localism*, Stop-BigMedia.com, 78, 89, http://www.stopbigmedia.com/=compendium (see, in particular, "Part 2: The Continuing Importance of Localism, Media Ownership and Television"); and John Helpin, James Heidbreder, Mark Lloyd, Paul Woodhull, Ben Scott, Josh Silver, and S. Derek Turner, *The Structural Imbalance of Political Talk Radio* (Washington, DC: Free Press and the Center for American Progress, 2007), 27, http://www.americanprogress.org/issues/2007/06/pdf/talk_radio.pdf.

32. Consumers Union et al., *Case against Big Media*, 87.

33. Common Cause, *Telecommunications Act of 1996*.

34. "News stories that have no clear connection to policy issues have increased from less than 35 percent of all stories in 1980 to roughly 50 percent today [2000]. Stories with a public policy component — hard news — have declined by a corresponding degree. News mediums differ somewhat in the amount of change, but the trend is the same for all of them — local TV news, national TV news, leading newspapers, local dailies, and weekly news magazines. Each has less policy-related coverage today than a decade or two ago . . . In sum, the news has softened considerably." Thomas E. Patterson, *Doing Well and Doing Good: How Soft News and Critical Journalism Are Shrinking the News Audience and Weakening Democracy — and What News Outlets Can Do about It* (Cambridge, MA: Joan Shorenstein Center on the Press, Politics and Public Policy, 2000), 3–5, http://www.hks.harvard.edu/presspol/publications/reports/soft_news_and_critical_journalism_2000.pdf.

CHAPTER 4. IN GOOGLE WE TRUST

1. Marcel Proust, *In Search of Lost Time: Within a Budding Grove*, trans. C. K. Scott Moncrieff and Terence Kilmartin (New York: Modern Library, 1998), 605.

2. Clay Shirky, "Why Abundance Is Good: A Reply to Nick Carr," Encyclopaedia Britannica Blog, entry posted July 17, 2008, http://www.britannica.com/blogs/2008/07/why-abundance-is-good-a-reply-to-nick-carr (accessed December 25, 2008).

3. A 2004 study of 52 daily U.S. newspapers by the Readership Institute at Northwestern University found that the average newspaper had about 65 broadsheet pages on weekdays and 137 broadsheet pages on Sundays, with an advertisement-to-editorial content ratio of 34 to 66 on weekdays and 44 to 56 on Sundays. Newspapers with larger circulations tended to have more pages and more advertisements. *An Analysis of Content in 52 U.S. Daily Newspapers: Summary Report* (Evanston, IL: Readership Institute, Northwestern University, 2004), 3, http://www.readership.org/new_readers/data/content_analysis.pdf. At the end

of 2008, Google News offered pages tailored to countries from Colombia and Cuba to Namibia, the Czech Republic, and the Philippines. At that time Google News was available in Arabic, Chinese, Dutch, English, French, German, Greek, Hebrew, Hindi, Italian, Japanese, Korean, Norwegian, Portuguese, Russian, Spanish, and Swedish.

4. Estimates based on data compiled by comScore.

5. Jesse Alpert and Nissan Hajaj, "We Knew the Web Was Big . . ." The Official Google Blog, entry posted July 25, 2008, http://googleblog.blogspot.com/2008/07/we-knew-web-was-big.html (accessed December 25, 2008).

6. See, for example, Marc Prensky, "Digital Natives, Digital Immigrants," http://www.marcprensky.com/writing/Prensky%20-%20Digital%20Natives,%20Digital%20Immigrants%20-%20Part1.pdf (accessed February 12, 2009); and Mark Bauerlein, *The Dumbest Generation: How the Digital Age Stupefies Young Americans and Jeopardizes Our Future* (New York: Penguin Group, 2008). For more scholarly examples, see the work of the New Literacies Research Team at the University of Connecticut.

7. Centre for Information Behaviour and the Evaluation of Research (CIBER), *Information Behaviour of the Researcher of the Future*, executive summary (London: University College London, 2008), 9, http://www.ucl.ac.uk/slais/research/ciber/downloads/ggexecutive.pdf. For student search behavior in particular, see idem, *Student Information-Seeking Behaviour in Context*, http://www.ucl.ac.uk/slais/research/ciber/downloads/GG%20Work%20Package%20IV.pdf (June 22, 2007).

8. CIBER, *Researcher of the Future*, 8.

9. Ibid., 8, 19.

10. Nicholas Carr, "Is Google Making Us Stupid?" *The Atlantic,* July/August 2008, http://www.theatlantic.com/doc/200807/google.

11. Joseph Weizenbaum, as cited in Lovink, "Society of the Query" (see part I intro., n. 1).

12. CIBER, *Researcher of the Future*, 23.

13. Sandra G. Hirsh, "Children's Relevance Criteria and Information Seeking on Electronic Resources," *Journal of the American Society for Information Science* 50 (1999): 1274, 1280.

14. Michael Lorenzen, "The Land of Confusion? High School Students and Their Use of the World Wide Web for Research," *Research Strategies* 18 (2001): 156, 159–62.

15. Nathan Bos, "High School Students' Critical Evaluation of Scientific Resources on the World Wide Web," *Journal of Science Education and Technology* 9 (2000): 161–73.

16. Andrew Large, "Children, Teenagers, and the Web," *Annual Review of Information Science and Technology* 39 (2006): 359.

17. CIBER, *Researcher of the Future*, 23.

18. Jay Moonah, "Episode #27: Information Literacy and Search Engines," Media Driving, podcast posted on October 15, 2008, http://mediadriving.com/2008/10/15/episode-34-information-overload-repost (accessed December 29, 2008).
19. Maggie Jackson, *Distracted: The Erosion of Attention and the Coming Dark Age* (Amherst, NY: Prometheus Books, 2008), 13.
20. Hindman et al., "Googlearchy" (see ch. 2, n. 15).
21. Lovink, "Society of the Query."

Part II

INTRODUCTION

1. Dennis Palmer Wolf, "The Art of Questioning," *Academic Connections,* Winter 1987, http://www.exploratorium.edu/IFI/resources/workshops/artofquestioning.html; and Instructional Assessment Resources, "Assess Students: Bloom's Taxonomy," University of Texas at Austin, 2007, http://www.utexas.edu/academic/diia/assessment/iar/students/plan/objectives/bloom.php.
2. Instructional Assessment Resources, "Assess Students."
3. The Urban Assembly School for Law and Justice graduation rates are according to Ms. Karopkin. The first graduating class was in the 2007–08 school year. See also Jennifer Medina, "Attention Goes a Long Way at a School, Small by Design," *New York Times,* June 30, 2008, http://www.nytimes.com/2008/06/30/education/30school.html?_r=1&pagewanted=1. The 56 percent graduation rate includes students who received their diploma by August 2007. Of the 2006 graduates, 44.3 percent planned to attend four-year colleges and 16.2 percent planned to attend two-year colleges. New York City Department of Education, *Graduation Rates Class of 2007,* 2008, 2, http://schools.nyc.gov/NR/rdonlyres/CE19A29E-DD2D-4EB4-981A-D3BF6EE4AD40/42079/0811_grad_rate.pdf; and idem, *2005-2006 Annual School Report Supplement: The Urban Assembly School for Law and Justice,* 5, http://schools.nyc.gov/OA/SchoolReports/2005-06/ASR_K483.pdf.
4. According to the U.S. Bureau of Labor Statistics, "The average person born in the later years of the baby boom held 10.8 jobs from age 18 to age 42." Almost two-thirds of the jobs were held between ages 18 and 27. *Number of Jobs Held, Labor Market Activity, and Earnings Growth among the Youngest Baby Boomers: Results from a Longitudinal Survey,* 2008, 1, http://www.bls.gov/news.release/pdf/nlsoy.pdf. See also U.S. Census Bureau, *Calculating Migration Expectancy,* October 21, 2008, http://www.census.gov/population/www/socdemo/migrate/cal-mig-exp.html.
5. U.S. Department of Education, "Statement by Secretary Spellings on History and Civics Reports Released by the Nation's Report Card," press release, May 16, 2007, http://www.ed.gov/news/pressreleases/2007/05/05162007.html (accessed December 26, 2008).

6. "President Bush Announces President's Advisory Council on Financial Literacy," White House Office of the Press Secretary, January 22, 2008, http://georgewbush-whitehouse.archives.gov/news/releases/2008/01/20080122-7.html (accessed February 7, 2009).

7. See "Financial Literacy: A Tough Teachable Moment," editorial, *Atlanta Journal-Constitution,* August 17, 2008; James Bowers, "Financial Illiteracy Plagues America," *Providence Journal-Bulletin,* October 22, 2008; and Braun Mincher, "We Teach Teens Trigonometry, Why Not Money 101?" *Christian Science Monitor,* September 23, 2008.

CHAPTER 5. THE THREE RS AND A WHY

1. Frank Oppenheimer, "Rationale for a Science Museum," *Curator* 11 (November 1968): 206–9, http://www.exploratorium.edu/frank/rationale/rationale.pdf.

2. Carnegie Corporation of New York and CIRCLE, the Center for Information and Research on Civic Learning and Engagement, *The Civic Mission of Schools* (New York: Carnegie Corporation of New York, and Medford, MA: CIRCLE, 2003), 11.

3. R. Freeman Butts, "Education for Civitas: The Lessons Americans Must Learn" (working paper, Hanna Collection on the Role of Education, Hoover Institution, Stanford University, 1997), http://www.civiced.org/papers/papers_butts01.html. The emphasis is Mr. Butts's.

4. Hindy Lauer Schachter, "Civic Education: Three Early American Political Science Association Committees and Their Relevance for Our Times," *PS: Political Science and Politics* 31, no. 3 (1998): 631–632.

5. Carnegie and CIRCLE, *Civic Mission of Schools,* 4.

6. Melissa K. Comber, *The Effects of Civic Education on Civic Skills* (Medford, MA: Center for Information and Research on Civic Learning and Engagement, 2005), 3, http://eric.ed.gov/ERICDocs/data/ericdocs2sql/content_storage_01/0000019b/80/28/04/74.pdf.

7. Karl T. Kurtz, Alan Rosenthal, and Cliff Zukin, *Citizenship: A Challenge for All Generations* (Washington, DC: National Conference of State Legislatures, 2003), 6, http://www.ncsl.org/public/trust/citizenship.pdf.

8. Alberto Dávila and Marie T. Mora, "Civic Engagement and High School Academic Progress: An Analysis Using NELS Data," CIRCLE Working Paper 52, part I of *An Assessment of Civic Engagement and High School Academic Progress* (Medford, MA: Center for Information and Research on Civic Learning and Engagement, 2007): 1 and 9, http://www.civicyouth.org/PopUps/WorkingPapers/WP52Mora.pdf.

9. Schachter, "Civic Education," 631.

10. National Center for Education Statistics, "Chronology of National Assessment of Education Progress (NAEP) Assessments from 1969 to 2007" (Washington, DC: U.S. Department of Education, 2008), http://nces.ed.gov/nationsreportcard/about/assesshistory.asp (accessed

December 26, 2008). Whether the civics test — and the writing, science, geography, history, economics, foreign languages, and arts tests — is offered depends on the availability of funding. Math and reading, on the other hand, must be administered every two years at the fourth- and eighth-grade levels.

11. National Center for Education Statistics, *The Nation's Report Card: Civics 2006* (Washington, DC: U.S. Department of Education, 2007), 1, 4, 9, 23, 27, 30, http://nces.ed.gov/nationsreportcard/pdf/main2006/2007476.pdf.

12. Ibid., 19.

13. Samuel L. Popkin and Michael A. Dimock, "Knowledge and Citizen Competence" in *Citizen Competence and Democratic Institutions,* ed. Stephen L. Elkin and Karol Edward Soltan (University Park: Pennsylvania State University Press, 1999), 142.

14. U.S. Senate Committee on Health, Education, Labor, and Pensions, *Putting the Teaching of American History and Civics back in the Classroom*: *Hearing on S. 504*, April 10, 2003, 1, http://frwebgate.access.gpo.gov/cgi-bin/getdoc.cgi?dbname=108_senate_hearings&docid=f:86582.pdf.

15. "President Introduces History & Civic Education Initiatives," White House Office of the Press Secretary, September 17, 2008, http://georgewbush-whitehouse.archives.gov/news/releases/2002/09/20020917-1.html (accessed February 7, 2009).

16. U.S. Department of Education, *Budget Summary and Background Information* for fiscal years 2002–2008, http://www.ed.gov/about/overview/budget/index.html (accessed February 14, 2009). In fiscal year 2003, We the People was funded at approximately $16.9 million in a proposed education budget that totaled $56.5 billion. Thus, We the People would have represented 0.03 percent of the Department of Education's budget that year.

17. Whereas the Center for Civic Education's We the People program primarily funds instructional civic engagement programs for students and community groups, the National Endowment for the Humanities' We the People provides grants for myriad different purposes. We the People grants in fiscal year 2008 included "a functional new home for the humanities" in Austin, Texas; a faculty workshop series on religious pluralism in Los Angeles; a preservation assessment of the Barnstable Historical Society's manuscript collections; and an endowment for graduate student summer research stipends, public engagement institutes, and symposia in the study of American material culture. See We the People, National Endowment for the Humanities, "2008 We the People Grants," http://www.wethepeople.gov/projects/2008grants.html (accessed December 28, 2008).

18. John T. Greenan, "The Case Method in the Teaching of Problems of Democracy," *The School Review* 38:202.

19. See U.S. Department of Education, *Estimated Total and School-Age Resident Populations, by State: Selected Years, 1970 through 2006* (2007).

20. See also Charles N. Quigley, "Civic Education: Recent History, Current Status, and the Future," *Albany Law Review* 62 (1999): 1427; Donovan R. Walling, "The Return of Civic Education," *Phi Delta Kappan* 89 (2007): 285, http://www.civiced.org/pdfs/centerInNews/Walling -CivicEdArticle.pdf; Mark C. Alexander, "Law-Related Education: Hope for Today's Students," *Ohio Northern University Law Review* 20 (1993): 57–98; and R. Freeman Butts, "The Morality of Democratic Citizenship: Goals for Civic Education in the Republic's Third Century," Center for Civic Education (1988), http://www.civiced.org/papers/ morality/morality_preface.html.

21. Quigley, "Civic Education," 1427–28, 1430.

22. Lowell C. Rose and Alec M. Gallup, "The 32nd Annual Phi Delta Kappa/Gallup Poll of the Public's Attitudes toward the Public Schools," *Phi Delta Kappan* 82 (2000), http://www.pdkintl.org/kappan/kpol0009 .htm.

23. Campaign for the Civic Mission of Schools and the Alliance for Representative Democracy, *From Classroom to Citizen: American Attitudes on Civic Education* (Calabasas, CA: Center for Civic Education, 2004): 5.

24. Deborah Meier, *In Schools We Trust: Creating Communities of Learning in an Era of Testing and Standardization* (Boston: Beacon Press, 2002), 120.

25. "Address of the President to the Joint Session of Congress," White House Office of the Press Secretary, February 27, 2001, http:// georgewbush-whitehouse.archives.gov/news/releases/2001/02/20010228 .html (accessed February 7, 2009).

26. U.S. Department of Education, "Secretary Spellings Answers Questions at the American Federation of Teachers Conference," transcript of questions and answers at QuEST 2005, July 8, 2005, http://www .ed.gov/news/speeches/2005/07/07082005.html.

27. National Center for Education Statistics, *Nation's Report Card*, 1, 7, 17.

28. See also Quigley, "Civic Education," 1429–30.

29. Peter Levine, *The Future of Democracy* (Medford, MA: Tufts University Press, 2007), xv.

CHAPTER 6. NO PIGGY BANK LEFT BEHIND

1. Jump$tart Coalition for Personal Financial Literacy, *2008 Survey of Personal Financial Literacy among High School Students* (Washington, DC: Jump$tart Coalition, May 6, 2008), 4.

2. U.S. Senate Committee on Governmental Affairs, *The Federal Government's Role in Empowering Americans to Make Informed Financial Decisions: Hearing before the Financial Management, the Budget, and International Security Subcommittee*, testimony of Dara Duguay, 33, http://

frwebgate.access.gpo.gov/cgi-bin/getdoc.cgi?dbname=108
_senate_hearings&docid=f:94201.pdf.

3. Lewis Mandell and Maykala Hariharan, "A Dream of Financial Litera-cy," *Credit Union Magazine, Savingteen Supplement* 40 (2004): 21A.

4. National Council on Economic Education, *Report Card—Survey of the States: Economic, Personal Finance, & Entrepreneurship Education in Our Nation's Schools in 2007* (New York: NCEE, 2007), 3, http://www.ncee.net/about/survey2007/NCEESurvey2007.pdf.

5. Working in Support of Education Financial Literacy Certification background document.

6. Consumer Bankers Association, *2003 Survey of Bank-Sponsored Financial Literacy Programs* (Washington, DC: Consumer Bankers Association, 2003), 8, 12, 26, http://www.cbanet.org/files/FileDownloads/2003%20Survey%20Overview.pdf.

7. In 2007 and 2008 the Senate and the House passed resolutions S. 126, S. 459, H.R. 273, and H.R. 1079 recognizing April as Financial Liter-acy Month. H.R. 2871 was introduced in the 106th Congress; H.R. 61 and S. 807 in the 107th Congress; S. 1181 in the 108th Congress; H.R. 5046 and S. 925 in the 109th Congress; and H.R. 4335 in the 110th Congress. H.R. 4335 had ninety-seven cosponsors, by far the most of any of the bills introduced (the next highest had fifteen).

8. U.S. Department of Education, *Elementary & Secondary Education Act, Subpart 13: Excellence in Economic Education*, http://www.ed.gov/policy/elsec/leg/esea02/pg78.html.

9. U.S. Department of the Treasury, "Office of Financial Education," http://www.ustreas.gov/offices/domestic-finance/financial-institution/fin-education (accessed December 26, 2008).

10. U.S. Department of the Treasury, "Integrating Financial Education into School Curricula: Giving America's Youth the Educational Foun-dation for Making Effective Financial Decisions Throughout Their Lives by Teaching Financial Concepts as Part of Math and Reading Curricula in Elementary, Middle, and High Schools," press release (2002), http://www.ustreas.gov/press/releases/docs/white.pdf.

11. The National Council on Economic Education was awarded a five-year grant in 2005 that is subject to annual congressional appropriations. National Council on Economic Education, "Excellence in Econom-ic Education," http://www.ncee.net/ea/program.php?pid=23 (accessed December 27, 2008). See also U.S. Department of Education, "Excel-lence in Economic Education: Funding Status," http://www.ed.gov/programs/econeducation/funding.html (accessed December 26, 2008).

12. "Executive Order: Establishing the President's Advisory Council on Financial Literacy," White House Office of the Press Secretary," Jan-uary 22, 2008, http://georgewbush-whitehouse.archives.gov/news/releases/2008/01/20080122-1.html (accessed February 7, 2009).

13. Sara Terry, "California Target: Economic Illiteracy," *Christian Science Monitor,* May 13, 1981.

14. Albert B. Crenshaw, "Md. Program May Help Disadvantaged Entrepreneurs Realize Dreams," *Washington Post,* June 5, 1989.

15. Ben Laurence, "How We Learnt to Coin a Phrase: We Have All Become Financial Experts — or Think We Have," *The Guardian,* September 19, 1992.

16. Jay Mathews, "Maybe They Also Think Convertible Debt Is a Car Loan," *Washington Post,* October 18, 1994.

17. Charles A. Jaffe, "Financial Literacy a Must," *Boston Globe,* January 8, 1996.

18. See Monica Chen, "Financial Literacy: Workshops Aim to Educate Public, Help Homeowners Avoid Foreclosure," (Durham, NC) *Herald-Sun,* June 27, 2008; Beckie Supiano, "For Students, the New Kind of Literacy Is Financial," *Chronicle of Higher Education,* September 5, 2008; and Lisa Schencker, "Economics and Education: Meltdown Makes for Fine Lesson," *Salt Lake Tribune,* October 15, 2008.

19. David Dieterle, as cited in Sven Gustafson, "Financial Literacy Curriculum Moving Forward," *Oakland Business Review,* weblog entry posted November 29, 2007, http://blog.mlive.com/oak_business_review/2007/11/financial_literacy_education_g.html (accessed December 26, 2008).

20. Practical Money Skills for Life, "Visa Back-to-School Survey Finds That Only 5% of Kids Learn Vital Life Skill of Money Management in Class," August 13, 2007, http://www.practicalmoneyskills.com/english/presscenter/releases/081307.php (accessed February 2, 2009).

21. National Council on Economic Education, "Department of Education Recognizes the Importance of Economic Education," press release, July 9, 2008, http://www.ncee.net/news/story.php?story_id=141. The funds are part of the Excellence in Economic Education awards cited previously. Bush did, however, request elimination of the Excellence in Economic Education funds in his fiscal year 2006 through fiscal year 2009 budgets. The housing legislation was the American Housing Rescue and Foreclosure Prevention Act of 2008 (H.R. 3221), which included a provision encouraging government partnerships with inner-city high schools, girls' high schools, and high schools with majority-minority populations to establish or enhance financial literacy programs. The higher education legislation was the Higher Education Opportunity Act, which, among other provisions encouraging the offering of financial and economic literacy programs, required the treasury secretary, the secretary of education, and the secretary of agriculture to "seek to enhance financial literacy" through "initiatives, programs, and curricula that improve student awareness of the short- and long-term costs associated with education loans and other debt assumed while in college, their repayment obligations, and their rights

as borrowers." U.S. House of Representatives, *The Higher Education Opportunity Act,* 110th Cong., 2nd sess., 2008, H.R. 4137, 412.

22. Comptroller of the Currency, Administrator of National Banks, "OCC Advisory Letter AL 2001-1: Financial Literacy," January 16, 2001, http://www.occ.treas.gov/ftp/advisory/2001-1.doc (accessed December 26, 2008).

23. Jump$tart Coalition, *2008 Survey,* 4.

24. Jeff Faux, *Globalization That Works for Working Americans,* EPI Briefing Paper (Washington, DC: Economic Policy Institute, 2007): 2, http://www.sharedprosperity.org/bp179/bp179.pdf.

25. Robert E. Scott, *The Importance of Manufacturing: Key to Recovery in the State and the Nation,* EPI Briefing Paper (Washington, DC: Economic Policy Institute, 2008): 2–3, 10, http://www.sharedprosperity.org/bp211/bp211.pdf.

26. "President Bush Signs Tax Relief Extension and Reconciliation Act of 2005," White House Office of the Press Secretary, May 17, 2006, http://georgewbush-whitehouse.archives.gov/news/releases/2006/05/20060517-2.html (accessed February 7, 2009).

27. Tax Policy Center, "Table T06-0251: Combined Effect of the 2001–2006 Tax Cuts, Distribution of Federal Tax Change by Cash Income Percentile, 2006" (Washington, DC: Urban Institute and Brookings Institution, October 31, 2006), http://www.taxpolicycenter.org/numbers/displayatab.cfm?Docid=1332&DocTypeID=2. For income of the top quintile of earners in the United States, see U.S. Census Bureau, "Table HINC-05: Percent Distribution of Households, by Selected Characteristics within Income Quintile and Top 5 Percent in 2006," *Current Population Survey: Annual Social and Economic (ASEC) Supplement* (August 28, 2007), http://pubdb3.census.gov/macro/032007/hhinc/new05_000.htm.

28. State tax revenues suffered from tax cuts enacted during the Bush administration because of linkages between state and federal tax codes. States are able to "decouple" from the federal government, and many have done so. However, as Isaac Shapiro and Joel Friedman of the Center on Budget and Policy Priorities note, "The states that have not decoupled are losing a total of about $9 billion during state fiscal years 2002 through 2005, a four-year period during which states have faced one of their most severe fiscal crises in half a century." The two primary culprits are changes in the estate tax and changes to the "bonus depreciation" provision that allows businesses to write off the cost of investments. *Tax Returns: A Comprehensive Assessment of the Bush Administration Tax Cuts* (Washington, DC: Center on Budget and Policy Priorities, 2004): 8–9.

29. National Council on Economic Education, "Contributors," http://www.ncee.net/contributors (December 26, 2008).

30. National Council on Economic Education, *What American Teens & Adults Know about Economics"* (New York: NCEE, 2005): 25, http://207.124.141.218/WhatAmericansKnowAboutEconomics_042605-3.pdf.

31. "If the United States stopped importing automobiles from Country X, who would be most likely to benefit?" The correct answer was "Automakers in the United States," with incorrect answers "Consumers in the United States" and "Automobile manufacturers in Country X." Ibid., 35.

32. National Council on Economic Education, "Campaign for Economic Literacy — NCEE Standards in Economics: Survey of Students and the Public," 1999, http://www.ncee.net/cel/results.php.

33. John Morton, "Economic Education: Is the Glass Half Full or Half Empty?" *Michigan Education Report* (2007): 11, http://www.educationreport.org/archives/2007/mer2007-04.pdf.

CHAPTER 7. QUESTIONING THE SYSTEM, OR BEATING IT?

1. See Christopher B. Swanson, *Cities in Crisis: A Special Analytic Report on High School Graduation* (Bethesda, MD: Editorial Projects in Education Research Center, 2008), 1, 9.

2. Operation HOPE, "The Citi Foundation Awards $500,000 to Operation HOPE" press release, June 23, 2008, http://www.operationhope.org/smdev/pressreleaselst.php?id=1373 (accessed February 7, 2009).

3. For instance, in an NPR interview in the summer of 2008, the economist Teresa Ghilarducci emphasizes that even when people think they are financially literate — in her example, by "diversifying" their 401(k) plans — it often turns out that they are not acting prudently after all. She contrasts 401(k) plans with pensions, noting that making personal investment decisions with a 401(k) plan probably makes workers worse off. Teresa Ghilarducci, interview by Terry Gross, "Preserving Your Pension in Tough Times," *Fresh Air*, National Public Radio, July 7, 2008, http://www.npr.org/templates/story/story.php?storyId=92213600.

4. U.S. House Appropriations Committee, *Role of the Arts in Creativity and Innovation: Hearing before the Subcommittee on Interior, Environment, and Related Agencies,* testimony of Jonathan Spector, April 1, 2008, 1, http://www.artsusa.org/images/news/press_room/Jonathan%20Spector%20testimony_040108.pdf.

5. See the Conference Board et al., *Are They Really Ready to Work? Employers' Perspectives on the Basic Knowledge and Applied Skills of New Entrants to the 21st Century U.S. Workforce* (New York: Conference Board, 2006), http://www.21stcenturyskills.org/documents/FINAL_REPORT_PDF09-29-06.pdf. As described in U.S. House Appropriations Committee, *Role of the Arts,* testimony of Jonathan Spector, 1.

6. The Conference Board, *Ready to Innovate — Key Findings: Are Educators and Executives Aligned on the Creative Readiness of the U.S. Workforce?*

(New York: Conference Board, 2008): 2, http://www.artsusa.org/pdf/ information_services/research/policy_roundtable/ready_to_innovate .pdf; and Conference Board, *Are They Ready to Work?*, 50.

7. Meira Levinson, "The Civic Achievement Gap," CIRCLE Working Paper 51 (Medford, MA: Center for Information and Research on Civic Learning and Engagement, 2007), 9, http://www.civicyouth.org/ PopUps/WorkingPapers/WP51Levinson.pdf.

8. Martin Luther King Jr., "Why I Am Opposed to the War in Vietnam," speech delivered April 30, 1967, Riverside Church, New York, http:// www.lib.berkeley.edu/MRC/pacificaviet/riversidetranscript.html.

9. JPMorgan Chase & Co., "Chase Mobilizes Employees to Help Delaware Youth Build Bright Financial Futures: Chase President and More than 100 Employees Will Teach Lessons on Financial Literacy," press release, April 10, 2008, http://investor.shareholder.com/jpmorganchase/press/ releasedetail.cfm?releaseid=307387&ReleaseType=Current. See Visa's "Encouraging Financial Literacy" Web site at http://www.corporate. visa.com/av/about_visa/csr/csr_financial_literacy.jsp; National Council on Economic Education, "Bank of America and National Council on Economic Education Launch a Comprehensive Education Program to Promote Financial Literacy for Students in Every Grade," February 26, 2002, http://www.ncee.net/news/story.php?story_id=20 (accessed December 26, 2008); and Merrill Lynch & Co. Foundation, Return of Private Foundation Form 990PF for 2003 and 2005. See also Merrill Lynch's "2007 Grants Recipient Listing" at http://philanthropy. ml.com/index.asp?id=66319_67031_67433_67436 (accessed December 26, 2008).

10. Jump$tart Coalition, *2008 Survey* (see ch. 6, n. 1).

11. See the following publications of the Jump$tart Coalition: *2008 Survey; 2006 Survey: Financial Literacy Shows Slight Improvement among Nation's High School Students* (April 5, 2006); *Financial Literacy Improves among Nation's High School Students: Jump$tart Questionnaire for Seniors Reveals Moderate Gains* (April 1, 2004); *From Bad to Worse: Financial Literacy Drops Further among 12th Graders: Jump$tart Urges States to Apply Newly Available Funds towards Innovative Personal Finance Education Programs* (April 23, 2002); *Financial Literacy Declining among 12th Graders: Coalition Urges States to Include Personal Finance in Curriculum Standards* (April 6, 2000); and *High School Seniors Lack Financial Smarts, Shows Survey* (May 22, 1997).

12. National Council on Economic Education, *What American Teens & Adults Know,* 44 (see ch. 6, n. 30).

13. Charles Schwab Corporation, *Charles Schwab Teens & Money 2007 Survey Findings: Insights into Money Attitudes, Behaviors and Concerns of Teens* (San Francisco: Charles Schwab, 2007): 1, http://www.aboutschwab .com/teensurvey2007.pdf; "Schwab Survey Reveals New Insights Into

Money Behavior and Concerns of Teens," press release, April 19, 2006, http://www.businesswire.com/portal/site/schwab/index.jsp?ndmViewId =news_view&ndmConfigId=1009912&newsId=20070919006225& newsLang=en (accessed December 26, 2008).

14. Although I visited during the 2007–08 school year, demographic data was available only for the 2006–07 school year, as of this writing. New York State Department of Education, *The New York State School Report Card Accountability and Overview Report 2006-2007: MS 224 Manhattan East School* (July 15, 2008), https://www.nystart.gov/publicweb-rc/ 2007/03/AOR-2007-310400010224.pdf.

15. According to Thomas Power, the New York program director of Banking on Our Future, standard training is at most two hours.

16. Working in Support of Education Financial Literacy Certification background document (see ch. 6, n. 5).

17. Jump$tart Coalition, *2006 Survey,* p. 6.

18. Operation HOPE, "Results: Banking on Our Future National Report, December 2008," table, http://www.operationhope.org/smdev/lf1.php ?id=1177.

19. St. Louis Federal Reserve's calculation of the personal savings rate. Federal Reserve's calculation of Consumer Credit Outstanding. Brian K. Bucks, Arthur B. Kennickell, and Kevin B. Moore, "Recent Changes in U.S. Family Finances: Evidence from the 2001 and 2004 Survey of Consumer Finances," *Federal Reserve Bulletin* (2006): A26, http://www .federalreserve.gov/PUBS/oss/oss2/2004/bull0206.pdf.

20. Operation HOPE, "Operation HOPE Performance Outline: Overview of Accomplishments to Date," http://www.operationhope.org/ dayofhope/downloads/hope.doc.

CHAPTER 8. THE MARXIST, ANTI-AMERICAN CONSPIRACY TO CONVERT YOUNG PEOPLE TO ENGAGED CITIZENSHIP

1. Sol Stern, "When Activism Masquerades as Education," *New York Daily News,* July 21, 2006.

2. Kathleen Kennedy Manzo, "Election Renews Controversy over Social-Justice Teaching," *Education Week,* October 29, 2008; and Rethinking Schools Online, "The History and Philosophy of Rethinking Schools," http://www.rethinkingschools.org/about/history.shtml.

3. Douglas Kellner, "Multiple Literacies and Critical Pedagogies," in *Revolutionary Pedagogies: Cultural Politics, Instituting Education, and the Discourse of Theory*, ed. Peter Pericles Trifonas (New York: Routledge, 2000), as cited in 21st Century Schools, "Critical Pedagogy," http:// www.21stcenturyschools.com/critical_pedagogy.htm. See also 21st Century Schools, "What Is Critical Pedagogy?," http://www .21stcenturyschools.com/What_is_Critical_Pedagogy.htm.

4. Sol Stern, "The Ed Schools' Latest — and Worst — Humbug," *City Journal*, Summer 2006, http://www.city-journal.org/html/16_3_ed_school.html.

5. Dávila and Mora, "Civic Engagement" (see ch. 5, n. 9).

6. New York State Department of Education, *Accountability Status Report: English Language Arts, Mathematics, Science, and Graduation Rate for George W. Wingate HS in NYC Geog Dist #17—RIC #6*, September 7, 2006, http://emsc32.nysed.gov/irts/school-accountability/2006-07/reports/331700011470.pdf.

7. Idem, *Progress Report 2007–08, High School: School for Democracy and Leadership*, http://schools.nyc.gov/OA/SchoolReports/2007-08/ProgressReport_HS_K533.pdf.

8. Matthew Spalding and David J. Bobb, "Federalism and Fiscal Responsibility: A Lesson in Civics Education," Heritage Institute Backgrounder #1874, August 3, 2005, http://www.heritage.org/Research/Education/bg1874.cfm.

9. Sol Stern, "Radical Equations: Marxist Pedagogues Are Hard at Work in New York's Public Schools," *City Journal*, March 19, 2007, http://www.city-journal.org/html/eon2007-03-19ss.html.

10. Stern, "Humbug."

11. The Campaign for Fiscal Equity, a group advocating school finance reform, challenged the constitutionality of New York State's school finance system in 1993, arguing that the finance system underfunded New York City's public schools. The case wound its way through the courts until 2003, when the New York State Court of Appeals ruled in favor of CFE. The court found that the New York State constitution requires all children to have the opportunity for a "sound basic education," meaning that students have the "opportunity for a meaningful high school education, one which prepares them to function productively as civic participants." Referees were appointed to resolve funding inequities that prevented students from receiving the sound basic education they are guaranteed, and subsequent court decisions ordered New York State to provide additional funds to New York City schools. See http://www.cfequity.org.

12. For the relationship between talking about current events and engagement, see Hugh McIntosh, Daniel Hart, and James Youniss, "The Influence of Family Political Discussion on Youth Civic Development: Which Parent Qualities Matter?" *PS: Political Science and Politics* 40, no. 3 (2007): 1. For the relationship between civic engagement and educational achievement, see Dávila and Mora, "Civic Engagement."

13. Stern, "Humbug."

14. Michael Neuschatz, Mark McFarling, and Susan White, "Reaching the Critical Mass: The Twenty Year Surge in High School Physics," *AIP Report: Findings from the 2005 Nationwide Survey of High School Physics*

Teachers (College Park, MD: American Institute of Physics 2008), iii, 2–3, http://www.aip.org/statistics/trends/reports/hs05report.pdf.

15. New York City Department of City Planning, *General Demographic Characteristics: 2005 American Community Survey (ACS) New York City Community Districts and PUMA Areas* (2006), 37; idem, *Selected Economic Characteristics: 2006 American Community Survey*, New York City Department of City Planning (2007): 56–57, http://home2.nyc.gov/html/dcp/pdf/census/acs_economic_pumas_2006.pdf (accessed December 27, 2008).

16. New York State Department of Education, *The New York State School Report Card Accountability and Overview Report 2006–2007: School for Democracy and Leadership* (2008), 3, https://www.nystart.gov/publicweb-rc/2007/f3/AOR-2007-331700011533.pdf.

17. David Horowitz, as quoted in Phyllis Schlafly, "Teaching 'Social Justice' in Schools," Eagle Forum, November 7, 2008, http://www.eagleforum.org/column/2008/nov08/08-11-07.html (accessed December 27, 2008).

18. Stern, "Humbug."

19. Sol Stern, "Radical Teach: N.Y.C. Schools' New Fad," *New York Post*, May 12, 2007. See also Sol Stern, "Radical Math at the DOE," *City Journal*, May 11, 2007, http://www.city-journal.org/html/eon2007-05-11ss.html.

20. President Bush put this, as he himself noted, bluntly: "I think you can spend your money better than the federal government can spend your money." "President Bush Visits Nashville, Discusses Budget," White House Office of the Press Secretary, July 19, 2007, http://georgewbush-whitehouse.archives.gov/news/releases/2007/07/20070719-3.html (accessed February 7, 2009). The year previous, James Sherk of the conservative Heritage Foundation congratulated President Bush and congressional Republicans for their commitment to the "principle" that "the American people know how to spend their money far better than Washington does." "Remember the Bush Tax Cuts This Labor Day," Heritage Foundation, September 1, 2006, http://www.heritage.org/Research/Economy/wm1204.cfm (accessed December 30, 2008).

21. Stern, "Humbug."

Part III

INTRODUCTION

1. Plato, *The Last Days of Socrates: Euthyphro, Apology, Crito, Phaedo*, ed. Harold Tarrant, trans. Hugh Tredennick (New York: Penguin Classics, 2003), 7.

2. Approximately 23 million young people voted in the 2008 presidential election, compared to 19.4 million in 2004. Young voters favored

Barack Obama over John McCain by more than 2 to 1. These youth voter turnout statistics are estimates based on the percentage of eligible 18- to 29-year-olds. Center for Information and Research on Civic Learning and Engagement, "Youth Turnout Rate Rises to at Least 52% with 23 Million Voters Under 30," November 7, 2008, http://www .civicyouth.org/?p=323; idem, *Fact Sheet: Young Voters in the 2008 Presidential Election*, November 24, 2008, updated December 19, 2008, http://www.civicyouth.org/PopUps/FactSheets/FS_08_exit_polls.pdf.

3. Bauerlein, *The Dumbest Generation* (see ch. 4, n. 6).

4. See Intercollegiate Studies Institute, *Failing Our Students, Failing America: Holding Colleges Accountable for Teaching America's History and Institutions* (Wilmington, DE, Intercollegiate Studies Institute, 2007), 9; and National Center for Education Statistics, *Nation's Report Card* (see ch. 5, n. 12), 30.

5. Thomas E. Patterson, *Young People and News* (Cambridge, MA: Joan Shorenstein Center on the Press, Politics, and Public Policy, 2007), 8, http://www.hks.harvard.edu/presspol/carnegie_knight/young_news _web.pdf.

6. National Conference on Citizenship, *America's Civic Health Index 2007* (Washington, DC: National Conference on Citizenship, 2007), 5, 16, http://www.ncoc.net/index.php?tray=series&tid=top5&cid=99 (accessed February 7, 2009).

CHAPTER 9. BLACK AND WHITE AND DEAD ALL OVER

1. Patterson, *Young People and News* (see part III, intro., n. 5), 8.

2. Pew Research Center for the People & the Press, *Audience Segments in a Changing News Environment: Key News Audiences Now Blend Online and Traditional Sources* (Washington, DC: Pew Research Center, 2008): 5, http://people-press.org/reports/pdf/444.pdf.

3. Patterson, *Young People and News*, 12.

4. "We're Broke and We Vote," a panel discussion at Demos's forum in Washington, DC, entitled "A Better Deal: Reclaiming Economic Security for a New Generation," Economic Agenda for Young Voters, C-SPAN, May 9, 2008, http://www.c-spanarchives.org/library/index. php?main_page=product_video_info&products_id=205252-4 &highlight= (accessed December 27, 2008).

5. Associated Press and Context-Based Research Group, *A New Model for News: Studying the Deep Structure of Young-Adult News Consumption* (New York: Associated Press, 2008): 37, http://www.ap.org/newmodel.pdf.

6. Patterson, *Young People and News*, 11.

7. Pew Research Center, *Audience Segments*.

8. Associated Press, *New Model for News*, 39–40.

9. Patterson, *Young People and News*, 17.

10. Associated Press, *New Model for News*, 37.

11. Ibid., 42.

12. D-Code and World Association of Newspapers, *Youth Media DNA: Decoding Youth as News & Information Consumers,* Phase Two Report (Paris: World Association of Newspapers, 2006), 10, http://www.d-code.com/pdfs/DCODE_YMDNA_Report.pdf.

13. Patterson, *Young People and News*, 22.

14. Center for Communication and Civic Engagement, http://cccc.com.washington.edu (accessed December 27, 2008).

15. Lovink, "Society of the Query" (see part I intro., n. 1).

16. See ch. 4, n. 10.

17. Dan Miller, comment on Shirky's "Why Abundance Is Good" (see ch. 4, n. 2).

18. Alfred Hermida, "Young Challenge Mainstream Media: A Quiet Revolution Is Taking Place in How People Get Their News," *BBC News,* May 3, 2006, http://news.bbc.co.uk/1/hi/technology/4962794.stm (accessed December 27, 2008).

CHAPTER 10. WHO'S AFRAID OF VIRGINIA YOUTH?

1. See the Hampton City Schools' Web site at http://www.sbo.hampton.k12.va.us/overview/overview.html (accessed December 26, 2008).

2. Ibid.

3. "Youth Civic Engagement—2005 Winner; 2004 Finalist: City of Hampton, VA," Harvard University Kennedy School Ash Institute for Democratic Governance and Innovation, Innovations in American Government Awards, http://www.innovations.harvard.edu/awards.html?id=7499 (accessed December 29, 2008).

4. See Hampton Coalition for Youth, *HYC History,* http://www.hampton.gov/youth/images/images/hyc_history.pdf (Hampton, VA: Hampton Coalition, n.d.); and Cindy Carlson, "Youth with Influence: The Youth Planner Initiative in Hampton, Virginia," *Children, Youth and Environments* 15 (2005), http://www.colorado.edu/journals/cye/15_2/15_2_12_YouthwithInfluence.pdf.

5. Carlson, "Youth with Influence."

6. Justin Smith, "Causes Enables 1.6 Million Strong Election Day Rally on Facebook," Inside Facebook, weblog entry posted on November 4, 2008, http://www.insidefacebook.com/2008/11/04/causes-enables-16-million-strong-election-day-rally-on-facebook (accessed December 28, 2008).

7. Allison Fine, *Social Citizens Beta,* "Millennials as Social Citizens," The Case Foundation (2008), http://www.socialcitizens.org/paper/millennials-as-social-citizens (accessed February 7, 2009).

8. Ibid.

9. The U.S. Census's Current Population Survey finds that the percentage of young people aged sixteen to twenty-four who volunteer rose from

21.9 percent in 2002 to 24.1 percent in 2003, 24.2 percent in 2004, and 24.4 percent in 2005. The percentage then declined to 21.7 percent in 2006 and 20.8 percent in 2007. See also the U.S. Bureau of Labor Statistics reports entitled *Volunteering in the United States* for 2002, 2004, 2005, 2006, and 2007.

10. Fine, *Social Citizens Beta,* "Blending Worlds," http://www.socialcitizens .org/paper/blending-worlds (accessed February 7, 2009).

CHAPTER 11. LIGHTS, CAMERA, DEBATE!

1. Commission on Presidential Debates, "The Second Clinton-Bush-Perot Presidential Debate (Second Half of Debate)," debate transcript, October 15, 1992, http://www.debates.org/pages/trans92b2.html (accessed December 29, 2008).

2. Lynn Sweet, "McCain, Obama Deal Puts Limits on 'Town Hall' Debate," *Chicago Sun-Times,* weblog entry posted on October 6, 2008, http://blogs.suntimes.com/sweet/2008/10/mccain_obama_deal _puts_limits.html (accessed December 29, 2008).

3. Minow and LaMay, *Inside the Presidential Debates* (see ch. 3, n. 20), 105.

4. See the Nielsen Company, Nielsen Wire weblog, http://blog.nielsen .com/nielsenwire/media_entertainment (accessed February 15, 2009); Lisa de Moraes, "It's Not Debatable: McCain-Obama Ratings Fall Far Short of Predicted Record," *Washington Post,* September 30, 2008; idem, "A Big Turnout for Debate 2," *Washington Post,* October 9, 2008; and idem, "VP Debate Appears to Be Most-Watched of 2008 Election," *Washington Post,* October 16, 2008. According to Nielsen, 52.4 million Americans watched the first presidential debate, 63.2 million watched the second presidential debate, and 56.5 million watched the third presidential debate. PBS, not included in the Nielsen totals, reported that an additional 2.6 million watched the first debate on PBS, 2.8 the second, and 3.2 the third. This would bring the average viewership to approximately 60.2 million.

5. International Institute for Democracy and Electoral Assistance, "Turnout in the World: Country by Country Performance," http:// www.idea.int/vt/survey/voter_turnout_pop2.cfm (accessed December 29, 2008). The International IDEA calculates turnout based on the voting-age population. Using that same measure of turnout for only the 2008 presidential campaign, the United States would rise to 123rd. United States Elections Project, "2008 General Election Turnout Rates," http://elections.gmu.edu/Turnout_2008G.html (accessed December 29, 2008).

6. Minow and LaMay, *Inside the Presidential Debates,* 9.

7. In fact, 87 percent of registered undecided voters responded that the debates would help them decide for whom to vote. Marist College Institute for Public Opinion, "Face Off: The First Presidential Debate?"

press release, September 25, 2008, 1–2, http://www.maristpoll.marist
.edu/usapolls/DB080925.pdf (accessed December 28, 2008).

8. Mitchell S. McKinney and Sumana Chattopadhyay, "Political Engagement Through Debates: Young Citizens' Reactions to the 2004 Presidential Debates," *American Behavioral Scientist* 50 (2007): 1176–77.

9. Ibid., 1170.

10. "Memorandum of Understanding," Kerry-Edwards, '04 and Bush-
Cheney, '04, September 20, 2008: 5, 24, http://www.c-span.org/pdf/
memounderstanding.pdf (accessed December 25, 2008).

11. Commission on Presidential Debates, "The Biden-Palin Vice Presidential Debate," debate transcript, October 2, 2008, http://www.debates
.org/pages/trans2008b.html (accessed December 28, 2008).

12. David Zurewik, "Jim Lehrer Looks Ahead to Friday's Presidential
Debate," *Baltimore Sun*, weblog entry posted September 23, 2008,
http://weblogs.baltimoresun.com/entertainment/zontv/2008/09/jim
_lehrer_looks_ahead_to_frid.html (accessed December 28, 2008).

13. The League of Women Voters sponsored the presidential debates in
1976, 1980, and 1984. After the Republican and Democratic parties
pressured for increased control of the debates between 1984 and 1987
and created the Commission on Presidential Debates, the League
withdrew its sponsorship for the third and final debate of 1988, which
the commission had asked the LWV to sponsor. In a now-famous press
release, League president Nancy M. Neuman said, "The League of
Women Voters is withdrawing its sponsorship of the presidential debate
scheduled for mid-October because the demands of the two campaign
organizations would perpetrate a fraud on the American voter . . . It
has become clear to us that the candidates' organizations aim to add
debates to their list of campaign-trail charades devoid of substance,
spontaneity and honest answers to tough questions. The League has no
intention of becoming an accessory to the hoodwinking of the American
public." The release added, "Most objectionable to the League, Neuman
said, were conditions in the agreement that gave the campaigns unprecedented control over the proceedings. Neuman called 'outrageous' the
campaigns' demands that they control the selection of questioners, the
composition of the audience, hall access for the press and other issues."
"League Refuses to 'Help Perpetrate a Fraud'; Withdraws Support
from Final Presidential Debate," League of Women Voters, October 3,
1988, http://www.lwv.org/AM/Template.cfm?Section=Press_Releases
&CONTENTID=7777&TEMPLATE=/CM/ContentDisplay.cfm. For
the mission of the Commission on Presidential Debates, see "Our
Mission," http://www.debates.org/pages/about.html. (Both sources
accessed December 29, 2008).

14. In 1996, Perot filed suit against the Commission on Presidential Debates
for excluding him and vice presidential candidate Pat Choate from the

1996 presidential debates. A federal appeals court upheld a lower court ruling dismissing the lawsuits. As a candidate in the preceding 1992 campaign, Perot had been included in all three presidential debates. See "Perot '96 and Natural Law Party v. FEC and the Commission on Presidential Debates," *Federal Election Commission Record* 22 (1996): 1, 5–6, http://www.fec.gov/pdf/record/1996/nov96.pdf.

15. Adapted from Lawrence Lessig, "Open Debates: Focusing the Call," Lessig 2.0, weblog entry posted October 10, 2008, http://lessig.org/blog/2008/10/open_debates_focusing_the_call.html (accessed December 28, 2008).

16. Sam Stein, "Lehrer Discusses Contours of Presidential Debate," *Huffington Post*, weblog entry posted September 19, 2008, http://www.huffingtonpost.com/2008/09/19/lehrer-discusses-contours_n_127728.html (accessed December 29, 2008).

17. Open Debate Coalition, Letter to Senator John McCain and Senator Barack Obama, September 23, 2008, http://lessig.org/blog/080923-opendebate.pdf (December 29, 2008).

18. Ibid.

19. Media Matters Action Network, *Change the Debate: How Gaffes, Games and Gotchas Dominated the 2008 Presidential Primary Debates* (Washington, DC: Media Matters Action Network, 2008), 4, http://mediamattersaction.org/static/pdfs/ctd-20080923.pdf.

20. There were thirty-five debates (nineteen Democratic and sixteen Republican), including four forums, as tabulated by the American Presidency Project at the University of California, Santa Barbara. "Presidential Debates: 1960–2008," http://www.presidency.ucsb.edu/debates.php (accessed December 29, 2008).

CONCLUSION: A CALL FOR SLOW DEMOCRACY

1. Plato, *The Last Days of Socrates* (see part III, intro., n. 1), 42.

2. Introductory paragraph on the Slow Food Web site, http://www.slowfood.com (accessed December 29, 2008).

3. The *New York Times* reported in late 2008 that Cox Newspapers (publisher of the *Atlanta Journal-Constitution*), Advance Publications (owner of the Cleveland *Plain Dealer*), and several smaller papers had decided to close their Washington bureaus. The article reported that the newspapers remaining in the capital had "cut back drastically on Washington coverage, eliminating hundreds of journalists' jobs at a time when the federal government — and journalistic oversight of it — matters more than ever." Richard Perez-Pena, "Big News in Washington, but Far Fewer Cover It," *New York Times,* December 17, 2008.

4. Susan Engel, "Open Pandora's Box: Curiosity and Imagination in the Classroom," Thomas H. Wright Lecture occasional paper, Child

Development Institute at Sarah Lawrence College (2006): 7, http://www.slc.edu/media/cdi/pdf/Occasional%20Papers/CDI_Occasional_Paper_2006_Engel.pdf.

5. Voter turnout in 2008 was 61.6 percent of the population eligible to vote, the highest since 1968, according to Dr. Michael P. McDonald of the George Mason University Department of Public and International Affairs, who calculates voter turnout based on eligibility criteria. The voter turnout based on the voting age population yields the same result: turnout based on this measure was 56.8 percent in 2008, the highest since 60.84 percent of the voting age population turned out in 1968. United States Elections Project, "2008 General Election Turnout Rates," http://elections.gmu.edu/Turnout_2008G.html (accessed December 29, 2008); "Voter Turnout Rate Said to Be Highest Since 1968," *Washington Post*, December 15, 2008; and American Presidency Project, "Voter Turnout in Presidential Elections: 1824-2004," http://www.presidency.ucsb.edu/data/turnout.php (accessed December 30, 2008).

Acknowledgments

I'M NOT SURE HOW OTHER AUTHORS DO IT, TYPING AWAY at their desks, shut off completely from the world, but I needed this to be a collaborative effort. I couldn't have asked for a better team with whom to collaborate.

Harry Moroz was the principal researcher on this book. He is intelligent, rigorous, and mature beyond his years and brings a pleasant disposition that belies his training at the University of Chicago. Hiring him was one of my best decisions. I know he is destined to do great things that put to good use his intellect and passion for social justice.

Jenny Williams was my hard-working and insightful editor. She helped me, on practically a daily basis, to craft and refine my arguments, going far beyond the call of duty to internalize my vision for the book to the point where I think she began to understand my thesis better than I did. She is as patient as she is smart, and working with me probably required more of the former than she had anticipated.

Johanna Vondeling, vice president at Berrett-Koehler, fought for me to have a chance to write this book, and supported me throughout. Though I don't think I "front-loaded" as much as she would have liked, I hope that she, more than anyone else, is proud of the final product.

Needless to say, any mistakes in thought, argument, research, or grammar are my own.

I am especially indebted to my colleagues at the Drum Major Institute. Bill Wachtel has entrusted me with the legacy of his father, and for that I will always be grateful. It was Bill who frequently reminded me that, through discussion, the best ideas will emerge. I have learned so much from Amy Traub, our director of research, over the past four years. Lauren Su manages to keep my life sane. Dan Morris has been so helpful in thinking about the relevance of the book to today's debates. Thanks to Mark, Tsedey, Kia, John, Cristina, and the rest of the DMI crew for drum majoring each and every day for justice. I thank the board of directors of DMI for giving me this opportunity, but most especially Deborah Sagner, Morris Pearl, Tom Watson, and Cecilia Clarke, for their daily support and friendship.

Dr. Pastora San Juan Cafferty gave me renewed hope in the book when she reviewed it, while recuperating on her couch, and told me I was on to something.

Michael Murphy was a regular support, from the very first days of the book proposal to the final hours, giving me comments on lines via Instant Messenger.

Thank you to Michael, Robert Ellman, Rebecca Buckwalter Poza, and Ellen Augustine for reviewing the entire manuscript and giving me such thoughtful comments. Thanks to Dean Freedman and Beth Douthirt Cohen and John Del Cecato and others who responded to my multiple e-mail surveys for feedback.

I have the best circle of friends, most of whom I've known for a very long time. Elana Karopkin is my best friend. She is my family, and so now is her husband, Michael. Randi designed the cover of this book (thank you, Randi!). Susan, Shannon, Beth, Gigi, Shreya, Esha, Katie, Karen—though I am an only child, I'm fortunate to have so many wonderful sisters.

I've had the honor of working for many professional mentors, from whom I have continued to learn long after I left their employ: Fernando Ferrer, Carolyn Lukensmeyer, Kathryn Wylde, and Stan Litow among them.

Rinku Sen made me write this book. I'm still angry about it.

My parents grew up very poor—my father in Coney Island, my mom in the Dominican Republic. They sacrificed everything to give me the childhood they dreamed of for themselves. I am grateful. Even if I don't always express it.

Thank you to Arturo Sr., Angela, Maria, Daniela, and Arturo Jr. for welcoming me into their family.

And, finally, my partner, Ana Maria Archila. Thank you for building a life with me.

Index

About the Author

SINCE 2002, ANDREA BATISTA SCHLESINGER HAS APPLIED her background in public policy, politics, and communications to lead the effort to turn the Drum Major Institute, originally founded by an advisor to Rev. Dr. Martin Luther King Jr. during the civil rights movement, into a progressive policy institute with national impact. During Andrea's tenure as executive director, DMI has released several important policy papers to national audiences; created its Marketplace of Ideas series, which highlights successful progressive policies from across the country; launched two policy blogs that reach several thousand readers each day; and launched a national program to foster careers in policy for college students from underrepresented communities.

In 2009, Andrea took a leave of absence from DMI to serve as a senior policy advisor to the re-election campaign of New York City mayor Michael R. Bloomberg.

Andrea studied public policy at the University of Chicago. Before joining DMI, she directed a national Pew Charitable Trusts campaign to engage college students in discussion about the future of Social Security and served as the education advisor to Bronx borough president and mayoral candidate Fernando Ferrer. She has been profiled in the *New York Times, The New Yorker,* and *Latina* magazine, and in *Hear Us Now,* an award-winning documentary about her tenure as the student member of New York City's Board of Education.

In media outlets from National Public Radio to the *Huffington Post,* Andrea is turned to for her forward-thinking analysis on America's greatest challenges. She has appeared on television shows such as CNN's *Lou Dobbs Tonight,* and her writing has appeared in various publications, including *The Nation, Newsday,* the *Chicago Sun-Times,* the Mississippi *Sun Herald,* the *New York Daily News,* Alternet.com, TomPaine.com, the *New York Sun, Colorlines* magazine, the *Chief-Leader,* and *City Limits* magazine.

Andrea was named a Forty Under 40 Rising Star by *Crain's New York Business.* She serves on the editorial board of *The Nation.* She grew up in Brooklyn and lives in Queens.

About Berrett-Koehler Publishers

Berrett-Koehler is an independent publisher dedicated to an ambitious mission: Creating a World That Works for All.

We believe that to truly create a better world, action is needed at all levels – individual, organizational, and societal. At the individual level, our publications help people align their lives with their values and with their aspirations for a better world. At the organizational level, our publications promote progressive leadership and management practices, socially responsible approaches to business, and humane and effective organizations. At the societal level, our publications advance social and economic justice, shared prosperity, sustainability, and new solutions to national and global issues.

A major theme of our publications is "Opening Up New Space." They challenge conventional thinking, introduce new ideas, and foster positive change. Their common quest is changing the underlying beliefs, mindsets, and structures that keep generating the same cycles of problems, no matter who our leaders are or what improvement programs we adopt.

We strive to practice what we preach – to operate our publishing company in line with the ideas in our books. At the core of our approach is *stewardship*, which we define as a deep sense of responsibility to administer the company for the benefit of all of our "stakeholder" groups: authors, customers, employees, investors, service providers, and the communities and environment around us.

We are grateful to the thousands of readers, authors, and other friends of the company who consider themselves to be part of the "BK Community." We hope that you, too, will join us in our mission.

A BK Currents Book

This book is part of our BK Currents series. BK Currents books advance social and economic justice by exploring the critical intersections between business and society. Offering a unique combination of thoughtful analysis and progressive alternatives, BK Currents books promote positive change at the national and global levels. To find out more, visit www.bkcurrents.com.

Be Connected

Visit Our Website

Go to www.bkconnection.com to read exclusive previews and excerpts of new books, find detailed information on all Berrett-Koehler titles and authors, browse subject-area libraries of books, and get special discounts.

Subscribe to Our Free E-Newsletter

Be the first to hear about new publications, special discount offers, exclusive articles, news about bestsellers, and more! Get on the list for our free e-newsletter by going to www.bkconnection.com.

Get Quantity Discounts

Berrett-Koehler books are available at quantity discounts for orders of ten or more copies. Please call us toll-free at (800) 929-2929 or email us at bkp.orders@aidcvt.com.

Host a Reading Group

For tips on how to form and carry on a book reading group in your workplace or community, see our website at www.bkconnection.com.

Join the BK Community

Thousands of readers of our books have become part of the "BK Community" by participating in events featuring our authors, reviewing draft manuscripts of forthcoming books, spreading the word about their favorite books, and supporting our publishing program in other ways. If you would like to join the BK Community, please contact us at bkcommunity@bkpub.com.

The Things We Do

The Things We Do
Using the Lessons of Bernard and Darwin
to Understand the What, How, and Why
of Our Behavior

Gary Cziko

A Bradford Book
The MIT Press
Cambridge, Massachusetts
London, England

This book was set in Sabon by Greg and Pat Williams, Gravel Switch, Kentucky, and was printed and bound in the United States of America.

Library of Congress Cataloging-in-Publication Data
Cziko, Gary.
  The things we do : using the lessons of Bernard and Darwin to understand the what, how, and why of our behavior / Gary Cziko.
    p.   cm.
  "A Bradford book."
  Includes bibliographical references and index.
  ISBN 0-262-03277-5 (hc : alk. paper)
  1. Social psychology. 2. Sociobiology. 3. Behavior evolution. 4. Social Darwinism. I. Title.
HM1033.C95 2000
304—dc21   99-051843

Copyright Acknowledgments
The author and publisher are grateful to the following for their permission to use excerpts from:
George Gershwin, DuBose & Dorothy Heyward, & Ira Gershwin. (1935). "Summertime." Copyright © 1935 (Renewed 1962) by George Gershwin Music, Ira Gershwin Music, and DuBose and Dorothy Heyward Memorial Fund. All Rights Administered by WB Music Corp. All Rights Reserved. Used by permission of Warner Bros. Publications U.S. Inc., Miami, FL 33014.
Steven Pinker. (1994). *The language instinct*. New York: Morrow. Copyright © 1994 by Steven Pinker. Reprinted with permission of Steven Pinker.
Steven Pinker. (1997). *How the mind works*. New York: Norton. Copyright © 1997 by Steven Pinker. Reprinted with permission of Steven Pinker.
Billy Roberts. (1966). "Hey Joe." Copyright © 1966 by Six Palms Music Corp. Reprinted with permission of Six Palms Music Corp.

To William T. Powers,
  for having led me to Bernard's lesson,
and to the memory of Donald T. Campbell,
  who introduced me to Darwin's

Contents

Preface

For as long as I can remember I have been fascinated by the behavior of living things. Although I grew up within the urban confines of New York, that did not prevent me from acquiring a variety of animal specimens for study, including newts, snakes, lizards, parakeets, gerbils, rabbits, and various tropical fish. My interest in living behavior led me to study psychology as an undergraduate in the early 1970s at Queens College of the City University of New York, and then to graduate study in experimental psychology in the mid and late 1970s at McGill University in Montreal.

As an undergraduate at Queens, I was much impressed by the theories of B. F. Skinner and saw in his radical behaviorism what I considered to be a truly scientific and grand theory of behavior; simply put, that animals and people alike do what they are rewarded for, with no need to be concerned about their desires, wants, or purposes. But my studies in language acquisition and bilingualism at McGill with Wallace Lambert and G. Richard Tucker, together with the influence of Donald Hebb (whose last year at McGill coincided with my first), led me to cognitive theories that, in contrast to Skinner's behaviorism, focused on the role of mental and neural processes in determining behavior.

Impressive developments in the so-called cognitive revolution accompanied my tenure at the University of Illinois at Urbana-Champaign during the 1980s and 1990s. But in spite of these developments, I sensed two important gaps in psychology's account of animal and human behavior. First, I felt that psychological theory provided no convincing explanation for the obvious purposefulness of behavior. Although cognitive psychology emphasized the role of internal mental processes in explaining behavior, these processes were seen as transforming input (stimuli, sensations, perceptions) into output (responses, behavior). But we observe that behavior is purposeful when actions are varied to achieve a certain outcome, and I could not see how any input-output or cause-effect model, behaviorist or cognitive, could account for this.

Second, the psychological theories I knew provided no explanation for the goals and preferences that animals and humans have. Behaviorism tries to explain animal and human actions as resulting from reinforcement in the form of rewards (for example, food for a hungry rat, money for a person). Cognitive psychology uses more complex theories of motivation. But why are things such as food, money, and sex rewarding or motivating in the first place?

These basic questions about behavior remained unanswered in my mind when, in 1989, I met two fascinating and very approachable men: the late Donald T. Campbell and William T. Powers. Don Campbell introduced me to Charles Darwin (actually, to Darwin's theory of evolution and its implications for psychology) and to his former associate and co-teacher Powers. Bill Powers in turn led me to a fascinating theory of purposeful behavior having its roots in the work of Claude Bernard.

It would take several more years before all the pieces started coming together, during which time my first book, *Without Miracles*, appeared. But by taking heed of the discoveries of two giants of biology and modern developments of their theories, I began to find answers to my very basic questions about animal and human behavior.

Although I consider myself extremely fortunate to have met Campbell and Powers when I did, I can't help feeling somewhat cheated by my undergraduate and graduate education in psychology, which completely ignored both Bernard and Darwin, whose revolutionary contributions to the life sciences create an essential foundation for understanding animal and human behavior. Consequently, the purpose of this book is to introduce the lessons of Bernard and Darwin to those interested in understanding the *what*, *how*, and *why* of animal and human behavior.

Campbell, Powers, Bernard, and Darwin are not the only individuals who had an important influence on the evolution of this book. Richard Marken and Hugh Petrie provided comments that greatly improved the book, as did several anonymous reviewers of the manuscript. Greg

Williams not only provided a thorough and detailed list of insightful and helpful comments, but also served as a rapid-turnaround copy editor and, with his wife Pat (the other half of the Gravel Switch Typesetting Team), transformed the manuscript into the formatted print and illustrations you now hold in your hands. I thank Michael Rutter of the MIT Press for his editorial assistance and for his company during a great day of mountain biking near Tucson in June 1997. The red pencil of Sarah Jeffries did wonders to transform my often wordy, loquacious, redundant, superfluous writing style into something more closely resembling readable modern English prose (this is the one sentence she didn't get to see). Fellow music lover Rich Palmer provided an invaluable service by somehow being able to "undue" the hundred or so overdue books I had in my possession from the vast stores of the University of Illinois library. And I must also recognize the stimulating environment, freedom, and support that the University of Illinois at Urbana-Champaign and its Department of Educational Psychology have provided over the last twenty years.

Last but certainly not least, I am truly appreciative of the love, support, and tolerance of my wife, Carol, who once again had to share me for an extended period with the demanding mistress that a book-in-progress becomes. I promised her it was just a temporary fling. But I am sure she will understand that some habits are hard to break.

1

Introduction and Overview

But if a thing is a product of nature . . . then this second *requisite is involved, namely, that the parts of the thing combine of themselves into the unity of the whole by being* reciprocally cause and effect *of their form.*
—Immanuel Kant (1790/1952, p. 556; second emphasis added)

As we enter the third millennium, we can look back at a century of unprecedented scientific and technological progress. We have learned to split and fuse atoms and in so doing convert minuscule amounts of matter into huge amounts of energy. We have walked on the moon and sent space probes to distant planets. We have discovered nature's clever trick for storing biological information in the double helix of DNA molecules and learned how to manipulate the genes of living organisms for our own agricultural, industrial, and medical purposes. Advances in chemistry and material science have provided new substances such as plastics, synthetic fibers, and metal alloys that have given us unbreakable shampoo bottles, inexpensive panty hose, jumbo jets, and superconducting materials. Progress in electrical engineering and computer science goes on at an accelerating pace so that the computer and software bought just a year or two ago is obsolete. Medical research has lengthened human life and improved its quality for those fortunate individuals having the means to take advantage of new drugs, equipment, and surgical techniques.

These accomplishments in physics, biology, chemistry, engineering, and medicine contrast sharply with our still limited scientific knowledge of the human mind and human behavior, the domain of those disciplines usually referred to as social, psychological, behavioral, and cognitive sciences. The field of psychology is fragmented into scores of different schools and theories, with those in one camp either ignorant of or openly hostile to the researchers, methodologies, theories, and findings of other camps. The very existence of the discipline of sociology is currently being threatened as it continues to lose turf to psychology, biology, and anthropology (Ellis 1966). And although expectations were great in the 1970s as psychologists, linguists, philosophers, anthropologists, neuroscientists, and computer scientists joined forces to create the new field of cognitive science, the ambitious goal of understanding how the human brain gives rise to intelligent behavior, thought, and consciousness remains largely unfulfilled.

The lack of clear progress in applied behavioral science becomes particularly evident when we examine the behavior-based ills of today's societies. In the United States, arguably the world's richest and most technologically advanced country, prisons are overflowing with people convicted of murder, rape, armed robbery, domestic violence, and drug dealing. Metal detectors are now commonly used to keep deadly weapons out of urban public schools where teachers are often more concerned with survival than with teaching. Throughout the world, ethnic, racial, and religious tensions regularly explode in horrifying acts of violence, leaving widespread suffering and misery in their wake. The AIDS virus, whose spread depends on human behaviors resulting in the transfer of bodily fluids from one individual to another, continues its deadly worldwide spread. And the increasing rate of global population growth poses a menacing danger to the earth's resources and continued survival of many species, including our own. So while stunning advances have been made in many fields of science and technology, we are still unable to solve the many serious social problems stemming from certain types of human behavior.

It is perhaps not surprising that our attempts to understand ourselves and solve these problems should be met with very slow progress if not outright failure. The fact that we humans can formulate questions concerning the things we do and feel, including why and how we do them and feel as we do, reveals a degree of intelligence that is not found in other species and may paradoxically lie beyond our ability to comprehend fully. The fact that the human mind is affected by studying itself, as pointed out by eighteenth-century philosopher Immanuel Kant, provides an additional difficulty that does not arise when we study physical phenomena or other species.

But there is another—and fortunately, correctable—reason for the slow progress of human behavioral and cognitive sciences. Simply put, certain essential findings from biology concerning the origin, evolution, and functioning of *all* forms of life have been largely ignored. Instead, for reasons to be explored in the following chapters, behavioral scientists have with few exceptions followed Sir Isaac Newton in applying the findings and methods of seventeenth-century classical physics to the study of life, disregarding the findings of two revolutionary nineteenth-century biological scientists—French physiologist Claude Bernard on the self-regulating nature of living organisms, and English naturalist Charles Darwin on the origin and evolution of species.

Newton's Legacy

Few individuals had as much impact on science and its continued development as Sir Isaac Newton (1643–1727). Among his many scientific achievements, he demonstrated that the movements of all bodies, whether on earth or in space, could be understood by his now famous three laws of motion.

Newton's first law is the law of inertia or momentum, stating that a body at rest will remain at rest and a body in motion will maintain its speed and direction unless acted upon by an external force. His second law, $a = F/m$, gives the acceleration that results from application of a force (F) on a body of a given mass (m). Newton's third law states that for every force (action) there is an equal and opposite force (reaction).

It is Newton's second law (of which the first is a special case) that is the most important, as it defines mathematically the effect that a force will have on a body, whether it be to cause a stationary object to move or a moving object to stop or change its speed or direction. And although Newton believed that the hand of God was required to stabilize the motion of the planets, further refinements of his theory, most notably those of Pierre-Simon Laplace (1749–1827), showed that his laws were sufficient to account for all observed motions of the planets (the anomaly of Mercury's orbit, which could not be explained without relativity theory, was unknown during Laplace's time).

Newton's second law remains a classic example of a *one-way cause-effect* theory that can be expressed as C —> E. The force applied to the object is the cause and the change in motion of the object is the effect. It is a one-way theory since while force determines acceleration, acceleration has no influence on force. For example, imagine a spaceship coasting at a constant speed between Earth and Mars. By igniting the engines and thereby applying a force to the rear of the vessel, the spaceship will accelerate at a rate determined by the amount of thrust provided by the engines and its own mass. In contrast, force provided by the engines is independent of the spaceship's mass, velocity, or acceleration. Thus we have a one-way cause-effect model in which force is the *independent variable* and acceleration is the *dependent variable*.

The laws that Newton discovered and formulated had a profound effect on science. This was not because they explained everything about the movements of inanimate bodies (for example, Newton didn't even attempt to formulate an explanation for how the gravity of one body could influence the movement of a distant body), but rather because they allowed for *prediction* and *control* of moving objects. Newtonian principles are still used to predict where the international space station will be at a given time and to control the trajectory of the space shuttle as it ferries supplies and passengers from Earth to the station.

It therefore seemed that a similar perspective could be applied to the behavior of living bodies. That is, if inanimate bodies react to forces in predictable ways, we should be able to predict (and consequently control) the behavior of living organisms once we uncover the cause-effect principles that apply to that behavior.

This is essentially what the field of psychology has been trying to do for the last hundred years or so. But although it could be argued that we have continued to make impressive gains since the time of Newton in predicting and controlling the behavior of inanimate objects and systems, we have made much less progress in predicting and controlling animate behavior, and little real progress in predicting and controlling human behavior where desires, goals, intentions, and purposes play such an important role.

The one-way cause-effect model that became Newton's legacy was also unable to provide scientific explanations for the origin and evolution of life forms and the physiological processes and purposeful behavior of living organisms. What was the cause that resulted in the emergence and evolution of living organisms? How is it that animals are able to maintain relatively constant conditions inside their bodies despite many disturbing environmental forces? How are organisms able to act purposefully in spite of these disturbing forces to achieve outcomes favorable to their survival and reproduction? To answer these questions, a different perspective on causality is required.

Bernard's Internal Environment

One nineteenth-century biologist whose work challenged one-way cause-effect models was Claude Bernard (1813–1878). As we will see in chapter 4, Bernard made many important discoveries concerning the internal processes of living organisms. But his most important contribution was a conceptual one in his recognition that these processes serve to maintain a relatively constant internal environment in spite of disturbing forces, and this regulation or control of the *milieu intérieur* is an essential condition for all forms of life. In other words, a necessary requirement for life is the achievement of a degree of independence or autonomy from the external environment so that the normal cause-effect relationships found in non-living systems no longer hold. A glass of warm water placed in a refrigerator will quickly chill to the temperature of its new environment. The cooler temperature is the cause and the cooled water the effect. But placing a bird in a cooler environment will have little or no effect on its body temperature, at least not while it remains alive. This phenomenon of the control of internal body temperature initially appears to violate the usual laws of physics in which external forces or causes have predictable effects.

Similarly, living organisms are able to control aspects of their external environments. A newly hatched gosling will stay in close proximity to its mother, scurrying around obstacles and avoiding its nestmates to do so. A mature salmon will fight strong currents and even jump up waterfalls in its drive to return to the stream in which it was hatched, to mate before it dies. And humans engage in an amazing variety of behaviors to provide food, comfort, and security for themselves and their families in an often uncaring and hostile world. What we see in these and all instances of purposeful behavior are not reactions to environmental forces, but rather actions that *compensate* for environmental forces to achieve the organism's goal, using behavior that appears outside the scope of Newton's laws of motion.

Bernard himself did not propose a formal alternative to the one-way cause-effect perspective, but those who continued this line of work on the self-regulating nature of living organisms eventually developed models incorporating what can be described as *circular causality* in which causes are also effects and effects are also causes. Also referred to as *closed-loop*, *cybernetic*, or *control* systems, models incorporating circular causality provide useful working models for both internal physiological processes and overt behavior of living organisms. In short, understanding circular causality is key to understanding how the behavior of living organisms, unlike that of nonliving entities, can be purposeful and goal directed whereas the underlying processes are physical and naturalistic.

Darwin's Selectionism

Bernard was interested in the internal mechanisms of living organisms, but Charles Robert Darwin (1809–1882) was most interested in why and how organisms emerged and evolved into the countless species that once lived or still do on our planet. And although Newton certainly had an influence on him (Depew & Weber 1995), Darwin had to break free of the one-way cause-effect model to provide a scientific theory of evolution. According to his theory of natural selection, the offspring of organisms spontaneously vary in form and behavior, resembling their progenitors, but not always exactly (never exactly for sexually reproducing species). By sheer luck, certain organisms are more successful in surviving and reproducing than their contemporaries, and these variations are inherited by *their* offspring, who also vary and enjoy differential survival and reproductive success, and so on. As Darwin theorized, and as understood by today's biologists, the environment does not cause these variations, but only winnows out less fit from better fit organisms.

Consider a tree frog whose back looks astonishingly like the bark of the tree on which it spends so much of its time. This remarkable camouflage is an adaptation that hides the frog from those who would have it for a meal. A one-way cause-effect analysis would attempt to explain this phenomenon as somehow transmitted from the environment (the tree's bark) to the organism (the frog's back), much as one can account for transmission of information from environment to film in the making of a photograph. But while the frog's back may appear to be analogous to a photograph of the tree's bark, the mechanism by which it evolved is quite unlike the one-way cause-effect process of taking a photograph. To take a photo, light reflecting from the object being photographed enters the camera through its lens and strikes the film, causing chemical changes in the film. The frog's camouflage arose only after many generations of frogs with varying backs enjoying differing rates of survival and reproduction. The environment did not cause these variations. Rather, these variations were spontaneously and randomly (and, of course, unknowingly) created by the frogs themselves, with the environment serving only as a type of filter selecting variations best suited to camouflage and eliminating the rest.

In a system operating according to Newton's second law, forces may interact in complex ways, but nothing truly new or creative emerges. Set the balls of a frictionless billiard table in motion and they will continue to bounce and collide, but that is all they will ever do. In contrast, in a system operating according to Darwin's principles of cumulative variation and selection, new complex and adapted entities—such as bacteria, bananas, beetles, baboons, and babies—can arise that are utterly unpredictable by Newton's or anyone else's one-way laws of cause and effect. One could argue that the physical processes underlying biological evolution are still Newtonian at their core. This may well be the case, but the fact remains that a one-way cause-effect model (such as that which explains how a photograph is made or where a thrown object will land) cannot account for the emergence of new, complex, and adapted forms (such as the back of the tree frog).

Circular causality is also an important part of evolution, acting in ways that we have only recently begun to understand and model. Since selection pressures are brought about by competing organisms of both the same and different species, selection influences evolution at the same time that evolution influences selection, each being both cause and effect of the other. For example, because cheetahs hunt and feed on gazelles, there is selection pressure on gazelles for running speed. But as gazelles evolve to be faster, this puts selection pressure back on the cheetahs for more speed, and so on. Unlike the circular processes studied by Bernard in which internal physiological conditions are tightly controlled, the runaway nature of evolutionary "arms races" tends to push organisms to extremes, as in California redwoods growing to over 300 feet in their quest to reach sunlight beyond the shadows of their giant neighbors.

The explanatory power of Darwin's discovery is not limited to biological evolution. As described in my previous book, *Without Miracles* (Cziko 1995), the process of variation and selection underlies the emergence of all sorts of complex, adapted entities. These entities include antibodies, brains, languages, computer programs, drugs, and other aspects of culture and technology, as well as the primary concern of this book—the behavior of living organisms. But, as we will also see, Darwin's more complex selectionist causality is not widely embraced by behavioral scientists, who still overwhelmingly prefer one-way cause-effect models consisting of independent variables (environmental causes) impinging on dependent ones (behavioral effects).

The central argument of this book is that when the revolutionary biological principles discovered by Bernard and Darwin are considered, updated with the best of our scientific knowledge, and applied to animal and human behavior, certain long-standing theoretical and practical problems in behavioral science disappear and new methods and topics for research in mind and behavior present themselves.

I recognize that this notion will not be an easy sell since it flies in the face of over 100 years of psychological theory and research based on one-way cause-effect theories. Also, the lessons of Bernard and Darwin are old news to biologists, at least with respect to the origin, evolution, and basic life functions of living organisms. But the case nonetheless can and must be made that further progress in behavioral and cognitive sciences can be achieved only by moving away from Newton and toward Bernard and Darwin.

This basic thesis is developed in the following parts and chapters. Part I presents philosophical (chapter 2) and psychological (chapter 3) overviews of past and current theories of behavior, and recounts how the progression from yesterday's psychic and spiritual to today's naturalistic and materialist[1] theories has thrown the purposeful baby out with the psychic, spiritualistic bath water.

The three chapters of part II show how a purely naturalistic and materialist theory of purposeful behavior is indeed possible and is being developed and applied by a small but growing group of behavioral scientists and practitioners. This theory, known as perceptual control theory, has its roots in the insights of Bernard (chapter 4) and the work of twentieth-century control systems engineers and cyberneticians (chapter 5), and was molded into its present form by William T. Powers and his associates (chapter 6). Chapter 6 provides both demonstrations and working models of animal and human behavior based on perceptual control theory. These demonstrations and simulations (many available on the World Wide Web at *www.uiuc.edu/ph/www/g-cziko/twd*) show and explain living organisms as purposeful systems demonstrating circular causality that behave to control their perceptions of the environment. They offer a new perspective for understanding what, why, and how living things, including humans, do what they do.

Part III applies Darwinian evolution to understanding animal and human behavior as well as to the human thought processes that underlie human behavior. Chapter 7 considers animal and chapter 8 human behavior from the evolutionary perspective provided by Darwin in an attempt to answer the ultimate, "big" question of why we and our animal cousins do what we do. Chapter 9 relates how the process of cumulative variation and selection that underlies biological evolution has been extended to provide new understandings of the maturation and functioning of the human organism, in particular, the human brain. On this view of the brain as a Darwinian machine operating under selectionist causality, variation and selection of organisms is replaced by variation and selection of synaptic connections, mental processes, and thoughts, giving rise to our uniquely human abilities in problem solving, imagination, and creativity, and indeed to consciousness itself.

Finally, part IV attempts to integrate the biologically inspired perspective of the three preceding parts with current theoretical and applied work in behavioral science. Chapter 10 shows how, by combining Bernard's and Darwin's lessons, we can understand how certain evolutionary processes, most notably those that occur within organisms, can be directed and purposeful, and provide the human brain with powerful mechanisms for lifelong adaptation to new environments and solutions to new problems.

Chapter 11 focuses on the problems of current psychological theory, showing that outdated one-way, push-pull theories of how the environment causes animate behavior are not only still widely held among behavioral and cognitive scientists but that their stubborn persistence is a major factor in the slow progress of these fields. Chapter 12 discusses theoretical advantages and practical uses of a theory of behavior that moves away from one-way cause-effect models to selectionist and circular models and to appreciation of the creative and self-regulating properties of life first recognized by Bernard and Darwin. (Readers wanting to see now a summary of the book's main conclusions can turn to the last section of chapter 12, "Toward a Unified Theory of Behavior.")

This book was written for both general readers interested in understanding what and how we (and animals) do what we do and why we do it, as well as for professional behavioral scientists, both theoretical and applied. I suspect that the main theses may actually be easier to grasp by readers with little or no formal study of behavioral, cognitive, and social sciences who are therefore "uncontaminated" by the orthodox perspective of viewing animate behavior as an organism's output (effect) determined by environmental input (cause). Behavioral scientists may well have a harder time suspending what they already believe about behavior and psychological theory, but once they do they may be better able to appreciate the full significance of Bernard's and Darwin's insights for understanding animate behavior and grasp the implications of demonstrations and computer simulations introduced in chapter 6.

My principal hope for this book is that it will help bring to completion two long overdue revolutions in behavioral and cognitive sciences that are already underway but still quite limited in their impact. Another hope is that the book will help interested readers see more clearly certain essential features of life; namely, how and why living organisms behave as they do. Such knowledge is of value not only for its own sake, but it also has important practical applications as we enter the twenty-first century and confront the behavioral challenges and problems of the third millennium.

I

Theories of Behavior:
From Psychic and Purposeful
to Materialist and Purposeless

2

Philosophical Perspectives on Behavior: From Animism to Materialism

I notice something and seek a reason for it: . . . I seek an intention in it, and above all someone who has intentions, a subject, a doer: every event a deed—formerly one saw intentions in all events, this is our oldest habit. Do animals also possess it?

—Friedrich Nietzsche (1901/1967)

As we observe the world around us, our attention is drawn to things that move and change. The sun makes its journey from east to west across the sky each day, and by night the moon, stars, planets, and occasional comets and meteors trace their luminous paths across the heavens. Drops of rain fall to the earth, collecting into rivulets and then streams that join together to form rivers that rush or leisurely meander to a sea that never seems to tire of sending waves crashing against the shore. Over many years, a fragile seedling grows into a towering oak and a helpless human infant somehow manages to transform itself into a musician, Olympic athlete, airline pilot, or neurosurgeon. Birds circle overhead while squirrels scamper among the branches of trees, and bees and butterflies busily collect nectar and pollen from flowers that open their brightly colored petals to the warm sun. In our cities we see a constant blur of movement as streams of people move along its sidewalks and vehicles clog its streets.

We humans are both affected by and constitute an important part of this movement and change as we go about our daily activities. So it is not surprising that we should be interested in the what, how, and why of the behavior of both nonliving objects and living organisms, including ourselves. In our attempts to understand, three major types of theories of motion and change have been developed. The first type appeals to immaterial, nonphysical explanations, including what may be called psychic, animist, supernatural, spiritual, or mystical entities and forces. The second type rejects such nonphysical explanations and sees all motion and change—whether of objects, plants, animals, or humans—as the result of processes involving only matter, energy, and physical laws that govern them and their interactions. The third type takes a dualist middle ground, combining both physical and spiritual entities and processes to account for all forms of behavior.

In this chapter we examine these three types of theories from a philosophical perspective, saving a psychological perspective for the next chapter. But before doing so, I have to provide some definitions.

Although the words *behave* and *behavior* are often meant to refer to actions of living organisms, they are also commonly used to refer to changes and movements that nonliving objects undergo. This more inclusive meaning is consistent with the definition of *behaviour* provided by the *Oxford English Dictionary*: "The manner in which a thing acts under specified conditions or circumstances, or in relation to other things." So though we speak of the behavior of a dog or child, we also consider how one chemical behaves in the presence of another and how the stock market behaved yesterday. Indeed, a better understanding of the differences underlying the behavior of inanimate objects on the one hand and living organisms on the other is a major goal of this book, and so I will use the unqualified term behavior and its derivatives to refer to either living or nonliving entities. When more specificity is required, the terms *inanimate behavior* and *animate behavior* will be used, recognizing that the discipline that refers to itself as *behavioral science* deals only with animate behavior (with physics usually restricting itself to the study of nonliving objects and systems; that is, inanimate behavior). To avoid the necessity of the adjective *nonhuman* when referring to animals other than *Homo sapiens*, the word *animal* is used, with its more usual meaning that excludes our own species (although, of course, our species is technically just another animal, if a rather special and peculiar one).

Mind Over Matter: Psychic Philosophies of Behavior

That humans possess self-awareness, consciousness, intentions, and desires that are not easily explained in terms of physical processes is a major motivator for immaterial theories of behavior, theories that have been extended by some to include all animals and plants and even inanimate objects. To explain motion and change, these theories appeal to non-physical entities and forces that remain beyond the domain of physical sciences as we know them.

Such theories of behavior are often referred to as *psychic* or *animist*, *psyche* being the Greek word for "mind" or "soul" that also forms the root of our modern terms *psychology* and *psychiatry*; *anima* is its Latin equivalent. Those theories that go the entire distance in using psychic explanations to account for all behavior involving humans, animals, plants, and objects are referred to as *panpsychic*. Panpsychic theories do not necessarily deny the existence of a physical world and mechanical processes, but see materialist explanations as insufficient to explain any of the phenomena occurring in the universe.

Animism

It has been stated that animist explanations of behavior characterized humankind's earliest attempts to make sense out of the world, a world containing other human beings, animals, and plants, as well as physical forces emanating from fire, wind, water, and the earth itself. At some point in the evolution of our species, our ancestors developed awareness of their own existence and desires as well as the strange and powerful force of life present in all living animals and humans, but obviously absent in the bodies of dead animals and humans. Therefore they developed belief in a soul or spirit that gave life to bodies and also accounted for human consciousness, thought, desires, and behavior. The phenomenon of dreams, in which one has experiences that seem detached from the physical location of one's body, would also suggest a life-giving spirit that normally inhabits the body but can also leave it. Belief in an immaterial, life-giving soul is consistent with belief in a spiritual life after death of the physical body, a creed that is characteristic of religions throughout the world.

But human imagination is such that it has also developed a belief in souls residing in apparently nonliving objects. In his *Natural History of Religion*, Scottish philosopher David Hume (1711–1776) attempted to make sense of the belief in the souls of objects (1757; quoted in Tylor 1871/1958, p. 61):

There is an universal tendency among mankind to conceive all beings like themselves, and to transfer to every object those qualities with which they are familiarly acquainted, and of which they are intimately conscious. . . . Nor is it long before we ascribe to them thought and reason, and passion and sometimes even the limbs and figures of men, in order to bring them nearer to a resemblance with ourselves.

Such animistic interpretations of the behavior of objects and physical forces allowed (and still allow) prescientific peoples to make better sense of their surroundings. Ascribing motives and intentions to other people and animals is the first step in this process. If I eat when hungry, flee when fearful, fight when angry, perform nurturing acts when loving, hunt to eat, and find or make shelter to stay warm and dry, it would not require much imagination to suppose that other humans and animals perform similar acts for similar reasons and purposes. It is but one more step to reason that kindness of the air and sun results in favorable weather and good crops while anger and jealousy of the spirits of water, earth, and fire bring floods, droughts, volcanic eruptions, landslides, earthquakes, wildfires, and other natural disasters. The next step is to attempt to influence these natural physical events by acts of propitiation, that is, by attempting to appease and favorably influence the spirits of the physical world through prayer, sacrifice, atonement, and other rituals (Kelsen 1946).

Sir Edward Burnett Tylor (1832–1917), one of the founding fathers of anthropology, provided the first systematic survey and description of animism throughout the world, describing animistic belief as a necessary first stage in the emergence of more fully developed religious systems (Tylor 1871/1958). That such beliefs serve the purpose of understanding and attempting to control natural events is demonstrated by their relative rarity in societies with modern science and technology and their persistence in societies that have had little or no contact with science and technology. However, as we will soon see, ignorance of science is not required for belief in an animistic world.

Ancient Panpsychism

It is also not the case that psychic theories of behavior are limited to "primitive" illiterate peoples not possessing sophisticated, carefully examined philosophies. Serious panpsychic theorizing goes back at least as far as the Greek pre-Socratic philosophers. Plato (428–348 B.C.) considered souls necessary to explain both the movements of heavenly bodies and the behavior of animals and humans. Concerning the former, Plato was struck by the orderly movements of stars, planets, sun, and moon and considered it evidence of a type of "world soul" provided by the Creator.

The primary cause of movement must be that which can move both itself and other things, and this he [Plato] identified as soul. Soul carries around the sun, moon, and stars but he leaves it doubtful whether this is because soul is present in the sun as it is in man or because soul pushes the sun from outside or because the sun is moved from outside by soul in some other way. (Kerferd 1967, p. 157)

Plato's rationale for rejecting purely materialist, mechanistic explanations of human behavior is offered in his *Phaedo* dialogue in which Socrates is about to be put to death. Here, Socrates insists that materialist explanations simply cannot provide satisfactory answers to the why of human action, such as why he decided to stay in Athens and face death rather than flee and save his life.

Among ancient Greek thinkers it was Plato's student Aristotle (384–322 B.C.) who provided the most ambitious account of motion and change in the universe, dealing explicitly with both inanimate objects and living organisms. Somewhat paradoxically, Aristotle's panpsychism seems to have been motivated by a rather mechanical notion of movement. For him, all movement had to be caused by a mover, so that if object B moves, it was because object A had moved it. But then what had caused object A to move? To avoid an infinite regress, Aristotle posited the existence of an unmoved mover that was eternal and immaterial. Whereas he referred to this unmoved, transcendent mover as the "outermost heaven," Christians later conceived of this prime mover as an all-powerful and personal God.

For Aristotle, even the actions of animals were ultimately due to outside causes. Although it might appear as if animals move themselves spontaneously, he explained that "many motions are produced in the body by its environment and some of these set in motion the intellect or the appetite, and this again then sets the whole animal in motion" (*Physics*, book VIII, chapter 2, p. 337).

Thus an animal is first at rest and afterwards walks, not having been set in motion apparently by anything from without. This, however, is false: for we observe that there is always some part of the animal's organism in motion, and the cause of the motion of this part is not the animal itself, but, it may be, its environment. (*Physics*, book VIII, chapter 2, p. 337)

Aristotle's cause-effect reasoning led to the notion of a *stimulus* that played such an important role in later psychological theory. But whereas Aristotle considered the environment ultimately responsible for the behavior of organisms, he also realized important distinctions between inanimate objects and living organisms and therefore attributed a soul to all forms of life, including plants, animals, and humans. His conception of soul was somewhat less mystical and spiritual than either Plato's or later Christian conceptualizations, and for this reason some scholars might well object to describing his philosophy as panpsychic. Nonetheless, it is clear that he saw the soul as that which gave life to living things.

Aristotle believed that plants had nutritive and reproductive souls that caused them to take in nourishment from the sun, air, and ground, and allowed their growth and reproduction. Animals had souls that were similarly nutritive and reproductive, but in addition allowed them to sense the world around them, move, and have desires so that they would seek some things but avoid others. The souls of humans, in addition to possessing all the abilities of those of plants and animals, were intelligent, making humans capable of thought and rational action. Through their rationality, they could develop plans and rules to impose on their cruder animal desires. Aristotle saw the human soul as quite distinct in its rational powers from the souls of plants and other animals, but his placing plants, animals, and humans on the same continuum showed an appreciation of the relationship existing among all living organisms that was not seen again until the time of Charles Darwin some twenty-two centuries later.

Even a cursory treatment of Aristotle's view must mention its strong teleological flavor. *Telos* in Greek means "end" or "goal," and a teleological explanation is one that attempts to explain a phenomenon as directed by its ultimate outcome. To quote Aristotle, "Nature, like mind, always does whatever it does for the sake of something, which something is its end" (*On the Heavens*; quoted in Peters & Mace 1967, p. 3). That such a view considers nature an intelligent, purposeful agent with a grand plan for the universe is additional evidence of the essentially panpsychic nature of Aristotle's thought.

Modern Panpsychism

Anyone acquainted with the success of modern science might suspect that panpsychic theories of behavior have long since disappeared, together with other obsolete scientific theories, such as the earth-centered theory of the solar system, the ether theory of space, and the phlogiston theory of fire. But this is actually far from the case. Although the success of the physical sciences and technology (especially Newton's physics and the technology of the industrial revolution) did help materialist theories of behavior eventually win out over psychic ones, panpsychic views of nature have been entertained by many influential thinkers of the nineteenth and twentieth centuries. Among prominent post-Newtonian panpsychists we find psychologist G. T. Fechner; philosophers G. W. Leibniz, Arthur Schopenhauer, C. S. Peirce, and A. N. Whitehead; and biologists Pierre Teilhard de Chardin, C. H. Waddington, and Sewall Wright.

A set of passages that vividly illustrates one nineteenth-century panpsychic perspective comes from Schopenhauer (1788–1860) who commented on the "strong and unceasing impulse with which the waters hurry to the ocean, [the] persistency with which the magnet turns ever to the North Pole, [the] readiness with which iron flies to the magnet, [the] eagerness with which the electric poles seek to be reunited, and which, just like human desire, is increased by obstacles [as well as] the choice with which bodies repel and attract each other, combine and separate, when they are set free in a fluid state, and emancipated from the bonds of rigidity." He noted that when we lift a heavy object we notice how it "hampers our body by its gravitation towards the earth" and that we "feel directly [how it] unceasingly presses and strains [us] in pursuit of its one tendency." He further observed how the stars and planets "play with each other, betray mutual inclination, exchange as it were amorous glances, yet never allow themselves to come into rude contact" (1818, 1836; quoted in Edwards 1967, p. 25).

Schopenhauer's observations appear amusing because he invokes well-understood physical phenomena as evidence of nonphysical psyches. Gravity and magnetism are understood today (indeed, as they were in his day) as mindless physical forces, and although we may still not completely understand why they act as they do, scientists today feel no need to invoke spirits, souls, ghosts, or other supernatural entities to account for their effects.

More recent, and perhaps more reasonably proposed, was the panpsychism of English embryologist and geneticist C. H. Waddington (1909–1975). Waddington felt that the voluntary and purposeful nature of our actions was evidence of an immaterialist cause of human behavior, arguing that "the experiences to which we give the name of free-will cannot depend wholly on the particular type of nervous activity which, when it is expressed in action, appears as a purpose, but most essentially involve a phenomenon of self-awareness in addition to this" (1962, p. 118).

He also held that biological evolution, together with the fact that human beings have self-awareness, logically leads to the view that all other organisms as well as inanimate objects also have at least some degree of self-awareness. In addition, since humans are undoubtedly aware of themselves and evolved from simpler forms of life, these simpler forms—indeed all forms of life—must also have some degree of self-awareness. And since, according to the theory of evolution, life arose from previous nonliving matter, all nonliving things must also have at least some degree of self-awareness.

So we see that panpsychic theories of behavior have a long history in philosophical attempts to make sense of the movements and changes of the world's objects and organisms. Arguments vary, but common to all of them is the belief that actions appearing to be deliberate and goal directed cannot be explained by completely mindless physical processes.

Having One's Ghost and Feeling It, Too: Dualist Philosophies of Behavior

In contrast to panpsychic philosophies, psychophysical dualism restricts an immaterial soul or mind to certain entities, typically not attributing a psyche to inanimate objects and perhaps also not to plants and animals. For dualists, certain behaviors can be explained as the results of purely physical processes and others are determined (or at least influenced by) a nonphysical soul or mind. Any theory that is not either panpsychic or purely materialistic must embrace psychophysical dualism to some degree.

Descartes: Putting the Ghost in the Machine

Influential French philosopher and mathematician René Descartes (1596–1650) is considered by many to be the father of modern philosophy.

Accordingly, his dualist philosophy had a great and continuing impact on Western thought.

Descartes's dualism has two major characteristics. The first concerns where he drew the line on the existence of souls. This line was very clear: only humans had souls; inanimate objects as well as plants and all animals were purely physical machines with no consciousness, desires, or purposes of any kind. It is reported that Descartes was amused at the howls, cries, and whimpers of live animals he dissected in his research, since he considered these to be but the hydraulically caused noises of unfeeling machines (Jaynes 1973, p. 170).

This may seem to be an absurd and downright inhumane attitude to take today, but it should be mentioned that during Descartes's time English physician William Harvey (1578–1657) showed that the heart, formerly thought by many to be the seat of the passions, was "only" a mechanical pump for the blood. Also, during that time hydraulically animated mechanical models of people and animals were popular fountain decorations. These developments likely encouraged Descartes's belief in the purely mechanical nature of animals.

The second defining characteristic of Descartes's dualism was his theory of the interaction between the physical machine of the living human body and the soul it somehow contained. It should be noted first that whereas he believed that all humans had a soul, he nonetheless considered the physical human body to be a machine in the same way that animals were machines. Accordingly, many human actions were purely physical phenomena that occurred without involving the soul, as when we reflexively pull our hand away from a hot object. This Descartes explained as the action of a mechanistic and automatic one-way cause-effect reflex from sensation to behavior. He believed erroneously that these automatic behaviors involved transmission of a fluid from sensory organs to brain to muscles. But his conceptualization of the reflex arc as a one-way physical connection between perceiving senses and acting muscles had a lasting effect on psychology's one-way cause-effect conception of animal and human behavior as consisting of responses to stimuli.

But actions involving human will involved the functioning of the soul. Descartes believed that the pineal gland at the base of the brain was the site of interaction between the spirit of the soul and the machine of the body. He chose the pineal gland for this function because it appeared to him that it was the only part of the brain that did not exist in other animals (we now know that it does). So unlike stimulus-response reflexes that took place without involvement of the soul, willful action involved the soul receiving information from the senses and determining action by moving the pineal gland, which set in motion "animal spirits" ultimately resulting in muscle movements and overt human behaviors. Although he had the physiological details wrong, his belief that willful or deliberate action involves mediation of a mind acting between stimulus and response anticipated the basic structure of later psychological theorizing, including modern cognitive psychology.

Some rather serious problems plague Descartes's dualism, and many post-Cartesian philosophers have based their careers on describing them. Even in his own day, many could not understand how a soul—which by Descartes's account possessed no physical properties such as shape, volume, position, or mass—could manage to move a physical organ, even one as small as the pineal gland. (The same problem, often unrecognized by cartoon and movie makers, arises for ghosts who are able to pass unimpeded through walls and doors but still somehow manage to make things go bump in the night and have other effects on physical objects.) But it should be recognized that Descartes did pursue a materialist philosophy of behavior as far as it seemed to him prudent to go. All animal behavior was a mechanical reaction to the environment, as is the behavior of a machine. Similar were certain types of human behavior, such as automatic reflexes we make when we are startled by a loud noise or sneeze when dust enters our nose.

But Descartes recognized something quite different about the purposeful behavior that humans consciously want to perform and do so by the exercise of their will. He did not see how a purely mechanical account could be sufficient to explain such actions in which humans do not merely *react* to their environment but instead autonomously and willfully *act* on their environment. In this respect, he was convinced that a human being was fundamentally different from a machine, no matter how cleverly designed such a machine might be.

Vitalism

Descartes's philosophy is just one of the many forms that dualism has taken in the history of human thought. Another form, still very much with us in popular thought if not in science, is known as *vitalism*, which recognizes a fundamental difference between living and nonliving entities. Whereas both inanimate objects and living organisms are subject to the materialist laws of physics and chemistry, vitalism posits a nonphysical entity that gives an organism life and powers that no inanimate body can possess. So whereas panpsychists see all objects possessing a nonphysical soul, and Descartes reserved souls for humans only, vitalism makes what most of us today would likely find to be a more reasonable distinction between objects and organisms, with a nonphysical life force, or *élan vital*, possessed only by the latter.

One of the best-known vitalists of the twentieth century was German physiologist and philosopher Hans Driesch (1867–1941). He defined vitalism as "the theory of the autonomy of the processes of life" (quoted in Beckner 1967, p. 255). For him, the life of an organism depended on "an autonomous, mindlike, nonspatial entity that exercises control over the course of organic processes" (Beckner 1967, p. 255). Driesch admitted that laws of physics and chemistry applied to living organisms and their behavior, but he found such mechanistic principles insufficient to account for an organism's stages of development. The development of a fertilized egg into an embryo and then into a viable, independent organism could be explained after the fact by laws of physics and chemistry. However, such mechanistic laws by themselves could not determine this development, but only put limits on the range of possibilities. It was the special life-giving entity that Driesch referred to as "entelechy" that determined the actual course of development from egg to mature organism.

A description of Driesch's most famous experiment will provide a useful illustration. In the late nineteenth century it was generally believed that a fertilized egg cell contained within it a miniature likeness of the mature organism that it used as a plan for the developing embryo, a theory known as *preformationism*. But in 1891 Driesch separated the two cells of the first division of a sea urchin's egg and was surprised to find that each separate cell developed into a normal, whole sea urchin. For Driesch, this was proof that the egg was more than a machine governed by ordinary laws of physics and chemistry, since no machine divided in half could still make what it had been designed to produce. He saw here evidence of a type of living agency—a regulatory, goal-based process that could not be explained mechanically.

Similarly, Driesch felt that a person's voluntary actions could not be accounted for mechanically, and here we see that he shares company with Descartes. As an example, take a moment to decide whether you want to raise your hand above your head and then act on your decision. If you did raise your hand, this behavior could be accounted for after the fact as the result of contracting muscles that had been stimulated by motor neurons carrying impulses from the brain. But Driesch thought that laws of physics and chemistry were inadequate to explain your *decision* to raise your hand or not.

Although Driesch's vitalism differs from Descartes's dualism concerning where the soul/no-soul line is drawn, they do share two important features. First, like Descartes's mind-body dualism, Driesch's vitalism runs into the problem of how an immaterial, vital entity could direct the physical processes of a living organism without being a physical entity itself. Second, both theories were inspired by the phenomenon of apparently purposeful, goal-driven life processes. Descartes saw such purpose only in the willful action of human beings; Driesch recognized it even in the development of a sea urchin egg that successfully overcame the disturbance of being divided into two parts by developing into two complete organisms. Neither man saw how such purposeful, goal-directed behavior could be accounted for mechanically and so had to reach outside the physical sciences to search for a spiritualist explanation.

Getting Extremely Physical: Materialist Philosophies of Behavior

Although dualist views of behavior are problematic on several counts, forms of dualism are surely the most widely held views of behavior today. Dualism is also an integral part of the world's major religions, which all make distinctions between body and soul, flesh and spirit. But many individuals throughout history, including most philosophers and scientists today, see no need to go beyond physics and chemistry to explain behavior. In contrast to both psychic and dualist theories, such materialist theories attempt to explain the behavior of objects and organisms using only physical explanations based on matter, energy, and their interactions, rejecting all immaterial entities and forces. According to materialism, "there are no incorporeal souls or spirits, no spiritual principalities or powers, no angels or devils, no demiurges and no gods (if these are conceived as immaterial entities). Hence, nothing that happens can be attributed to the action of such beings" (K. Campbell 1967, p. 179).

Ancient Materialists

Although the doctrine of materialism is often associated with modern science, materialism has a long history and has been in competition with psychic and dualist theories since at least the time of ancient Greek philosophers. Among classical Greek thinkers, Leucippus (fifth century B.C.) and his student Democritus are best known for the development of materialism. They were the first to come up with the notion of atomism, the belief that the universe consisted of nothing but bits of tiny, indivisible matter and empty space between them—atoms and void. For Leucippus and Democritus, all that happened in the universe was the result of the mechanical action of these atoms as they collided with and exerted pressure on each other, with all movement and changes due to the combination and separation of atoms. As is consistent with our current theory of the conservation of matter and energy, these pioneering materialists asserted that nothing can arise out of nothing, and nothing can be destroyed. Thus they excluded from their system all teleology of the type embraced by Plato and Aristotle.

Three other early Western philosophers who developed materialistic theories should also be mentioned. Empedocles (fifth century B.C.) divided all matter into the four elements of earth, wind, water, and fire, a system that was also used by Aristotle. Epicurus (342–270 B.C.) saw all motion and objects as the result of an infinite number of atoms falling through infinite space during unlimited time, with resulting collisions leading eventually to every possible arrangement of atoms, including those in living organisms. Lucretius (c. 99–55 B.C.) was the only notable Roman to expound a materialist theory of behavior. These last two thinkers were similar in wanting to liberate people from religious anxieties and so argued with vigor against an immaterial soul and for the mortality of human existence.

Materialists of the Seventeenth Century and Later

Due to renewed popularity of Aristotle's philosophy and the power of the Roman Catholic Church, materialism did not form an important part of European thought until the Renaissance of the seventeenth century. One person who helped to bring about its revival was the well-known English philosopher Thomas Hobbes (1588–1679).

Influenced by the physics of Galileo (whom Hobbes met during a visit to Italy in 1636) and the notion of inertia, according to which objects in motion tend to stay in motion, Hobbes attempted to provide a purely materialist, mechanistic account of human sensation and behavior. Like other materialist theorists we have encountered, he understood all change in the universe as the result of physical bodies in motion and all movement as caused by contact of one moving body with another. He also considered the human body to be a complicated machine as did Descartes, although devoid of Descartes's immaterial soul.

But unlike classical materialists, Hobbes rejected the idea of empty space, believing instead that all space was filled with an intangible material substance. Accordingly, he rejected all notions of souls, angels, and a purely spiritual God, but instead saw God as making up the physical matter that filled what only appeared to be empty space.

A bit later on the European continent, French physician and philosopher Julien Offroy de La Mettrie (1709–1751) was promoting materialist ideas (and getting into trouble for doing so, such as being exiled in Holland). After a bout of serious illness during which La Mettrie experienced his mental powers declining along with his physical health, he became convinced that thought is nothing but the physical functioning of the brain and nervous system. His books *L'histoire naturelle de l'âme* (*The Natural History of the Mind*) and *L'homme machine* (*Man the Machine*) described humans as self-energized machines whose body parts functioned in purely mechanical ways. He also explained perception and learning as the results of changes in the brain, a concept that although wrong in its specific details is similar to the modern view of the essential relationship among brain, mind, and behavior. By showing that muscles and bodily organs could continue to function when removed from a living body, La Mettrie believed he had demonstrated that a soul was not necessary for life. But in contrast to Descartes's passive, purely reactive view of the functioning of animal and human bodies, La Mettrie conceived of the living body "as a purposively self-moving and self-sufficient system, consisting of dynamically interrelated parts" (Popkin 1967, p. 381).

In the *Système de la nature* published in 1770 by German-born Frenchman Paul Heinrich Dietrich d'Holbach (1723–1789), we find a well-developed and thoroughly atheistic materialism. Holbach saw all events in the universe as the result of the redistribution of matter and its energy. Human behavior, which might appear spontaneous and uncaused by physical forces, was for him the result of motion already existing within the body. He also explained emotional feelings and personality as dependent on arrangements of internal states of matter and explained behavior that appeared to be based on free will as the result of spontaneous modifications of the brain.

Progress in science, notably in physics, chemistry, and biology from the seventeenth century to the present day, has done much to make materialism more appealing and respectable. The influence of Galileo on the materialism of Thomas Hobbes has been noted. But it was the remarkable breakthrough in physics achieved by Sir Isaac Newton that had the most significant and lasting effect on these theories. Newton's grand achievement was a precise, mathematical understanding of the motion of bodies through space.

Kepler had derived laws of motion for the planets, and Galileo had developed laws describing the motions of bodies on earth. Newton's system of three laws (described in chapter 1) was more general than either and applicable to all objects, terrestrial and celestial. In Newton's system, all physical objects are fundamentally inert and can only move or change as a reaction to outside forces such as gravity, or by coming into contact with another moving object. This is very unlike Aristotle's teleological system of physics in which, for example, a heavy object falls toward the center of the earth not because of the influence of an external force but rather because of the object's own goal to be as near the center of the earth as possible. By convincing scientists that the behavior of all physical bodies could be understood as quantifiable reactions to external forces, Newton had an enormous impact on science, philosophy, and even psychology.

But whereas the success of Newton's mechanics eliminated the full-time job that angels had of pushing the planets around the sun, Newton himself did not believe his laws of physics completely eliminated the need for God. Instead, God was still required to prevent the stars from collapsing into one giant heap of mass under the force of gravity and to maintain the regular motion of the planets that would otherwise be disrupted by gravitational attraction as they passed close to each other in their orbits around the sun. Thus he maintained a decidedly dualist philosophy of the universe.

The same could not be said for French astronomer and mathematician Pierre Simon de Laplace (1749–1827). One of the advantages Laplace had over Newton was the improved calculus developed by his colleagues, especially that of Italian-French mathematician Joseph Louis de Lagrange (1736–1813). With this tool in hand, Laplace went about polishing up Newton's system of mechanics, eliminating from it all known problems and anomalies, such as the varying speeds of Saturn and Jupiter. He was therefore convinced that no divine intervention was necessary to maintain the observed regular motion of the planets. His confidence in the adequacy of a purely mechanical and deterministic account of the motions of objects was such that when Napoleon questioned him about the absence of God from his theory, Laplace confidently replied that he had no need of that hypothesis!

To illustrate the power of his new and improved Newtonian mechanics, Laplace proposed a thought experiment involving superhuman intelligence that knew the position of every particle of matter in the universe and all the forces currently acting on each of them. To a being with this knowledge of initial conditions, together with the now-understood laws of motion, "nothing would be uncertain and the future as the past, would be present to its eyes" (Laplace 1814/1902, p. 4).

Laplace's materialist theory of the universe's behavior, based entirely on the idea of moving particles of matter interacting with each other, is clearly reminiscent of the classical materialist views of Leucippus, Democritus, Empedocles, Epicurus, and Lucretius. But one important difference is that he had mathematics and empirical results to back up his claim, at least with respect to the regular behavior of inanimate matter such as the motion of planets around the sun. And although it is less clear that even improved Newtonian mechanics could do much to explain the more complex behavior of living organisms, we will see that the one-way cause-effect perspective was eventually to become—and remains—the principal model on which psychological theories of animal and human behavior are founded.

The world today is divided along many lines. One of the most obvious is the line dividing the wealthy, industrialized countries of Europe, North America, and Oceania from the poorer, less industrialized countries of much of the rest of the world. Perhaps less obvious, but just as striking, is the line separating materialist (physical, natural) methodologies and beliefs of science and scientists from overwhelmingly psychic (spiritual, supernatural) or dualist methodologies and beliefs of the rest of the world's human population. While science is now thoroughly materialistic in orientation and methodology, most individuals doubt that life, its origin, its meaning, and its experiences can be accounted for by physical properties of matter, energy, and their interaction, and hence believe in a God or gods, spirits, angels, paranormal happenings, and other supernatural entities and phenomena. In the next chapter we will see that there is good reason to doubt the adequacy of widely held materialist explanations of animate behavior.

3

Psychological Perspectives on Behavior: From Purposeful to Purposeless

From a purposeful perspective on behavior . . .

The pursuance of future ends and the choice of means for their attainment are thus the mark and criterion of the presence of mentality *in a phenomenon. We all use this test to discriminate between an intelligent and a mechanical performance. We impute no mentality to sticks and stones, because they never seem to move for the sake of anything, but always when pushed, and then indifferently and with no sign of choice. So we unhesitatingly call them senseless.*
—William James (1980, p. 8)

. . . to a purposeless one (one hundred years later) . . .

It is possible to step back and treat the mind as one big monster response function from the total environment over the total past of the organism to future actions.
—Allen Newell (1990, p. 44)

In moving from philosophical to psychological perspectives on behavior, we should first consider what distinguishes them from each other. Both are concerned with many of the same issues, such as the nature of perception, thought, and consciousness; what and how we are able to learn from our environment; and the underlying causes of behavior. So it is not so much their contents that differentiates the two disciplines as their methodologies. Philosophy relies primarily on verbal reasoning, logic, and sometimes mathematics to understand the world, our perception of it, and our actions within it; psychology for the most part claims to be an empirical science based on data derived from both laboratory-based and naturally occurring data.

Wundt's Voluntaristic Psychology

It is fitting that Wilhelm Wundt (1832–1920), who founded in Leipzig the first laboratory for experimental psychology in 1879, is widely considered to be the father of psychology. Wundt believed that psychology, like the older and respected science of physics, should rely on experimental methods to test and refine its theories. But Wundt saw the domain of "raw," immediate human experience, comprising both feelings and sensory perceptions unmodified by reflection or abstraction, as the primary subject matter of psychology. Relying on introspective reports of trained subjects who would report their experiences to controlled stimuli such as a ticking metronome, Wundt attempted to understand human psychological experience by relating it to its basic elements, an approach that has been described as a type of mental chemistry. As part of this project, he developed his tridimensional theory of affect, by which all emotions can be classified according to the three dimensions of pleasantness-unpleasantness, strain-relaxation, and excitement-calm.

Wundt held that a careful analysis of immediate experience would reveal to the psychologist the basic properties of the human mind, including its lawful changes from one state to another, a principle he referred to as "psychic causality." But whereas he made a distinction between psychic and physical causality, he nevertheless recognized the psychological importance of the physical function of the brain and nervous system, stating that "there is no psychical process, from the simplest sensation and affective elements to the most complex thought-processes, which does not run parallel with a physical process" (1912, p. 186). Wundt's contrasting of psychic and physical processes might make him appear to be a mind-body dualist, which indeed is the usual description of him in psychology textbooks. But that is not an accurate characterization. Instead, he maintained that there were both psychological and physical aspects to thought, perception, and animate behavior, and both had to be studied in order to understand the underlying phenomena (see Blumenthal 1988, p. 196).

Still, he felt that there were serious limitations in restricting oneself to physical approaches to studying animate behavior:

Wundt acknowledged . . . the theoretical possibility of reducing psychological observations to physiological or physical descriptions. Still, he argued, these physical sciences would then describe the act of greeting a friend, eating an apple, or writing a poem in terms of the laws of mechanics or in terms of physiology. And no matter how fine-grained and complicated we make such descriptions, they are not useful as descriptions of psychological events. Those events need be described in terms of intentions and goals, according to Wundt, because the actions, or physical forces, for a given psychological event may take an infinite variety of physical forms (Blumenthal 1988, p. 198).

We see here that he recognized the importance of purpose in understanding animate behavior and that many different behaviors can be effective in achieving the same goal. Indeed, the notion of purposeful animate behavior played such a central role in his psychology that he referred to his psychological theory as "voluntaristic," based on the Latin word *voluntas* meaning "will." For Wundt, such purposeful behavior required central control processes that were fundamentally different from mechanistic processes of physical causality.

William James: Varying Means to a Fixed End

At the end of the nineteenth century and beginning of the twentieth, no one had a greater influence on psychological theory in the United States than William James (1849–1910). James was (and still is) widely respected for his two-volume *Principles of Psychology* that took him twelve years to complete before being published in 1890.

In the opening chapter of the *Principles*, James took great pains to make what he considered to be an important distinction between the behavior of physical objects and that of living organisms. First, he described the behavior of iron filings in the presence of a magnet and the behavior of air bubbles blown into the bottom of a pail filled with water. We observe the filings "fly through the air for a certain distance to stick to its [the magnet's] surface" and the air bubbles "rise to the surface and mingle with the air" (1890, p. 4). But if obstacles are introduced, such as a card placed on the magnet or a water-filled jar inverted over the bubbles, neither the filings nor the bubbles will end up as before. Instead, now the filings will stick to the intervening card and the bubbles will remain trapped inside the jar.

James went on to contrast the behavior of the iron filings with that of Romeo in the presence of Juliet and the behavior of the bubbles with that of a frog, and showed how living organisms can circumvent such obstacles, achieving their goals in spite of disturbances.

Romeo wants Juliet as the filings want the magnet; and if no obstacles intervene he moves towards her by as straight a line as they. But Romeo and Juliet, if a wall be built between them, do not remain idiotically pressing their faces against its opposite sides like the magnet and the filings with the card. Romeo soon finds a circuitous way, by scaling the wall or otherwise, of touching Juliet's lips directly. With the filings the path is fixed; whether it reaches the end depends on accidents. With the lover it is the end which is fixed, the path may be modified indefinitely.

Similarly, the frog will not, like the bubbles,

perpetually press his nose against its [the jar's] unyielding roof, but will restlessly explore the neighborhood until by re-descending again he has discovered a path around its brim to the goal of his desires. Again the fixed end, the varying means! (1890, p. 4)

Thus living things distinguished themselves from nonliving objects in their purposeful behavior and intelligence in obtaining fixed goals by varying their actions. A nonliving thing showed only "a mechanical performance" and naturally "we impute no mentality to sticks and stones, because they never seem to move for *the sake of* anything, but always when pushed, and then indifferently and with no sign of choice" (1890, p. 5).

It would seem that James was a soul-body dualist in dismissing the possibility that the apparently purposeful behavior of living organisms could have mechanical explanations. But he also considered mental phenomena and the behavior of humans and animals to be aspects of the same natural world in which we find nonliving objects. So in keeping with the provisional and undogmatic character of his treatment of complex and controversial topics, he admitted that brain and mind "hang indubitably together and determine each other's being, but how or why, no mortal may ever know" (1898, p. 119).

The Rise of Behaviorism

In addition to the immediate impact that James's *Principles* had on psychological thought, other events in Russia and the United States a short time later had an even greater influence on the growth of the still-young field of psychology, leading to the rise of what eventually became known as *behaviorism*.

In St. Petersburg, physiologist Ivan Pavlov (1849–1936) was studying the digestive system of dogs in the 1890s when he and his assistants noticed a curious phenomenon. The animals would secrete gastric juices not only when food was placed in their mouths but also at the mere sight of food and even at the sight of anyone who regularly fed them. Pavlov explained this change in behavior (now known as Pavlovian, classical, or respondent conditioning) as modification of a stimulus-response reflex. This involved linking a new stimulus (for example, the sound of a bell that regularly preceded the introduction of food into a dog's mouth) to an old response (in this case, salivation).

It is interesting to note that Pavlov's student, Anton Snarsky, who had done the original research on Pavlovian conditioning, attempted to explain this change in behavior by appealing to the dog's higher mental processes involving feelings, expectations, and thoughts. But Pavlov rejected this interpretation, wishing to remain "in the role of a pure physiologist, that is, an objective observer and experimenter" (quoted in Boakes 1984, p. 121). He therefore rejected all mentalistic interpretations, preferring to consider all animate behavior as the result of one-way stimulus-response reflexes, and all changes in animate behavior as the result of environmentally caused modifications of these reflexes.

While Pavlov restricted his research to dogs, American psychologist John B. Watson (1878–1958) applied Pavlov's theory to both animals and humans. In an influential paper published in 1913 entitled "Psychology as the Behaviorist Views It," Watson criticized the method of introspection used by Wundt and his followers, and declared that psychology should abandon all study of consciousness and mental processes, and be concerned only with publicly observable behavior and its causes. He even went so far as to hold that thinking was actually a form of silent speech that involved tiny, imperceptible movements of the larynx.

Pavlov and Watson explained animal and human behavior as the functioning of stimulus-response reflexes and learning as the pairing of new stimuli with old behaviors. Edward Thorndike (1878–1949), however, was interested in understanding how new behaviors were learned and spent considerable time observing how animals such as dogs and cats managed to escape from a box that required a new action, such as pulling on a loop of string, to open the door. Based on this and other animal research, Thorndike concluded that all learning in all animals (including humans) followed certain fundamental laws. The most well-known of these is his law of effect, stating that behaviors that are followed by "satisfaction to the animal" will most likely recur, while actions followed by "discomfort to the animal" will be less likely to recur.

Thorndike was the first psychologist to propose that all new learned behavior results from the selective reinforcement of random responses. It was fellow American B. F. Skinner (1904–1990) who made behaviorism widely known among both psychologists and the larger public in the second half of the twentieth century. Skinner called such learning "operant conditioning" since it involved organisms learning new ways of operating on their environments. Like Thorndike, he saw such new, useful behaviors as resulting from the reinforcement of those actions that were followed by a rewarding consequence. So, for example, if a hungry rat's push of a lever resulted in the delivery of a food pellet, the rat would soon learn to push the lever repeatedly. In addition to his extensive technical research on animal learning, Skinner, who had originally intended to be a novelist, wrote several popular books about behaviorism and its application to social and educational problems (1948, 1971, 1974). Skinner's name remains most firmly connected to the theory of *radical behaviorism*, a perspective that denies a causal role to internal mental states, purposes, and thought processes, and instead sees animate behavior and all changes in animate behavior as determined by the environmental consequences of actions.

It is important to realize that Skinner did not deny that human thinking and consciousness existed. But, like Watson, he did not see how such mental phenomena could offer any useful explanation of animate behavior, stating that "behavior which seemed to be the product of mental activity could be explained in other ways" (1954, p. 81). And consistent with his stimulus-response view of learned behavior, he denied that motives, desires, or purposes could provide an explanatory account for animal or human behavior. He argued instead that "a person disposed to act because he has been reinforced for acting may feel the condition of his body at such time and call it 'felt purpose,' but what behaviorism rejects is the causal efficacy of that feeling" (1957, p. 224).

Behaviorism can be seen as a bold attempt to make the study of animal and human behavior as objective and as scientific as the physical sciences.

It was reasoned that since behavioral scientists cannot have objective access to the subjective experiences of another animal or person, such mental states must be omitted from study. Instead, what could be studied objectively were overt behaviors of organisms and environmental factors that caused them. As described by Gardner (1987, pp. 11–12):

A strong component of the behaviorist canon was the belief in the supremacy and determining power of the environment. Rather than individuals acting as they do because of their own ideas and intentions, or because their cognitive apparatuses embody certain autonomous structuring tendencies, individuals were seen as passive reflectors of various forces and factors in their environment. . . . It was believed that the science of animate behavior, as fashioned by such scholars as Ivan Pavlov, B. F. Skinner, E. L. Thorndike, and J. B. Watson, could account for anything an individual might do, as well as the circumstances under which one might do it. (What one thinks was considered irrelevant from this perspective—unless thought was simply redefined as covert behavior.) Just as mechanics had explained the laws of the physical world, mechanistic models built on the reflex arc could explain human activity.

In other words, the behaviorist approach could be characterized as an attempt to extend Newton's one-way cause-effect mechanics to living organisms. From this perspective, animate behavior is not autonomous or purposeful in any way but is composed of mechanically determined reactions to physical forces, with the reflex arc as a type of connecting rod between environmental inputs (causes or stimuli) and consequent behavioral outputs (effects or responses).

Such a characterization may be an accurate description of Pavlov's and Watson's classical conditioning in which one stimulus (such as the sound of a bell) becomes substituted for another (such as food). But it does not do complete justice to Thorndike's and Skinner's view of learning in which new, adapted behaviors are acquired. For an animal to learn a new response, behaviors that have not occurred before must occur spontaneously. These random behaviors, as shown by cats and dogs in Thorndike's puzzle boxes, and rats and pigeons in Skinner boxes, are not reactions to environmental stimuli but are rather emitted by an active organism seeking food, water, or escape from an unpleasant situation. So an essential component of Thorndike's law of effect and Skinner's operant conditioning is behavior that is essentially *uncaused* by the environment. In this way this view of animate behavior departs from a one-way cause-effect model.

But whereas operant conditioning requires such spontaneous, random behavior, this does not make it any less mechanistic or more purposeful for the behaviorists. Although neither Thorndike nor Skinner speculated on the precise cause of such emitted behavior, it could be readily accounted for by some type of random behavior-generator within the organism that performed the equivalent of tossing a die or selecting a value from a table of random numbers and acting on the result. Nonetheless, for both men the environmental consequences of a random action—for example, the degree to which it was successful in obtaining food for a hungry animal—determined the likelihood that such an action would be repeated in similar circumstances. So Gardner is essentially correct in the quotation concerning behaviorists' "belief in the supremacy and determining power of the environment." Living organisms, unlike inanimate pieces of matter, emit spontaneous behaviors uncaused by their physical environment, and it is from this repertoire that some behaviors are selected. But the environment nonetheless determines the behavior that is learned during this process in much the same way that environmental factors determine the motions of nonliving objects.

Skinner saw a striking analogy between his theory of operant learning and the theory of natural selection for biological evolution, remarking that "in certain respects operant reinforcement resembles the natural selection of evolutionary theory. Just as the genetic characteristics which arise as mutations are selected or discarded by their consequences, so novel forms of behavior are selected or discarded through reinforcement" (1953, p. 430). In the same way that Darwin's materialist and mindless theory of natural selection replaced a purposeful God in providing a scientific explanation for the evolution of species, Skinner considered the mechanical and mindless selection of animate behavior by the environment to be a replacement for the notions of mind and purpose operating at the level of individual organisms. We will return to his theory of learning and its curious mix of Newtonian and Darwinian causality in chapters 7 and 11.

Tolman's "Purposeful Behaviorism"

Skinner and the earlier behaviorists removed all consideration of mind and purpose from their analysis of animal and human behavior. This was possible, however, only by ignoring what Wundt and James had earlier emphasized—that animate behavior often varies markedly while its consequences remain constant. A rat does not take the exact same steps every time it runs through a maze, nor does it push a lever exactly the same way each time to obtain food. Neither does a man move the steering wheel of his car exactly the same way each time he drives from home to work. Skinner showed that he was aware of this phenomenon by defining the term "operant" as a class of animate behaviors that all had the same effect on the environment. But he provided no explanation as to how reinforcing individual actions could serve as a reinforcement for the infinity of actions not performed that also produced the same environmental effects. For example, if individual actions are selected by their consequences, how would reinforcing a rat with food for pushing a lever with its right paw lead it subsequently to push the same lever with its left paw or with its nose?

Edward C. Tolman (1886–1959) identified this problem in Skinner's behaviorism and recognized the goal-directed nature of animate behavior. He made a distinction between what he called *molar* and *molecular* descriptions of animate behavior. A molar description referred to the consequences of the behavior, and a molecular description referred to the specific muscular and limb movements performed by the organism. As examples of molar descriptions of behavior he offered (1932, p. 8)

a rat running a maze; a cat getting out of a puzzle box; a man driving home to dinner; a child hiding from a stranger; . . . my friend and I telling one another our thoughts and feelings—*these are behaviors* (qua *molar*). And it must be noted that in mentioning no one of them have we referred to or, we blush to confess it, for the most part even know, what were the exact muscles and glands, sensory nerves, and motor nerves involved.

To demonstrate that rats do not learn specific, fixed responses when learning new tasks, Tolman and his associates at the University of California in Berkeley conducted a number of ingenious and influential experiments from the 1920s to 1950s. Among the best-known was one conducted by Tolman's student D. A. Macfarlane in which rats learned to swim through a maze to obtain a food reward (see Tolman 1932, pp. 79–80; Boakes 1984, p. 232). After they had learned to do this well, a raised floor was installed in the maze so that the rats now had to wade through the maze to get to the box containing the food. It was hypothesized that if the rats' learning consisted of acquiring specific swimming behaviors (that is, specific responses to specific stimuli), they would have to relearn the maze in the wading condition, as the movements and stimuli involved in wading are very different from those involved in swimming. It was found instead that after a very brief period of adjustment to the new situation (just one run through the maze), the rats performed as well in the wading condition as they had in the swimming condition. This was a clear demonstration that what the rats learned while swimming the maze could not be described as the formation of stimulus-response connections. Rather, the acquisition of a more abstract form of knowledge about the location of the goal box and how to get there was involved, since it made no difference to the rats whether they swam or waded to their destination. Similarly, once a person knows how to reach a specific location by driving a car, he can also go there by bicycle (if he knows how to ride one) or by walking (if it is not too far). The destination can be reached despite the fact that stimuli and responses differ greatly from one mode of transportation to another.

But in spite of these findings and many others like them, Tolman was never able to eliminate the concept of stimulus-response connections from the very core of his theory of purposeful behavior. Indeed, his attempt to explain how animate behavior can vary and yet reach a consistent goal involves imagining long, complicated chains of such connections existing within the organism in the form of intervening variables, and conceiving of responses not as specific muscular contractions but rather as a "performance." With respect to the latter, Tolman wrote (1959, p. 100):

It is to be stressed . . . that for me the type of response I am interested in is always to be identified as a pattern of *organism-environment rearrangements* and not as a detailed set of muscular or glandular activities. These latter may vary from trial to trial and yet the total "performance" remains the same. Thus, for example, "going towards a light" is a *performance* in my sense of the term and is not properly a response (a set of muscular contractions).

But substituting the word "performance" for "response" does nothing to explain how an organism is able to accomplish a repeatable "organism-environment rearrangement" by responding to stimuli; it simply states that it somehow happens. If "behavior may vary from trial to trial and yet the total 'performance' remains the same," how is it that the organism is able continually to adjust its behavior to arrive at a desired goal?

Tolman made an important initial step toward solving this problem in his realization that sensory feedback was important; that is, the rat's behavior changed the stimuli it perceived and this feedback was essential in guiding the organism toward its final goal (1959, p. 103). But he never provided an explicit model for how such a system could work, so he never managed to break free of the behaviorist tradition of regarding stimuli as causes of animate behavior.

Hebb's Bridge from Behaviorism to Cognitive Psychology

Another important and influential North American psychologist who attempted to overcome the shortcomings of behaviorism was Donald O. Hebb (1904–1985) of McGill University in Montreal. Hebb was particularly interested in applying newly discovered principles of brain functioning to understand better how the brains of humans and animals worked to influence behavior. Watson and Skinner considered the brain as a type of black box whose inner workings were both invisible and irrelevant for understanding animal and human behavior. In contrast, Hebb dared to try to peer inside the brain and was convinced that it was only by understanding details of the brain's operations that animal and human behavior could be explained. He called his brain-based approach to animate behavior "neuropsychology."

He saw animal and human behaviors as varying along a continuum with respect to the amount and type of brain processes involved in the behavior. At one end of this continuum were behaviors that appeared to involve automatic, rapid reactions to stimuli, such as the startle response to a loud, unexpected sound, or withdrawing a hand from a hot surface. At the other end of the continuum were behaviors requiring a great deal of brain, or cognitive, processes between stimulus and response, such as finding the answer to a complex problem in mathematics or making a difficult decision. Since these brain processes occurred between stimulus and response, he referred to them as "mediating processes" in which thought, ideas, and images were involved. Toward the middle of this reflex-cognitive continuum were activities that were more than automatic responses to stimuli but did not require a great deal of mental activity, such as easy arithmetic tasks.

Hebb was thus able to build a bridge between the stimulus-response behaviorist psychology that was beginning to wane in the second half of the twentieth century and the "cognitive revolution" that was gaining momentum. In addition, he considered the neural mechanisms by which such cognitive processes could work. The behaviorists' conception of the brain was that of a one-way telephone switchboard that directly connected incoming stimuli to outgoing responses (with learning being a modification of these direct connections based on experience). Hebb instead imagined more complex brain processes that could account for cognitive processes such as thought, motivation, and attention (1949, 1972). In so doing he replaced the stimulus-response model of behaviorism with what has been described as a stimulus-organism-response model of animate behavior.

Hebb's major contribution in this regard was his theory of the "cell assembly," a group of brain cells (neurons) that formed a closed circuit in the brain and could remain active for quite some time after an initial stimulus by a type of nervous reverberation. These reverberations, which he believed were the basis of all higher cognitive processes, mediated or intervened between incoming sensory information and outgoing motor responses. An example he used involved presenting a schoolboy with the words "please add" followed five seconds later by the words "four, seven" (1972, pp. 85–86). The schoolboy's response of "eleven" is evidence that the initial stimulus of "please add" was somehow being kept active in the brain until the words "four, seven" were heard. Even though there was no immediate response to the initial words, they influenced behavior regarding the words subsequently heard and thus mediated the response to the numbers (the response would have been different if the instructions "please subtract" had been given instead). Thus all cognition could be understood as such mediating brain processes between stimulus and response.

This neuropsychological-based stimulus-organism-response account of animate behavior had important advantages over the direct stimulus-response theories of the behaviorists, but it still encountered difficulties in accounting for voluntary and purposeful animate behavior. This is because animate behavior was still ultimately determined by sensory stimulation, either directly (as in reflexes) or through mediating cognitive processes involving the reverberation of circular neuronal circuits in the brain. As Hebb put it (1972, p. 84):

The typical problem of higher behavior arises when there is a delay between stimulus and response. What bridges the S-R gap? In everyday language, "thinking" does it: the stimulus gives rise to thoughts or ideas that continue during the delay period, and then cause the response.

But if "higher behavior" involves stimuli eliciting thoughts with thoughts in turn causing responses, how can this mechanistic, one-way cause-effect system account for the goal-directed nature of animate behavior in which behavior varies as it must to produce a consistent outcome? If, as Hebb believed, "all behavior is under sensory guidance, through the switchboard of the central nervous system" (1972, p. 92), it would appear that animate behavior could not be any more purposeful or voluntary than the behavior of wind-blown clouds or falling drops of rain.

The Cognitive Science Approach to Behavior

Hebb recognized the mechanistic implications of his neuropsychological theory of animate behavior and consequently dismissed the notions of will and voluntary behavior, stating that "in modern psychology the terms 'volition' and 'will' or 'will power' have disappeared" (1972, p. 92). He could have easily added "purpose" to his list. Although cognitive psychology in the 1980s and 1990s developed in ways that he could not have foreseen, it has remained purely materialistic and for the most part continues to see animal and human behavior as the mechanical product of sensory stimulation processed by a brain that consequently produces behavioral outputs.

As mentioned, behaviorists thought the brain was analogous to a telephone switchboard that permitted only direct one-way connections between stimuli and their corresponding responses. To this switchboard Hebb added reverberating groups of neurons that he called "cell assemblies." Cognitive scientists of the second half of the twentieth century replaced the switchboard theory with one based on the digital computer, and used these electronic machines to attempt to simulate animal and human brains and the behavior they produce.

But a particularly intriguing development occurred around the middle of the twentieth century that promised to provide what had until then appeared unimaginable—a completely materialist, mechanistic model of purposeful animate behavior. In a 1943 paper with the title "Behavior, Teleology, and Purpose," Arturo Rosenblueth, Norbert Wiener, and Julian Bigelow proposed that machines designed in a certain way could demonstrate goal-directed behavior. It seemed that during the early decades of the twentieth century, while psychologists were not paying attention, engineers found a way to build machines called "control systems" that, like Shakespeare's Romeo and James's frogs, could vary their behavior as necessary to produce consistent outcomes.

We will save for the next chapter a more detailed account of the revolution begun by Rosenblueth, Wiener, and Bigelow. But it should be pointed out here that this new approach to understanding animate behavior constituted the first real break with the one-way cause-effect view that was a part of all previous theories. Instead of seeing external events as causes for animate behaviors, this new "cybernetic" approach recognized that the behavior of a living organism (or that of a machine designed as a control system) has an effect on its environment. Therefore its behavior must also affect what it senses or perceives of this environment. So instead of a one-way behaviorist stimulus-response, or a one-way cognitive stimulus-computation-response conception, cybernetics closed the loop by connecting response back to stimulus while maintaining the normal Newtonian cause-effect relationships for components within the overall system. But if it is the case that response influences stimulus and stimulus influences response, one can no longer speak of independent external causes for animate behavior. This is because the one-way causal chain has been turned into a closed loop in which stimulus and response both *cause* and *are caused by* each other. The familiar one-way, push-pull, cause-effect model inherited from Newton, in which an independent environmental stimulus causes a dependent behavior, was for the first time replaced by something quite different, a theory of animate behavior based on a closed loop exhibiting *circular causality*.

A number of other pioneering cognitive scientists were influenced by cybernetics (see Miller, Galanter, & Pribram 1960); however, this new field and its radically different view unfortunately had little lasting impact on behavioral and cognitive science. With few exceptions, behavioral scientists working in the last decades of the twentieth century stuck with the familiar one-way cause-effect approach.

This is not to say that important recent advances have not been made in understanding the brain, cognitive processes, and their roles in animal and human behavior. But the dominant view in behavioral and cognitive sciences remains consistent with—and seriously limited by—the input-output, stimulus-organism-response model developed by Hebb in the 1950s in which animate behavior remains dependent on past and present environmental influences. "Cognitive psychology comes in various forms, but all share an abiding interest in describing the mental structures and processes that link environmental stimuli to organismic responses . . ." (Kihlstrom 1987, p. 1445).

Conclusion to Part I: Embracing Materialism, Spurning Purpose

It is obviously not possible to provide a comprehensive account of 2500 years of human thought on inanimate and animate behavior in just two book chapters. But this summary does indicate two important trends.

The first trend is movement away from immaterial, psychic theories of behavior to materialist, physical ones. The animism of early nontechnological societies, including the panpsychic physics of Plato and Aristotle, gradually gave way to the materialist physics of Newton and Laplace that remains with us. And what is true for physics is also true of psychology, a discipline that became thoroughly and unashamedly materialist in both its behaviorist and cognitive versions in the twentieth century.

The second trend is movement away from a conception of behavior as goal-directed toward a view of it as being essentially purposeless. For the behavior of inanimate objects this is linked to the trend from psychic to materialist theories in physics. Whereas Plato and Aristotle shared a goal-directed view of the universe, Newton, Laplace, and their successors were able to purge all notions of purpose from the behavior of nonliving objects and systems. Concerning animate behavior, Wundt's voluntaristic psychology and James's emphasis on purposefulness were replaced by twentieth-century theories of purposeless animate behavior by psychologists, whether they be in the behaviorist or cognitive camp.

The result of these two long-term trends is that today mainstream philosophical and psychological theories of both inanimate and animate behavior are thoroughly materialist and overwhelmingly purposeless in orientation. One could make a strong argument that the popularity of materialism is justified by the success of our modern, materialist science that discovered physical mechanisms and forces underlying a broad range of phenomena—from sickness to supernovas—that could previously be understood only as actions of gods or angels or other forms of spirits and ghosts. Newton's physics relieved angels from their full-time jobs of pushing the planets around in their orbits and required only an occasional helpful shove from God himself; Laplace's improved mechanics did away with God completely. Even more amazing was Darwin's audacity and success a century later in accounting for the diversity and complexity of living organisms without God's help. Some scientists continue to include God or other spiritual entities in their science, but they constitute a small minority whose work is excluded from mainstream scientific journals.

But does a thoroughly materialist view of the universe necessarily lead to a purposeless view of all its behavior as well? One reason that this might appear to be the case has to do with a conception that requires purposeful behavior to be caused by a future event or state. In this view, if the purpose of rain is to allow trees, flowers, and grass to grow, the *future* growth of these plants would have to somehow influence the *present* actions of clouds and raindrops. According to our present conception of physics, effects cannot precede their causes, or causes follow their effects. So it may well be the case that attributing purpose to naturally occurring inanimate behavior is inconsistent with modern materialist science.

Can the same case against purposeful behavior be made for living organisms? Our everyday observations certainly suggest otherwise. What William James noticed in the behavior of Romeo and frogs—variable actions leading to consistent consequences—we see everyday in the behavior and achievements of animals and humans. Our experience as human beings—each with our own long-term financial, career, and family goals together with our more mundane daily trials against the unpredictable disturbances provided by traffic, illness, accidents, and often uncooperative family members and co-workers—makes it obvious that our behavior is goal directed and purposeful. This is the case even if such behavior can ultimately be reduced to the buzzing of neurons and the twitching of muscle fibers.

Fortunately, we do have a thoroughly materialist, physical explanation for the purposeful behavior of living organisms that does not involve spiritual agents or require that the future influence the present. Unfortunately, it is not widely known and appreciated by behavioral and cognitive scientists. Having its roots in nineteenth-century biology, we will see that in its modern and expanded form this theory provides a revolutionary framework for understanding the what, how, and why of animal and human behavior.

II

Purpose Without Spirit: From Constancy of the Internal Environment to Perceptual Control of the External Environment

4

A Biological Perspective on Purpose: The Physiology of Bernard and Cannon

We must therefore seek the true foundation of animal physics and chemistry in the physical-chemical properties of the inner environment. The life of an organism is simply the result of all its innermost workings. All of the vital mechanisms, however varied they may be, have always but one goal, to maintain the uniformity of the conditions of life in the internal environment.
—Claude Bernard (1878; quoted in Rahn 1979, p. 179).

Claude Bernard and the Internal Environment

The seven years from 1859 to 1865 are noteworthy for several revolutionary advances that took place in the life sciences. In 1859 Charles Darwin published *The Origin of Species* in which he convincingly argued for a common ancestor to all living organisms on earth and explained the great diversity of their forms as resulting from evolution by natural selection (the application of Darwin's insight to understanding behavior will be taken up in the next two chapters). From 1860 to 1865, French chemist Louis Pasteur (1822–1895) conducted a series of experiments that laid to rest the theory of spontaneous generation of life (showing, for example, that yeast and bacteria would not grow in decaying matter that had been sterilized and protected from exposure to air and dust) and laid the foundation for modern medicine with his germ theory of disease. In 1865 Austrian monk and pea gardener Gregor Mendel (1822–1884) discovered certain regularities of heredity that eventually led to the development of the fields of genetics and molecular biology. And also in 1865, Claude Bernard published his now classic *Introduction à l'étude de la medicine experimentale* (English translation 1927).

The contributions of Darwin, Pasteur, and Mendel are well known even among nonscientists. Bernard's name is much less familiar despite his numerous important contributions to our understanding of internal systems and their functioning, or physiology, of living organisms. Bernard's contributions include the following (Fruton 1975, p. 35):

1 The discovery of the role of the pancreatic secretion in the digestion of fats (1848)

2 The discovery of a new function of the liver—the "internal secretion" of glucose into the blood (1848)

3 Induction of diabetes by puncturing the floor of the fourth ventricle [of the brain] (1849)

4 The discovery of the elevation of local skin temperature on section of the cervical sympathetic nerve (1851)

5 Production of sugar by washed excised liver (1855) and the isolation of glycogen (1857)

6 The demonstration that curare specifically blocks motor nerve endings (1856)

7 The demonstration that carbon monoxide blocks the respiration of erythrocytes (1857)

It could be held, however, that Bernard's most important contribution to our understanding of the phenomenon of life is not included among any of these discoveries. Through his exhaustive research on internal systems of living organisms, Bernard came to understand that the function of physiological processes was to *regulate* or *control* the internal environment (*milieu intérieur*) of the organism. And he understood that this control, so essential to life, was achieved by normal laws of chemistry and physics, not by any special vitalist entities or processes.

As an example of control of the internal environment, let us consider the topic of the doctoral dissertation Bernard submitted in 1853. The countless living cells in a mammal's body require a continuous supply of food that must be present at all times in blood as glucose. If too little glucose is present, a condition known as hypoglycemia, the body's tissues will starve and, most important, the brain will no longer be able to function, leading to loss of consciousness and ultimately death. A very high concentration of glucose in blood, or hyperglycemia, is also dangerous since it may result in loss of consciousness and death, and less extreme hyperglycemia can cause thickening of capillaries and circulatory disease. So in healthy humans the level of blood sugar is maintained within quite narrow limits to 90 milligrams per 10 deciliters of blood. This control is maintained even if we go for many hours and even days without eating or if we instead stuff ourselves beyond reason over a few hours at a restaurant or holiday family meal.

How is this precise control of blood sugar level maintained? Bernard correctly identified the liver as a reservoir for glucose (where it is actually stored in a modified form known as glycogen), releasing it into the blood as necessary by the body's cells. He believed that the central nervous system played a direct role in the control of glucose levels, but we know today that the control center is located in the pancreas in clusters of cells called pancreatic islets or islets of Langerhans. Within these clusters are two types of cells, alpha and beta cells. Both have chemical sensors that are sensitive to the amount of glucose in the blood, but each has a different concern. Alpha cells become active when they detect blood glucose levels below 90 ml/10 dl and respond by producing glucagon, an enzyme whose principal effect is to stimulate the liver to release some of its store of glucose into the blood. Beta cells work in a complementary fashion, since they are sensitive to high levels of blood glucose and react by producing insulin, an enzyme that has the effect of removing glucose from blood. Through this complementary action of pancreatic alpha and beta cells, blood sugar level is controlled within narrow limits in spite of disturbances provided by fasting, eating, and physical activity. This vital control is conveniently accomplished automatically without awareness or conscious effort on our part.

Blood sugar is just one of the many aspects of our internal environment that must be closely controlled for the normal functioning of our cells. Other essential variables are body temperature, water and salt concentrations, oxygen and carbon dioxide levels, and acid-base balance. It is probably no coincidence that their control provides us with an internal liquid environment that in many respects is similar to the warm sea in which our first single-celled ancestors evolved. As Bernard wrote in 1878, the year of his death:

The living organism does not really exist in the *milieu extérieur* (the atmosphere, if it breathes air; salt, or fresh water, if that is its element), but in the liquid *milieu intérieur* formed by the circulating organic liquid which surrounds and bathes all the tissue elements; this is the lymph or plasma, the liquid part of the blood, which in the higher animals is diffused through the tissues and forms the ensemble of the intracellular liquids and is the basis for all local nutrition and the common factor of all elementary exchanges.

The *stability of the milieu intérieur* is the primary condition for freedom and independence of existence; the mechanism which allows of this is that which ensures in the *milieu intérieur* the maintenance of all the conditions necessary to the life of the elements (Bernard; quoted in Robin 1979, p. 258).

By "freedom and independence of existence," Bernard was not referring to metaphysical freedom of will. Rather he was describing the physical autonomy that allows organisms such as humans to survive in many different and often quite harsh environments despite the chemical and physical fragility of cells that make up our bodies. He saw this control of the inner environment as the primary distinguishing feature of life, what makes life possible and can be understood without recourse to vitalistic principles or phenomena.

It is intriguing to consider that although Bernard was an important proponent of a materialist view of life that made use of then-current knowledge of physics and chemistry, his conception of the organism as a regulator of its internal environment was in an important sense inconsistent with one-way cause-effect models of the physical sciences. If I pour sugar into a glass of water, the concentration of dissolved sugar in the water will increase. If I put a glass of cool water in the warm sun, the temperature of the water will rise. If I apply force to a chair by giving it a shove, it will either slide across the floor or fall over (depending on the amount of friction between chair and floor). These are all examples of the one-way, input-output causality of Newtonian physics in which a physical cause has a direct physical effect.

But Bernard pointed out that living organisms can and do react quite differently to such physical events. If I inject 200 milliliters of a 50% sugar solution into a vein in my arm, my blood sugar concentration may increase for a short while, but the activation of beta cells in my pancreas will soon produce enough insulin to restore my blood to its normal level of sugar. If I leave a cool room to sit in the warm sun (or vice versa), it will have little if any effect on my core body temperature (although the clothes I am wearing will slowly become warmer). And if I give another person a shove, it may well have no effect other than to have him stand his ground and shove me right back.

It seems as if the body actually "wants," "intends," "desires," or "wills" to maintain a certain concentration of blood sugar (90 mg/10 dl), temperature (98.6° F), and physical location (its current one). And it does what it has to to maintain these variables in spite of the types of physical disturbances that would have a noticeable effect on a nonliving object (for contrast, consider what effects these actions would have on a dead body). Although it would always be possible to apply a disturbance so large that the organism would lose control (such as a rapid intravenous injection of a liter of corn syrup, or an eight-hour stay in the sauna, or a shove from a bulldozer), control of important, life-sustaining variables is usually quite well maintained despite many typical disturbances we and other organisms continually confront.

In other words, although he did not describe it exactly this way, Bernard discovered that physiological systems are *purposeful and goal-directed*, designed to maintain constant conditions despite physical disturbances. In this sense, in their stubborn and active resistance, these systems were quite unlike anything that Newton or subsequent physicists had studied. Bernard's unprecedented knowledge of the materialist internal workings of organisms led to an appreciation that they functioned in a purposeful manner to maintain the physical conditions essential for life.

Walter Cannon and Homeostasis

It appears that Bernard's closest associates were much less impressed by this new understanding of the organism's control of its internal environment than they were by his experimental findings listed earlier. It was not until the twentieth century that this knowledge would be appreciated, expanded, and disseminated on the other side of the Atlantic, primarily by Walter Cannon (1871–1945) of Harvard University who, in his research on digestion, was the first to use X rays in the study of physiology. (Like Marie Curie, another pioneer in the use of X rays, Cannon's death was apparently due to the lethal accumulation of radiation he received while conducting his research.)

In his 1932 book *The Wisdom of the Body* (revised in 1939), Cannon published the results of his research team at Harvard's physiological laboratory on the functioning of many mammalian physiological systems, introducing a term that would become universally recognized in the field (1939, p. 24):

The constant conditions which are maintained in the body might be termed *equilibria*. That word, however, has come to have a fairly exact meaning as applied to relatively simple physico-chemical states, in closed systems, where known forces are balanced. The coordinated physiological processes which maintain most of the steady states in the organism are so complex and so peculiar to living beings—involving as they may, the brain and nerves, the heart, lungs, kidneys and spleen, all working cooperatively—that I have suggested a special designation for these states, *homeostasis*. The word does not imply something set and immobile, a stagnation. It means a condition—a condition which may vary, but which is relatively constant.

In addition to making the concept of homeostasis widely known and continuing the line of physiological research begun by Bernard, Cannon made other important theoretical contributions. One of these was the evolutionary perspective that he brought to homeostasis through which he saw the evolution of "advanced" or "higher" organisms as involving attainment of more sophisticated systems of control. He recognized the influence here of Belgian physiologist Léon Fredericq who in 1885 wrote:

The higher in the scale of living beings, the more numerous, the more perfect and the more complicated do these regulatory agencies become. They tend to free the organism completely from the unfavorable influences and change occurring in the environment.

Expanding on this idea and obviously influenced by Bernard as well, Cannon noted that "lower animals" such as the frogs can control neither the water content of their bodies nor their internal temperature and can therefore live only in and near water and at moderate temperatures. During cold winter months, a frog must burrow into the mud at the bottom of its pond or lake and remain there until warmer temperatures return. The "more highly evolved" lizard is able to control against loss of water and therefore can live in dry environments like deserts. But because reptiles are also unable to control their body temperature, they, like frogs, cannot remain active when the temperature falls. "Only among higher vertebrates, the birds and mammals, has there been acquired that freedom from the limitation imposed by cold that permits activity even though the rigors of winter may be severe" (Cannon 1939, p. 24). Evolutionary biologists usually refrain from using potentially misleading terms such as "lower," "higher," or "advanced" to compare organisms. Nonetheless, the notion that evolution can provide organisms with increasingly sophisticated control systems is an important insight to which we will return in a later chapter.

Cannon also understood that the mammalian nervous system was divided into two main parts, "one acting outwardly and affecting the world about us [today known as the somatic or 'voluntary' nervous system], and the other [the autonomic nervous system] acting inwardly and helping to preserve a constant and steady condition in the organism itself" (1939, pp. 25, 26). It is here that he appeared to come very close to recognizing that an organism's external actions, like its internal physiological ones, are also part of an essential process of control.

In retrospect, however, one can find serious limits to Cannon's understanding of the control achieved by biological systems. For instance, he provided no formal functional or mathematical analysis of the homeostatic systems he investigated, although he did implicitly recognize that such systems involved the functioning of a circle or loop. Notice, for example, how in the following sentence he begins and ends at the same place—the carbonic acid level of the blood (1939, p. 288):

If the hydrogen-ion concentration of the blood is altered ever so slightly towards the acid direction, the especially sensitive part of the nervous system which controls breathing is at once made active and by increased ventilation of the lungs carbonic acid is pumped out until the normal state is restored.

On the other hand, Cannon did not explicitly recognize or appear to appreciate the essentially non-Newtonian character of physiological control processes, as is evident in his one-way, cause-effect, push-pull account of body temperature regulation that makes no mention of an internally specified goal state or purpose (1939, pp. 200, 201).

If conditions are such that there is a tendency to tip the organism in one direction, a series of processes are at once set at work which oppose that tendency. And if an opposite tendency develops, another series of processes promptly oppose it. Thus quite automatically the remarkable uniformity of the temperature of the internal environment is preserved, in opposition to both internal and external disturbing conditions.

Nor did Cannon recognize that many mammalian physiological systems are not strictly homeostatic but rather are capable of achieving and maintaining themselves at different states according to changing needs. This phenomenon, called *rheostasis* (Mrosovsky 1990), is similar to changing the setting on a thermostat resulting in a cooler, though still controlled, room temperature. Despite these limitations, Cannon made a major contribution to understanding the body's "internal wisdom," and his concept of homeostasis eventually found its way into all modern physiology textbooks.

5

The Engineering of Purpose:
From Water Clocks to Cybernetics

He devoted himself to alchemy, in which he claims to have uncovered miraculous things, and inventions of wonderful furnaces, among them one that will maintain the fire at any degree of heat desired, whether hotter or colder.
—N. C. Fabri de Peiresc (1624; referring to Cornelis Drebbel's thermostatic furnace; translated in Mayr 1970, p. 56)

Let us consider a car following a man along a road with the clear purpose of running him down. What important difference will there be in our analysis of the behavior of the car if it is driven by a human being, or it is guided by the appropriate mechanical sense organs and mechanical controls?
—Arturo Rosenblueth & Norbert Wiener (1950, p. 319)

The Use and Understanding of Feedback Control

Although Bernard and Cannon recognized the self-regulatory nature of the living systems they studied, an explicit, formal understanding of such systems did not develop from this physiological research but rather had to await the attempts of engineers to make purposefully behaving machines using what is now called *feedback control.*

Devices making use of feedback control go back at least as far as the Hellenistic period (Mayr 1970). The first documented device was designed by Ktesibios, a barber and mechanic living in Alexandria during the third century B.C. when that north African city was the scientific and intellectual center of the world (Euclid, Archimedes, and Eratosthenes were just three of Ktesibios's fellow Alexandrians whose names students of astronomy and mathematics will recognize).

Ktesibios's water clock required a steady, unvarying flow of water to measure accurately the steady, unvarying flow of time. But because water flows more quickly from a full container and more slowly when it is less full, Ktesibios had to devise a way to keep the vessel at a constant level while water was flowing from it into the clock mechanism. As he did this in a manner not unlike that of the modern flush toilet to which it is assumed the reader has handy access, I will use this more modern invention instead of the water clock as our first example of a feedback-control device.

The modern flush toilet must have a certain amount of water on hand for each flush to be effective. For this purpose, most residential toilets make use of a holding tank into which water accumulates between flushes. Since too little water in the tank does not allow adequate flushing and too much is wasteful (it will simply flow out through an overflow drain), a mechanism is used to maintain the water at the desired level. This mechanism consists of a float resting on the surface of the water that is connected to a valve. When the water level falls after a flush, the float falls with it and in so doing opens a valve, admitting water into the tank. But as the tank fills and the water level rises, so does the float, eventually closing the valve so that the tank does not overfill.

For the reader who has not already peered inside a flush toilet tank, it is well worth lifting the lid and taking a look. With the tank lid off and the flush lever activated, one can observe in live action the events described: the tank empties, the float falls, the valve turns on, the tank refills, and the valve shuts off. It is also informative to push lightly on the flush lever for a few seconds so that just a portion of the water in the tank escapes into the bowl. This will show that the tank need not be emptied completely before the float valve mechanism acts to refill the tank. If all is operating properly, the float-valve mechanism will not let the water remain very much below the desired level.

What is this desired level? Inside most tanks a line indicates the optimal amount of water for flushing the toilet. If the water level in your tank is above or below this line, it can be changed by adjusting the float's position on the link that connects it to the valve. By changing the distance between the float and the valve, you can control the water level that will be reached before the valve turns itself off.

Notice the phrase I used in the preceding sentence—"the valve turns itself off." Is this actually the case? Isn't it rather that the rising float causes the valve to close? Yes, of course. But what is it that causes the float to rise? Obviously, the water that is filling the tank. And why is the water entering the tank? Because the valve is open. And what will cause the valve to close? The rising water level. So the valve, through a series of events, does in a sense close itself, since the valve's opening eventually causes it to close again.

If it seems that we are going around in a circle here, it is because we are. All feedback-control devices make use of what is called a *feedback loop*, meaning that the effect the device has on its environment is *fed back* to the device. In the case of the toilet tank, the falling of the float causes the valve to open, but the resulting inflow of water causes the float to rise again. So the action of the float is fed back to itself, having the consequence that the float simultaneously *affects* the water level and is *affected by* the water level. And since a low water level results in opening the valve, which raises the water level, this is called a *negative*-feedback system. This contrasts with a *positive*-feedback system, which tends to drive itself to extremes, as when a microphone is placed too close to an amplifier's loudspeaker, resulting in an annoying howl or squeal as sounds are continuously amplified, picked up by the microphone, and reamplified. A positive-feedback toilet tank (if such a useless thing existed) would be one that filled itself when it already had too much water. Since all positive-feedback devices drive themselves to extremes, they cannot be used alone to establish control and so cannot be referred to as feedback-*control* systems (although it is possible to establish certain kinds of control by using a negative-feedback system to control a positive-feedback one).

All feedback control must therefore ultimately rely on negative feedback. We can see now why such a system is called a feedback-control device, since the effect (feedback) of the environment on the device is controlled by the device itself. The operation of the feedback loop should also make it clear that a type of *circular causality* is involved that is quite unlike the one-way, push-pull causality characteristic of physical objects and systems not organized as feedback-control systems.

The usefulness and convenience of the toilet tank feedback-control system becomes more apparent when the system malfunctions. If the valve no longer opens when the water level drops, the human user must then refill the tank manually after each use, taking care not to add too much or too little water. It can be appreciated that the float valve provides a very convenient form of automation that replaces irksome human labor.

Many other feedback-control devices have been designed and used since Ktesibios's water clock, from a Byzantine oil lamp of the third century B.C. that automatically maintains a proper level of oil for burning, to the "fantail" used in eighteenth-century England and Scotland to keep windmills facing the wind. But the device that first attracted worldwide attention and use was the speed governor for steam engines invented in 1788 by Scottish engineer and inventor James Watt (1736–1819).

The invention of the steam engine marked a turning point in human history since it provided a source of mechanical power that for the first time did not depend on the vagaries of wind or water, or the muscles of human or beast. But one problem with the early steam engine was that its speed was sensitive both to the amount of steam pressure generated in the boiler and to the work load placed on the engine. Watt's ingenious solution was to make use of a combination of centrifugal force and gravity acting on a pair of metal balls (called flyweights) spinning on each side of a vertical rotating shaft so that if the speed of the engine increased, the flyweights would spread apart due to centrifugal force. This operated a valve that decreased the flow of steam to the engine so that the slower speed would be restored. If instead the engine's speed decreased, the centrifugal force acting on the flyweights would decrease so that they would be pulled down by gravity, thereby increasing the amount of steam delivered to the engine. In this way, the engine's speed remained constant in spite of fluctuating steam pressure and work loads without requiring a human operator to monitor it and attempt to keep it constant by manually operating a steam valve or changing the amount of heat applied to the boiler. The negative nature of this feedback control is apparent since anything that would tend to decrease the engine's speed would result in an increase in steam delivered to the engine, thereby keeping its speed constant, whereas anything that would tend to increase the speed would result in a decrease in steam delivered to the engine, thereby maintaining its speed.

An early important application of feedback control to electrical systems was achieved by Harold S. Black, an engineer for Bell Laboratories in New Jersey. Black had been wrestling with the problem of designing amplifiers for a transoceanic telephone system. In 1927 he figured out how to use negative feedback to amplify telephone signals by a known amount in undersea cable amplifiers using vacuum tubes that aged and lost amplification year by year and had to be placed on the ocean floor where they were needed to function for perhaps twenty years without maintenance. Black achieved this by building amplifiers with much more amplification than required and then "throwing away" most of it by using negative feedback. The result was an amplifier whose characteristics were almost immune to changes in the vacuum tubes. As a bonus, the fidelity of amplification was greatly increased, changes in available electrical power had practically no effect on the telephone signal, and noise generated in the electronic circuits was markedly reduced relative to the signal (see Bode 1960 for details).

Black's electronic invention used different components from those in the mechanical control systems described above, but the two kinds of systems—the telephone amplifier with negative feedback and the electromechanical negative-feedback control devices—share fundamental similarities, and the same basic laws govern both. In addition, the practice of using schematic diagrams for designing electrical circuits made it clear to Black and other engineers just how feedback-control devices operated: through a feedback loop the system's varying output was used to control its input.[1]

The Birth of Cybernetics

Once the general principles of feedback control were understood, control systems (as engineers refer to them) found widespread use in engineering for automatically controlling processes that were previously not possible or that would otherwise require a constantly attentive human operator. And this brings us back to Walter Cannon, or rather to one of his associates, Mexican physiologist Arturo Rosenblueth.

Rosenblueth, who learned to appreciate the self-regulating nature of living physiological processes through his work with Cannon at Harvard, met and collaborated with MIT mathematician Norbert Wiener and engineer Julian Bigelow. Rosenblueth was knowledgeable about living physiological systems, and Wiener and Bigelow were familiar with new developments in engineering, having developed negative-feedback systems during World War II for aiming antiaircraft guns at enemy airplanes.

They realized that for a machine to behave as a human operator would, it had to be goal directed, and this could be achieved only by designing it as a negative-feedback-control system. This design constraint provided an important clue about the organization and behavior of living organisms. In their influential 1943 paper "Behavior, Purpose, and Teleology," the three men were the first to establish a clear link between animate behavior and that of feedback-control systems designed by engineers. In addition, they maintained that purposeful behavior, whether that of human or machine, did not require the usual impossible teleological assumption of a future cause having a present effect. Instead, purposeful behavior could be explained by present causes having present effects, although now with causation acting in a circular manner.

Pursuing these ideas further, Wiener published a groundbreaking book in 1948, *Cybernetics*, that promised to revolutionize the study of animal and human behavior. In *Cybernetics* (revised in 1961), Wiener continued his application of the principles of feedback control to living organisms and in so doing developed the first formal, mathematical analysis of the types of self-regulatory systems that Bernard and Cannon studied.

But Wiener went beyond physiology. One way of appreciating the breadth of his cybernetic work is to recall Cannon's division of the nervous system into inward-acting (autonomic, involuntary) and outward-acting (somatic, voluntary) systems. Cannon, like Bernard, realized that the function of the autonomic system was to ensure a stable internal environment, maintaining vital conditions such as blood pressure (by varying heart rate and blood vessel constriction and dilation), blood oxygen concentration (by varying respiration), and body temperature (by varying the rate of metabolism and by initiating perspiration or shivering). Cannon, being a physiologist and not a behavioral scientist, was not particularly interested in the function of the somatic or outgoing nervous system, the one that innervates muscles attached to limbs permitting locomotion and other voluntary actions on the external environment. But if the purpose of the autonomous, involuntary nervous system is to control the organism's *internal* environment, why not at least consider the possibility that the purpose of the somatic, voluntary nervous system is to control the organism's *external* environment?

This is essentially what Wiener proposed. Indeed, the word *cybernetics* can be roughly translated from its Greek origin as "steersmanship," referring to the process of steering a ship on a course to a desired destination. Recognition that such behavior was purposeful and was used to control aspects of an organism's external environment (in much the same way as physiological functions controlled aspects of an organism's internal environment) promised a radically new foundation for understanding animal and human behavior. This new perspective is diametrically opposed to the traditional one-way cause-effect view that the environment controls an organism's behavior, either directly through stimulus-response connections or indirectly by initiating intervening cognitive processes between stimulus and response. We will see in the next chapter that this new view has revolutionary implications for behavioral science.

6

A Psychological Perspective on Purpose: Organisms as Perceptual Control Systems

The analysis of behavior in all fields of the life sciences has rested on the concept of a simple linear cause-effect chain with the organism in the middle. Control theory shows both why behavior presents that appearance and why that appearance is an illusion. The conceptual change demanded by control theory is thus fundamental; control theory applies not at the frontiers of behavioral research but at the foundations.

—William T. Powers (1989, p. 127)

Two of the three necessary steps toward a thoroughly materialistic model of purposeful behavior have now been described. The first step was Bernard's and Cannon's discovery of self-regulation in the physiological processes controlling internal body conditions such as temperature and sugar level, acidity, and carbon dioxide concentration of the blood. The second was the cybernetic understanding of circular causality as it recognizes the essential role played by the closed loop of action and feedback in control systems designed by engineers and in self-regulating physiological processes and overt behavior of animals and humans.

But something is still missing: we have yet to come to a clear understanding of how *purpose* operates in such systems, including how it can be represented, where it comes from, and how it manages to bring about controlled consequences by varying actions in the face of unpredictable disturbances. In this regard it is noteworthy that in Cannon's influential book *The Wisdom of the Body* the word "purpose" is not even included in the index. And although it is featured prominently in the title of Rosenblueth, Wiener, and Bigelow's seminal 1943 paper, it again is conspicuously absent from the index of Wiener's *Cybernetics* except for its supporting role in referring to the pathological condition known as purpose tremor.

The Purposeful Behavior of a Cruise Control System

To address these crucial issues concerning purpose, we must go beyond our rather mundane toilet tank example and consider a somewhat more complex feedback-control device that will be familiar to many readers who drive cars. This is the cruise control system commonly found on automobiles that automatically maintains a steady speed with no assistance from the driver.

An automobile cruise control system is engaged by first turning it on and then pushing the "set" button after the car has reached the desired speed. This speed, say 65 miles per hour, somehow becomes the system's goal or purpose (we will soon see how), and the system acts to increase or decrease the amount of fuel it delivers to the motor as necessary to maintain it. So if the car begins to climb a hill or a stiff headwind begins to blow, the system will sense a reduction in speed (being equipped with a speedometer that measures the rate of rotation of the wheels) and will provide more fuel to the engine through a mechanical link to the throttle. This will increase the engine's power output so that speed is maintained despite the hill or wind. As the car begins to descend the other side of the hill or the wind subsides, the cruise control system will sense the increasing speed and close the throttle, reducing the amount of fuel delivered to the engine so that again the desired speed is maintained. Because it responds to too-high speeds by reducing the amount of fuel delivered to the motor and to too-low speeds by increasing the flow of fuel, the system can be easily recognized as a negative-feedback-control system, identical in function to Watt's steam engine regulator.

Now that we have seen that a cruise control system automatically maintains a steady speed in spite of varying road conditions, let's take a closer look at its internal functions to see how it manages to accomplish this. Figure 6.1 is an adaptation of Wiener's control system diagrams from *Cybernetics* (Wiener 1961, pp. 112, 114). The three boxes indicate the three essential components of a feedback-control system: *sensor*, *comparator*, and *effector*. In a cruise control system, the sensor is a speedometer that converts the rate of wheel rotation to an electrical signal. The signal provided by the sensor is compared with another signal, here labeled "input," which represents the desired or goal speed of the car.

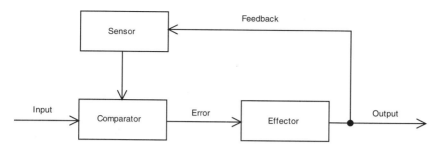

Figure 6.1
Wiener's feedback-control system

The comparator compares the actual speed indicated by the sensor with the desired speed represented by the input signal by subtracting the latter from the former. This comparison results in an error signal, which indicates not only the difference between actual and desired speeds but also the direction in which the actual speed must be changed to match the desired speed. So, for example, if the current speed is 70 miles per hour but the desired speed is 65, subtracting 70 from 65 yields negative 5, indicating that speed has to be reduced by 5 miles per hour. This error signal is then normally amplified and sent to the effector, in this case the throttle that will reduce the amount of fuel provided to the engine until the actual speed matches the desired speed, thereby closing the loop. It should be noted that this is once again a *negative*-feedback system, since the effector increases the amount of fuel sent to the engine if the sensed speed is less than the goal speed, but decreases the delivery of fuel if the measured speed is more than the goal.

It should now be a bit more obvious how the purpose of the system is represented and how it controls the speed of the car. In this diagram, the desired speed, or purpose, is represented by input into the system, which is an electrical signal that indicates the speed of the car when the "set" button is pushed. In this system, as in most engineered feedback-control systems, the desired level of the controlled variable is designed to be manipulable by the human operator. Setting the desired room temperature on a thermostat is another example. In these cases, the goal is provided to the system by a human operator, and is represented in the control system by a signal that is sent to the comparator. The system will then act in a purposeful manner, varying its output as necessary so that the two signals entering the comparator—the signal representing the vehicle's actual speed and the signal representing the desired or goal speed—are the same or very nearly so.

As mentioned earlier, one of the most important insights of the original cyberneticians was the realization that purposefully acting humans and engineered feedback-control systems are alike in certain essential respects. So let us now see how we can use Wiener's diagram to explain the behavior of a human driver controlling the speed of a car the good old-fashioned way, that is, without the assistance of a cruise control system.

We will start again with the sensor. The driver can sense the speed of the car in a number of ways. The speed at which the driver sees road surface approach the car and engine and wind noise (both loudness and pitch) can all be perceived as indicators of speed. But none of these perceptions provides a very precise measure of speed (although I did once know a musician with absolute pitch who claimed she could keep her car at a given speed by keeping the frequency of the engine noise close to a particular musical note!). Fortunately, all cars come equipped with a speedometer that provides the driver with an accurate visual indicator of speed. So the sensor is the driver's eyes and what is sensed is the speed indicated by the speedometer.

But this, of course, is not enough. The driver also has to have a target or goal speed to provide a purpose to his speed-controlling behavior. Let's assume that this goal is the legal speed limit posted as 65 miles per hour. Something within the driver's brain must compare the speedometer reading with the goal speed, subtract the latter from the former, and send the difference (error) to an effector to be acted on. The effector now consists of the muscles of the driver's right leg and foot that act to push down on the accelerator pedal if the perceived speed is less than the goal speed, release the pedal if the perceived speed is above the goal speed, or hold its current position if the perceived and goal speeds match (zero error). Of course, any movement of the accelerator will influence the speed of the car, and this result will be fed back to the speedometer, where the feedback loop from sensor through comparator to effector and back once again to sensor is completed.

So we see that Wiener's basic diagram of a feedback-control system can be readily applied to the purposeful behavior of both machine (cruise control system) and human (driver), even though the physical make-up of the two systems is quite different—electrical wires, sensors, and motors in the former, but living nerves, eyes, and muscles in the latter. However, there is one fundamental difference between machine and driver that seems to have escaped the notice of some early cyberneticians—the origin of what we referred to above as the desired speed or goal speed, but what control systems engineers usually refer to as the *reference level* of the system.

In Wiener's diagram, the reference level is supplied from outside the system and is therefore labeled as an input, since in engineered control systems the reference level can usually be set and manipulated by a human operator. For a cruise control system, the reference level can be changed by pushing the "accelerate" (faster) or "coast" (slower) button until the new desired speed is reached. But there are no "accelerate" or "coast" buttons to be found on the human driver. In fact, the only way to provide input to a human driver is through his senses, as when he sees a speed limit sign or his driving companion asks him to slow down. But there is no guarantee that he will observe such signs or requests. Indeed, our driver may instead decide to speed up when the legal speed limit drops or he is requested to slow down (for example, if traffic decreases or he wishes to annoy his passenger). Or he may slow down when the limit increases or he is requested to speed up (for example, if snow begins to fall or he again wishes to annoy his passenger). So in contrast to the reference level of an engineered control system that is typically provided from the outside by a human user, the reference levels that serve as human goals and purposes seem to originate somewhere inside the brain. If this is the case, it means that the goals of human beings (as well as all other living organisms) are not subject to direct environmental control, as is the case for engineered control systems.

Properties of Engineered and Living Control Systems

We will return shortly to the question of the origin of human reference levels, but only after we first consider some additional ways in which engineered and human control systems are similar. First, although both cruise control systems and human drivers must compensate for many disturbances that would otherwise change the car's speed, they need not perceive the disturbances themselves. The cruise control system has no way of determining whether the road is climbing or descending. Nor can it know if there is a stiff headwind or tailwind, that a heavy trailer was just attached to the car, that a tire is losing air and offering steadily increasing rolling resistance, or that a spark plug has fouled, causing the engine to lose power. All it can sense, and therefore control, is the car's speed. Yet despite its complete ignorance of a multitude of potential and actual disturbing factors, it nonetheless does a good job of maintaining the desired speed. Whereas a human driver may be able to perceive at least some of these disturbances (although wind speed, potentially a very important disturbing factor, is not usually one of these), the performance of the cruise control system suggests that he may not require or use any of this information as long as, like the cruise control system, he pays careful attention to the speedometer reading.

Second, a control system *does not control what it does*. Rather, it *controls what it senses*. The word *control* is used here in its technical sense of maintaining some variable at or near a specified fixed value or pattern of values despite disturbances. Both the cruise control system and human driver can control only what they are able to sense or perceive to be the speed of the vehicle, and they do so by changing output (behavior). Technically speaking, behavioral output is not controlled since the only way the car's speed can be kept close to the reference level speed despite disturbances is by varying the output (that is, changing behavior) as necessary. So we see that a feedback-control system, whether artificial or alive, controls its input (what it senses) and not its output (how it behaves). Consequently, maintaining a constant speed using either a cruise control system or an attentive human driver allows one to predict accurately how long it will take to cover a certain distance. But it will not let one predict how much fuel will be used to drive the distance because fuel consumption is not controlled, varying as it must to compensate for unpredictable disturbances. Since a control system controls what it senses, and since an organism's sensing of the environment is generally referred to as perception in behavioral science, application of control theory to the behavior of living organisms is called *perceptual control theory*. Including the word *perceptual* distinguishes this application of control theory to the behavior of living organisms from the control theory applied by engineers and physicists to artificial (that is, nonliving) control systems.

Third, it is important to realize that whereas a control system's behavior is clearly *influenced* by its environment, it is *not determined* solely by its environment. Rather, its behavior is determined by what it senses (or perceives) of the environment *in comparison with its goal or reference level*. It is worth emphasizing again the crucial difference between nonliving control systems designed by engineers and living ones fashioned by biological evolution: an engineered control system is usually designed so that its reference level can be manipulated by the operator, for example, by pushing the "accelerate" button of the cruise control system or by turning up the room thermostat; however, no such direct manipulation of the reference levels of living control systems is usually possible. We can certainly ask a taxi driver to drive more slowly or tell a teenage child to be home by midnight, but we have no way to guarantee, other than by using overwhelming physical force, that either person will comply with our wishes.

Finally, both engineered and living control systems behave in a clearly *purposeful* manner, varying behavior as necessary in the face of unpredictable disturbances to control some perceived variable, in the same way that William James's frog purposefully sought to reach the surface of the water and Romeo sought to reach Juliet's lips (recall chapter 3). This is not achieved by some future state having present effects, but by having a goal state (reference level), comparing it with current conditions (perception), and acting on the difference (error) until it disappears or is made very small.

Note that nothing mystical, psychic, or spiritual is required for this to occur. It is certainly the case that specifying, perceiving, and controlling something like car speed, temperature, or water level in an engineered control system is orders of magnitude simpler than specifying, perceiving, and controlling something like building a house, writing a book, or having a successful career. Nonetheless, the fact that the former can be achieved in a completely mechanistic, materialist way using fairly simple wires, levers, valves, motors, and sensors suggests that the latter can also be achieved just as mechanistically and materialistically using the much more complex neural networks, sensory equipment, muscles, and limbs of the human body.

The cybernetic ideas of Wiener and his associates were greeted with considerable enthusiasm by several leading scientists around the middle of the twentieth century. Between 1946 and 1953 these ideas became the theme of a series of ten meetings sponsored by the Josiah P. Macy Foundation under the title "Feedback Mechanisms and Circular Causal Systems in Biology and the Social Sciences Meeting" that would later incorporate Wiener's new term in the revised title "Cybernetics: Circular Causal and Feedback Mechanisms in Biological and Social Systems." But although many leading figures in the biological, social, and behavioral sciences as well as prominent philosophers, physicists, and mathematicians attended these meetings,[1] the revolution in behavioral science that appeared so ready to occur never did.

One reason was that many participants of the Macy meetings were more interested in applying cybernetics to issues in information theory and communication than to biological, behavioral, and social sciences. Those who were eager to apply these new ideas to the life sciences often lacked basic technical knowledge concerning the design and operation of negative-feedback-control systems. One such individual, who later became president of the American Society for Cybernetics, stated that purposeful behavior could be explained in the same way that Newton's theory of gravity explained the behavior of a drop a water sliding down an inclined plane, totally disregarding the closed-loop character of purposefully acting systems (reported by Powers 1989, p. 261)!

Another factor in cybernetics' lack of lasting impact on the behavioral and cognitive sciences was the emergence of reliable and powerful digital computers in the middle of the century. The digital computer, with its binary zero-one mode of operation, was better suited to symbolic representations and their logical manipulation as practiced in what has become known as the artificial intelligence (AI) approach to investigating brain, cognition, and behavioral processes. Analog computers, with their use of continuously varying electrical currents that is more amenable to a cybernetic approach to modeling nervous systems, were largely replaced by their digital successors.

Many other reasons could be invoked for cybernetics' failure to revolutionize the behavioral and social sciences (see Powers 1989, pp. 129–136). But a major factor that is still operating to impede acceptance of the basic cybernetic insight is the difficulty replacing the well-entrenched one-way cause-effect (stimulus-response, input-output) model of animate behavior with the more complex cybernetic notion of circular causality. And just such a replacement is needed to account for purposeful behavior in which causes are simultaneously effects and effects are simultaneously causes. It wasn't until the 1960s when another combination of two engineers and a medical researcher began to formulate a general feedback-control theory of human behavior.

Understanding Behavior as the Control of Perception

The Contributions of William T. Powers and His Associates

These three individuals were physicist and electrical engineer William T. Powers, physicist Robert D. Clark, and clinical psychologist Robert L. McFarland, who in the 1950s worked together at the Veterans Administration Research Hospital in Chicago. In 1960 they published a two-part article with the title "A General Feedback Theory of Human Behavior." Thirteen years later in 1973 Powers published the first book that focused exclusively on the application of cybernetic and control-system concepts to animal and human behavior. His book finally made good on the cybernetic promissory note issued by Rosenblueth, Wiener, and Bigelow thirty years earlier.

Powers made three important contributions in extending cybernetic concepts to animal and human behavior. The first was to appreciate fully the revolutionary implications that cybernetics had for behavioral science and to share this insight. As indicated by the title of his book, *Behavior: The Control of Perception*, he recognized that organisms, organized as living networks of negative-feedback-control systems, behaved as they do to control their perceptions. This was a blatant reversal of the then- and still-current mainstream view in behavioral science that perception (of environmental stimuli) controls behavior, either directly (as in behaviorist theory) or through intervening brain-based psychological processes (as in cognitive theory). By turning behavioral theory upside-down, Powers achieved what the preceding ninety-four years of psychological research and theory had not: liberation of psychology from the one-way cause-effect view that sees the behavior of living organisms, like that of inanimate objects, as determined by external forces.

Related to this liberation was Powers's realization—mentioned above in anticipation—that unlike engineered control systems such as thermostats, steam pressure regulators, and cruise control systems, reference levels specifying the goals of living control systems originate from *within* the organism and are neither provided nor directly manipulated by the environment. This raises the question as to what within the organism provides these reference levels and how and why they are provided, leading to Powers's second important contribution: a theory and working model of the *hierarchical* organization of control systems operating within the organism.

A Hierarchy of Perception and Control

To understand this hierarchical organization of control systems and its functioning, it will be useful first to take another look at a simple control system. But this time we will use a more complete diagram inspired by Powers's work that is more appropriate to living control systems than Wiener's diagram.

Figure 6.2 differs in several ways from Wiener's original diagram. First, the reader should take note of the purely cosmetic change from Wiener's horizontal orientation to a vertical one.

Second, a dashed horizontal line divides the control system from its environment. This makes it clear that the system is influenced by the environment only through its sensors (for a living organism this could be any sense organ such as eyes, ears, nose, or touch receptors in the skin), and it acts on the environment only through effectors such as those provided by muscles attached to limbs.

Third, input to the system on the left of Wiener's diagram has been replaced by an entity labeled purpose (6) which provides the reference signal (5) to the control system's comparator (4). Whereas in Wiener's diagram it appeared as if the reference signal came from outside the control system, here its source is clearly within the organism itself. We will return shortly to this important component labeled purpose (6) when we consider the hierarchical organization of living control systems.

Finally, three additional components have been added to the bottom environmental side of the diagram. Controlled variable (1) refers to the particular physical aspect of the environment that the organism is controlling. This can be anything that the organism can see, hear, smell, feel, or otherwise sense. In our example of maintaining driving speed, this envi-

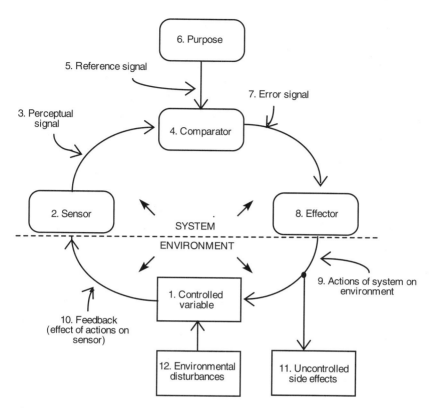

Figure 6.2
Elementary control system

ronmental variable is the position of the needle on the speedometer that the driver must be able to see in order to control the car's speed.

The box on the lower left, environmental disturbances (12), represents all the factors that influence the controlled variable other than actions of the control system itself. In our driving example these disturbances are factors such as wind speed and its direction, and the slope and condition of the road. These are influences for which the driver must compensate so that the car's speed remains under control.

The last addition is the box on the lower right that is labeled uncontrolled side effects (11). This box shows that the actions of a control system, whether engineered or living, will almost certainly have effects on its environment *other* than the desired effect on the controlled variable. Thus, delivering more fuel to the engine while climbing a hill will have effects beyond that of maintaining the speedometer needle at 65 mph. These effects include greater engine noise and vibration, increased use of fuel, higher engine temperature, and faster flow of emissions from the exhaust pipe. These are all unintended effects of maintaining the car's speed, and we will see later how the distinction between intended (purposeful) and unintended (nonpurposeful) consequences of an organism's behavior is crucial for understanding what a living organism is really doing.

Now that we have a more complete diagram showing what is involved in purposeful behavior, let's take a trip around the closed loop it illustrates to ensure that the functions of all its components, labels, and connections are clear. Staying with the example of a human driver maintaining a constant automobile speed of 65 mph, we will start at the controlled variable (1), which is a reading of 65 mph on the speedometer. But as this is an aspect of the driver's external environment (note that it is in the environment half of the diagram), it must be sensed by the driver to be controlled by him. This is done with his light sensor (2), or eyes. (Obviously, if the controlled variable were a sound, taste, smell, feeling, or some combination of these, other sensory systems would be involved.) The driver's visual system converts the speedometer reading into a perceptual signal (3) that is then provided to the comparator (4) that compares this signal with the reference signal (5) of 65 mph provided by the system's purpose (6). The difference between these two signals (3 and 5) constitutes the error signal (7) that causes the effector (8) to act, which in this case is the driver's foot acting on the accelerator pedal. The action of depressing or releasing the pedal (9) influences the driver's environment in many ways. The intended effect of the behavior is its influence on the car's speed and consequently on the driver's perception of the speedometer reading. This effect of behavior on perception through the system's environment is what is referred to as feedback (10). It is this feedback link from actions through the environment back to sensor that completes the loop from controlled variable (1) to sensor (2) to comparator (4) to effector (8) back to controlled variable (1). The box labeled environmental disturbances (10) represents all of the influences on the car's speed that must be compensated for by the driver. Finally, uncontrolled side effects (11) refer to all the unintended consequences of the driver's manipulation of the accelerator pedal (for example, engine and wind noise, fuel consumption, air pressure on the windshield, and engine and tire temperature).

We are now ready to consider where the all-important reference signal (5) comes from. And important it is, since changing this signal from 65 mph to 55 mph will result in an error if the car had been traveling at the previous goal speed of 65 mph, causing the driver to slow down to and maintain this lower speed. Similarly, increasing the reference signal to, say, 80 mph will cause an error in the opposite direction, leading the driver to accelerate to and maintain the higher speed, perhaps even resulting in a speeding ticket (which is probably one good reason why the reference signal will probably not be increased to 80 mph). Since this reference signal representing the control system's goal does not come from the environment (notice how figure 6.2 shows no connection from the environment to the reference signal), it must be provided as the output from some other component of the nervous system. This other component is a higher-level control system that, instead of sending its output to muscles, sends it to the comparator of a lower-level control system.

Powers hypothesized that the nervous systems of animals and humans are made up of many networks of control systems with the basic hierarchical arrangement shown in figure 6.3 whereby higher-level systems send their outputs as reference signals (and thereby constitute higher-level goals) to the comparators of lower-level ones (note that to save space in figure 6.3 comparators are indicated by the letter C, sensors by I for input, and effectors by O for output). For humans, Powers proposed eleven levels of perception. And since each higher-level control system must be able to sense what is happening in the control systems below it, the human control-system hierarchy also requires eleven levels of perception, with higher-level perceptions being made up of weighted combinations of lower-level ones.

Although combining many basic control systems in this hierarchical fashion adds much complexity (and capability) to the overall network, it should be kept in mind that each elementary control system compares its perceptual signal with its reference signal and acts on any difference to reduce it to close to zero. But instead of sending its output to a muscle or group of muscles to act on some aspect of the environment, a higher-level system sends its output to one or more lower-level control systems where it acts as a reference signal for the lower-level systems.

CONNECTIONS TO HIGHER LEVELS

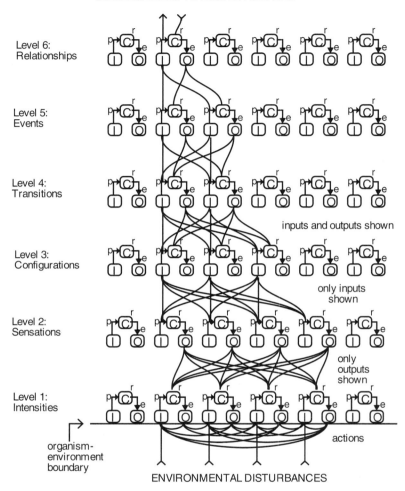

Figure 6.3
A hierarchical network of control systems

This model of the nervous system makes certain predictions about behavior, some of which can be easily demonstrated. But we will save this for a bit later in this chapter where several interesting demonstrations of perceptual control will be described. Instead, let us now consider how Powers's proposed organization provides a new perspective on the physiological control of an organism's inner environment as studied by Bernard and Cannon.

It will be recalled that Bernard wrote of the "constancy of the internal environment" and Cannon introduced the term homeostasis to describe the process by which the body maintains constant internal conditions in spite of the disturbances to which it is continually subjected. But it turns out that at least some of these internal conditions are not so constant after all, and vary in functional ways.

Human body temperature is a particularly interesting example. It is normally maintained close to 98.6° F regardless of ambient air temperature. But we have all experienced fevers during which body temperature increases to 100° or even 102° or 103° F. It used to be thought that these higher temperatures were the harmful effects of bacterial or viral infections. Research has shown, however, that the elevated body temperature characteristic of fever is actually an adaptation in that it helps the immune system eliminate harmful microorganisms. This is accomplished by setting a higher reference level (often called a set point by physiologists) that, like 98.6° F, is also defended against disturbances.

Consider the stages of a typical fever. First, your body temperature begins to rise. But even though it may already be higher than normal, you feel cold and may shiver and put on additional clothing or blankets. This is an indication that the reference level for body temperature has been reset to a higher setting by a higher-level control system. Until your body reaches this new temperature goal you feel cold despite the fact that your body may already be warmer than normal. When your temperature attains the new reference level, you are more comfortable but you feel very warm to anyone who touches you. Finally, your fever "breaks," which means that your reference level for body temperature has been reset once again to its normal temperature of close to 98.6° F. But since it takes a while for your body to cool down to the reference level of the new target temperature, you feel very warm during this time and may perspire profusely until your body temperature once again matches its normal reference level.

While it is not yet completely clear how the reference level for body temperature is manipulated, it is clear that homeostasis is not the best word to describe a control process that involves a changing reference level. Consequently, physiologist Nicholas Mrosovsky (1990) used the term rheostasis[2] to describe such changing reference levels, and he described many such varying reference levels, including those involved in body weight, calcium stores, blood acidity, blood gases, and blood pressure.

Control of body temperature holds further interest since for humans and many other animals it may involve voluntary overt behavior in addition to involuntary internal physiological processes. Shivering and constriction of blood vessels close to the skin are two automatic physiological responses designed to raise body temperature by generating and retaining heat. But a human may also act on the external environment to raise body temperature, as when a person puts on a sweater, adds another log to the fire, prepares and consumes a hot drink, turns up the room thermostat, or adds insulation to the attic. Behavioral means of regulating body temperature are particularly noticeable in cold-blooded animals (technically *ectotherms*) that have no internal physiological means of controlling body temperature. Lizards climb up the sides of rocks and walls in the early morning to catch the first warming rays of the sun. The desert iguana will move closer to a source of heat (such as an electric lamp in laboratory conditions) when infected with a pathogen, thus producing a reptilian version of fever that facilitates elimination of disease-causing microorganisms (see Mrosovsky 1990, p. 77).

Humans can control many variables that are much more complex than body temperature. Imagine for example that Mary, living in San Francisco, learns that her son has become ill in New York City and is being cared for in a hospital there. It is very likely that this situation would be disturbing to Mary in many ways and she would likely feel compelled to make arrangements to visit her son during his illness. We could invoke all kinds of reasons for why Mary is going off to New York, such as love for her son, concern for his well-being, or even that she was rewarded in some way for previous visits she made either to her son or to other individuals in similar situations. But another way of understanding Mary's actions is that she sees herself as a good and loving mother, and not visiting her son during his illness would constitute a serious disturbance to her self-perception.

This is surely a much more complex variable than body temperature or driving speed, but the basic principles of perceptual control are still applicable. For Mary to control her perception of herself as a good mother, she will have to manipulate many lower-level reference levels and control the many perceptions they specify. This is just another way of saying that she will have to accomplish many subgoals to accomplish her higher-level goal of visiting her son. To go from San Francisco to New York, she will have to obtain an airline ticket. To obtain her ticket, she must telephone an airline or travel agent. This involves pushing buttons on her telephone, accomplished by manipulating the tension of her arm muscles in a certain pattern. Only if all these (and many other) lower-level perceptual-control systems are successful in achieving their goals (each subject to unpredictable disturbances) will Mary be able to visit her son and thereby control her perception of herself as a good mother. Doing so, however, will likely cause disturbances to other goals she has, such as those related to her family and work in San Francisco. Thus goals can be related to each other within the same hierarchy as lower-level and higher-level, but can also be situated in different hierarchies, creating the possibility of someone being "of two minds" with accompanying stress and conflict.

The What, Why, and How of Behavior

Powers's model of a hierarchy of perceptual control systems provides a new way of understanding the what, how, and why of animal and human behavior and how this understanding is very different from views provided by other psychological theories.

We will first consider the what of behavior. When behaviorism came to dominate American psychology at the beginning of the twentieth century, one of its major goals was to make psychology a "real" science like physics, and *objective* measurement of behavior became an essential part of its methodology. The number of seconds taken by a rat to run through a maze, the rate at which a pigeon pecked at a key, and the number of times a child disrupted his class during a day at school are examples of behaviorists' objective measurement of behavior. But whereas many aspects of an organism's behavior can be measured by such apparently objective means, such an approach ultimately fails to be either objective or useful. This is because every behavior has very many consequences, and all that a behavioral scientist can ever do is describe one or more *subjectively selected consequences*.

Take the example of Mr. Smith walking down the street. By mentioning walking, I already described one of the consequences of his behavior, namely, that his legs are moving in such a way as to propel him over the ground. I could conceivably obtain more quantitative data about his behavior, such as the frequency of his gait, the speed of his travel, or the force with which he pushes his feet against the ground. But he is also doing many other things that I might have described. He may be out for exercise, calming himself after an argument with his wife, breaking in a new pair of shoes, or going to buy a newspaper at the corner store. He is probably also breathing, perspiring, and even slowly wearing out the soles of his shoes. These are all possible consequences of his behavior, but it is not at all obvious from simply observing Mr. Smith walk down the street which of these descriptions, if any, provides the best answer to the question, what is he doing?

So how does one provide an objective account of behavior when there are so many possible behavioral consequences from which to choose? Figure 6.2 provides a clue. Note that when a control system acts on its environment it has two major types of behavioral consequences. One is that some aspect of the environment, what we called the controlled variable (1), is affected. But many "uncontrolled side effects" (11) are also brought about. Objective observation and measurement do not themselves tell us which of the many effects that one's behavior has on the environment is being controlled—that is, which is the one for which there is a reference level and therefore matters to the individual.

A perceptual control system analysis informs us that one or more of these behavioral consequences matter to the behaving system, and others do not. But how do we find which consequences are being controlled by the individual's behavior and which are unintended side effects? Fortunately, the nature of perceptual control is such that it may be quite easy to find out which is the controlled variable because disturbances to this variable will be resisted whereas disturbances to uncontrolled aspects of the environment will not be resisted. This method of finding out what a particular behavior is intended to accomplish is called the test of the controlled variable by Powers, or more simply, the test.

Let us consider how we might apply the test to Mr. Smith. If we guess that he is out for exercise we might offer him a ride to wherever he is going. His refusal to accept would be consistent with the hypothesis, since a car ride would disturb his goal of getting exercise; but if he accepted, the hypothesis would not look good. If we suspected that he is out to buy a newspaper, we might tell him that the corner store is out of newspapers but the vending machine in the other direction still has some and then observe his actions. A change of heading toward the vending machine would be consistent with the newspaper hypothesis and no change of direction would be evidence against it.

In the case of human behavior, we might save ourselves considerable trouble by simply asking what someone is doing, or more accurately, what he or she is attempting to achieve by his or her actions. But although we may obtain useful information in this way, we have no guarantee that it will be accurate, particularly if the individual has some reason to conceal the real motives for his or her actions or is not conscious of them. And asking is not an option when dealing with very young children or animals.

So we see that perceptual control theory provides a new approach to understanding the what of behavior. Because an action on the environment is initiated when there is a difference (error) between a goal (as represented by a reference signal) and one's current perception, a useful answer to what one is doing is the intended consequence of the behaving organism. Jack may knock over a glass of wine into the lap of his dining companion while reaching for the salt, but a wine-stained skirt was not the intended consequence of his behavior, only the rather unfortunate unintended side effect of the combination of a reference signal for more salt on his steak and the location of the salt shaker behind his glass of wine. The goal-based analysis of behavior provided by perceptual control theory not only provides a new approach but in so doing provides, by the test, a scientific method for distinguishing between the intended (purposeful) and unintended (accidental) consequences of behavior, a distinction that is not even considered meaningful in the objective behaviorist approach. Indeed, the key to understanding behavior as the purposeful control of perception is to attempt to perceive the world from the perspective of the behaving organism. In this important sense, behavior is best understood from a subjective viewpoint, not an objective one.

From a control theory perspective, the answer to the question concerning the why of behavior partially overlaps with the answer to the what. To return to our example of Mr. Smith's walk, knowing what he is doing in terms of his goals (say buying a newspaper) is also to answer why he is walking down the street. But as every parent of a young, inquisitive child knows, one can always continue the why game to the next level and ask why he is getting a newspaper.

To answer this question we must make use of the hierarchy of control systems as shown in figure 6.3. As can be seen in this diagram, comparators receive their reference levels (goals) from the output of higher-level control systems. So obtaining the newspaper is a subgoal on the path to satisfying some higher-level goal, one specified in the reference signal to a higher-level perceptual control system. This higher-level goal could be to check the closing stock market prices. And why is Mr. Smith interested in the closing stock quotes? This brings us up one more notch to a yet higher-level perceptual control system that has as its goal the accumulation of wealth. Why accumulate wealth? Perhaps to be able to retire comfortably at age sixty. If, like the perpetually inquisitive child, we keep on asking why, we will eventually run out of reasonable higher-level goals and be tempted to answer with a simple unadorned "because." But the important point for the present discussion is not to provide an accurate list of higher-level goals for this particular example but rather to show that such why questions can in principle be answered by discovering what the next higher-level control system is controlling, and understanding all goals (except perhaps the one or ones at the very top of the hierarchy—more on that later) as being in the service of still higher-level goals.

The final question about behavior concerns how, and once again the hierarchy of control systems suggests an approach. Just as the why question can be answered by finding the reference level of the next-higher control system, the how question can be addressed by considering the reference levels of lower-level control systems. This is because higher-level goals typically require the control of many lower-level perceptual variables, and higher-level systems control their perceptions by manipulating reference levels they send as outputs to lower-level systems. If Mr. Smith discovers in the newspaper that he is not accumulating wealth according to his plan, he will have to modify certain lower-level goals so that, say, he will change his portfolio from 60 percent bonds and 40 percent stocks to 60 percent stocks and 40 percent bonds. Or, more drastically, he may have to modify his plans, postponing retirement from age sixty to sixty-five to ensure that he will have sufficient funds to retire in comfort.

We can now appreciate that answering a what question about behavior is actually more complicated than first suggested whenever we are dealing with a hierarchy of control systems. This is because the control of a variable such as buying a newspaper involves simultaneous control of many lower-level perceptions (such as reaching the store, taking the newspaper off the shelf, and putting a certain quantity of money on the counter). Yet buying a newspaper is itself a lower-level goal from the perspective of the higher-level goal that has set it, such as checking one's investments or preparing for retirement.

So it turns out that there is usually no one simple answer to a what question concerning behavior (e.g., what is he doing?) but rather the answer must be a description of a set of interrelated goals, some of which may be consciously accessible to the individual (if human) but others not necessarily so. Mr. Smith may be consciously aware of his goal to buy a newspaper, but he is certainly not consciously aware of the complex pattern of perceptual control that is involved in walking down the street (so complex, in fact, that no robot has mastered the bipedal gait). He may not even be conscious at the moment of his goal to retire at age sixty. The test, however, can still in principle be applied to any of these controlled variables, and answers to why questions of behavior can be answered only by moving up the hierarchy, whereas answers to how questions can be addressed only by moving down.

Demonstrations of Perceptual Control

We now come to Powers's third and final (as least as presented here) major contribution. Many behavioral scientists have produced block diagrams of their theories of behavior and perception of the types shown in figures 6.2 and 6.3, as well as verbal arguments to go along with them. But Powers took an important step beyond diagrams and words in producing several convincing demonstrations of the phenomenon of perceptual control and simulations of control-theory models of behavior. These models and demonstrations also inspired several other researchers to develop additional working demonstrations. Since they provide a useful hands-on approach to understanding perceptual control, we will explore several of them and see how they exemplify the concepts introduced above.

The Classic Rubber-Band Demonstration

Our first demonstration, developed by Powers (1973, pp. 242–244), only requires for equipment two rubber bands, a coin, a table, and a willing participant. The two rubber bands are knotted together as shown in figure 6.4 and the coin is placed on the table.[3] Seated across from you, your participant puts a finger through one of the two rubber-band loops and you do the same with the other loop. You then ask your participant to keep the knot that joins the two rubber bands centered over the coin while you gradually and repeatedly move your end of the rubber band toward and away from the coin, keeping it taut, but not so taut that it might break.

If your participant understood your request, you will see that the hand he is using to hold his end of the rubber bands mirrors the actions of your own hand. As you pull your end of the rubber bands away from the coin, he pulls in the opposite direction to keep the knot over the coin. And as you move your hand toward the knot, he does the same.

Since the movements of your participant's hand mirror those of yours, a third person observing this demonstration might well conclude that the participant was simply copying your actions with the position of your hand as the stimulus and moving his hand in response. But it is easy to show that this stimulus-response appearance is really just a seductive illusion (referred to by Powers as the behavioral illusion) and not at all what is really happening. This can be shown by blocking your participant's view of your hand by putting a large book (or magazine or newspaper) between your hand and the knot while taking care not to interfere with your participant's view of the knot and coin. You will then see that even with your hand hidden from your participant's view, he will have no difficulty keeping the knot over the coin in spite of your hand's movements. So contrary to what may appear to be happening, your participant is not responding directly to your hand's movements.

We can get a better idea of what is going on here by referring back to figure 6.2. In this demonstration, the participant is the control system above the horizontal system-environment boundary and you are acting as

Figure 6.4
Knotted rubber bands

a source of environmental disturbances (12). The participant is able to keep the knot above the coin and achieves this by observing the controlled variable (1) with his eyes serving as sensors (2) that provide a perceptual signal (3) to the comparator (4) that compares the perceived position of the knot with the reference signal (5) provided by his purpose (6). The error signal (7), indicating the discrepancy between the intended perception and actual perception, is sent to the effector (8) that causes muscle contractions to increase or decrease tension on the participant's end of the rubber bands. So whereas your disturbances (12) do result in the participant counteracting them, the diagram makes it clear (as did blocking the participant's view of your hand) that he is responding to disturbances to the position of the knot only because of their effect on the controlled variable (1).

So is it not your movements in themselves but rather their effect on the position of the knot relative to the coin that causes the participant to move his hand. But then isn't it also the case that the participant's actions influence the position of the knot? So what is causing what? Is the position of the knot causing the participant to move his hand, or are his hand movements causing the position of the knot to change? The correct answer, which I hope is obvious by now, is that *both* are happening at the same time: changes in the position of the knot lead to movements of the participant's hand that simultaneously lead to changes in the position of the knot. Here we once again find circular causality operating in a closed loop from perception to action back to perception that defies a one-way, cause-effect analysis.

Computer-Based Demonstrations of Perceptual Control

Although the rubber-band example is a simple and useful demonstration of the phenomenon of perceptual control (and countless variations of it demonstrate other aspects), it does not permit a quantitative analysis of the relationships among disturbance, controlled variable, and action. For this reason, Powers developed a computer demonstration, called Demo 1, that runs on any IBM-compatible computer running DOS (or a DOS window) and that can be obtained on the Internet at *www.uiuc.edu/ph/www/g-cziko/twd*.

Demo 1, the phenomenon of control, provides a computer version of the rubber-band demonstration called a tracking task. The participant's task is to keep a short horizontal line, the cursor, between two target lines (see figure 6.5) by manipulating a computer mouse or trackball, referred to generically as the handle. Instead of pulling on the end of a rubber band, the participant moves a mouse or trackball up and down. Instead of keeping the knot centered over the coin, the participant keeps the cursor horizontally aligned between the two target lines. And instead of you as demonstrator providing disturbances by pulling on your end of the rubber band, disturbances are generated automatically by the computer program.

But now the similarities with the rubber-band demonstration end as the computer demonstration is able to store, display, and analyze relevant data. Figure 6.6 shows a typical run of step F of Demo 1 called compensatory tracking. Time is represented along the horizontal axis, which also serves as an indication of target lines. The positions of the handle, cursor (C. Var), and disturbance are represented by the three lines as they change over time during the course of the 30 or so seconds of the run.

The most striking pattern of this graph is the symmetrical relationship between the disturbance and handle, the latter forming a mirror image of the former. This corresponds to the symmetrical movement of the participant's and your hands in the rubber-band demonstration. This result is even more striking using the computer since we know that the participant never saw the disturbance but only its effect on the cursor while the cursor's position was simultaneously being influenced by the participant's movement of the handle. Yet the disturbance and handle movements are

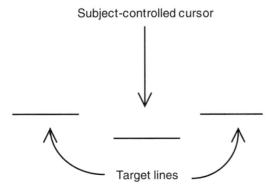

Figure 6.5
Cursor display for Demo 1, compensatory tracking task

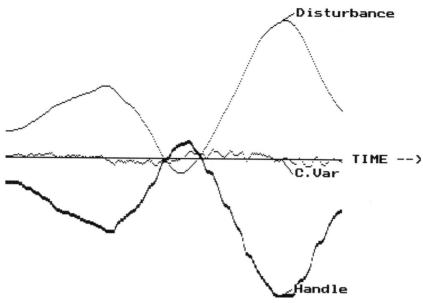

Figure 6.6
Results of Demo 1, compensatory tracking task

very highly corrrelated, with the program indicating for this particular run a correlation coefficient of negative 0.996 between the variables (see box 6.1 for an explanation of correlation coefficients).

Box 6.1
The Correlation Coefficient and Causality

To measure the direction and strength of the relationship between two continuous variables, behavioral scientists use an index called the *correlation coefficient* (usually denoted by the letter *r*), which was developed by Karl Pearson (1857–1936), a British applied mathematician and philosopher of science.

The value of the correlation coefficient varies from -1.00 to 1.00. Its sign (negative or positive) indicates the *direction* of the relationship between two variables, let's call them *x* and *y*. A positive sign indicates a direct relationship, so that as *x* increases *y* also increases and as *x* decreases so does *y*. A negative sign indicates an inverse relationship, so that as *x* increases *y* decreases, and vice versa. As examples, a positive correlation would most likely be found between the height and weight of a group of individuals (since taller people tend to be heavier than shorter people). A negative correlation would likely be found between weight and the number of pull-ups a person can do (since heavier people tend to be able to do fewer pull-ups than lighter individuals).

The *strength* of the relationship between x and y is indicated by the absolute value of the correlation coefficient, that is, its distance from zero and closeness to either negative one or positive one. Correlation near zero would likely be found between weight and intelligence since heavier people would not be expected to be more or less intelligent than slimmer people. A correlation around 0.7 would likely be found between the height and weight of a group of people, indicating a fairly strong but less than perfect relationship between the variables (it is not perfect since some people will be shorter but heavier than some other people). Perfect (or close to perfect) correlations are not usually found in the behavioral sciences, but can be found in Newtonian physics, such as for the relationship between the mass of an object and the force necessary to accelerate it at a given rate.

It is generally well understood among behavioral scientists that a strong correlation between variables x and y does not mean x is the cause of y. First, it may be that y is really the cause of x. For example, a strong positive correlation may be found for a sample of people between wealth and level of education. Although it may be that wealth leads people to pursue education, it could also be the other way around so that one's education level determines wealth (more highly educated people may earn more money than less-educated individuals). Second, it may be that another variable (or variables) may cause both x and y, so that wealthy people receive both wealth and educational opportunities from their wealthy parents.

But although a strong correlation does not imply causation, we nonetheless should expect to see a strong correlation between two variables if one of them *is* the cause of the other. For example, if smoking really does cause lung cancer, we should find a strong positive correlation between smoking behavior and incidence of this disease, and we do. This is why in Powers's Demo 1 it is of such interest to find a near-zero correlation between what the participant sees and what he does, since this is strong evidence that what the participant does (response) is *not* directly caused by what he sees (stimulus). Instead, what the participant does *controls* what he sees.

Less striking, at least initially, is the relationship between the cursor (which is what the participant saw) and his handle movements (what he did). The small movements of the cursor above and below the horizontal axis of the graph indicate that the participant was successful in keeping the cursor close to the target position but did not achieve perfect control. And the correlation between the cursor and handle in this run was only 0.179, which is quite close to zero as far as its strength is concerned. But it is this near-zero relationship that is remarkable since we might naively expect what the participant saw to influence what he did. Once we realize, however, that what he *did* also influenced what he *saw* (he was, after all, using his behavior to control his perception of the cursor), the lack of relationship makes more sense. The lesson being, once again, that the circular causality characteristic of perceptual control does not work according to rules of one-way cause-effect phenomena characteristic of the behavior of nonliving objects. In Demo 1 the indication that the participant is actually controlling his perception of the cursor is that there is virtually no measurable one-way relationship between what the participant saw and what he did.

This rather curious characteristic of perceptual control is demonstrated more clearly in step I of Demo 1, intentional vs. accidental effects. In this demonstration, there are now three cursors between the target lines (see figure 6.7). All three are influenced by the participant's movement of the handle, but each is affected by a different disturbance. This would correspond to a task in which three knotted pairs of rubber bands were looped around a participant's finger with three separate disturbers on the other ends. Although the participant's actions move all three cursors, having three disturbance patterns means that only one of the three cursors can be kept between the target lines. The participant's task is to pick one of the three cursors to control, and it is the computer's task to figure out which one it is.

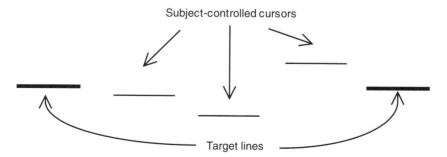

Figure 6.7
Screen display for Demo 1, Step I tracking task

Someone watching the participant do this task would have no difficulty deciding which cursor was being controlled since it is the one that remains close to the target position while the others wander up and down the computer screen. But this is not how the computer makes its decision. It does so by computing correlations between handle movements and all three cursors and picking the cursor that has the *weakest* (closest to zero) correlation with the handle. This counterintuitive approach works very well. In a typical run, correlations between 0.70 and 0.90 are obtained between the handle and the two uncontrolled cursors, while a virtually zero correlation (such as negative or positive 0.10) is obtained between the actually controlled cursor and the participant's handle movements.

An interesting variation of this method of distinguishing the intentional effects of actions from their unintended side effects was developed by psychologist Richard Marken. In his Mind Reading demonstration (developed for Macintosh computers and for Java-enabled Web browsers such as current versions of Netscape Navigator and Internet Explorer) on any computer platform, several numbers (boxes in the Java version) roam the computer screen, each continuously pushed around in two dimensions by its own disturbance. What is seen is not unlike a few scattered fallen leaves being blown around on the ground by its own gusts of wind. But the participant's computer mouse, along with the disturbances, also influences the movements of each number, pushing them all in the same way. By focusing on one number, the participant can control its position on the screen. The participant can decide to keep the chosen number stationary (counteracting its disturbances) while the other numbers continue to be buffeted by their disturbances. In this case it would easy for an observer to find the number being controlled, as it would be the only nearly stationary number on the screen.

But the participant could also decide to move his chosen number in any desired pattern, as in tracing out a circle, square, or figure eight, or even writing his name across the screen with the number. In these cases, since all the numbers will be moving around the screen in irregular patterns, an observer would be hard pressed to tell which one was being controlled by the participant. But the computer only has to find the weakest correlation between the movements of each number and the movements of the participant's mouse to determine which number the participant is intentionally moving. When found, the program indicates the controlled number by highlighting it in boldface. This mind reading of the participant's intentions works no matter what type of pattern the participant imposes on his number, as long as he has an intention concerning where he wants the number to be and varies his behavior to bring about the desired perceptions.

Another program developed by Marken called Find Mind allows the subject to do some mind reading of her own. Now we have numbers (boxes again in the Java version) roaming around the screen as before, but one of them is different from all the others, although this is not at first apparent from watching them move. All the numbers but one have been programmed to move around the screen not "caring" where they roam. If one of these numbers had been programmed to move one inch to the left while a disturbance pushed them all an inch upward, the number would simply move about an inch and a half toward the upper left corner by combining its own movement with that of the disturbance. But one of the numbers represents the actions of a control system with a varying reference signal specifying where it should be at any given instant and the means to counteract disturbances to achieve its goals. As in the previous demonstration all the numbers are influenced by the computer operator's mouse movements, but the one acting as a control system will go where it intends to go (the intention, of course, having been provided in the computer program by the programmer) and will resist disturbances to its movements. By trying successively to keep each number contained in a box at the center of the screen, the user will soon find the one number that has a mind of its own in not "wanting" to be in the box. This one number actually "feels" quite alive in its resistance to the user's mouse-induced disturbances.

These demonstrations were designed to give the user a better understanding of the phenomenon of perceptual control and to show some of its rather surprising characteristics, such as near-zero correlation between perception and action when one's actions are used to control one's perceptions. But Powers and his associates did not stop there. They wanted to show not only that perceptual control is a real phenomenon but that control systems can provide useful working models for animal and human behavior.

Powers's Demo 2, modeling compensatory tracking, leads the user step by step to the construction of a working control system whose behavior in a tracking task is compared with that of the user. In step F, closing the loop, the user sees how a working control system keeps the cursor centered on a target location and how changing the system's reference signal influences the consequences of its behavior. In step J, matching the model to real behavior, the user can compare his behavior to that of the model control system and make adjustments to the model until its behavior closely matches his own. In figure 6.8, the top diagram portrays the computer model's behavior (with plots of cursor, handle, and disturbance provided) and the bottom diagram is that of the human operator. The smaller

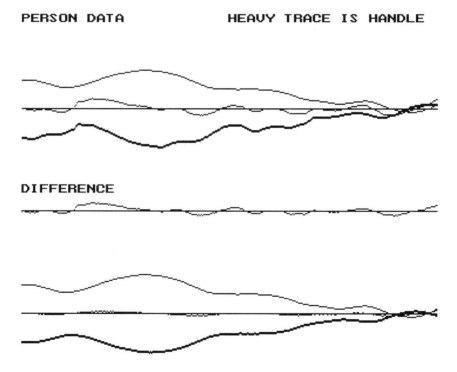

PERSON DATA   HEAVY TRACE IS HANDLE

DIFFERENCE

MODEL DATA

Figure 6.8
Matching person and model data in Demo 2

graphic separating the two shows the difference in their behavior. In the particular case shown, the difference was very small, with the correlation between the control system's behavior and the human's (in this case yours truly) equal to a very strong correlation of 0.986. This near-perfect correlation indicates that the control-system model fits the human's behavior extremely well (it should be noted that correlations stronger than 0.70 are quite rare in the behavioral and social sciences). Thus, Powers's Demo 2 goes well beyond the typical diagram of a psychological theory in that it can be turned into a working model that does what it was designed to do, that is, control some aspect of its environment as a purposeful human performs this same task.

Demonstrating a Hierarchy of Perceptual Control

Powers and his associates also developed a number of demonstrations of the hierarchical organization of human control systems that was described earlier and illustrated in figure 6.3. Recall that in a hierarchy of control systems, higher-level systems send their outputs as reference signals to lower-level systems. In this way the higher-level control systems do not tell the lower-level ones what to do but rather what to perceive as the consequence of their actions. This proposed hierarchical organization has at least two implications. First, it makes some interesting predictions about the performance of certain tasks. Second, it should prove useful in modeling certain types of animal and human behaviors.

Our first demonstration requires a human participant and you as experimenter. First, ask your participant to extend her arm fully toward the front so that her hand is at the same level as her shoulder, and to maintain it in this position. Now you apply disturbances to her extended arm by pushing her hand gently up and down and from side to side. If the participant indeed has the goal of maintaining her arm in this fixed position (as you have asked her to do), she will resist your disturbances, pushing back on your hand with the force required to keep her arm more or less stationary. This is a rather simple feedback-control system of the type shown in figure 6.2, with you acting as the environmental disturbance. You will notice that your participant's control of her arm is not perfect, but she should be able to keep her arm fairly close to her intended position as long as you don't apply too great a force to her hand or make very rapid changes in the force you apply.

Now as your participant maintains her extended arm position, place your own hand above and lightly touching hers and tell her that when given a certain signal she should bring her arm quickly down along her side. The signal will not be a verbal one, however. You will give it by pushing down on her extended hand (remember your hand is already touching hers) when you want her to change the position of her arm. When you provide the signal as described, you will notice a curious reaction from your participant. Instead of quickly bringing her arm down to her side as soon as you push down on it, she will at first resist your push for a fraction of a second. You can do this again and again, and each time this momentary resistance and hesitation will occur. This resistance seems at first rather odd since you are pushing her hand in the direction that she intends to move it. So why does she initially resist your push?

The hierarchical organization of control systems makes it clear why this must happen. By asking your participant to move her hand down when you push on it, you are actually asking her to change her reference signal (goal) for the position of her hand from straight out to down. But the only way this reference signal for hand position can be changed is by the output of the control system above it, the one that supplies the reference signals to the lower control system and is concerned with your participant's higher-level goal of complying with your request. It would be a disturbance to this higher-level system if your participant were to keep her arm and hand extended after you have pushed down on it, and so to correct for this error the higher-level system changes the reference level for the arm-position control system below. But before the higher-level system can perceive the push on her hand, the lower system has already sensed it (since it is lower in the hierarchy) and taken appropriate action to maintain the original position before the reference level can be changed to the new position by the higher-level system. So this momentary resistance and hesitation in bringing her arm down when pushed are exactly what a hierarchical control-system model of behavior predicts.

Many other manual demonstrations of the hierarchical organization could be described (see, for example, Robertson & Powers 1990, p. 21). But we will now move on to another interesting computer program developed by Powers known as Arm 1.

This computer demonstration (which again can be run on any IBM-compatible computer running DOS or in a DOS window) shows both how a hierarchy of control systems could be used to model human pointing behavior and how such a model could be used to create a robot arm. The task for the computer-simulated arm involves bringing its fingertip in contact with the center of a suspended triangular target and maintaining contact while the target is moved anywhere within reach in the three-dimensional space in front of the arm. This may seem to be a rather simple task for a robot arm to accomplish, but it turns out to be quite complicated, as least when pursued in the typical manner of using what the robot sees to compute what it should do. For this one-way cause-effect approach to work, the robot first has to see the target, determine its position in space, convert this position to the angles required at the shoulder and elbow joints for its fingertip to touch the target (this calculation is known in robotics as *reverse kinematics*), and finally calculate the forces required to bring the arm to this position without undershooting or overshooting the target using what is known as *reverse dynamics* (see Bizzi, Mussa-Invaldi, & Giszter 1991 for evidence of the extreme complexity of this feed-forward approach to pointing to a target).

But this pointing behavior is actually quite easy to accomplish using seven simple control systems, with six of them organized into a two-level hierarchy. At the higher level are three visual control systems, each of which sees both the target and the robot arm's fingertip and also has a reference level of zero for the perceived distance between fingertip and target. One of these visual control systems controls horizontal distance between fingertip and target by sending its output as a reference signal to the comparator of a lower-level kinesthetic control system that controls the side-to-side angle of the shoulder joint. The second of the upper-level visual control systems controls the vertical distance between fingertip and target by sending a reference signal to another lower-level system that controls the up-and-down angle of the shoulder joint. And the third upper-level visual control system makes sure that the fingertip is not behind or in front of the target by controlling for zero perceived difference in the distance of the target and fingertip from the eyes by manipulating the reference level sent to the elbow joint. These six simple control systems, plus a separate seventh one that keeps the robot facing the target, are sufficient to keep the simulated robot pointing to the target as the user manipulates the position of the target in simulated three-dimensional space using the keyboard or a mouse (see figure 6.9). Powers's Arm 2 program does the same, but is more realistic (although slower) in that it includes the effects of gravity on the arm, real arm dynamics (related to the physical characteristics of human arms and muscles), and the possibility for the robot to learn to point more effectively over time (Powers 1999).[4]

Demonstrating Social Systems

Social systems composed of interacting purposeful individuals also were modeled using perceptual control theory. Powers, together with sociologists Clark McPhail and Charles Tucker (1992), developed a program called Gather[5] that models the movements of temporary gatherings of individuals (persons or animals). In these simulations, individuals are programmed as control systems that begin their existence at a certain point on the screen and move to satisfy the reference levels they are given for their locations. Each individual's location goal is either a fixed point on the computer screen or a certain proximity to another individual who also has a goal of either a fixed location or distance to another individual. Each individual also has reference levels for avoiding too-close proximity to other individuals and the fixed obstacles that are scattered across the screen. The user can manipulate the number of individuals, their goals, the number of obstacles present, and various other parameters

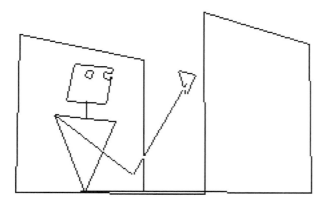

Figure 6.9
Pointing arm simulation

of the individuals' control systems, and see the effects on their collective behavior.

Figure 6.10 is the result of one run of Gather in which one individual, labeled M, moves from the left of the screen to its destination goal in the circle on the right side of the screen. The goals of the four individuals labeled G are not fixed locations but rather the intention to remain close to M without being too close to each other or run into any of the obstacles indicated by small circles.

With the choice of the right control-system parameters, all of the individuals are successful in achieving their goals (as the traces on figure 6.10 indicate) regardless of the distribution of the obstacles they must avoid. Their collective behavior is similar to that of a human mother being followed by her four children across a shopping mall while avoiding other individuals and objects, or a mother goose followed by her four goslings as they waddle from meadow to lake avoiding rocks and trees along the way. It is also of interest to note that the arc formed by the four Gs does not exist as a goal for any of the individuals but rather emerges as an uncontrolled (but reliable) side effect of the outcomes that the Gs are controlling, namely, maintaining a certain distance between themselves and M.[6]

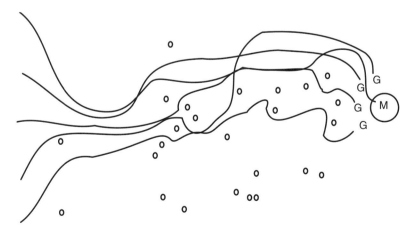

Figure 6.10
Gather simulation of four individuals (G) following another (M) (after McPhail, Powers, & Tucker 1992)

Three Final Demonstrations: Controlling Another Person, "Ballistic"
Movements, and the Coin Game

Three final demonstrations, none requiring a computer, are worth describing since each shows another interesting characteristic of perceptual control. The first requires the same knotted rubber bands (see figure 6.4) used in the first demonstration, a table, two coins placed about 10 inches apart on the table, and, of course, our indispensable willing human participant. As in the first demonstration, you and your participant each grasp an end of the two knotted rubber bands, and you ask your participant to keep the knot over the coin that is farther from him. But this time as you watch the position of his hand, you move your hand so that he places his hand over the other coin.

What you have done is controlled the behavior of your participant by "making" him put his hand over the other coin. This control was achieved by knowing what perceptual consequence he was controlling and providing the disturbances that would lead him to put his hand where you wanted it to be. But this control of your participant's behavior works only as long as he maintains his goal of keeping the knot over the more distant coin and *does not care* (that is, has no higher-level goal or reference signal for) where his hand is located over the table. If either of these conditions no longer holds (your participant either no longer wishes to comply with your request to keep the knot over the one coin, or does not want to keep his hand over the other coin) you will no longer be able to control his behavior without recourse to overwhelming physical force. This indicates a general principle of the control of one person's behavior by another: Other than using irresistible physical force, an individual can control another individual's behavior (or more accurately, the *outcome* of his behavior) only by causing disturbances to goals that will elicit the desired behavior, and only if the desired behavior does not disturb the goals of higher-level control systems.

Another example shows the fallacy of the common belief that certain so-called ballistic behaviors take place too quickly for continuous sensory feedback to be involved in their execution. Two such behaviors are hammering and throwing a ball or stone. Neurobiologist William Calvin (1990, p. 239) made just such an argument and proposed it as a factor contributing to the evolution of the human brain:

. . . ballistic movements [are] quite unlike the ones where an intention and feedback corrections suffice to get the job done: Brief movements have to be carefully planned in advance. Any trial and error has to be done while planning, checking a proposed movement against memory as you "get set," and discarding the plans that don't jibe.

To see if feedback can actually be used in these actions, one has to figure out how to apply a disturbance to the behavior while it is occurring and see if it is resisted to any extent. This can be easily done by attaching an elastic band to your participant's wrist (I use a large loop of rubber about an inch wide cut from an old bicycle inner tube) and have him throw or hammer while you apply a disturbance by pulling on the elastic band after his action has begun (still better would be to use two elastic bands with two disturbers pulling on one, or the other, or both, or neither so that the participant could not anticipate what the disturbance would be).

For throwing I have my participant throw a tennis ball underhand from a distance of about 15 feet against a chalkboard on which a target consisting of a circle of about 1.5 feet in diameter has been drawn. For hammering, I place a coin on a table and let the participant hammer on it with his closed fist (it's technically pounding, not hammering, but much easier on the table if not on the fist). While disturbances applied by the elastic band will likely have some effect on the accuracy of throwing or hammering, the effects are quite small compared with the magnitude of the disturbance. This is something you should also experience as the thrower or pounder with your participant attempting to disturb your actions, since you will experience how you automatically adjust your actions "on the fly" to compensate for the disturbances.

The fact that these disturbances can be corrected after the throwing or hammering action has begun indicates that negative-feedback control *is* involved in these supposedly ballistic behaviors. If they were the result of preplanned motor commands (as Calvin and many others believe), no real-time corrections would be possible at all. The results of these demonstrations are instead consistent with the operation of a hierarchy of control systems in which upper-level systems do not tell lower-level systems what to *do* (that is, provide motor commands) but specify what lower-level systems should *perceive*. The controlled perception is that of a certain sequence of joint angles (known as *proprioception*) that has been associated with the perception of previously successful throwing or pounding and that will itself be adjusted by still higher-level systems depending on the perceived outcome of each trial. It is important to note that a form of associative learning is occurring here. But it is not that of associating a stimulus with a behavior. Rather, it is associating higher-level controlled perceptions with lower-level ones.

The final demonstration is the coin game devised by Powers (1973, pp. 235–236). It shows how difficult it can be to figure out what perception another person is controlling, even when you have the opportunity to make repeated disturbances and guesses.

To play the game you need four coins, a table, and your human participant. Have your participant first arrange the coins in any configuration she wishes (for example, rectangle or square, or even something like two coins closer to each than the other two coins are to them or to each other) and ask her to write down in words on a piece of paper the configuration or condition that she has adopted as her goal. You as experimenter attempt to guess what your participant is controlling by disturbing the coins any way you wish and having the participant say "no error" or correct the error (by moving a coin or coins) that you have created. Once you are fairly certain that you know what the participant is controlling, test your hypothesis by making three moves, each of which you believe will be corrected by the participant, followed by three moves you believe will cause no error. If successful, you then describe what you believe to be your participant's controlled variable (such as, any three coins in a straight line) and compare it with what the participant wrote down.

Playing the coin game will reveal how difficult it can be to determine what the participant is "doing" (actually, what perception she is controlling) even though her actions are completely visible to you, and you can repeatedly disturb the configuration of coins and observe her reaction. Of course, the game is none other than a form of the test for the controlled variable mentioned earlier and provides an illustrative example of how the test can be used to understand another person's behavior.

I hope that I have provided useful descriptions of these demonstrations and what they reveal about the process of perceptual control. Verbal descriptions alone, however, cannot come close to providing the understanding and insights that hands-on experiences with these demonstrations can provide. For this reason, I strongly urge that readers take the time to do at least the rubber-band demonstrations, and that those with access to a personal computer and the Internet obtain and try out the computer demonstrations. Only in this way can one realize that seeing behavior as the control of perception is not just another cute slogan or cliché, and that cybernetic models of perceptual control are more than just boxes and lines on pieces of paper. Rather, perceptual control is a real and easily demonstrated phenomenon that cannot be understood from the traditional one-way cause-effect view of animal and human behavior, and networks of negative-feedback perceptual control systems can be fashioned into working models that behave remarkably like the purposefully behaving animals and humans that they were meant to simulate. Most important, however, is understanding that we now have a basic theory (and model) of animal and human behavior that can explain its purposeful nature in purely materialist and mechanistic terms, but which requires a rejection of the one-way cause-effect view of living behavior.

The Puzzle of the Ultimate Why Question

We have now seen how considering animate behavior as an organism's means to control aspects of its environment provides a new way of addressing questions concerning the what, how, and why of behavior. From this perspective, what questions are addressed by considering the perceptual variable that an organism is controlling, keeping in mind that any given action may have many uncontrolled side effects that are of no concern to the behaving organism, and that the behavioral consequences specified in reference levels need not be static but instead can be continually changing.

How questions are answered by considering the subgoals, or lower-level reference levels, that must be controlled for a higher-level perceptual variable to be controlled. From this perspective, a professional golfer is able to drive her ball onto the green not because her nervous system is able to send a certain fixed sequence of motor commands to her muscles, but because she has learned to control a sequence of lower-level perceptions involving the positions and velocities of her limbs, head, and trunk, as well as the relationship of these kinesthetic and proprioceptive perceptions to the visual perception of the green she is aiming at.

In contrast to behavioral how questions that focus our attention on lower-level control systems and their reference levels, why questions about behavior are addressed by moving up the hierarchy of control systems to find higher-level reference levels (or goals) that determine lower ones. Someone observing my behavior at this moment would notice that I am currently tapping keys on my computer. Why? To make certain letters and words appear on my computer screen (not to make the tapping sound that accompanies each keypress, although objectively my typing is creating noise as well as words). Why make these words appear? Because I want to write and publish a book. Why write and publish a book? Maybe to became famous and make lots of money from royalties (not very likely). Or perhaps so that I can make a lasting contribution to human knowledge (somewhat more likely?). But why bother contributing to human knowledge (I could be outside enjoying this beautiful late spring day rather than sitting in my office in front of a computer)? Good question. As we have noted earlier, as we continue to ask why questions about behavior we usually come to a point at which we no longer can easily imagine what words to put after "because."

But the hierarchy of goals posited by perceptual control theory provides at least a framework for considering answers to why questions. And the answers we find are very different from the ones proposed by one-way cause-effect theories that look for answers not within the organism but rather in the effects that the environment has on the organism. Because we attempt to answer these questions by searching for the next higher-level control system and its reference level, these can be considered the proximate causes of behavior.

But for any theory of behavior to be complete, ultimate causes of behavior must also be considered. We observe a robin pecking in the soft earth during a rainstorm and understand its behavior as a way of getting food in the form of earthworms into its stomach. But why earthworms and not the seeds that the sparrows and finches consume? A male robin pursues a female until she allows him to mount her. From where did this urge to copulate come? We later see the female robin regurgitating her food into the gaping mouths of her newly hatched chicks. But why should she share her hard-earned food with this chorus of seemingly insatiable little beaks?

Similar questions concerning the ultimate reasons for behavior could easily be posed for humans, but answers cannot be found by staying within an individual organism's hierarchical network of perceptual control systems. Instead, we have to consider the process responsible for life itself and its continued evolution.

III

Behavior and Evolution: Then and Now

7

The Evolution of Animal Behavior:
The Impact of the Darwinian Revolution

Darwin's theory of natural selection came very late in the history of thought. Was it delayed because it opposed revealed truth, because it was an entirely new subject in the history of science, because it was characteristic only of living things, or because it dealt with purpose and final causes without postulating an act of creation? I think not. Darwin simply discovered the role of selection, a kind of causality very different from the push-pull mechanisms of science up to that time. *The origin of a fantastic variety of living things could be explained by the contribution which novel features, possibly of random provenance, made to survival. There was little or nothing in physical or biological science that foreshadowed selection as a causal principle.*

—B. F. Skinner (1974, p. 36; emphasis added)

People and animals are most remarkable for the things they do. Inanimate objects and forces certainly can impress us, as when a tornado plows through an American prairie town, a volcano erupts in Indonesia, an earthquake wreaks havoc on a Japanese city, or a comet pays a visit to our corner of the cosmos. But most of the objects that we encounter tend to stay in one place unless pushed or pulled in some way by an animal or person.

Living animals and people are different. They can burrow, crawl, walk, run, hop, climb, swim, and even fly to get where they want to go. Many animals engage in complex rituals for attracting mates and employ clever tricks for finding food, avoiding enemies, and raising their young. They build elaborate structures such as spider webs, beehives, coral reefs, bird nests, and beaver dams to provide shelter and to obtain food and store it for themselves and their associates. Some even make and use tools. One particular species, *Homo sapiens*, has transformed a considerable portion of the earth's surface, covering it with farms, highways, parking lots, houses, shopping centers, and skyscrapers.

Watching all this activity, the curious mind must wonder why all these organisms do what they do. Further reflection suggests that there are really two different types of why questions to consider about the behavior of animals and humans. One concerns immediate or *proximate* explanations. In the previous chapter we learned how seeing animate behavior as the means by which organisms control perceived aspects of their environment provides one set of answers to why questions. A cybernetic, control-system perspective allows us to understand purposeful behaviors in terms of the goals they achieve, such as attracting mates, obtaining food, finding (or building) shelter, avoiding enemies, or caring for offspring.

But we have also seen that this goal-based view does not address the ultimate questions having to do with why such goals (and the perceptual control systems that serve them) appeared in the first place. This is a particularly interesting question when we consider the many complex behaviors (and their consequences) of animals and humans.

This chapter focuses on these questions concerning animal behavior and chapter 8 deals with human behavior. We will see how the proposed answers go beyond the model inherited from Newtonian physics to arrive at a very different type of explanation first proposed by a reclusive English naturalist well over a hundred years ago.

The How and Why of Animal Instincts

When we observe the actions of animals we notice two rather distinct types of behaviors. One type consists of acts that every individual of a given species is somehow able to perform without first having to experience them performed by others, and without being in any way guided or instructed in them. Thus a mother rat will build a nest and groom her young even if she is raised in total isolation and has never seen other female rats engage in those acts (Beach 1955). The behaviors involved in the caterpillar's spinning a cocoon, the spider's weaving a web, the beaver's constructing a dam, and the honeybee's sculpting a honeycomb are additional examples of complex behavior that seem to be somehow built into these organisms.

The other type of behavior consists of acts that appear to be influenced by an animal's own particular experiences, and it is here that we notice striking differences in individuals of the same species. A circus performance shows us what dogs, bears, horses, lions, tigers, and elephants can do when provided with certain types of experiences. Dogs do not normally walk upright on their hind legs, bears are not to be seen riding motorcycles through the woods, or seals balancing beach balls on their noses in the Arctic. Yet these creatures can perform these and other unnatural acts if given a special type of environment provided by a circus and its animal trainers.

Similarly, whereas all normal, healthy children manage to breathe, laugh, cry, walk, and even talk without explicit instruction, such is not the case for reading, writing, mathematics, and music performance skills. The development of these latter abilities normally requires many years of explicit instruction coupled with many long hours of practice. Of the two types of behaviors, the first is typically referred to as *instinctive*, *innate*, or *inherited*, and the second as *learned* or *acquired*.

Two interrelated questions can be asked concerning instinctive behaviors of animals. The first deals with their origin and the second deals with their propagation. It is important to address the questions separately, but we will see that the most satisfactory answer we have to each turns out to be very much the same. We will also see that the answer to the ultimate why question provides an answer to the question of how these behaviors originally came about.

Instinct Through Divine Providence

One view of instinctive animal behavior came to us in the Western philosophical tradition through the writings of Aristotle, Thomas Aquinas, and Descartes, and remained popular and virtually unchallenged through the eighteenth century. This view attributes the source of instinctive behavior to an all-knowing creator. As Thomas Aquinas reasoned in the thirteenth century:

Although dumb animals do not know the future, yet an animal is moved by its natural instinct to something future, as though it foresaw the future. Because this instinct is planted in them by the Divine Intellect that foresees the future. (1265–1273/1914, p. 470)

Later in the eighteenth century the views of followers of Aristotle and those of Descartes differed in many respects concerning animal behavior. But like Thomas Aquinas they agreed that complex animal behavior could be explained by an appeal to instincts that they understood as blind, innate urges instilled by God for the welfare of his creatures.

It is within this tradition of Christian thinking that we find William Paley (1743–1805), an English archdeacon, theologian, and philosopher. The Reverend Paley saw in the instinctive behavior of animals convincing evidence for the existence, goodness, and wisdom of God. He made his point by emphasizing those behaviors that could not possibly have been the result of learning during the lifetime of the organism. Thus he described (1813, p. 306) how moths and butterflies

deposit their eggs in the precise substance, that of a cabbage for example, from which, not the butterfly herself, but the caterpillar which is to issue from her egg, draws its appropriate food. The butterfly cannot taste the cabbage—cabbage is no food for her; yet in the cabbage, not by chance, but studiously and electively, she lays her eggs. . . . This choice, as appears to me, cannot in the butterfly proceed from instruction. She had not teacher in her caterpillar state. She never knew her parent. I do not see, therefore, how knowledge acquired by experience, if it ever were such, could be transmitted from one generation to another. There is no opportunity either for instruction or imitation. The parent race is gone before the new brood is hatched.

Paley emphasized that if the animal has no opportunity to learn behaviors that are essential to the survival and continuation of a species, the originator of the behaviors must be God. From this supernatural perspective the question of transmission of behaviors to the next generation simply does not arise, since the behaviors are an integral part of the organism as designed by its creator.

Although such supernatural accounts are no longer held by behavioral scientists, providential thinkers such as Paley must be credited for noticing an important characteristic of these behaviors—that they are essential to the survival and reproductive success of the animal, even though it is unlikely that the animal is mindful of their ultimate function. The providentialists saw the mind of God as the explanation, but other scientists of the nineteenth century were seeking more naturalistic, materialist explanations.

Instinct Caused by the Environment

The work of Charles Darwin's grandfather, Erasmus Darwin (1731–1802), offers one materialist alternative to the providential view of instinct. Erasmus Darwin's annoyance with that view can be seen in his observation that from this perspective, instinct "has been explained to be a kind of inspiration; whilst the poor animal, that possesses it, has been thought little better than a machine!" (quoted in Richards 1987, p. 34). He and other "sensationalists" of the time emphasized the role of *sensory* experience. They believed that all behavior was based on the experience and intelligence of the individual organism, and described ways in which apparently instinctive behavior could be explained as such. But this explanation fared less well with behaviors performed immediately after hatching or birth. A French naturalist's theory appeared, at least initially, to do better.

Although early in his career Jean-Baptiste Lamarck (1744–1829) believed that all species had originally come into existence in much the same form as he observed them during his lifetime, he eventually accepted and promoted a theory of transformation by which over long periods of time organisms could change into new species. He also formulated a materialistic account of how the habits of animals of one generation could be changed into the instincts of their descendants, an account that bypassed Paley's God[1] and proposed instead mechanisms of environmental influence on organisms and their response to these factors.

According to Lamarck, changing environmental conditions forced organisms to change their habits. These changed habits involved increased use of certain body structures and organ systems along with the decreased use of others, with resulting organic changes being passed on to succeeding generations. Since behavior is clearly influenced by biological structures including internal organs and appendages, the inheritance of such modified structures would result in the instinctive behavior dependent on the structures in succeeding generations. In this way Lamarck attempted to provide explanations both for the origin and transmission of new instinctive behaviors.

This materialist theory was well in keeping with the growing scientific naturalism of the nineteenth century, as was its one-way cause-effect character. The latter can be seen in its three necessary components. First, the environment causes a change in an animal's behavior (imagine a bird's environment becoming drier, so that it now has to find, crack open, and eat bigger and harder seeds than it did when smaller, softer seeds were more readily available).[2] Second, this change causes structural changes in the animal, both a result of the new behavior and facilitator of it (the bird develops a larger, more powerful beak, better able to crack bigger and tougher seeds). Third, these changes in structure and behavior are transmitted to the animal's offspring who thereby inherit the new high-performance beak and the (now instinctive) behaviors for using it. As Lamarck explained (1809; quoted in Løvtrup 1987, p. 53),

> Everything which has been acquired . . . in the organization of the individuals in the course of their life, is preserved through the reproduction, and is transmitted to the new individuals which spring from those who have undergone these changes.

In his view the environment causes changes in behavior, which cause changes in body structures, which in turn cause changes in the germ (egg and sperm) cells, which cause instinctive behavior in offspring. This causal chain from environment to behavior to bodily structure to germ cells to offspring has the ultimate effect of producing new organisms that possess as instincts the acquired habits of their parents.

But although Lamarck's theory successfully avoids a supernatural creator, it runs into serious problems of its own. First, how is it that a changing environment causes animals to assume adaptive behaviors? If soft seeds are no longer available, how does the environment cause the bird to search out and attempt to eat larger, tougher seeds? Particularly problematic in this regard are behaviors that cannot be imagined as the result of individual learning, as the egg-laying behavior of the moth and butterfly (in Paley's observation quoted above).

Second, according to Lamarck's principle of use and disuse, body parts that are used a great deal will develop and become more adapted to such use, whereas those that are not used will shrink and atrophy. But, to remain with our example, how will a bird's attempting to crack a seed that is too big and tough for its beak cause its beak to become bigger and stronger? We all know from our attempts to repair things that using a tool that is too small or weak will usually ruin the tool (and often what we are trying to fix), not make it bigger and stronger. As another example, consider that our shoes do not grow thicker soles the more we walk in them, nor do they become thin by being left unused in the closet. On the contrary their soles wear out from extended use and maintain their original condition only if not used. Now it is clearly the case that among living organisms we see what appear to be Lamarckian effects of use and disuse, as when someone begins to exercise and develops larger muscles and then stops and loses them again. But something more than a direct physical cause-effect phenomenon must be involved here because these adaptive results are not what we see happening in the objects we use where continued use leads to wear and tear and eventual breakdown, but disuse results in preservation.

Third, we must consider if the structural and behavioral changes an organism undergoes during its lifetime actually cause similar changes in its offspring. Lamarck was so convinced that such acquired changes were passed on to offspring that he wrote that the "law of nature by which new individuals receive all that has been acquired in organization during the lifetime of their parents is so true, so striking, so much attested by facts, that there is no observer who has been unable to convince himself of its reality" (1809; quoted in Burkhardt 1977, p. 166).

Indeed, the belief that acquired characteristics were inherited by one's offspring was well accepted in Britain and Europe throughout most of the nineteenth century, yet it turns out that there was never any good evidence for it whatsoever. A man and a woman who develop large and strong muscles either through hard physical labor or sport do not have a son or daughter who is born with similarly well-developed muscles. A man and woman who both become proficient pianists will not produce a child who can instinctively play the piano. And as German embryologist August Weismann (1834–1914) rather gruesomely demonstrated, chopping off the tails of several generations of mice does not produce successive generations of tailless mice or even mice with shorter tails. Weismann consequently made an important distinction between those cells of the body that are passed on to the next generation in reproduction (germ cells) and other cells that are not (somatic cells). He held that changes to somatic cells could in no way cause corresponding changes to germ cells. Separation of these two types of cells remains today as a generally recognized barrier to Lamarckian inheritance of physical or behavioral characteristics so that the habits acquired by one generation cannot become innate instinctive behaviors in a later one.[3]

So we see that while Lamarck attempted to provide a naturalistic, non-providential account of instinctive behavior, his theory (referred to by some as *instructionist*, since it assumes that the environment can somehow directly cause or instruct adaptive changes in behavior) failed at every posited cause-effect relationship, from environment to behavior, from behavior to somatic cells, and from somatic cells to germ cells. Clearly, a radically different explanation was needed.

Instinctive Behavior as Naturally Selected

Just such a radically different explanation was proposed by Charles Darwin. Darwin's initial attempt to explain instincts had much in common with Lamarck's theory. He believed that beneficial habits that persisted over many generations would make heritable changes in the organism leading to instinctive behavior in later generations. Gradually, however, he became dissatisfied with the idea of inherited habits as the sole explanation for instinctive behaviors, particularly when he realized (as Paley had before him but Lamarck apparently had not) that many of these behaviors (such as the moth laying eggs in cabbage) could not have originated as habits. Another example is provided by British natural theologian Henry Lord Brougham who wrote in 1839 about the female wasp who provides grubs as food for the larvae ("worms") that will hatch from its eggs "and yet this wasp never saw an egg produce a worm—not ever saw a worm—nay, is to be dead long before the worm can be in existence—and moreover she never has in any way tasted or used these grubs, or used the hole she made, except for the prospective benefit of the unknown worm she is never to see" (quoted in Richards 1987, p. 136). We know that Darwin was intrigued by this observation since he wrote in the margin of Brougham's book "extremely hard to account by habit." It was, in fact, more than "extremely hard" since "an act performed once in a lifetime, without relevant experience, and having a goal of which the animal must be ignorant—this kind of behavior could not possibly have arisen from intelligently acquired habit" (Richards 1987, p. 136).

So in keeping with his theory of natural selection for the origin of species, Darwin began to see instincts not as results of inherited useful habits but as consequences of the reproductive success of individuals already possessing useful habits (although he never completely abandoned the former idea). Natural selection thus provided an explanation for instinctive behaviors that never could have originated as habits, such as the wasp's egg-laying behavior.

Darwin's selectionist theory of instinct differs fundamentally from Lamarck's one-way cause-effect (or instructionist) theory of evolution. For Lamarck, the environment somehow caused (directed, instructed) adaptive changes in organisms that were passed on to future generations. It is this direct, causal effect of environment on organism that constitutes the one-way push-pull character of Lamarckian theory. But in Darwin's selectionist theory, individuals of a species naturally vary their behavior, with the environment playing no active, instructive role in causing this variation. Instead, the environment's role is restricted to that of a type of filter through which more adaptive behaviors pass on to new generations and less adaptive ones are eliminated. Darwin's selectionist explanation is distinctly different from Lamarck's in that the behaviors offered to the scrutiny of natural selection are not caused by the environment but are rather generated spontaneously by the organisms.[4]

An example may be useful here. Among Darwin's finches in the Galápagos Islands, one particular species, appropriately called the vampire finch, foregoes the vegetarian diet of seeds and nuts of other finches and prefers instead the taste of blood, obtaining it by perching on the back of a booby (a larger bird) and jabbing it with its pointed beak until it draws blood (see Weiner 1994, p. 17). Since this is the only bloodthirsty finch on the islands, it is reasonable to assume that the species descended from birds that did not drink blood. But because of natural variation in the behavior of its ancestors, some of these finches must have tried pecking at other birds and found some nutritional advantage from the practice, producing more offspring than birds that tried pecking at other objects. Within any one generation, these birds would show natural variation in feeding behavior; and after many generations of variation and selection the vampire finch that we know evolved. So unlike Lamarck's theory, which assumed that an animal's learned behaviors were inherited by its offspring, Darwin's selectionist account of instinctive behavior can work only with a *population* whose individuals already vary in their behavior, selecting behaviors leading to greater survival and reproductive success. Darwin, unfortunately but understandably, hadn't a clue as to why individuals of a species varied in form or behavior, or how these variations could be inherited by following generations. Our current knowledge of genetics and the molecular basis of mutation and sexual reproduction provides answers to these questions and strong support for Darwin's conclusion.

But one particularly thorny problem remained for Darwin concerning instinct, that of the evolution and behavior of neuter insects. The *Hymenoptera* order of insects includes bees and ants together with some wasps and flies. Many of these insects live in well-structured societies where survival depends on a specialized division of labor among the members that is reflected in different castes, such as the queen, drones, and workers in a beehive. Particularly intriguing and troublesome for Darwin's theory of natural selection was the fact that worker castes are often made up of insects that are sterile and therefore have no genetic means of passing on their instinctive behaviors to the next generation of workers. This posed a serious threat to Darwin's theory, as he was well aware.

A solution came after he learned how cattle were selected for breeding to produce meat with desirable characteristics. As described in a book by William Youatt published in 1834 and read by Darwin in 1840, animals from several different families would be slaughtered and their meat compared. When a particularly desirable type of meat was found, it was, of course, impossible to breed from the slaughtered animal. But it was possible to select for breeding cattle most closely related to it to produce the desired meat. In like manner, a colony of insects that produced neuters that helped the survival of the community (say, by taking care of young, providing food, or defending against enemies) would be naturally selected to continue to produce such neuter insects even if the neuter insects themselves could not reproduce. Darwin concluded that "this principle of selection, namely not of the individual which cannot breed, but of the family which produced such individual, has I believe been followed by nature in regard to the neuters amongst social insects" (1856–1858/1975, p. 370).

The concept of kin and community selection became powerful in understanding the evolution of altruistic behavior (to which we will return shortly) and it provided Darwin with an explanation for complex and useful instinctive behaviors that could not be explained by Lamarckian inheritance. But where the inheritance of acquired habits seemed conceivable, particularly when Darwin could see no selective advantage for the behavior, he made use of Lamarckian principles. And since for some reason Darwin was unable or unwilling to see survival or reproductive advantages accruing from the expression of emotions, he explained these as inherited useless habits that existed only because they accompanied more useful ones.

Despite the enormous impact that Darwin had on the life sciences during his own lifetime, he had relatively little immediate impact on the scientific study of animal behavior. One reason for this has to do with methodological difficulties of both naturalistic and experimental research on animal behavior. Another was the heavy use of anecdotal evidence and anthropomorphic interpretation practiced by George Romanes (1848–1894), Darwin's young disciple and defender who wrote extensively about animal behavior and mind from a Darwinian perspective while maintaining belief in the inheritance of acquired habits.

It was not until the 1930s that a serious attempt to study animal behavior from evolutionary and selectionist perspectives was begun. Konrad Lorenz (1903–1989) grew up sharing his family's estate near Vienna with dogs, cats, chickens, ducks, and geese. His observations in this setting eventually led to the founding of the field of ethology, which he defined as "the comparative study of behaviour . . . which applies to the behaviour of animals and humans all those questions asked and methodologies used as a matter of course in all other branches of biology since Charles Darwin's time" (1981, p. 1).

As suggested by this definition, Lorenz was primarily interested in finding evolutionary explanations for instinctive behavioral patterns characteristic of a species. For example, it was brought to his attention that greylag geese reared by humans would follow the first person they had seen after hatching in the same way that naturally hatched goslings waddled after their real mother. Lorenz confirmed these findings and extended them to several other species of birds. This pattern of behavior, resulting from a type of bonding with the first large moving object seen by the hatchling, he called imprinting, and it is for this finding that Lorenz is still best known.

By extending Darwin's theory of natural selection to animal behaviors observed in the field, Lorenz posited a genetic basis for specific behaviors that was subject to the same principles of cumulative variation and selection that underlie the adapted complexity of biological structures. In the case of the greylag goose, goslings that maintained close contact with the first large moving object they saw (which would normally be their own mother) would be in a better position to enjoy her protection and nurturance. Consequently, they would be more likely to survive and to have offspring that would similarly show this behavioral imprinting than goslings lacking this behavioral characteristic. In much the same way that we now understand how a tree frog can become so well camouflaged over evolutionary time through the elimination by predators of individuals that are less well camouflaged, we can understand how instinctive behavior can be shaped through the elimination of individuals whose behaviors are less well adapted to their environment.

Another example of Lorenz's conception of instinctive behavior is the egg-rolling behavior of the greylag goose. When the goose sees that an egg has rolled out of her nest, she stands up, moves to the edge of the nest, stretches out her neck, and rolls the egg back into the nest between her legs, pushing it with the underside of her bill. Lorenz called this a "fixed motor pattern" (1981, p. 108), that is, a sequence of actions generated in the central nervous system of the goose that is released or triggered by the sight of an egg (or other egglike object) outside the nest. In other words it is a fixed sequence of actions released by a specific type of stimulus. The purpose of this instinctive act is clearly to return the egg to the security of the nest, and it is easy to appreciate its value for the continued survival of the species.

But a serious problem with this concept becomes apparent when one realizes that an invariant pattern of actions will not be successful in returning a wayward egg to the nest unless all environmental conditions are exactly the same for each egg-rolling episode. This is, of course, the same problem with all one-way cause-effect theories. Instead, for the goose to be consistently successful in returning an egg to her nest she must be able to modify her behavior not only from episode to episode but also within each episode to compensate for variability in conditions and disturbances that she inevitably encounters, such as differences in the distance between herself and the egg at the beginning of the behavior, and irregularities in the terrain between the egg and the nest. This is another instance of consistent outcomes requiring variable means that William James described as the essence of purposeful behavior. And it is for this reason that Lorenz's stimulus-response analysis ultimately fails to explain the typical success of instinctive actions.

Many good examples of the variability of instinctive behaviors that are directed to fixed, consistent outcomes can be found in a book published in 1945 by E. S. Russell entitled *The Directiveness of Organic Activity*. Here are just three.

1. The larva of the caddis fly (*Molanna*) builds itself a protective case made of grains of sand. If this case is overturned, it will try a remarkable range of behaviors to right it. It will normally first extend its body out of the tube of the case and grip the ground with its forelegs in an attempt to flip the case over sideways. If this does not work, the larva will reverse its position and make a hole in the tail end of the case. Then it will either extend its body out the rear of the case and attempt to twist the case around the long axis of its body, or reach under the case and flip the case over its head. If the ground is very fine, loose sand, the larva will produce silk to bind grains together to make a firmer platform for righting its case. Or it may try to pull its case to another spot where the ground provides better traction. If all this fails, the caddis larva may bite a piece off the roof of the case and use that as a platform for its righting attempts, or even remove an entire wing of the case to flip it over. If the larva is still unsuccessful after several hours of work, it will abandon its case and build a new one somewhere else (Russell 1945, pp. 123–124).

2. The burying beetle (*Necrophorus vestigator*) is so called because it buries small dead animals on which it deposits its eggs. These insects often cooperate in this endeavor, working together to remove soil from under the animal so that it sinks into the earth. If the corpse lies on grass-covered soil, they will bite through the impeding stems and roots. If a mat of woven raffia is placed under the corpse, the beetles will cut through that as well. If a dead mole is tethered to the ground by raffia strips, the beetles will start their usual digging, but when the mole does not sink they will crawl over it, find the tethers, and cut them. If a small mouse is suspended by wires to its feet, the beetles will bite through the mouse's feet. If the suspended mouse is large, the beetles will be unsuccessful, although they may work for nearly a week before abandoning the project. Russell also

reported that when a dead mouse was placed on a brick covered with a thin layer of sand, the beetles spent a few hours trying unsuccessfully to bury it. Then they spent several more hours pulling the mouse in various directions until it was finally dragged off the brick and buried (1945, pp. 125–126).

3. The shore crab (*Carcinus maenas*) moves its legs in a fixed progression when walking forward. If one or more legs are amputated, it is still able to move about, but the order of movement of the remaining legs is changed, clear evidence that locomotion is not achieved by a fixed motor pattern that is inherited and unmodifiable. Similarly, "an insect which has lost a leg will at once change its style of walking to make up for the loss. This may involve a complete alteration of the normal method, limbs which were advanced alternately being now advanced simultaneously. The activities of the nervous system are directed to definite end, the forward movement of the animal—it uses whatever means are at its disposal and is not limited to particular pathway" (Adrian; quoted in Russell 1945, pp. 127).

So it appears that Lorenz was mistaken in insisting on innate fixed motor patterns as the basis for instinctive behavior. But he must nonetheless be acknowledged as the first to attempt to provide a Darwinian account of species-specific behavior patterns, and he was recognized for his achievement in 1973 when he shared a Nobel prize with fellow ethologists Nikolaas Tinbergen and Karl von Frisch. In the same way that biologists constructed evolutionary trees (phylogenies) by comparing the anatomical similarities and differences among living organisms and fossils, Lorenz used patterns of instinctive behavior, basing his comparative study "on the fact that *there are mechanisms of behavior which evolve in phylogeny exactly as organs do* (1981, p. 101). His evolutionary perspective also led him to emphasize that understanding animal behavior involved appreciating its purposefulness in preserving the species, its role in the entire repertoire of the animal's activities, and its evolutionary history.

Whereas Lorenz was successful in going beyond a one-way cause-effect view of the origins of instinctive behaviors, he nonetheless maintained a rather stimulus-response view of the actual behaviors performed. He concluded that evolution works in a selectionist manner, resulting in the emergence of those organisms with adaptive stimulus-response systems that contribute to survival and reproductive success. He was apparently unaware of the need for and existence of an alternative to this account that was as necessary as his selectionist explanation of its origins. And he would have no doubt been intrigued by the type of behavior generated by the Gather computer simulation described in chapter 6 that provides a striking simulation of the mother-following behavior of his beloved geese.

Foundations and Misconceptions

Lorenz placed the study of instinctive animal behavior within a thoroughly Darwinian framework, but his work initially had rather limited impact, especially in the United States. One reason for this was his association with the Nazis during World War II (see Richards 1987, pp. 528–556). Another reason was the then-dominant behaviorist paradigm in North America that was much more interested in learned behavior of rats and pigeons in artificial experimenter-controlled laboratory settings than in naturally occurring behavior of a variety of animals in their natural habitats. But Lorenz's Darwinian initiative eventually had an important impact on both sides of the Atlantic.

Before discussing this impact, it will be useful to outline in a bit more detail the necessary components of a standard evolutionary view of instinctive animal behavior. For evolution by natural selection to occur, three conditions must be met. First, there must be variation in the population of organisms making up a species. Although we may be most accustomed to thinking of this in terms of the physical make-up of organisms (morphology) such as size or coloration of body parts, variation in species-typical behavior can also be observed among individuals of a species, such as in feeding and mating behaviors.

Second, this variation in behavior must have consequences for reproductive success. Measured as the number of viable offspring produced, it requires both survival to the age of reproductive maturity (for which obtaining food and avoiding predators and serious diseases are essential) as well as the ability to find mates and, for some species such as birds and mammals, feed and protect one's offspring.

Finally, variation in behavior influencing reproductive success must be heritable; that is, it must be able to be passed on to the next generation.

Although this inheritance of behavior need not be limited to genetic inheritance (since forms of cultural learning are also possible for many animal species), evolutionary accounts usually emphasize the genetic component.

The importance that a Darwinian view of instinct ascribes to survival and reproductive success should come as no surprise for two reasons. First, if variation in behavior exists and behavior can be inherited by the next generation, clearly those behaviors that were not conducive to survival and reproduction would eventually be eliminated from the species. Any male squirrel that attempted to mate only with pine cones or engaged only in oral sex with other squirrels would simply not have any descendants to continue these innovative (for squirrels) sexual practices. Similarly, any mammal (other than humans or mammals raised by humans) that refused to nurse at its mother's breast would not survive long enough to find a mate and produce nipple-avoiding offspring of its own.

Second, the survival or reproductive function of many striking instinctive behaviors that we see among animals are rather obvious. The spider spins an intricate web. Why? If we watch what happens after the web is complete the answer becomes obvious—to obtain food. A wasp paralyzes a caterpillar with her venom and buries it alive with her eggs. Why? So that her hatched larvae will have fresh food (and not decayed, putrid flesh) when they emerge from their eggs. The male ruff, a European shore bird, spreads its wings, expands the collar of feathers around his neck, and shakes his entire body when a female ruff comes in sight. Why? To attract a mate. The parasol ant carries bits of freshly cut leaves back to its nest. Why? To grow a certain type of fungus that it uses for food. Countless other examples could be given, and indeed much of the appeal of books, films, and television programs about nature lies in their portrayal of such instinctive behaviors that have obvious survival and reproductive functions. And although we certainly need not assume that these animals are in any way conscious or aware of the survival, reproductive, or evolutionary consequences of their actions, the survival or reproductive role that most instinctive behaviors play is either initially obvious or made clear by further research into the life and habits of the particular species.

An evolutionary perspective on behavior can be misleading in at least three ways, however. The first has to do with Lorenz's original conception of instincts as fixed motor patterns. As we saw in the previous chapter, invariant sequences of actions cannot be adaptive in an environment containing unpredictable disturbances. An assembly-line robot may be able to assemble an automobile part by repeating the same motion over and over again, but it is successful only to the extent that its environment is carefully controlled to prevent disturbances from affecting the production line. The real world of living organisms, with its changing weather conditions and the presence of many other (often competing and hostile) organisms, is anything but a carefully controlled production line. In its natural environment an animal's action patterns cannot remain invariant if they are to be functional; rather its behavior must compensate for such disturbances. It is now recognized by at least some ethologists that animal instincts are modifiable by feedback received during execution of behaviors (see Alcock 1993, pp. 35–37).

We saw in chapter 6 how organisms organized as networks of hierarchical perceptual control systems can be effective in producing repeatable, reliable outcomes despite unpredictable disturbances. For an evolutionary perspective on instinctive behavior to make sense, we have to discard the commonly accepted notion that specific behaviors can evolve and be usefully inherited, and instead recognize that it is perceptual control systems and reference levels that are selected and fine-tuned for their survival and reproductive value across generations. We also have to be on guard against the behavioral illusion demonstrated in the previous chapter that makes it seem as though environmental factors (or stimuli) cause behavior, when in fact organisms vary their behaviors to control aspects of their perceived environment.

The second potential danger lurking in evolutionary accounts of instinctive behavior is the tendency to regard genes as *determiners* of instincts and consequently to regard instinctive behaviors as essentially inborn or innate. We know that genes do influence an organism's behavior, as it has been shown repeatedly and clearly that certain genetic differences are associated with striking behavioral differences. For example, changing a single gene in the fruit fly *Drosophila melanogaster* results in male flies referred to as *stuck* since they do not dismount from females after the normal period of copulation (Benzer 1973). Another single-gene difference affects the daily activity cycle of fruit flies. Normally this period is twenty-four hours long, but flies with a particular variation of a gene (referred to as an *allele*) have no fixed activity cycle. Flies with a second type of allele have shortened nineteen-hour activity cycles, and flies with a third allele have lengthened cycles of twenty-nine hours (Baylies et al. 1987).

But whereas individual genes and groups of genes have an important influence on behavior, they alone cannot determine behavior since all development and consequent behavior depend on the interaction of genes and environmental factors, the latter including physical factors such as nutrition and temperature as well as various sensory experiences. In this respect, genes can be thought of as a type of basic recipe for building an organism, while the environment provides the necessary materials and additional crucial information in the form of certain sensory experiences. When viewed in this way, questions concerning whether a given behavior depends more on nature or nurture can be seen to be meaningless, as would be asking whether the appearance and taste of an apple pie depend more on the recipe or on the ingredients. Of course, both are crucially and 100 percent important, since without the recipe (or equivalent knowledge of apple-pie baking) the ingredients are useless, as would be the recipe without the ingredients.

Some striking examples of the necessary interaction of genetic and environmental factors in determining behavior have been provided by the common laboratory rat. A mother rat will normally build a nest before bearing offspring and then groom her newborn pups. That she performs these behaviors even if she is raised in total isolation from other female rats, and so has never seen other rats engage in such behaviors, is the reason that such activities are referred to as instinctive. Nonetheless, certain experiences are necessary for these behaviors to take place. For example, when provided with appropriate nesting materials a pregnant rat will not build a nest if she had been raised in a bare cage with no materials to carry in her mouth. Also, a mother rat will not groom her young if she had been raised wearing a wide collar that prevented her from licking herself (Beach 1955). And failure to groom her babies can have serious consequences, since a newborn rat cannot urinate until its genital area has been first so stimulated, resulting in burst bladders for the unfortunate unlicked pups (Slater 1985, p. 83).

These and other findings indicate that instincts are not behaviors that are somehow completely specified in the genome of an animal, as stated by Lorenz. Rather, they are species-typical behaviors that emerge from the interaction of an animal's genes with the usual environmental conditions. As research shows, a change in either genes or environment can result in a change in instinctive behavior.

A final danger to guard against in taking an evolutionary view of animal instincts is thinking that all instinctive behaviors must be well adapted to the organism's present survival or reproductive needs. Although most instincts appear to have current survival or reproductive value, it does not follow from evolutionary theory that *all* such behaviors do. Certain behaviors may be neutral or even maladaptive side effects of other adaptive behavior. Reasons have been advanced for how certain forms of homosexual animal behavior can improve reproductive success; for example, cows mounting other cows may signal to nearby bulls that the cows are sexually receptive (see also Bagemihl 1999 for a comprehensive review of animal homosexuality). Research suggests, however, that at least some forms of homosexuality, such as that among female macaque monkeys, serves no clear direct or indirect reproductive function and may be simply a side effect of natural selection of animals with high sex drives (see Adler 1977). Such "useless" behavior may be tolerated by natural selection if it has negligible effects on ultimate reproductive success. But we should not expect it to persist for long if it has negative effects on survival and reproduction unless it appears as an unavoidable side effect of some other adaptive behavior that compensates for the effects of the maladaptive one.

In addition, because of the long periods of time required for evolution to shape adaptive instinctive behaviors, there is no guarantee that such behaviors are still adaptive today. Moths used the moon and stars to navigate during their nightly forays for millions of years when these celestial bodies were the only nocturnal sources of light. But the appearance of countless sources of artificial illumination in areas inhabited by humans now has moths spending the night flying in dizzy circles around electric light bulbs, into flames, or onto the electrocuting grid of bug zappers. The distinction between the environment in which a behavior evolved and the current environment where it may be less well suited will become particularly important when we consider human behavior in the next chapter.

The Problems of Altruism and Cooperation

Keeping in mind these potential problems of evolutionary accounts of behavior, we can now turn to some other aspects of animal behavior that first challenged and then showed the value of such an approach. The role of instincts in promoting the survival and reproduction of individual organisms (and therefore continued existence of copies of their genes in future generations) puts a distinctive selfish spin on instinctive behavior. It would initially seem that any behaviors that were helpful to others but costly to the originator should simply not evolve as instincts.

So-called *altruistic* acts, such as sharing food or putting oneself at risk by crying out to warn others of an approaching predator, would appear to reduce the ultimate reproductive success of the altruistic donor while increasing that of its recipients and genetic competitors. Yet these and other apparently altruistic behaviors are commonly observed among animals. A ground squirrel emits an alarm call upon noticing a predator, thereby warning other squirrels but putting itself at greater risk of predation (Alcock 1993, p. 517). A vampire bat regurgitates blood for a neighbor that was unsuccessful in finding its own meal (Slater 1985, p. 178). It was this problem of accounting for the evolution of altruistic acts that attracted the attention of a new generation of British and American biologists in the 1950s, 1960s, and 1970s who were interested in solving this and other evolutionary puzzles about animate behavior.

Among these scientists was British geneticist, biometrician, and physiologist J. B. S. Haldane (1892–1964) who in 1955 provided an important clue. He noted that a gene predisposing an animal to save another animal from some danger, with the potential "hero" running a 10 percent risk of being killed in the attempt, could spread in the population through natural selection if the animal thus saved were a close relative of the hero, such as an offspring or sibling. This is because a closely related individual would have a good chance of sharing the same altruistic gene as the hero, so that a copy of the gene in question would likely be saved even if the hero were to perish by his actions. Haldane also noted that such a gene could even spread, although not as quickly, if the saved individual was more distantly related to the hero, such as a cousin, niece, or nephew. "I am prepared to lay down my life for more than two brothers or more than eight first cousins" (reported in Hamilton 1964, 1971, p. 42) was his way of summarizing this phenomenon.

This was the beginning of the formulation of what is known as *kin selection*, the idea that a gene is not "judged" by natural selection solely on its effects on the individual who carries it, but also on its effects on genetically related individuals (that is, kin) who are also likely to carry a copy of the gene. From this perspective, altruistic behavior toward kin can be understood as a form of selfishness on the part of the gene necessary for the behavior, since the related individuals who receive assistance are likely to carry a copy of the same gene and pass it down to their offspring.

As there are different degrees of relatedness (the closest being identical twins; followed by offspring and full siblings; then half siblings, grandchildren, nieces, and nephews; followed by first cousins, etc.) it would make evolutionary sense for altruistic behavior to be scaled according to the degree of relatedness so that it would most likely be directed toward the closest relatives. British biologist William Hamilton developed these ideas in papers published in 1963 and 1964, noting that evolution should be expected to bias altruistic behavior toward close relatives and therefore also select for the ability of altruistic animals to discriminate close relatives from more distantly related individuals so that their acts could be preferentially directed toward the former and not the latter.

But whereas kin selection is an important factor in the evolution of behavior, we also see apparently altruistic acts directed toward unrelated individuals.[5] How can evolution account for this?

The modern answer was first hinted at in 1966 by American biologist George C. Williams in *Adaptation and Natural Selection*, a book that became a classic in evolutionary biology. Williams suggested that beneficent behavior toward another unrelated individual that was initially costly for the donor (for example, giving away food) could in the long run be advantageous if the favor was later returned.

This idea was further developed and refined in 1971 by American biologist Robert Trivers with the theory of *reciprocal altruism*, as in "I'll scratch your back if you'll scratch mine." Here, cooperative and seemingly altruistic behavior can evolve among individuals who are not closely related. Indeed, it can also account for mutually advantageous relationships observed between different species, such as that between cleaner-fish and the larger fish that they clean. During cleaning, the cleaner-fish obtains a meal and the cleaned fish gets rid of troublesome parasites, but only as long as it refrains from gobbling down the much smaller cleaner-fish. Through such symbiotic behavior both cleaner and cleaned profit in ways that would not be possible without mutual co-operation (see Trivers 1971).

Another topic much studied by researchers taking an evolutionary approach to animal behavior is sex differences. No matter how successful an animal is in finding shelter and food and defending itself from disease and enemies, none of these achievements can have evolutionary significance if the animal does not reproduce and have offspring that survive until they in turn reproduce. For sexually reproducing species, reproduction means finding a mate, and offspring of many species require some form of parental care.

The importance of finding a mate and factors determining mate selection were first pointed out by Charles Darwin in *The Descent of Man and Selection in Relation to Sex*, published in 1871. Darwin observed that males often compete with each other for access to females and that females in contrast tend to be choosy in their selection of partners, often preferring males with alluring courtship displays or some physical characteristics that could well interfere with their day-to-day survival. Darwin understood that such selection pressure was responsible for the elaborate "ornaments" possessed by males of many species, such as the bright and striking plumage of the paradise bird and peacock, and deer antlers.

But sexual selection and its consequences for animal behavior were largely ignored for the next century until Robert Trivers's 1972 paper, which drew attention to the fact that sex cells (gametes) produced by males (sperm) are much smaller and more numerous than those produced by females (eggs). An individual male may well provide enough sperm cells (many millions) during a single mating theoretically to impregnate every female of the species. This is in sharp contrast to the females of most species who produce a much smaller number of much larger eggs (in birds, a single egg may equal from 15 to 20 percent of the female's body weight). This marked discrepancy in potential reproductive potential (being much greater for males) should have important consequences for differences in sexual behavior, and as we will soon see, it does.

Making Darwinian Sense of Animal Behavior

Darwin's theory of evolution by natural selection turned out to be remarkably successful in providing answers to many ultimate why questions about animal behavior. Animal behavior scientists have repeatedly found that behaviors appearing at first quite puzzling often make good sense when seen from the Darwinian perspective, especially when principles of kin selection, reciprocal altruism, and sexual selection are taken into account. Let us take a brief look at some examples that can be understood using these evolutionary principles.

Since Hamilton's formulation of kin selection, many studies of animal behavior yielded results that are consistent with the theory. Parental care for offspring, such as that often observed in birds and mammals (and also practiced by certain species of insects and fish) is one obvious form. In one setting where it might appear difficult for parents to recognize their offspring, the communal cave nurseries of the Mexican free-tailed bat that may contain many thousands of crowded young pups, mothers find and feed their own offspring greater than 80 percent of the time (McCracken 1984). For certain birds whose young receive assistance from nonparents, these helpers are typically closely related individuals such as siblings (Harrison 1969; Brown 1974).

It was mentioned earlier that insects of the order *Hymenoptera* live in societies with a strict division of labor. Particularly intriguing are workers who diligently care for the queen's offspring and yet are sterile and therefore unable to have offspring of their own—certainly an extreme form of altruism. It turns out that these species are *haplodiploid*, meaning that each female receives the normal half of its mother's genes but *all* of its father's genes. Because of this genetic quirk, sterile female workers are actually more closely related to their siblings than they would be to their own offspring!

Similar societies in which most individuals are sterile and raise the offspring of their mother have been found that are not haplodiploid, for example, the naked mole-rat. Kin selection theory would predict that these altruistic individuals should show a very high degree of genetic relatedness to each other so that the altruistic genes they carry have a high probability of also being present in the individuals they assist even though they have no descendants of their own. This fact was found for the naked mole-rat (Reeve et al. 1990).

Examples of reciprocal altruism in which one individual assists another that is not closely related in order to receive some benefit in return (either at the same time or later) are widely reported in studies of animal behavior. The relationship between cleaner-fish and their cooperative hosts was mentioned earlier. Another interesting example is provided by olive baboons (*Papio anubis*). Sexually receptive females of this species are usually closely attended by a single male consort on the lookout for opportunities to mate. A rival male, however, may solicit the aid of an accomplice male who engages the consort in a fight. While distracted, the rival has uncontested access to a female. What is in this for the accomplice who fights but does not mate? He will likely get his chance at mating the next time when his buddy will take his turn in distracting another consort (Packer 1977).

What about differences in male and female behavior related to the roles they play in reproduction, with males' billions of tiny cheap sperm and females' much fewer, much larger, and much more costly eggs? The huge quantity of sperm cells that a male produces means that gaining access to as many mates as possible increases his reproductive success. But this is usually not the case for a female, whose reproductive success depends more on the fate of her fertilized eggs. This would lead us to expect that males should be more eager to mate and less discriminating in their choice of mates than females, who should be more restrained and more choosy in their selection of mates. And this is just what was found across a very wide range of animal species including insects, amphibians, reptiles, birds, and mammals.

A good example of discriminative mate choice is provided by female insects that demand a "nuptial gift" from the male before allowing copulation to take place. The female black-tipped hangingfly (*Bittacus apicalis*) will reject the advances of any male that does not first offer a morsel of food. And the larger the male's gift, the better the male's chances of inseminating the female, since a quickly consumed tidbit may lead the female to cut short the mating process and seek another gift-bearing male (Thornhill 1976). Such behavior puts selection pressure on males to provide larger bits of food since males with little or no gifts are not likely to have their "stingy" genes represented in the next generation, whereas those with larger gifts are more likely to reproduce.

This is just one example of many in the animal world of eager males having to provide resources to females for sperm to gain access to eggs. But it is not always food that is offered. Many female birds will mate only with males that control a food-producing territory. Female bullfrogs prefer mating with the largest males (as indicated by the strength and pitch of their singing), and it is not likely coincidental that the largest males usually control the breeding locations that are best suited to the development of fertilized eggs. Female birds often select males based on their song repertoire, plumage, size, or courtship ritual, which are indicators of health, strength, and parental ability as well as the likely mating success of male offspring fathered by the male (see Alcock 1993, chapter 13, for many similar examples).

But there are some fascinating exceptions to these typical male-female differences in reproductive strategies. In some species we find a complete reversal of the typical sex roles. Among pipefish of the species *Syngnathus typhle* the male receives from the female the eggs he has fertilized and keeps them in his brood pouch until they hatch. Since females can produce eggs more quickly than males can rear them, brooding pouches are in great demand among females. So as one would expect, it is the male pipefish who is picky about his mates, preferring large, well-decorated females who appear to be able to provide many high-quality eggs for him to carry.

Another interesting example of sex role reversal is the Mormon cricket (which, curiously, is neither a cricket nor Mormon but rather a katydid with no known religious preference). The male produces for his mate a large, nutritious meal in the form of what is called a *spermatophore*. Since the spermatophore may weigh as much as 25 percent of his body weight, he can usually produce only one in his short lifetime, thereby limiting his mating opportunity to just one female. Since he invests so much in his single mating, he is choosy, preferring to mate with large females who carry a greater number of eggs, and females compete for access to him.

These examples are of particular interest since they demonstrate that it is not gender itself or any intrinsic property of egg or sperm cells that normally makes males competitors for and females selectors of mates. Rather it is the gender with the higher reproductive costs that is choosy in selecting a mate, whereas the gender with the lower costs is less dis-criminative and more competitive. The fact that exceptions are so nicely accounted for by the struggle for survival and maximization of reproduc-tion is an indication of the power of the Darwinian perspective on animal behavior.

A particularly striking example that can be explained from an evolu-tionary perspective involves the grisly act of infanticide. Hanuman langurs are monkeys found in India that live in bands consisting of one sexually active male and a harem of females with their young. Occasionally, the resident male is expelled from the group by another male after a series of violent confrontations. When this occurs, the incoming male attacks and kills the infants that were fathered by the previous resident male.

Many reasons could be proposed for this behavior. Perhaps high testos-terone levels left over from fighting result in heightened aggression and attacks on easy victims. Or maybe the new male makes use of the infants as a source of high-protein food after a period of great physical exertion. Or it could be that infanticide is a pathologial reaction to the high stress accompanying the artificially high population densities of langurs in the many locations where they are fed by humans.

An evolutionary explanation, however, would look first at the repro-ductive consequences of langur infanticide, and these turn out to be con-siderable. Nursing females provide resources to the offspring of the previous male. In addition, lactating females do not ovulate and so cannot be impregnated by the new male. So by killing the infants the incoming male both eliminates the reproduced genes of his male rival and makes the females sexually receptive once again. That male langurs have never been observed to eat the infants they kill and that infanticide occurs also in areas of low population density lend support to the hypothesis that infanticide is a means of achieving reproductive advantage (Hrdy 1977). Also consis-tent with this interpretation is the observation of infanticide in similar con-ditions by other animals including the lion (Pusey & Packer 1992) and the jacana (Emlen, Demong, & Emlen 1989), a water bird.

Of course male langurs need not be conscious of the reasons for their killing ways, any more than they are conscious of why they have a tail or fingers. It is extremely unlikely that they have figured out that lactating females do not ovulate and that killing infants will make their mothers fertile and sexually receptive. It is more reasonable to suppose that incoming males simply have an instinctive desire to eliminate from their band all infants, a goal (or reference level) that was repeatedly selected in past generations because of the reproductive advantages it conveyed.

These are just a few examples of how an evolutionary perspective focusing on reproductive success provides answers to the ultimate why questions concerning a wide range of animal behaviors. Many other examples could be given showing the survival and reproductive function of behaviors animals use to find and make places to live, obtain food, defend themselves from predators, cooperate with other animals, mate, and care for offspring (see Alcock 1993, and McFarland 1993). Indeed, it can be said that evolutionary theory now provides the core explanatory framework for studies of animal behavior in natural settings. In addition, it is strongly supported by countless experiments in both field and laboratory settings (again, see Alcock 1993, for descriptions of many such studies).

But when invoking evolutionary answers to these ultimate why questions, we must be on guard against the tendency to see specific behaviors as being selected for their survival and reproductive benefits. Instead, we know that what are selected and inherited are not fixed patterns of action but rather goals in the form of reference levels and the physical means to achieve them despite continual and unpredictable disturbances provided by an uncaring Mother Nature.

To illustrate this essential point, let's consider a spider spinning its web. The webs of any given species of orb-weaving spider are all of the same basic design, but actual dimensions must vary because of variations in the locations where they are installed, such as branches of a tree or bush. So it is obvious that no invariant sequence of actions will be successful in installing a web in all locations. Instead, each web must be custom-designed for the site it is to occupy.[6]

The spider is able to fit web to site not by engaging in a fixed pattern of actions but by *varying* its behavior for each stage of web building until certain goals are met before it proceeds to the next stage. First, the spider, perched on a branch, releases a strand of silk into the wind until it catches on another branch. Since the distance to the other branch will be different for each site, the spider cannot release a fixed length of silk each time and therefore it has no fixed sequence of behavior. Instead, it must continually let out silk until it feels that its sticky end is attached to another branch (probably not unlike the way an angler fishing for bottom fish lets out line until he feels the weighted hook come to rest on the bottom of the lake). The amount of silk it will then pull back in for the proper tension must also vary from one web to another, depending on the distance between the branches and the stiffness of the branches themselves. After tying the near end to its branch, the spider uses this first strand to drop a looser second strand and then a third to form a Y configuration with three stands meeting at what is to become the center of the web. The spider then begins to construct additional radials, like the spokes of a bicycle wheel, checking angles between the radials with its outstretched legs and continuing to add radials until the angle between each spoke and its neighbor falls below a certain value. Each radial is also carefully cinched in so that it has the proper tension.

Next, the spiral portion of the web is constructed. Using a temporary nonsticky strand as a scaffold, the spider works first from the center outward and then from the periphery back toward the center, laying down permanent, sticky silk that will trap its future meals. The spider again carefully controls the spacing between spirals, since too much space would allow insects to pass through the web and too little would be wasteful of precious silk. Finally, the spider determines how much the web sways in the breeze. If sway is excessive, it may attach weights in the form of small pebbles or twigs to one of the web's lower corners. If after all this work the spider judges the web to be unsatisfactory, it will abandon the site and construct another web elsewhere.

Due to the nature of web building and the varied conditions in which it occurs, sensory feedback is essential to all stages of construction. It is only by varying its behavior as required to achieve each subgoal that the spider is successful in recreating the same basic design that evolved over millions of years for its prey-catching ability. As noted by William James (1890, p. 7): "Again the fixed end, the varying means!" In the case of the spider's web, the fixed end can be brought about only by achieving a number of subgoals in a particular order. It is these subgoals and the means for achieving them, not the spider's actions themselves, that evolved because of their value in providing the spider with a means for its livelihood.

Learned Behavior

We have seen that instinctive animal behaviors are (and must be) more flexible than originally understood by Lorenz for them to remain adaptive in a world of unpredictable obstacles and disturbances. But these behaviors nonetheless have real limits to their flexibility. A spider's web catches prey, and the spider must custom-build each web to fit its site. But the design it uses is the same basic one that has been successful over many thousands of years. If this design now turns out to be unsuccessful for a particular spider in securing food, the spider cannot make another kind of web, like the more productive one being used nearby by another species. It is stuck with the design of its species in much the same way that it is stuck with having eight legs, a hairy body, and an appetite for juicy insides of insects.

Other animals show more flexibility, being capable of learning. Whereas an insect-eating spider will eat only insects, rats will nibble on just about anything that might be edible and learn to distinguish what is nutritious from what is not (more on this type of rat learning later). Thus individual rats of the same species may have very different diets and food preferences according to their dining experiences. The circus examples given at the beginning of this chapter of dogs walking on their hind legs, bears riding motorcycles, and seals balancing beach balls on their noses are particularly striking cases of animal learning that appear unrelated to such naturally occurring instinctive behaviors as barking, scratching, and catching fish. But these unnatural acts arise only in a specially arranged environment where they are instrumental in obtaining food and achieving other goals. Although psychologists recognize several different forms of learning, we will focus here on the kind that involves acquisition of what appear to be novel behaviors as a result of the animal's particular experiences.

One way of looking at such learning is to see it as a behavioral adaptation to environmental changes that happen too quickly to be tracked by natural selection. Gradual changes in climate or the gradual appearance and extinction of pathogens, prey, and predators can affect instinctive behavior through the differential survival and reproduction of organisms with adaptive behaviors. But more rapid environmental changes taking place from one generation to the next or even within a generation cannot be tracked by evolution. As Skinner (1974, p. 38) observed, "contingencies of survival cannot produce useful behavior if the environment changes substantially from generation to generation, but certain mechanisms have evolved by virtue of which the individual acquires behavior appropriate to a novel environment during its lifetime." These "mechanisms" refer to ways of learning that allow animals to adapt their behavior to unpredictably changing environments.

We considered several approaches to learning theory in chapter 3, including classical conditioning theories of Pavlov and Watson as well as instrumental and operant conditioning theories of Thorndike and Skinner. But since that chapter came before the discussion of perceptual control theory in chapter 5 and before the evolutionary perspective presented in this chapter, it will be worth while to take another look at learning and modification of animal behavior from these new perspectives, focusing on the type of learning that Skinner was interested in.

As described in chapter 3, Skinner included both one-way cause-effect and selectionist components in his theory of how animals acquire new behaviors, in much the same way that Lorenz included both of these in his account of instinctive behavior. The selectionist component for Skinner had to do with the learning process itself; that is, how new behaviors are first emitted (random variation) with certain ones selected by the environment according to their consequences. It is for this reason that Skinner emphatically rejected the frequently applied characterization that his was a stimulus-response theory because of the "unstimulated" nature of the originally emitted novel behaviors.

But despite his protests, an important one-way cause-effect component of Skinnerian theory comes into play after a new behavior has been learned. This is because the new behavior is then elicited or caused by sensory stimuli that are the same as or similar to environmental stimuli experienced when the behavior was originally selected. The rat may stumble upon pushing the lever to obtain food in a haphazard, random way, but after it learns this new way of feeding itself it will immediately approach and push the bar (if hungry) when placed into the same or similar box in which the behavior was learned. It is for this Newtonian-inspired one-way cause-effect conception of performance of already learned behaviors that Skinner's theory was and still is characterized by many behavioral scientists as a stimulus-response theory. This characterization is understandable, if not completely justified, when it is realized that Skinner repeatedly referred to the "stimulus control" of behavior. Although he understood stimulus broadly as the cumulative effects of all previous sensory stimuli experienced by the organism, he emphasized that "the environmental *history* is still in control" (Skinner 1974, p. 74). By control he actually meant cause. This view of behavior is in striking contrast with the circular causality of perceptual control theory, which sees organisms purposefully varying their behavior to control perceived environmental consequences of those behaviors. In other words, instead of Skinner's selection *by* consequences we have Powers's selection *of* consequences.

A good way to contrast the difference between these theories of how organisms modify their behavior is to consider an intriguing pattern of behavior Skinner observed. He found that he could obtain very high rates of a behavior (such as a hungry pigeon pecking at a key to obtain food) by gradually *decreasing* the rate of reinforcement. These high rates could be obtained by starting out with a relatively generous reinforcement schedule that provided a grain of food for each key peck, and then using progressively more stingy schedules requiring more and more pecks (for example, 2, 5, 10, 30, 50, 75, and 100) for each reward. Skinner was thereby "able to get the animals to peck thousands of times for each food pellet, over long enough periods to wear their beaks down to stubs. They would do this even though they were getting only a small fraction of the reinforcements initially obtained" (Powers 1991, p. 9).

But if, according to this theory of operant conditioning, reinforcement increases the probability of the behavior that resulted in the reinforcement (note that this describes a *positive*-feedback loop) how could it be that *reducing* the reinforcement leads to an *increase* in the rate of behavior? This puzzle is solved when we see reinforcement not as an environmental event but rather as a goal the organism achieves by varying its behavior as required. If circumstances are arranged so that the hungry Skinner-box-trained rat must perform more bar presses to be fed, and it has no other way to obtain food, it will adapt its behavior by increasing the rate of bar pressing. If the rate of reinforcement is increased to the point at which the rat can maintain its normal body weight, a control-system model of behavior based on circular causality would predict that further increases in reinforcement should lead to decreases in the rate of behavior. This is exactly what happens (see Staddon 1983, p. 241, figure 7.18).

Skinner also believed that any behavior an animal was physically capable of could be brought about through contingencies of reinforcement. He took particular delight in demonstrating the games that he taught pigeons to play, such as the one in which the bird used its beak to roll a midget bowling ball down a miniature alley to a set of tiny pins (Skinner 1958).

But other research on animal learning has discovered clear constraints on the types of behaviors that animals can learn, and that instinctive behaviors can often interfere with learning new ones. Keller and Marian Breland, who worked for many years training animals for commercial purposes, reported several such examples in their informative and entertaining 1961 paper "The Misbehavior of Organisms." Included in their report are accounts of chickens that could not learn to stand on a platform for twelve to fifteen seconds without vigorously scratching it; raccoons that could learn to put one coin in a container but when given two coins would spend minutes rubbing them together and refuse to deposit them; and pigs that, after having learned to pick up and place large wooden coins in a piggy bank, would after several weeks or months begin repeatedly to drop the coin, push it with their snout (called "rooting"), and pick it up again, taking up to ten minutes to transport four coins over a distance of about six feet. Other researchers reported that male three-spined sticklebacks (a North American fish) were successfully trained to swim through a ring to gain access to a female, but they could not learn to bite a glass rod for the same reward since they attempted instead to mate with the rod (Sevenster 1968, 1973)! In all these cases we see the animal's normal instinctive behaviors related to eating and reproduction interfering with the new behavior the researcher wanted it to learn, a phenomenon referred to by the Brelands as "instinctive drift."

Other interesting evolutionary constraints on learning were investigated in the laboratory rat. For example, rats are quite handy with their front paws and so a hungry rat normally learns quite quickly to press a bar to obtain food. But it is very difficult to get a rat to press a bar to avoid a shock (Slater 1985, p. 87). This seems due to the rat's freezing in response to fear, an instinctive behavior incompatible with bar pressing.

Rats also can make certain associations between stimuli and their effects, but not others. If a rat is made sick after consuming a food with a certain taste, it will consequently avoid all foods having the same taste. And if a sound or visual stimulus regularly precedes an electric shock, a rat will associate this as a signal of the impending shock and will learn to make an appropriate avoidance response. But rats cannot learn to associate taste with electric shock or use auditory or visual cues to learn that a food is noxious (Garcia & Koelling 1966; Garcia et al. 1968).

These findings may be puzzling for the psychologist who has no appreciation of the evolutionary past of the rat, but they make quite good sense from an evolutionary perspective. For rats, which often scurry about in dark places and eat an amazing variety of foods, taste is a better indicator of the quality of food than its visual appearance or the sounds they make while eating. In contrast, physical dangers are usually accompanied by visual and auditory signals, not gustatory ones. So it makes sense that evolution would have selected rats that learn what is bad to eat by taste and what is physically dangerous by sight and sound.

That rats can learn food aversion based on taste is itself a quite remarkable adaptation that led psychologists to seriously revise their theories about learning. It was once widely believed (based on Pavlov's and other studies of classical conditioning) that two stimuli had to be presented several times and within a very short time if one was to become associated with the other. But in 1955 John Garcia and his associates fed rats a harmless substance with a characteristic taste and later made the animals sick using radiation (Revusky & Garcia 1970). Contrary to expectations, rats would learn to avoid the new food even if they were made sick several hours after ingesting it. And this food-avoidance learning appeared permanent.

The findings of this and several similar studies were quite surprising to psychologists at the time, although this type of learning ability again makes good evolutionary sense. Rats live in a wide variety of rapidly changing (now usually human-made) environments and consume a wide range of foods, often those intended for humans or discarded by them. Since they cannot know beforehand whether a new food is toxic or nutritious, they are very cautious and at first take only a small quantity of it. And since it may take a few hours for food poisoning to take effect, they have evolved a learning mechanism that can operate over an interval of hours so that they forever avoid the taste of a food that has made them ill just once. This well-adapted learning is why rat poisons have limited success. On the other hand, a rat whose normal diet is deficient in an essential nutrient (such as the B vitamin thiamine) has a stronger inclination to try a new food. If the new addition happens to be followed by recovery from the dietary deficiency, the rat will develop a marked preference for it (Rodgers & Rozin 1966).

These examples of how the learning ability of animals is adaptively constrained by evolution show that whereas theories of learning may be able to provide some answers to proximate why questions about animal behavior (such as why is that pigeon pecking that key? Answer: Because it is hungry and has discovered that it can obtain food by doing so), learning alone cannot provide answers to ultimate why questions. Ultimate questions must consider the evolutionary origin of the animal's learning abilities.

But what exactly is learned when an animal escapes from a puzzle box of the type Thorndike used, presses a bar to obtain food in a Skinner box, or develops a preference for a food that contains some essential nutrient? We saw in chapter 6 and from the preceding discussion of instinctive behavior that fixed patterns of behavior cannot remain adaptive in a world characterized by variable circumstances and unpredictable disturbances. Learning can be adaptive only if learned behaviors remain flexible and permit the organism to obtain its goals in the face of these disturbances.

The hierarchy of controlled perceptions introduced in chapter 6 provides a quite different perspective on learning. It will be recalled (see figure 6.3) that it shows how higher-level goals are achieved through manipulation of combinations of lower-level goals (subgoals). A spider is able to catch prey only by achieving a rather large number of subgoals that involve spinning a web (which itself requires achieving additional subgoals as described earlier), catching prey, and injecting its venom to kill or paralyze it. Fortunately for the spider, it inherits a control system hierarchy in which these goals and subgoals are specified, and so it requires no learning to be able to feed itself. This is what is referred to as instinctive behavior.

But other animals are more adaptable. A rat inherits certain taste preferences, and as long as it can find sufficient quantities of these foods, it may live its entire life without having to try new ones. But a starving rat must try new foods if it is to survive. It will then come to prefer tastes associated with feelings of wellness and avoid those associated with sickness. The rat is not learning specific new eating behaviors, but rather to reset reference levels for lower-level perceptions based on consequences for higher-level goals.

The rat placed in the Skinner box also demonstrates learning, but this involves learning which patterns of proprioceptive, auditory, and visual perceptions lead to the delivery of a food pellet (another perception). A rat's behavior is more flexible than that of a spider in that the rat is able to reset reference levels based on experience, whereas the spider's reference levels are less modifiable. However, we saw that evolution allows certain types of flexibility but not others; recall that a rat quickly learns in a single trial which taste leads to nausea and which sounds are followed by skin pain. In perceptual-control-theory terms, the rat learns to set a very low or zero reference level for these tastes and sounds to avoid the nausea and pain that follow them. But its behavioral flexibility is limited in that it cannot change its reference level for taste based on sound or for a certain sound based on nausea.

Learning from a hierarchical-perceptual-control-theory perspective is actually finding out, by a form of trial and error, which combinations of lower-level perceptions are successful in bringing about a higher-level goal. Powers refers to this process as *reorganization* (1973, p. 179):

Reorganization is a process akin to rewiring or microprogramming a computer so that those operations it can perform are changed. Reorganization alters behavior, but does not produce *specific behaviors*. It changes the parameters of behavior, not the content. Reorganization of a perceptual function results in a perceptual signal altering its *meaning*, owing to a change in the way it is derived from lower-order signals. Reorganization of an output function results in a different choice of means, a new distribution of lower-order reference signals as a result of a given error signal.

This way of looking at what is normally considered learning combines the two alternative causal processes that provide the major themes of this book. First there is cybernetic circular causality in recognizing the purposeful nature of animal behavior and learning. Animals act on their world based on what they perceive and thereby change their environment and what they consequently perceive of it. Animals also change how they act on the world when old ways are no longer effective in getting what they want. But this change in behavior is based on a Darwinian process involving spontaneous variation and selection; not variation and selection of specific behaviors as conceived by Skinner and his behaviorist followers, but rather variation and selection of goals as the organism discovers which new combinations of controlled lower-order perceptions lead to the attainment of higher-level goals.

We will consider in more detail this notion of within-organism evolution and its purposeful nature in chapters 9 and 10 after we consider the evolutionary bases of human behavior in the next chapter.

8

The Evolution of Human Behavior: The Darwinian Revolution Continued

The challenge of Darwinism is to find out what our genes have been up to and to make that knowledge widely available as a part of the environment in which each of us develops and lives so that we can decide for ourselves, quite deliberately, to what extent we wish to go along.

—Richard Alexander (1979, pp. 136–137)

A fast-food restaurant is a little monument to the diet of our ancient ancestors.

—Leda Cosmides (quoted in Allman 1994, p. 50)

Oh, yo' daddy's rich, an' yo' ma is good look-in'
So hush, little baby, don' yo cry.

—"Summertime" (G. Gershwin, D. & D. Heyward, & I. Gershwin 1935)

Hey, Joe. Where you goin' with that gun in your hand?

Goin' down to shoot my old lady. You know I caught her messin' around with another man.

—"Hey Joe" (Billy Roberts 1966)

As we saw in the previous chapter, the evolutionary approach pioneered by ethologists provides answers to many ultimate why questions concerning animal behavior. The basic notions of survival and reproductive success, further refined by concepts of kin selection and reciprocal altruism, have time and again provided compelling answers concerning why animals naturally do the things they do and are able to modify their behavior in adaptive, functional ways.

But what about our own species? The Darwinian conclusion that human beings are also a product of biological evolution is scientifically inescapable, meaning that our behavior must also be compatible with and explainable by natural selection. But we humans are undisputably different from all other known organisms in the remarkable flexibility and variability of our behavior and the planning, consciousness, emotions, awareness, and moral sense that often accompany what we do.

In this chapter we will consider both the successes and problems of attempts to use natural selection to understand human behavior since the time of Darwin.

Darwin and His Critics on Animate Behavior

Although Darwin was the first scientist to consider in print the implications of natural selection for human behavior, he took a rather long time to do so. In *The Origin of Species* (published in 1859), in which he introduced the theory of natural selection, he made no explicit mention of human evolution or behavior. It was, however, quite clear from the central argument of this revolutionary book that he believed humans, like all other living organisms, gradually evolved to their present form from nonhuman ancestors. It was this unwritten but clear implication of his work that raised the most criticism and debate. As the wife of the Bishop of Worcester is reported to have worried, "Descended from monkeys? Let us hope that it is not true. But if it is true, let us hope that it does not become widely known" (quoted in Giddens 1991, chapter 2).

Unfortunately for the good bishop's wife, the theory of natural selection turned out to be both true and widely known. But it wasn't until over a decade later (after first publishing two revisions of the *Origin* followed by a book on orchids and another on domesticated animals) that Darwin tackled the emotionally charged and highly controversial issue of human evolution in *The Descent of Man and Selection in Relation to Sex*, first published in 1871 (see Darwin 1874, 1952). Here he maintained that human behavior was in some respects like that of other animals, while in other respects it was unique. He attempted to explain both the similarities and differences as arising naturally from the evolutionary process.

Like all other sexually reproducing animals, humans are (as were our nonhuman ancestors) subject to sexual selection of males by females and of females by males. Darwin saw in human sexual selection an explanation for human racial differences. Since he saw no obvious survival advantages for racial differences in physical attributes such as stature, hair, skin color, and body shape,[1] he reasoned that these variations were the results of differences in perceived sexual attractiveness among different races and the resulting selection of mates.

But more interesting from a behavioral perspective are his conclusions concerning the evolutionary basis for differences in behavioral and mental dispositions of men and women. Here he forged a bold link between humans and the sexual differences found in other animals (1874, pp. 583–584):

No one disputes that the bull differs in disposition from the cow, the wild-boar from the sow, the stallion from the mare, and, as is well known to the keepers of menageries, the males of the larger apes from the females. Woman seems to differ from man in mental disposition, chiefly in her greater tenderness and less selfishness. . . . Woman, owing to her maternal instincts, displays these qualities towards her infants in an eminent degree; therefore it is likely that she would often extend them towards her fellow-creatures. Man is the rival of other men; he delights in competition, and this leads to ambition which passes too easily into selfishness. These latter qualities seem to be his natural and unfortunate birthright.

He also used sexual selection to explain what he saw as the more violent, aggressive nature of the male sex (1874, p. 583):

There can be little doubt that the greater size and strength of man, in comparison with woman, together with his broader shoulders, more developed muscles, rugged outline of body, his greater courage and pugnacity, are all due in chief part to inheritance from his half-human male ancestors. These characters would, however, have been preserved or even augmented during the long ages of man's savagery, by the success of the strongest and boldest men, both in the general struggle for life and in their contest for wives; a success which would have ensured their leaving a more numerous progeny than their less favored brethren.

It was rather straightforward to provide evolutionary accounts of the human male's more aggressive characteristics. In contrast, understanding the evolutionary origins of the ethical, moral, and religious aspects of human nature was not so easy. Even Darwin's friends and supporters of his theory of evolution (including geologist Charles Lyell, cousin and gentleman scientist Sir Francis Galton, and fellow discoverer of natural selection Alfred Russel Wallace) could not imagine how survival and reproductive success could be at the origin of the kinder and gentler characteristics that often distinguish humans from other animals. According to Richards (1987, p. 206),

Lyell could not conceive that man's intellect and moral sensibility naturally grew by slow degrees from animal stock. Galton and Greg isolated another crucial problem for the Darwinian approach to man: as soon as protomen formed social bonds and through sympathy became solicitous for their mutual welfare, natural selection ought to be disengaged; for sympathy would prevent the salutary elimination of mentally and morally inferior individuals. Wallace . . . pressed these difficulties home. He urged that man's great intellect and refined moral sense far exceeded what was required for mere survival in the wild; hence, natural selection could not have produced them.

Darwin's three responses to these challenges are remarkable for their keen insight and anticipation of theories that became widely appreciated and accepted only much later the next century. First, he imagined that as their reasoning powers increased, our early ancestors would have realized that aiding another individual would increase their chances of being helped later by that individual in return. We saw this idea in the previous chapter, now referred to as reciprocal altruism.

Second, Darwin proposed that natural selection occurring at the level of the *group* could result in the evolution of behavioral traits that, although possibly of no use or even detrimental to the survival and reproductive success of the individual possessing them, would confer a selective advantage to the individual's community. As he reasoned (1874, p. 137):

It must not be forgotten that although a high standard of morality gives but a slight or no advantage to each individual man and his children over the other men of the same tribe, yet that an increase in the number of well-endowed men and an advancement in the standard of morality will certainly give an immense advantage to one tribe over another. A tribe including many members who, from possessing in a high degree the spirit of patriotism, fidelity, obedience, courage, and sympathy, were always ready to aid one another and to sacrifice themselves for the common good, would be victorious over most other tribes; and this would be natural selection.

Finally, he recognized the powerful influence that social praise and blame had on the behavior of individuals (1874, p. 136), an influence that would have been obvious to anyone living in Victorian England. Otherwise, individuals who refused to act for the good of the group (for example, by refusing to fight in the group's wars or not sharing food or other valuable resources) and instead acted only for their own and their family's interest would have greater survival and reproductive success than those who acted for the good of the larger social group. This would prevent the natural selection of altruistic behavior.

All this is not to imply that Darwin's views on the evolutionary origins of human behavior were unproblematic. For one thing, he did not seem to recognize the important role that the environment could play through social and cultural factors in influencing human behavior. This is evident in one of his descriptions of differences between men and women. He noted that "if two lists were made of the most eminent men and women in poetry, painting, sculpture, music (inclusive both of composition and performance), history, science, and philosophy, with a half-a-dozen names under each subject, the two lists would not bear comparison" and therefore "the average of mental power in man must be above that of woman" (1874, p. 504). It seems inexcusable to us today that he ignored the limited educational and employment opportunities afforded to women in his day and their impact on their lives and career options.

Also evident from this conclusion concerning male-female differences was Darwin's reliance on anecdotal observations of human behavior. This approach may have served him well in his research and conclusions on animal behavior, but animal behavior has much less variation than human behavior. The fact that a male peacock spreads and shakes his tail before a peahen to encourage her to mate is in itself suggestive that other peacocks act similarly. Observing that a panda bear eats bamboo leaves provides a good clue concerning the dining habits of all pandas. But seeing a single instance of human behavior tells us very little indeed about the behavior of humans in general, since humans have so many distinct ways to feed themselves (from hunting and gathering to writing computer programs), dress themselves, shelter themselves, and procure mates. (We will take a look at the large apparent variation in human behavior from another perspective later in this chapter.)

Darwin was also completely unaware of the genetic basis of heredity and so could not understand how traits were passed down from one generation to another, even though Mendel's ground-breaking work on genetics (based on the 30,000 pea plants he had grown) was published in 1865. Without this knowledge, Darwin could not understand how kin selection could be such a powerful force in the evolution of altruistic and cooperative behavior among humans.

Finally, he never abandoned the Lamarckian notion of the inheritance of acquired characteristics in his belief that habits learned during an individual's lifetime could show up as unlearned instincts in one's descendants. He made extensive use of this notion in his book *The Expression of the Emotions in Man and Animals* (1872/1955).

In spite of these limitations, Darwin must be credited for insisting on and providing thoroughly naturalistic explanations for the evolution of human behavior that did not require the divine intervention insisted on by both his harshest critics and some of his closest friends and supporters, such as Lyell, Wallace, and American botanist Asa Gray.

The Post-Darwinian Gap

Because Darwin's theory of evolution had such a great and immediate impact on the scientific world (the entire first edition of the *Origin* was sold out the first day it was put on sale), one might well expect that it would have had a great impact on those social and behavioral scientists interested in accounting for human behavior. But that impact was delayed for quite some time.

One reason for this lack of immediate effect on human psychology was that in spite of Darwin's arguments as summarized above, many simply could not see how evolution by natural selection could account for the emergence of the human mind. Among those who, like Darwin, sought thoroughly naturalistic explanations for the origin of the human species, many remained unconvinced of the theory, preferring instead Lamarck's notion of the inheritance of acquired characteristics. Why was natural selection rejected as the motor of evolution? There were at least three reasons.

First, since natural selection requires gradual accumulation of small variations appearing in each generation, it would take a very long time before an organism as complex as a giraffe or human could evolve from the simplest one-celled organisms. But the best estimates of the age of the earth available in the nineteenth century (provided by Lord Kelvin) were between 10 and 15 million years, far too young even by Darwin's reckoning to have allowed enough time for the evolution of all known extinct and extant species. Lord Kelvin's estimates were based on the temperature of the interior of the earth and rate of decrease of the sun's energy output. However, both radioactivity (which plays a major role in maintaining the earth's high interior temperatures) and nuclear fusion (which is the source of the sun's energy) were unknown phenomena in the nineteenth century. So although the earth is now considered to be about 4.5 billion years old, providing ample time for evolution to do its stuff, the best estimates during Darwin's time were considered incompatible with his theory of natural selection.

Another reason to doubt the effects of natural selection was the problem of inheritance. Darwin and other naturalists and biologists of his day (except Mendel) believed that inheritance in sexual species involved *blending* characteristics of male and female parents. Reasoning from this assumption, Scottish engineer Fleeming Jenkin pointed out that any new favorable variation would be diluted as the organism possessing it bred with other organisms. Over time, this repeated dilution of new traits meant that little or none of the originally advantageous variation would be retained by succeeding generations, making the emergence of new species impossible.

As noted, Darwin was unaware of Mendel's pioneering experiments in genetics that showed that inheritance did not involve a blending of male and female characteristics but rather was *particulate*; the fact that the offspring of a male-female couple is either male or female and not a blend of the two sexes is just one obvious example of the particulate nature of inheritance. Indeed, the basic notion of the gene that Mendel developed is that of an indivisible unit of biological inheritance that does not blend or dilute itself in the process of reproduction. The modern particulate theory of genetics is therefore thoroughly compatible with Darwin's theory of evolutionary change arising through natural selection of spontaneous variations produced by genetic mutation and sexual recombination of genes. Unfortunately, commonly held but erroneous ideas about inheritance in Darwin's own time were not entirely compatible with the concept of natural selection as the motor behind the evolution of species and emergence of new ones.

The third widely respected argument had to do with how the initial stages of a complex adaptation could become established. It was maintained by one of Darwin's harshest foes (the converted, and later excommunicated, Catholic zoologist St. George Mivart) that a complex adaptation such as a bird's wing was of no use to the animal that possessed it as a tool of flight unless it was fully formed and functional. From this line of reasoning it would seem that if natural selection were a gradual process involving accumulation of very small changes from one generation to the next, there would be no way that such a complex adaptation could ever begin to evolve.

Darwin had a good rebuttal to this objection, and one that is still considered valid today. He recognized that a complex adaptation may have had its beginning in a form that served a quite different function than its current one. For example, it is now believed that wings did not originally emerge as organs of flight but rather as protuberances allowing insects and birds to regulate their body heat. Nonetheless, this was seen by many as another valid argument against natural selection and is still used today by creationists and other opponents of evolution.[2]

But if Darwin was not swayed by Mivart's argument, he was troubled by those of Kelvin and Jenkin. So much so that by the sixth and final edition of *Origin* he considerably softened his position on natural selection, putting more emphasis on the role of the Lamarckian inheritance of acquired characteristics that he incorporated into his ill-fated theory of *pangenesis*.

His concessions to the antiselectionists did nothing to help his theory gain acceptance. The result was that, beginning in the years shortly before his death in 1882 until well into the twentieth century, biological evolution involving descent with modification was widely accepted among scientists but natural selection was not. Instead, the inheritance of acquired characteristics was seen as the primary motor of evolution, in spite of now obvious fatal flaws of Lamarckian theory.

But whereas the theory of natural selection was rejected by biologists and zoologists, it was embraced by many prominent philosophers and psychologists in Europe and America who saw in the process of variation and selection a mechanism to elucidate the functioning of the human mind. This application of Darwinian theory to the mental realm is part of what I call the "second Darwinian revolution" that is discussed in the next chapter.

Sociobiology's Search for Ultimate Causes

We saw in chapter 7 how biologists such J. B. S. Haldane, William Hamilton, George Williams, and Robert Trivers applied Darwinian concepts in the 1950s through 1970s to find answers to many perplexing ultimate why questions about animal behavior—including instances of cooperative social behavior—using theories of kin selection and reciprocal altruism. They also applied evolutionary reasoning to human behavior, but since their work was often couched in the complex mathematics of population genetics and directed to other evolutionary biologists, it had little impact at the time on behavioral science. This changed dramatically with the appearance of a book in 1975 that brought a broad Darwinian perspective to the behavior of a remarkable variety of organisms, from microorganisms and slime molds to gorillas and human beings.

The book was *Sociobiology: The New Synthesis* written by Edward O. Wilson, a Harvard entomologist recognized as one of the world's leading experts on ants and other social insects. Defining sociobiology as "the systematic study of the biological basis of all social behavior" (1975, p. 4), Wilson provided many fascinating examples from the world of insects and other animals of the types of behaviors and evolutionary reasoning described and formulated by Hamilton, Williams, and Trivers. Due to the accessibility of his writing and attractive illustrations, *Sociobiology* quickly attracted widespread attention. Although only the last of the twenty-seven chapters dealt with human behavior, it made it clear that Wilson's evolutionary, genetic, and essentially selfish account of the origins of social behavior was fully intended to be applicable to our species as well.

Wilson's book earned him both popularity and notoriety. Many biological and behavioral scientists appreciated the grand scale and synthesis of his work, but others (including some of his Harvard colleagues) accused him of being a racist, sexist, imperialist, right-winger, and genetic determinist. His public appearances were boycotted and disrupted, and he was even doused with a pitcher of ice water at one of his lectures.

But this negative reaction did not stop additional applications of Darwinian theory to human behavior. One year after the publication of Wilson's book, Oxford zoologist Richard Dawkins published *The Selfish Gene*, the first in what was to become a series of popular and influential books on evolution. Dawkins also explored the evolutionary and genetic bases for behavior, including the apparently altruistic behavior of humans toward their fellows. Like Wilson and the new generation of behavioral Darwinians, he emphasized the inherently selfish genetic nature of what may appear to be the kind, altruistic behavior of both animals and humans.

Why did this new application of a Darwinian perspective to human behavior meet with such resistance from so many behavioral scientists and indifference from others? To understand this reaction, we must take a closer look at some of the assumptions, reasoning, and conclusions of Wilson and his sociobiologist colleagues.

The first assumption is that the human species, like all other species of living organisms, evolved from simpler forms of life by natural selection. The second assumption is that since the evolution of a species is directed by the survival and reproductive success of individual organisms (including the survival and reproductive success of new generations), and that this success is influenced by an organism's behavioral characteristics, various human behaviors can be understood as adaptations that promote (or at least promoted in the past) survival and reproductive success. The third assumption is that there is a genetic basis for human behavior in the same way that there is an inherited, genetic basis for the behavior of other animals and for the physical structure of both.

All three of these assumptions are quite in keeping with modern biological theory and clearly consistent with what was learned from studies of animal behavior as discussed in chapter 7. So why all the fuss about applying them in an attempt to discover ultimate explanations for human behavior?

At least part of the resistance was (and is) due to misinterpretation of certain aspects of sociobiological theory. Perhaps the most common charge is that of *genetic determinism*, the idea that humans inherit genes that in effect force them to behave one way or another. It is true that Wilson and other sociobiologists discussed the possibility of human genes underlying such human behavioral characteristics as homosexuality and social conformity (for example, see Wilson 1975, pp. 555, 562). But it is also clear that these scientists were aware that genes must interact with environmental factors for them to have any effect on the structure or behavior of an organism, human or otherwise. As Wilson explained (1975, p. 26):

Blue eye color in human beings can be proved to be genetically different from brown eye color. But it is meaningless to ask whether blue eye color alone is determined by heredity or environment. Obviously, both the genes for blue eye color and the environment contributed to the final product. The only useful question . . . is whether human beings that develop blue eye color instead of brown eye color do so at least in part because they have genes different from those that control brown eye color. The same reasoning can be extended without change to different patterns of social behavior.

Wilson also included a section in the last (human) chapter of *Sociobiology*, entitled "Plasticity of social organization," in which he presented the hypothesis "that genes promoting *flexibility* in social behavior are strongly selected at the individual level" (1975, p. 548; emphasis added).

However, he and other sociobiologists were on occasion less careful in describing the role of genes in human behavior. For example, Wilson asserted in his Pulitzer prize-winning book *On Human Nature* that "the question of interest is no longer whether human social behavior is genetically determined; it is to what extent" (1978, p. 19). The use of the word "influenced" (which implicitly recognizes the effect of other factors) instead of "determined" (which can be easily taken to mean that genes are the *only* cause of human behavior) would have given his opponents less cause for criticism.

Another charge is that sociobiologists often infer a specific genetic basis for apparently universal human behaviors without considering how such behaviors could have arisen from more general aspects of the form and abilities of the human organism interacting with the environment. For example, Wilson stated that "in hunter-gatherer societies men hunt and women stay at home. This strong bias presents in most agricultural and industrial societies and, on that ground alone, appears to have a genetic origin" (1975; quoted in Lewontin, Rose, & Kamin 1984, p. 255). But it is quite easy to imagine how this division of labor could be the indirect effect of physical differences between men and women such as men's greater size, strength, running speed, and throwing ability, which are characteristics best suited to hunting, and women's ability to bear and nurse babies, which is better suited to staying at or near one's home and taking care of children. As three of sociobiology's harshest critics remarked, Wilson's "argument confuses the observation noted, with the explanation. If its circularity is not evidence, one might consider the claim that, since 99 percent of Finns are Lutheran, they must have a gene for it" (Lewontin, Rose, & Kamin 1985, p. 255).

Another example is that all normal able-bodied humans use their hands to eat. This could therefore be considered a universal, species-specific aspect of human behavior (and a social behavior insofar as it is done with other humans). But does this then indicate that a specific human gene or group of genes causes us to use our hands to eat, which if changed would result in a human who did not use his or her hands to eat? This appears unlikely, as it is obvious that a hungry human who has learned to use his or her hands for manipulating objects would also use them to place food in his or her mouth. Of course, there is a genetic basis for the human behavior of eating with one's hands, since without human genes a human would not have hands to begin with, or the neurological system to achieve fine motor control of its fingers. But it is simply unconvincing to argue that a specific gene or set of genes must exist for a particular behavior simply because all (or nearly all) humans do it. Philosopher Daniel Dennett has made this same point using yet another example (1995, p. 486):

Showing that a particular type of human behavior is ubiquitous or nearly ubiquitous in widely separated human cultures goes *no way at all* towards showing that there is a genetic predisposition for that particular behavior. So far as I know, in every culture known to anthropologists, the hunters throw their spears pointy-end-first, but this obviously doesn't establish that there is a pointy-end-first gene that approaches fixation in our species.

None of this is to deny that using one's hands to eat, dividing labor between the sexes, and throwing spears pointy-end-first may well be adaptive behaviors that facilitated the survival and reproduction of individuals who practiced them. But given the structure and abilities of human brains and bodies together with the environments in which they live, it seems implausible that any such universal human behaviors have a *specific* determining genetic basis. Instead, it is more likely that such behaviors are the outcome of the more general problem-solving abilities our species possesses that are themselves products of the interaction of our genetic endowment with our environment. As will be proposed later in this chapter, the entire enterprise of attempting to separate genetic from environmental (or social) causes of behavior is itself an indication of confusion.

These criticisms and problems notwithstanding, the evolutionary approach taken by sociobiologists has been of considerable value in addressing certain ultimate why questions about human behavior. The major contribution to our understanding is the realization that human behavior, like the behavior of all organisms, was shaped over evolutionary time as a function of its survival and reproductive consequences. As for any other species, a human behavior having an inherited basis that increases an individual's survival and reproduction, or the survival and reproduction of closely related individuals, will over time spread through the population. In contrast, heritable behaviors with less positive effects will over time be eliminated.

The Darwinian approach taken by sociobiologists to study human behavior yielded interesting hypotheses, predictions, and answers. We will now consider some of these as they relate to male-female differences and parental care of children.

Men and women differ in many obvious ways, but an important one that is not immediately apparent is their capacity for reproduction. With each ejaculation a man can provide up to 100 million sperm that are then quickly replaced. In contrast, a woman produces only about 400 eggs during her entire lifetime. In addition, a woman must make a very large investment in producing and rearing a child. The fetus develops in her body from which it draws its nourishment, the woman gives birth to the child at considerable risk to her own health, and the child must be nursed and cared for a considerable length of time. In contrast, a man needs do nothing more than copulate to produce a child, although, of course, many men (but certainly not all) also make substantial investments in their children. Thus a man's potential reproductive capacity is much greater than a woman's.

As in other animals, these striking differences in reproductive functions and capacities should, from an evolutionary perspective, lead to similarly striking differences in certain behaviors. Since the limiting factor for male reproductive success is the availability of fertile women, we should expect to find keen competition among males for fertile female mates, and evidence shows that such competition exists in all human societies. In fact, many cases of homicide are related to men competing for women (Daly & Wilson 1988).

Also, since each copulation by a man with a fertile woman has the potential of producing one or more children carrying half of the man's genes even with no further involvement by him, we would expect men to be more easily sexually aroused and more interested in mating with many different women. Because women have much less to gain from multiple partners (only one man at a time can father a child), they should be less easily sexually aroused and less interested in having several sex partners. The facts that married men are much more likely to engage in sex outside of marriage than their wives (Symons 1979), that many men pay women for sex but women do this much more rarely, and that a huge worldwide pornographic industry is supported by men who are willing to pay to just look at images of young scantily clad and nude women, are all consistent with evolution-based predictions by sociobiologists concerning male-female differences in sexual behavior. These findings are also consistent with male-female differences in animal behavior as discussed in chapter 7.

Men and women also differ in mate choices. A man may maximize his reproductive potential by establishing a relationship with a younger woman with many reproductive years ahead of her. So we should expect men to prefer younger mates, especially as they grow older. In contrast, a woman may maximize her reproductive success by finding a man with sufficient material resources to provide for her and her children, and such a man is likely to be older than she. As expected, men's preference for younger women and women's preference for older men were found in at least thirty-seven countries (Buss 1989; Kenrick & Keefe 1992). A rather blunt way to summarize these findings is to note that men tend to see women as sex objects (preferring mates and wives who are young and physically attractive), and women tend to see men as resource objects (preferring older and wealthier men with less concern for physical attractiveness).

But youthfulness is just one factor involved in female reproductive capability, with health and fertility being others. One indicator of female health and fertility is the ratio of waist to hip size. Healthy women in their prime childbearing years (early teens to middle age) have waist-to-hip ratios between 0.67 and 0.80, although conditions such as hypertension, diabetes, gallbladder disease, and (obviously) pregnancy tend to increase this ratio. A small waist-to-hip ratio is also indicative of high levels of the female hormone estrogen and therefore of fertility. We should thus expect men to find young women with low waist-hip ratios to be most attractive. This was in fact found in the United States and many other cultures where a ratio of 0.7 is considered most attractive by men (Singh 1993, 1997).

The care that parents invest in raising children has also been a subject of considerable interest among sociobiologists, using as their basic working hypothesis that men should invest less in their mate's child if they know or suspect that the child was fathered by another man. Perhaps one of the most interesting findings concerning parental care of children has to do with the Ifaluk people of the Caroline Islands in the South Pacific. Their society is characterized by a relatively high degree of sexual permissiveness so that a man has little certainty that he is the father of his wife's children. Evolutionary analysis would predict that a man in this situation would withhold at least some parental support from his wife's children. In the case of the Ifaluk, a man provides support not for his wife's offspring but rather for his sister's, to whom he is more likely to be related, by becoming their "uncle-father" (Alexander 1979). In the somewhat less exotic setting of the Canadian city of Hamilton, Ontario, children over the age of four living with a step-parent were forty times more likely to suffer some form of parental abuse than those living in families with both biological parents (Daly & Wilson 1985).

A final example of the value of a sociobiological approach to human behavior deals with two major practices that are used throughout the world to help one's child obtain a desirable spouse. Because a man's reproductive capacity is limited primarily by his access to fertile women, we would expect that a man and his parents would be willing to give up some material resources to obtain a wife, the payment of which to the woman's family is often referred to as a *bride price*. This was the custom among the inhabitants of southern Sudan when I made several visits there in the early 1980s. I found it interesting to compare prices for brides in different localities, with a typical price being in the neighborhood of fifteen goats. But when I explained to my male Sudanese hosts that in other places such as India it is the bride's family that provides money and other goods (that is, a *dowry*) to the groom's family, they were incredulous. Why on earth would a young woman's parents pay an unrelated man's family in addition to giving away the services of their daughter?

At the time I could provide my African friends with no reasonable explanation for the Indian custom of the dowry. Since then I learned that providing a bride price is much more common than paying a dowry throughout the world (Murdock 1967). Paying for a bride is particularly prevalent in societies where men often take more than one wife (polygyny) since this practice increases competition for wives (if some men have more than one wife, other men must have none) and hence their worth to men. In contrast, the woman's family providing a dowry is about fifty times more likely to be found in socially stratified, monogamous societies than in nonstratified, polygynous societies (Gaulin & Boster 1990). In such societies men's wealth and earning potential vary greatly, and because a man's resources cannot be diluted by the acquisition of many wives, it pays for a woman's family to find her a wealthy husband, even if considerable cost is incurred in doing so. So these strikingly different practices of bride price versus dowry can be understood as different ways of achieving the common goal of maximizing reproductive success in two different cultural contexts.

Evolutionary Psychology's Search for Proximate Causes

The work of sociobiologists provides interesting hypotheses and useful explanations for aspects of human behavior by focusing on the survival and reproductive consequences of behaviors in different social contexts. It must be kept in mind, however, that uncovering the ultimate, evolutionary origins of certain preferences and behaviors does not explain proximate here-and-now reasons for a behavior. To use an analogy, studying and understanding the history of the invention and development of the automobile does not provide an explanation for why my car (usually) accelerates when I step on the gas.

This is perhaps made most clear by an example of animal behavior. The European cuckoo is a bird that is referred to as a *brood parasite*, meaning that the female lays each of her eggs in other birds' nests and then abandons them. The cuckoo egg hatches before those of the host bird, and the intruding hatchling proceeds to dump the other eggs out of the nest by balancing each egg on its back between its extended wings while walking backward up the side of the nest.

Coming up with an ultimate, evolutionary explanation for the young cuckoo's egg-dumping behavior is not difficult. By eliminating the eggs of its genetically unrelated hosts, the cuckoo monopolizes the care and food given to it by its duped adoptive parents. Since today's cuckoos descended from cuckoos that practiced egg dumping, they continue the practice. But eliminating its nestmates to have more food for itself is not likely what the cuckoo has in mind when it sends its hosts' eggs tumbling out into the void. Its actual proximate goal is almost certainly something much simpler, such as to remove all objects of a certain size, shape, and color from the nest with no knowledge that achieving this immediate goal will have a longer-term positive effect on its survival and later reproductive success. That this behavior had the effect of increasing the survival and reproduction of cuckoos in the past provides no proximate explanation at all for why the individual cuckoo still does what it does. The latter can be determined only by empirical testing of various hypotheses by introducing objects of varying shapes, colors, and sizes into the cuckoo's adoptive nest and observing its behavior to determine what perceptual variables it is controlling. In this way, the young cuckoo's immediate behavioral goals can be determined, goals that evolution selected because of their ultimate side effects of facilitating survival and reproductive success.

Now let us consider an example of human behavior. It was noted that men throughout the world, particularly older men, prefer women who are considerably younger than themselves. The ultimate, evolutionary explanation for this preference that was offered was that younger women are fertile and have many reproductive years ahead of them. Men who in the past chose younger mates left more descendants than those who chose older, less fertile mates, so this inherited preference for younger women spread throughout the population of human males.

But this ultimate, evolutionary explanation does not necessarily provide information concerning the proximate reasons as to why an individual man prefers and pursues younger women. In the case of the cuckoo, the ultimate, evolutionary explanation for any behavior or preference need not correspond to the proximate explanation. But since humans can plan ahead and consider the long-term consequences of behaviors, choices, and preferences, the proximate reason may be that older men prefer younger women because they really do consciously desire to have many children and see a younger woman as a means to this goal. But a more likely explanation is that men have evolved a preference for young women because our male ancestors who had such a preference left more descendants than those who did not, and that preference may have nothing to do with any perceived reproductive advantages. Again, the ultimate, evolutionary explanation for a behavior need not necessarily provide information concerning proximate mechanisms. This is particularly clear for nonhuman organisms that are unable to consider the long-term survival and reproductive consequences of their behavior. But the distinction between ultimate and proximate explanations is valid for humans as well.

Sociobiologists have not always been careful to distinguish between the two types of behavioral explanations, sometimes taking ultimate, evolutionary explanations as proximate ones. As John Tooby commented (quoted in Allman 1994, p. 49):

> Many sociobiologists have this view of people as *fitness maximizers*. They assume that since evolutionary biology says "We all evolved to propagate genes," the purpose of humans is to propagate genes. They believe that beneath all of our complicated human behaviors there is an underlying hidden logic of "gene propagation." So when you are being nice to your child, they say, all you are *really* doing is selfishly trying to propagate your own genes. A lot of sociobiological work carries this cynical interpretation of human behavior—a view of the world for which sociobiologists have been rightly criticized. The problem is that sociobiologists confuse the mechanisms of the mind with the *process* that built the mind, and in fact these are two separate things. Evolutionary biology is not a theory of human nature. Rather, it is a theory for how human nature *came to be*—and a useful tool for discovering what human nature actually is. A mother really does love her child—it's not that somewhere deep inside her mind there is a selfish motive to spread her genes. In fact, it's really the other way around: Human beings love their children because those ancestors who loved their children had more surviving children, and we're descended from them and not the others who didn't love their kids. So in the "grand evolutionary biological" sense of *Why do you love your kids?* You love them because it is part of your human nature that evolved as part of our ancestors' brain mechanisms. There is nothing in those brain mechanisms that says *That kid has your genes; he's propagating your genes, and so you should love him.*

John Tooby and his wife, Leda Cosmides, two founders of the new field of evolutionary psychology, are primarily interested in discovering psychological mechanisms that serve as the proximate causes of human behavior while looking to evolutionary theory for clues to these mechanisms and their ultimate origins. This Darwinian approach is still in its beginning stages, but it has already made two important theoretical contributions. The first, as mentioned, is the distinction between ultimate (evolutionary) and proximate (psychological) causes of human behavior. The second is the realization that almost all human evolution took place while our species lived in small groups of hunter-gatherers, long before the development of agriculture, large urban communities, and modern technology. This means that many behaviors and preferences that were adaptive in their original evolutionary contexts may no longer be adaptive today.

An example is our taste preference for sugar, salt, and fat—which are, coincidentally, the main ingredients of concoctions served in fast-food restaurants that have invaded almost all corners of the world. During the Pleistocene epoch, which ended 10,000 years ago, such nutrients were difficult for our hunter-gatherer forebears to obtain, yet vital for their survival. So individuals who consumed as much sugar, salt, and fat as they could when available would have had survival and reproductive advantages over those who did not. Because there was little danger during this time of consuming too much of these nutrients (being in such scarce supply), humans evolved a strong craving for the taste of foods with these nutrients.

But today millions of people live where they have virtually unlimited access to foods containing all the sugar, salt, and fat they can eat, and the associated health problems of obesity, diabetes, hypertension, and heart disease are all too common in modern industrial societies. So whereas a craving for these nutrients was adaptive in early human environments, recent changes in the environment for many modern humans rendered these dietary preferences less adaptive if not downright maladaptive. This distinction between what evolutionary psychologists call the "environment of evolutionary adaptiveness" (often abbreviated EEA) and our current environment is important in understanding how certain human preferences and behaviors that appear nonadaptive today may nonetheless have an adaptive evolutionary origin.

Changes in survival and reproductive consequences of certain behaviors and preferences in modern environments not anticipated by evolution often give useful clues to the proximate mechanisms of human behavior. For example, behaviors and preferences that in the past typically resulted in many offspring were selected by evolution. But what was actually selected? Is it a basic human desire to have many children? Or is having many children a side effect of achieving other proximate goals?

The finding that over the last century family size declined in Western societies and that today it tends to be smaller for wealthier families

(Vining 1986) suggests the latter. This decline and its negative correlation with wealth is one consequence of the availability of contraceptive methods that permit heterosexual couples to copulate while limiting the number of children they have or avoiding having children altogether. The fact that contraception is widely used, particularly by wealthier couples who in the past would have been expected to produce the most children and grandchildren, is a good indication that having many children is not a universal human goal resulting from natural selection, but is rather a side effect of other inherited preferences, notably the desire for frequent sexual intercourse, particularly with young, attractive females (for men) and wealthy, high-status men (for women).

The picture that emerges is one in which evolution selected organisms who had goals (and the means to achieve them) that resulted in better than average survival and reproductive success. But survival and reproduction are not the goals per se that the organism pursues. Rather, organisms, humans included, evolved preferences (and the means to achieve them) that in past environments led to survival and reproductive success with no guarantee that they will do so today. Overconsumption of sugar, salt, and fat and the practice of birth control are two examples of the lessening fit of evolved preferences and behaviors to survival and reproduction.

But humans do differ from other organisms in the flexibility they show in achieving their goals. A farmer can change the crops he plants depending on weather and economic conditions. In contrast, the leaf-cutting ant, having discovered agriculture millions of years before humans did, is limited to its crop of leaf-based fungus and cannot change its way of feeding if for some reason cultivating fungus is no longer practical or possible. In other words, humans have higher-order goals that are achieved by manipulating lower-order goals as necessary. Other organisms also provide evidence of a hierarchy of goals in their behavior (recall the examples of flexible insect behavior in chapter 7), but their hierarchies are not as extensive as those of humans. Thus certain goals (such as what to eat) cannot be varied to the extent that humans can adaptively modify their goals (which is why you will never find a vegetarian dog or a cat on a self-imposed diet).

This emphasis on the flexibility of human behavior is another way in which evolutionary psychology distinguishes itself from sociobiology. In the terminology of Robert Wright whose book *The Moral Animal* (1994) introduced evolutionary psychology to a large audience, we can look at human nature as made up of "knobs and tunings." Knobs are basic preferences selected by human evolution, and tunings are influenced by environmental factors. The preference for a variety of sex partners may be a basic knob that all human males inherit as part of their evolutionary legacy. But the extent to which this preference is realized (tuning) may well depend on the particular experiences of the particular man. Learning that other men who are sexually promiscuous pay no obvious penalty for their adventures and are able to maintain a stable family life and high social status may result in the knob being set on the high end of the scale. In contrast, living in a society where male sexual promiscuity is punished (for example, by exposure as scandalous, leading to loss of social status and esteem) may result in a much lower setting of that specific knob.

Such variation in tunings of basic inherited preferences may well explain much of the cultural diversity that is found among human societies, a diversity that has led many anthropologists and sociologists to reject the notion of universal human behavioral characteristics that were shaped by our evolutionary past. But we have seen that whereas the cultural practices of bride price and dowry are superficially very different, both can be understood as having positive effects on reproductive success in their social contexts. Still, these positive reproductive consequences are likely only a side effect of men competing for wives in polygynous societies and women attempting to secure high-status, resourceful husbands in monogamous, stratified societies.

When one looks under the surface in this way, similarities among diverse human societies are more striking than differences. Donald Brown, in his book *Human Universals* (1991), described characteristics that appear to be universally present in all human cultures. Steven Pinker (1994, pp. 413–415) outlined some of them, summarized here.

With respect to oral language, all human societies have:

Gossip. Lying. Verbal humor. Humorous insults. Poetic and rhetorical speech forms. Narrative and storytelling. Words for days, months, seasons, years, past, future, body parts, inner states (emotions, sensations, thoughts), behavioral propensities, flora, fauna, weather, tools, space, motion, speed, location, spatial dimensions, physical properties, giving, lending, numbers (at the very least "one," "two," and "more than two"), proper names, possession. Kinship categories, defined in terms of mother, father, son, daughter, and age sequence. Binary distinctions, including male and female, black and white, natural and cultural, good and bad. Measures. Logical relations including "not," "and," "same," "equivalent," "opposite," general versus particular, part versus whole. Conjectural reasoning (inferring the presence of absent and invisible entities from their perceptible traces).

Concerning nonlinguistic vocal communication, all human communities have:

Cries and squeals. Interpretation of intention from behavior. Recognized facial expressions of happiness, sadness, anger, fear, surprise, disgust, and contempt. Use of smiles as a friendly greeting. Crying. Coy flirtation with the eyes. Masking, modifying, and mimicking facial expressions. Displays of affection.

With respect to emotions we find all human communities having:

Sexual attraction. Powerful sexual jealousy. Childhood fears, especially of loud noises, and, at the end of the first year, strangers. Fear of snakes. "Oedipal" feelings (possessiveness of mother, coolness toward her consort).

Concerning activities, humans everywhere have:

Dance. Music. Play, including play fighting.

Aspects of universal human technology include:

Manufacture of, and dependence upon, many kinds of tools, many of them permanent, made according to culturally transmitted motifs, including cutters, pounders, containers, string, levers, spears. Use of fire to cook food and for other purposes. Drugs, both medicinal and recreational. Shelter. Decoration of artifacts.

For social conventions, we find in all human communities:

A standard pattern of time for weaning. Living in groups, which claim a territory and have a sense of being a distinct people. Families built around a mother and children, usually the biological mother, and one or more men. Institutionalized marriage, in the sense of publicly recognized right of sexual access to a woman eligible for childbearing. Socialization of children (including toilet training) by senior kin. Children copying their elders. Distinguishing of close kin from distant kin, and favoring of close kin. Avoidance of incest between mothers and sons. Great interest in the topic of sex. Exchange of labor, goods, and services. Reciprocity including retaliation. Gifts. Social reasoning. Coalitions. Government, in the sense of binding collective decisions about public affairs. Leaders, almost always nondictatorial, perhaps ephemeral. Laws, rights, and obligations, including laws against violence, rape, and murder. Punishment. Conflict, which is deplored. Rape. Seeking of redress for wrongs. Mediation. In-group/out-group conflicts. Property. Inheritance of property. Sense of right and wrong. Envy.

Concerning sex and age differences, found universally are:

Division of labor by sex and age. More child care by women. More aggression and violence by men. Acknowledgment of differences between male and female natures. Domination by men in the political sphere.

As discussed, universal human behavioral patterns and preferences cannot in themselves be used as evidence that they have a specific genetic basis. Instead they may be the result of the interaction of more general abilities and desires with physical and social environments that are similar enough in all cultures to produce these behaviors. But this essential interaction of genes and environment does not in any way detract from a Darwinian approach to explaining their origins since any behavior, preference, or trait depends on an interaction of genes and environment, of nature and nurture.

Sociobiologists and evolutionary psychologists respect this essential gene-environment interaction insofar as they usually refrain from stating that any human trait or behavior is either solely genetically or environmentally determined, but they make other errors as a result of not adequately respecting this interaction. For instance, it is not unusual for a Darwinian-inspired behavioral scientist to state that some behavior or trait is more due to genes than environment, or vice versa. E. O. Wilson commented on the extent to which human social behavior is genetically determined. A more blatant and potentially pernicious example of such thinking can be found in Herrnstein and Murray's controversial book *The Bell Curve* (1994). The authors used a maze of statistical analyses to argue that differences between American blacks and whites in performance on general intelligence tests are almost exclusively due to genetic racial differences and not to striking differences in environments in which individuals of these two races typically grow up and remain. Yet if all behavior and psychological abilities result from an interaction of genes and environment, what can it actually mean to say that either genes or environmental factors are more important for a behavior or trait?

One way of simplifying this issue is to consider the surface area of a rectangle, which is a function of both its length and width. Specifically, its length and width interact in a multiplicative fashion so that its area in square units is its length multiplied by its width. The way in which the length and width interact in determining area means that the effect of length on area depends on width. Similarly, the effect of width on area depends on length. So increasing a rectangle's width from 5 to 6 units will have more of an effect on its area if it is 16 units wide rather than 15 units wide. Increasing width from 16 to 17 units will have more effect on area if it is 6 units rather than 5 units long. Note that this interactive relationship makes it nonsensical to ask whether a rectangle's length or width is more important in determining its area.

Consider the implications of a similar multiplicative gene-environment interaction for human abilities and behaviors, such as those related to a child's success in school. If genes and environmental factors interact in determining school achievement, it makes no sense to consider whether nature or nurture is more important or which contributes more to the observed differences in this regard among a group of children.

Here's another example, a hypothetical case I call "The Case of the Stuttering Triplet," like the surface area example above, inspired by psychologist Donald Hebb's important 1953 paper on the roles of heredity and environment in behavior. Two psychologists, Dr. A and Dr. B, are interested in the causes of stuttering. Dr. A finds a boy named Stu who stutters and learns that Stu has a fraternal (dizygotic) twin living in the same house who does not stutter. Dr. A concludes from these findings that Stu's stuttering is genetically determined, since his brother, who has a different genome but shares the same home environment, does not stutter.

Meanwhile, Dr. B discovers a boy, also named Stu, who stutters. During his investigation Dr. B learns that this Stu has an identical (monozygotic) twin who was separated from Stu at birth, lives with a different family, and does not stutter. Dr. B concludes that Stu's stuttering is due to environmental factors since Stu's identical brother, who has an identical genome but lives in a different environment, does not stutter.

The punch line is that Dr. A and Dr. B have both found and studied the very same stuttering boy but have learned different things about him. Stu is actually one of *triplets*, two of them identical (one of them being Stu) and one fraternal. Dr. A's knowledge of Stu's nonstuttering fraternal twin living in the same home led him to conclude that Stu's stuttering had a genetic cause. In contrast, Dr. B's discovery of Stu's nonstuttering identical twin in a different home led to a very different conclusion, that Stu's stuttering must be due to his environment. What is really going on (obvious to us since we know of both Stu's identical and fraternal nonstuttering brothers) is that a certain *combination* of environmental and genetic factors led to Stu's stuttering, with neither genes nor environment being more or less important than the other in bringing about this phenomenon.

But there is yet another way in which genes and environment interact to influence behavior that goes beyond the multiplicative model suggested by the rectangle example. Research indicates that certain environmental factors can cause chemical changes in the body that affect certain genes that in turn produce proteins that ultimately influence the brain. Since changes in the brain influence behavior and the resulting environment, we have another circle of causality that defies one-way cause-effect analysis. We will see in the next chapter a particularly striking example of how at least a portion of a person's genes are not fixed at birth but rather continue to evolve throughout life in response to certain environmental conditions. To return briefly to the rectangle, it is as if changing its length also influences its width, which then influences its length, and so on.

What all this means for a Darwinian approach to human behavior is that neither genes nor environment (including culture) can be considered in isolation. Even to ask the question as to whether nature or nurture is more important in determining a human structural or behavioral trait is an indication of confusion. Since so much of humankind's environment is a function of human behavior and preserved for succeeding generations in the form of culture (which includes homes and schools), we must consider coevolution of both to make sense of human behavior. As the noted Ukrainian-born American geneticist Theodosius Dobzhansky remarked (quoted in Wilson 1978, p. 21), ". . . in a sense, human genes have surrendered their primacy in human evolution to an entirely new, nonbiological or superorganic agent, culture. However, it should not be forgotten that this agent is entirely dependent on the human genotype." And, of course, the human genotype has from its very beginning also been dependent on human culture.

This interaction of nature and nurture also blurs the distinction that is still often made between innate and learned behavior. We noted in the preceding chapter how the learning capabilities of animals were shaped by natural selection. That is, the ability to modify behavior in useful ways as a result of experience is inherited. Insofar as such learning abilities have survival and reproductive consequences, they in turn help to shape further evolution of the organism.

Strengths and Dangers of a Darwinian Approach to Human Behavior

The Darwinian approach to human behavior that emerged in the 1990s in the form of evolutionary psychology has begun to offer new insights into the behavior of our species.[3] Like its sociobiological forerunner, evolutionary psychology recognizes the importance of Darwinian evolution, including kin selection and reciprocal altruism, to provide ultimate explanations. In addition, it attempts to discover proximate psychological mechanisms underlying various human actions, recognizing that certain evolved behaviors and preferences may no longer be adaptive in a world so very different from the physical and social world in which we evolved.

But this approach has potential dangers that must be guarded against. One is the tendency to analyze human behavior by attempting to separate genetic from environmental factors, when these factors interact so that any such separation is meaningless at best and seriously misleading at worst.

Another potential danger is application of basic human universals or observed group differences (such as those based on sex or race) to individuals. By way of illustration, let us consider a proposed human universal from the preceding list where it was noted that all human societies make use of music and dance for various social functions. But finding music and dance in all human societies does not mean that all individual humans engage in musical behavior. Rather, since evolution depends on variation in traits and abilities, we should expect to find individual variation in participation in and abilities for such activities. Similarly, not all mature humans engage in sexual activities (while others do so frequently) and not all individuals participate in gift giving (while the great majority of us do). It is therefore important to keep in mind that human universals suggested by an evolutionary perspective are universal only in the sense that they are found in all human cultures and societies, and not in the sense that they apply to every human being on earth.

We must also guard against applying observed group differences to individuals. For example, consideration of human spatial abilities from an evolutionary perspective led to the hypothesis that since our male ancestors were primarily hunters of mobile, far-ranging game while our female forebears were mostly foragers of immobile, nearby vegetable foods, there should be sex differences in those abilities that are most important for hunting (where men should show an advantage) and foraging (where women should be superior). As predicted, men as a group are better in tasks involving mental rotations of objects, map reading, and maze learning, whereas women as a group show superiority in recalling objects and their locations. To take an ability where women show an advantage, a test for object memory, a group of 115 women correctly recalled on average 1.9 more objects from a diagram containing 27 objects than a group of 63 men (Silverman & Eals 1992, p. 539).

But in spite of this statistically significant difference favoring women ($p < 0.01$), the variability of individuals in each group (pooled standard deviation 4.03) resulted in a large enough overlap between men and women in this ability so that one cannot predict with confidence that a given woman will actually have a better memory for objects than a given man. Instead, since the mean difference between the groups is less than half the difference between a typical individual and his or her group's mean, a given man has close to a 7 out of 10 chance of being either above the woman's mean or not being more below that value than would be expected for a typical woman.

Even when group mean differences equivalent to one standard deviation are found (which is not common in psychological studies; an example would be a difference in means between two groups of 15 IQ points), it is still the case that a given individual in the lower group has an even chance of being either above the mean of the higher group or not farther below it than a typical individual of the higher group.

The lesson to take away from this is that a Darwinian approach to human behavior may lead to the discovery of interesting pancultural human universals and group differences, but such findings rarely if ever allow one to make accurate or useful predictions concerning the abilities or behavior of a given individual. So even if it is true, as Herrnstein and Murray claim, that American blacks score on the average 15 points below American whites on measures of general intelligence, such a group difference would be of virtually no use for making predictions about the intelligence of an individual white or black American.

Evolutionary psychology, unlike behaviorism, also recognizes the central importance of desires and goals in explaining human behavior. But, curiously, its practitioners have yet to discover proximate psychological mechanisms that can explain how such goals and desires influence behavior. This is because the mechanisms they propose continue to be one-way cause-effect models in which sensory input is transformed (that is, cognitively processed) into behavioral outputs. To illustrate this perspective, here are Cosmides and Tooby stating their view of the proximate psychological mechanism (1987, p. 282):

> Behavior is not randomly emitted; it is elicited by information which is gleaned from the organism's external environment, and, proprioceptively, from its internal states. Natural selection gave us information processing machinery to produce behavior, just as it gave us food processing machinery to produce digestion. . . . The evolutionary function of the human brain is to process information in ways that lead to adaptive behavior; the mind is a description of the operation of a brain that maps information input onto behavioral output. . . . Behavioral output differs with informational input; the information processing machinery that maps informational input onto behavioral output is a psychological mechanism.

But we saw in chapter 6 how such a one-way cause-effect mechanism is simply incapable of accounting for purposive behavior. If such a model cannot explain how a person can maintain the knot joining two rubber bands at a certain spot in spite of continuous disturbances, or keep a car centered in a highway lane despite curves and gusting winds, it certainly is inadequate to the task of accounting for how we are able to find food, procure mates, protect our children, defeat our enemies, and further our careers and reputations in complex, constantly changing, disturbance-filled environments.

This continued reliance on a one-way input-output mechanism of behavior leads to other problems. One is that evolutionary psychologists are susceptible to the behavioral illusion described in chapter 6 in which the covariation between some observable aspect of the environment and a person's behavior makes it appear as if a stimulus is causing behavior when in fact behavior is being used to control a perception that may not be apparent to the researcher. A second problem is that the one-way cause-effect model of behavior cannot distinguish between the intended consequences of human action and its unintended, accidental side effects. And a third problem is that an input-output view of behavior cannot account for the way in which certain desires or goals serve as subgoals, that is, as a means of achieving other goals, and how these subgoals are varied in response to disturbances to achieve the higher-level goals.

Perceptual control theory, with its hierarchy of perceptions and goals, provides an explicit, working model for these important characteristics of human behavior. But it is able to do so only by rejecting a one-way cause-effect view and replacing it with a hierarchy of closed loops, each involving the simultaneous functions of perception, comparison with a reference level, and action.

Whereas evolutionary psychologists recognize the Darwinian *origin* of many human desires and goals, as a group they have not yet escaped the grasp of one-way cause-effect reasoning in their attempts to understand the proximate *mechanisms* of behavior. Neither do they recognize the existence and importance of Darwinian processes occurring within the brain as humans constantly adapt their behaviors and desires to new environmental challenges for which our evolutionary past could not have prepared us. This application of Darwinian theory to adaptive processes occurring during the lifetime of organisms constitutes a veritable second Darwinian revolution that is the subject of the next chapter.

9

Evolution Within the Body: The Darwinian Lesson Extended

Evolution builds brains using evolution itself as a design tool. As it matures, a brain literally adapts to its body.
—Terrence W. Deacon (1997, p. 194)

Our present understanding of Darwinian evolution offers some answers and suggests others to many ultimate and proximate why questions concerning behavior. However, it must be recognized that the natural selection of organisms has a serious adaptive limitation. Natural selection can lead only to the evolution of organisms whose structure and behavior are adapted to *past* environments, with no guarantee that they will be adapted to the environment in which they live today and will inhabit tomorrow.

To the extent that an organism's environment is similar to that in which its predecessors evolved, we can expect its physical structures, physiological systems, and behavior to fit the demands of its current environment. But if the environment is significantly different in any way from that of its ancestors, we should not be surprised to find the organism maladapted in some way to the demands of living and reproducing. Changes in climate or in a species' food supply, or the arrival of a new predator or parasite may lead to extinction. The consequences of this inability of natural selection to prepare organisms for future environments can be quite serious, as indicated by the fact that the normal fate of a species is extinction; there are many times more extinct species than extant ones.

Psychologist Henry C. Plotkin referred to this as the "uncertain futures problem" (1994, p. 135), and it poses a serious challenge for all living organisms. Obviously, an organism's chance of surviving and reproducing would be improved if it could somehow solve the uncertain futures problem by changing its behavior to adapt to changes in the environment. Indeed most, if not all, organisms can adaptively modify their behavior to at least some degree, although some species are much better at this than others. In this respect, the human species is distinguished by remarkable flexibility that permits us to survive in a range of environments unmatched by any other species yet encountered (excluding parasites and bacterial companions for which we serve as host), from tropical forests and deserts to arctic tundra and, thanks to modern technological advances, from the ocean floor to the lunar surface.

The ability to change one's behavior (and thoughts, in the case of humans) as a result of environmental experiences is generally referred to as *learning* by psychologists and animal scientists. We surveyed in chapter 3 several attempts to understand how humans and other organisms are able to make adaptive changes to their behavior. But we also noted how these proposals—from behaviorist theories of Pavlov, Thorndike, Watson, and Skinner to cognitive theories of learning—fail to account for the purposeful nature of behavior, relying as they do on one-way stimulus-response or stimulus-computation-response mechanisms.

This chapter considers a more satisfactory materialist understanding of how it is that human behavior and thought can be adaptively modified as a result of experience. In keeping with the book's major themes, the mechanism offered will most assuredly not be one in which environmental stimuli cause behavior, but rather one that extends Darwin's selectionist lesson to processes occurring *within* organisms.

The Immune System as Within-Organism Darwinian Selection

Although it may seem odd to begin our discussion of learning with a look at the mammalian immune system, there are actually very good reasons for doing so. They will not become apparent, however, until we consider some basic facts about the functioning of the immune system.

The human immune system's primary function is to protect our bodies from microscopic pathogens such as bacteria, viruses, and chemical toxins that are collectively known as *antigens*. It does this by producing cells called *antibodies* that are able to recognize invading antigens and bind with them so that other cells produced by the immune system can find and neutralize or destroy them. What is both striking and essential about antibodies is that they have a very close physical match to the antigens to which they bind. An effective antibody fits an antigen in much the way that a jigsaw puzzle piece fits its neighboring piece (although for antibodies and antigens the fit is in three dimensions, not just two).

For over 100 years scientists puzzled over how antibodies managed to achieve this close fit with antigens. During the 1890s the first important immune system researcher, Paul Ehrlich (1854–1915) of Germany, theorized that mammals were born with a large innate set of antibodies, at least one of which was able to bind to any possible antigen. In this view, information essential for the production of all possibly needed antibodies is contained in the animal's genes (see Ehrlich 1900). Ehrlich's theory was therefore known as a *germ-line theory* of antibody production, with germ line referring to the entire set of genes (or *genome*) that is passed from parents to offspring.

But this theory soon encountered a major difficulty. During the 1900s Karl Landsteiner (1868–1943) of Austria demonstrated that antigens could be produced in response to the introduction of completely new artificial substances. This indicated that the germ-line theory is inadequate since an animal could not possibly possess in its finite genome the information required to produce an infinite number of all possibly needed antibodies. In effect, Landsteiner showed that the immune system somehow manages to solve the uncertain futures problem by producing new antibodies able to bind with antigens never before encountered in its host's life or evolutionary past.

The theory that first attempted to account for the immune system's ability to generate antibodies in response to novel antigens was the *template theory* that appeared in Europe in 1930 and was further developed by Nobel prize-winning chemist Linus Pauling (1901–1994) in the United States. According to the template theory, antigens themselves are used by the immune system to construct well-fitting antibodies, similar to the way that a cookie cutter makes cookies out of dough. Since antibody formation is considered the result of the direct action of antigens on antibodies, this can be referred to as an *instructionist* theory with antigens somehow directly causing or "instructing" adaptive changes in the production of antibodies. In this way the template theory is similar to Lamarck's instructionist theory of evolution that saw the environment as directly causing adaptive changes in organisms (see chapter 7).

Also like Lamarck's theory, the template theory of antibody production ultimately failed. As British-Danish immunologist Niels Kaj Jerne (1911–1994) pointed out in the 1950s, it could not account for several key immunological findings. These include the increasing rate of antibody production during the initial immune response, the system's memory of previously encountered antigens, and the fact that antibodies produced during the latter stages of an immune response are more effective in binding with antigens than antibodies initially produced.

In addition to making strong arguments against the template theory, Jerne offered an alternative for which he received a Nobel prize in 1984. His natural selection theory of antibody production held that a mammal initially possesses a relatively small number of antibodies. Successful binding of an antibody to an antigen—which fortunately does not require an exact fit between them—triggers the antibody to produce a large number of copies of itself. In this way a preexisting antibody is effectively *selected* by the antigen that in turn stimulates the chosen antibody to produce a multitude of clones. Australian virologist Sir Frank Macfarlane Burnet (1899–1985), yet another Nobel laureate, further developed this theory, calling it the *clonal selection theory* of antibody production.

Whereas this rather sketchy account of antibody production has omitted much (for a more detailed summary see Cziko 1995, chapter 4), it nonetheless reveals its essentially Darwinian operation. Indeed, the clonal-selection production of antibodies is a veritable microcosm of Darwinian evolution with the three major principles of overproduction, variation, and selection each playing an essential role. Overproduction is evident in the production of far more antibodies than are effective in binding with an antigen; variation is achieved by the random recombination and mutation of antibody genes; and selection occurs as only those antibodies that bind with an antigen can reproduce and thus be represented in the next generation.

It should be now somewhat clearer why this chapter on learning and cognitive development began with an introduction to the mammalian immune system. It is because the immune system is an adaptive system that has overcome the uncertain futures problem by employing its own version of Darwinian evolution. This evolution takes place not over long periods of geological time, but rather over the much shorter lifetime of individual organisms as certain antibodies are naturally selected for reproduction and others are eliminated. Whereas adaptive biological evolution proceeds by cumulative natural selection occurring *among* organisms, we now understand that the immune system is able to adapt to new, unpredictable pathogenic threats by cumulative variation and selection occurring *within* organisms. Might it also be the case that organisms are able to devise behavioral and mental solutions to problems posed by uncertain futures using a similar process of within-organism variation and selection?

Darwinian Theories of Behavioral and Cognitive Change

Just such a Darwinian approach to cognitive functioning and behavior played an important role in psychological theory, particularly at the end of the nineteenth century and beginning of the twentieth. In the late nineteenth century, theories involving mental or cognitive variation and selection were used to attempt to understand how scientific discoveries are made. Scottish philosopher and psychologist Alexander Bain (1818–1903) emphasized that scientific discoveries required the generation of a great number of ideas and then trying them out (1868, pp. 593 ff.). Another early cognitive Darwinian was English economist and logician W. Stanley Jevons (1835–1882) who stated that "in all probability the errors of the great mind exceed in number those of the less vigorous one. Fertility of imagination and abundance of guesses at truth are among the first requisites of discovery; but the erroneous guesses must be many times as numerous as those which prove well founded" (1874; quoted in Campbell 1974, p. 428).

Other respected nineteenth-century writers who were quick to apply Darwinian selectionism to the understanding of human thought and behavior included American psychologist James Mark Baldwin (1861–1934), Austrian physicist and philosopher Ernst Mach (1838–1916), and

French mathematician Henri Poincaré (1854–1912). Central to all these men was the notion that useful thoughts (beliefs, ideas) could be found only if the thinker generated a large number of varied guesses that were somehow filtered so that only the better ones were retained and the others discarded.

In the United States, mathematician and philosopher Chauncey Wright (1830–1875) was so taken by the theory of evolution that he visited Darwin in England in 1872 and went on to apply concepts of natural selection to the workings of the human mind. Instead of Darwinian competition among organisms, Wright described a process of mental competition among beliefs, with both other current beliefs and the environment acting to eliminate less fit beliefs and leaving better-adapted ones.

Wright's ideas apparently also had some influence on America's first great psychologist, William James. James, who recognized the purposeful character of animal and human behavior (recall his description of the frog seeking air and Romeo striving to place his lips on those of Juliet), applied the ideas of Darwinian random variation and selection to the psychological realm (1880, pp. 456–457).

> . . . new conceptions, emotions, and active tendencies which evolve are originally *produced* in the shape of random images, fancies, accidental outbirths of spontaneous variation of the excessively unstable human brain, which the outer environment simply confirms or refutes, preserves or destroys—selects, in short, just as it selects morphological and social variation due to molecular accidents of an analogous sort . . .

But the rise of behaviorism in the United States during the first half of the twentieth century put a rather abrupt end to James's cognitive Darwinism and replaced it with a Darwinism oriented to overt behaviors. The theory of operant conditioning introduced by Thorndike and further developed and advocated by Skinner was described and critiqued in chapters 3 and 7. It will be recalled that Skinner's dismissal of purpose and his emphasis on the environment's role in determining an organism's behavior resulted in a theory in which external factors cause the organism's behavior and cannot account for the way in which the organism acts to control aspects of its environment. Skinner saw behavior as determined by its consequences (reward and punishment), however, a true appreciation of the purposeful nature of animate behavior must include understanding behavior as a means of controlling consequences.

In retrospect, it is unfortunate that Skinner used an evolutionary analogy for his theory of animate behavior and learning, since this provided a reason for those involved in the cognitive revolution of the second half of the twentieth century not only to reject his narrow focus on overt behavior and environmental control but to purge all Darwinian thinking from psychology as well. The Skinnerian image—organisms (including humans) emitting random behaviors with the environment providing consequences to determine which of these behaviors should be repeated—was (and still is) considered simplistic, unrealistic, and even repugnant to cognitive scientists. They instead attempt to understand behavior and its change by focusing on mental and neural processes that underlie what often appears to be initially highly intelligent behavior, not the randomly emitted fumblings Thorndike and Skinner described.

Perhaps the best example of this anti-Skinnerian and anti-Darwinian attitude among cognitive scientists is that of linguist Noam Chomsky and his innatist theories of language structure and acquisition. Indeed, Chomsky's 1959 review of Skinner's book *Verbal Behavior* is typically taken as the beginning of the cognitive revolution in psychology. Curiously, his anti-Darwinism goes so far as even to deny Darwinian evolution an important role in the evolution of the human capacity for language.[1]

Donald T. Campbell's Cognitive Darwinism

At least one behavioral scientist was able to reject Skinner's narrow focus on overt behavior while recognizing the power of the Darwinian process working within organisms. Donald T. Campbell (1916–1995), who spent most of his academic career at Northwestern University near Chicago, is best known among behavioral and social scientists for his development of research methods (see, for example, Campbell & Stanley 1966; Cook & Campbell 1979). But although this work remains important and influential, Campbell was actually more interested in developing a general theory of knowledge processes that used as its engine the Darwinian mechanism of variation and selection.

Campbell made three major accomplishments in this area. First, he documented and described Darwinian theories of thought and behavior of philosophers, psychologists, and other scientists since the time of Darwin (Campbell 1974). Second, over more than thirty-five years he provided strong arguments that Darwinian variation and selection underlie all processes by which adaptation of some type is achieved. These include the fit of our perceptions to aspects of the environment they represent, the fit of our thoughts and mental processes to real-world problems we confront and solve, and the fit of our scientific theories and predictions to the universe they describe. Finally, he devised a hierarchy of knowledge processes to explain how the development of all forms of knowledge—whether over long periods of evolutionary time or during the relatively short lifetime of a single organism—can be accounted for by the general Darwinian process of variation and selection.

For the purpose of this chapter, it is Campbell's description of what he called "vicarious blind variation and selective retention" that is of most interest. Campbell saw such vicarious processes as adaptive mental processes "substituting for overt locomotor exploration or the life-and-death winnowing of organic evolution" (1974, p. 421). Let us turn to a concrete example for a better idea of what he had in mind.

Imagine that a desired object, such as a piece of food, is placed in view behind a fence so that an animal can obtain it only by first moving away from it to go around the intervening barrier. This is known as the *Umweg* (German for "detour") task and has been used to test the problem-solving abilities of chimpanzees, chickens, and other animals (see Boakes 1984, pp. 184–196).

It turns out that chickens and chimpanzees differ markedly on the Umweg task. Whereas chickens can solve the problem only if their frantic movements bring them by chance to a spot where they can see the path around the obstacle, chimpanzees can more calmly examine the situation and then simply walk around the barrier to obtain the object. So chickens must rely on the variation and selection of overt behaviors, but larger-brained chimps are able to substitute the variation and selection of mental processes for overt behavior.

Here's another example that you can try yourself. Examine the maze shown in figure 9.1 and by visual examination alone (using no pen or pencil or tracing actions) try to find the path from the upper left corner to the lower right one. You should try this now before reading further.

Notice how you were able to solve the maze problem with no overt behavior at all (other than moving your eyes, if you consider that overt). To find the path, you almost certainly made a number of mental errors,

Figure 9.1
Maze

running into cul-de-sacs and backtracking to find an alternative successful route. This is an example of the vicarious variation and selection of mental processes that in humans—and presumably other "higher" animals such as apes and perhaps even dogs and cats—can substitute for the overt variation and selection of behaviors that Skinner emphasized.

As a final example, imagine trying to rearrange the furniture in your living room to accommodate a piano. In looking over the room as currently furnished, you could readily imagine other possible arrangements. You might think, "The sofa could be moved from the back wall to under the window freeing up wall space for the piano, and the armchair currently next to the window could be moved to the empty corner." On second thought, this plan may not prove to be feasible, as the piano would block access to the built-in bookcase. But other arrangements could easily be imagined as you observe the room's current configuration and contents and think about other ways it could be arranged.

The usefulness of this variation and selection of mental processes as a substitute for more costly (in terms of time and energy) and potentially dangerous overt behaviors provides what may be an important clue in understanding the evolution of consciousness itself. While the topic of consciousness and its purpose continues to intrigue and mystify both philosophers and cognitive scientists (for example, see Dennett 1991; Searle 1992), one important use of consciousness is the vicarious mental variation and selection it makes possible. This perspective on consciousness does not provide answers to the question of why we have the particular conscious experiences we have, but it does suggest an important functional role for consciousness. Consciousness as vicarious variation and selection allows us to try out possible solutions mentally using a type of simulated or virtual reality as a substitute for more effortful and possibly dangerous overt behavioral trials.

It is largely because of Campbell's writings that a general Darwinian approach to human knowledge, thought, and behavior survived through both the behaviorist and cognitive phases of twentieth-century psychological theory. Campbell coined the term *evolutionary epistemology* that is still widely used, at least among philosophers, for a general Darwinian account of the emergence of knowledge. For more than thirty-five years he provided important philosophical, logical, historical, and anecdotal reasons for seeing creative thought, problem solving, technological advances, and scientific progress as involving the cumulative blind variation and selection of thought trials. But he did not undertake empirical research to provide evidence for his claims and so his Darwinian account of knowledge processes has not had much impact on mainstream psychological theory. But we will see in the following sections that there is increasing evidence from both behavioral and neuroscientific research for Campbell's cognitive extension of Darwin's lesson.

Evidence for Cognitive Darwinism

When Campbell first proposed his extension of Darwinian theory to psychology, he anticipated difficulty finding empirical support, noting "the unfavorable ratio of hypothesized unobservable processes to observable input-output variables" (1960, p. 397). Thoughts and ideas do not leave fossils that can be dug up and examined, nor are they readily accessible to other means of scientific observation and measurement. But now, forty years later, a growing body of evidence suggests that some cognitive processes do involve the Darwinian variation and selection of thought trials. These findings are not only consistent with Campbell's theory but are difficult to account for otherwise. Much of this research deals with human creativity and invention and was reviewed by Simonton (1999b). We will now take a look at some of these studies, as well as some others not discussed in Simonton's book.

If it is true that problem solving and other adaptive forms of human creativity depend on blind variation and selection of thought trials, we should expect them to be enhanced by factors that increase the variability and number of such thoughts. This was found in a number of experimental studies. Subjects in one study were provided with shapes and forms to create objects having certain functions (Finke, Ward, & Smith 1992). They came up with the best and most imaginative inventions when both the forms they were given and the target function were randomly selected from a large set of possibilities. In another study, randomly generated associations facilitated problem solving on a marketing task (Proctor 1993).

Other investigations, known as psychometric studies, examined relationships between certain psychological traits and creativity. They found that above a certain basic level, IQ is not related to creative ability (Simonton 1985). Instead, creative individuals tend to produce many varied ideas (see, for example, Eysenck 1993, 1994, 1995). Accordingly, tests that attempt to measure creativity typically do so not by replicating the types of items found on intelligence tests but rather by assessing an individual's ability to generate many diverse ideas. The Remote Associations Test (Mednick 1962) assesses creativity by measuring one's ability to create associations between dissimilar ideas. Other tests assess an individual's ability in what is called divergent thinking, that is, the ability to generate many novel and diverse responses to a problem or question. An example is the Alternate Uses Test in which one attempts to come up with as many different uses for an object as one can.

Other aspects of personality that are associated with creativity also support a within-organism Darwinian view of cognition. Simonton (1999a) summarized this research by noting that:

. . . creative personalities tend to possess those characteristics that would most favor the production of ideas both numerous and diverse. In particular, creative individuals tend to be independent, non-conformist, unconventional, even bohemian; they also tend to have wide interests, greater openness to new experiences, and a more conspicuous behavioral and cognitive flexibility and boldness.

Also of interest are studies of creativity and invention that use historical measures. Historiometric studies conducted by Simonton (1979, 1987, 1997) showed that individuals who are most prolific are also the most successful in creative achievements. This relationship between quantity and quality holds across as well as within individuals and thus provides some evidence that creativity is a function of variations. The more an individual produces, the more likely he or she is to be successful in some creative endeavor, not unlike biological evolution in which organisms that produce the most offspring are most likely to produce a variation that will be better adapted to survival and reproduction. Of particular interest is the finding that the proportion of produced variations that are successful does not increase as an individual gains experience in his or her field. Rather, individuals appear to be most creative around the age of 40, which is when they produce the greatest number of variations. In addition, a Darwinian view of creativity can account for the output of scientific communities (Kantorovich 1993).

Finally, in the field of cognitive development, Siegler (1996) found a high degree of variation in the problem-oriented thinking of children and held that "variability and selection functions seem essential to any developing system. Thus, they may be a basic part of many, if not most, mechanisms of cognitive development" (1989, p. 376).

These are just a few of the studies from the considerable (and growing) body of empirical research that supports a within-organism Darwinian theory of creative thought and behavior as suggested by Campbell. The reader is referred to Simonton's recent book (1999b) for a thorough treatment of this topic.

The Rise of Neural Darwinism

In addition to evidence from psychological studies of thought, personality, and behavior, the rapidly developing field of neuroscience has uncovered findings having clear Darwinian implications for our understanding of the development, structure, and functioning of the human brain.

One of the principal puzzles in the neurosciences is understanding how something as complex as the human brain can develop from a single fertilized egg cell. The adult human brain contains about 11 billion specialized nerve cells, or *neurons*, and each neuron may have up to 10,000 connections, or *synapses*, with other neurons. It is widely believed by neuroscientists, psychologists, and even some philosophers that all knowledge that the brain contains—from knowing how to walk to being able to perform abstract mathematical reasoning—is a function of neurons and their interconnections. Therefore, understanding how the functional complexity of the brain develops is a major goal of behavioral and brain sciences.

It was thought at one time that the brain's complex organization was fully specified in the genome as a result of many millions of years of natural selection. Research findings now cast doubt on such a view. For one thing, it is estimated that the human neocortex alone (the most recent addition to our brain) has about 10^{15} (1 followed by 15 zeros, or 1 thousand million million) synapses (Eccles 1989, pp. 1, 4). Since the entire human genome has only about 3.5×10^9 (3.5 billion) bits of information stored as nucleotide base pairs, some scientists (for example, Deacon 1997, p. 197) have concluded that our genes simply do not have enough storage capacity to specify all these connections, in addition to including information on the location and type of each neuron plus similar information for the rest of the body.

How then is the brain able to achieve the very specific and adaptive wiring required to function in so many remarkable ways? For example, how does a motor neuron know to which particular muscle fiber it should connect? How is a sensory neuron in the visual system able to connect itself to the correct cell in the visual cortex of the occipital lobe of the brain? If this detailed neuron-to-neuron wiring plan is not provided by the genes, from where does it come?

It turns out that the precise wiring of the brain and nervous system is accomplished by a process that *eliminates* many neurons and synapses. As far back as 1906 it was known that some embryonic neurons did not survive birth (Changeux 1985, pp. 216, 217), with later research finding that of the 20,000 neurons present in a particular location of a chicken embryo's spinal cord, only 12,000 remained in the adult bird (Hamburger 1975).

In addition to entire neurons, countless synaptic connections are eliminated during the development of the mammalian nervous system. But how does the nervous system know which connections to retain and which to eliminate? The work of David Hubel and Torsten Wiesel in the 1970s (who shared a Nobel prize in 1981) provided an important clue. They conducted their ground-breaking experiments by sewing closed the lid of one eye of newborn cats and found that even one week without sight altered the connections of the eyes to the brain (layer 4 of the occipital cortex, to be more precise). Neurons carrying nervous signals from the closed eye made fewer connections with the cortex, whereas those from the open eye made many more connections than was normal. This finding suggests that visual system neurons engage in a form of Darwinian competition for space in the visual cortex, with the result of the competition dependent on the amount and type of sensory stimulation carried by the axons.

We know that normal development of the brain is a function of interaction between genetic inheritance and environmental experience. The genome provides the general structure of the central nervous system, and nervous system activity and sensory stimulation provide the means by which the system is fine-tuned and made fully operational. But this fine-tuning does not depend on adding new components and connections in the way that a radio is normally assembled in a factory. Instead it is achieved by eliminating much of what was originally present. It is as if the radio arrived on the assembly line with twice as many electrical components and connections than it needed. If such an overconnected radio were plugged in and turned on, nothing but silence, static, or a hum would be heard from its loudspeaker. However, careful removal of unnecessary components and judicious snipping of redundant wires would leave just those components and connections that result in a functioning radio. This snipping is analogous to the elimination of synapses in the human brain as part of its normal development.

Psychologist William Greenough of the University of Illinois at Urbana-Champaign has studied in microscopic detail the process by which brain connections change over time as maturing animals interact with their environments. Using sophisticated techniques to determine the numbers of neurons and synapses in specific regions of the rat's brain, he and his associates found a rapid spurt in the growth of synapses during the first months of the rat's life that occurs regardless of the amount or type of sensory experience (Greenough & Black 1992). This period of synaptic "blooming" is followed by a sharp decline in the number of synapses. That is, elimination or "pruning" of synapses takes place based on the activity and sensory stimulation of the brain, ultimately resulting in the pattern of connections characteristic of the mature rat's brain.

Greenough refers to this initial blooming and pruning of synapses as *experience-expectant* learning, since the initial synaptic overproduction appears to be relatively independent of the animal's experiences. It is as though the brain is expecting important things to happen during the first months of life and is prepared to profit from these experiences with an overabundance of synapses, only a fraction of which will be selectively retained. The work of Greenough and his associates has been limited to rats and monkeys, but autopsy studies of human cortex have also found a decrease to about 60 percent of the maximum number of synapses as the human brain matures (Huttenlocher & Dabholkar 1997, p. 167).

In a recent book on the evolution of language, neuroscientist and biological anthropologist Terrence Deacon (1997, p. 199) summarizes the role of within-organism Darwinism for brain development:

In the same sense that Darwinian processes have created new design information for building organisms during the course of the evolution of life, Darwinian-like processes in brain development are responsible for creating the new information required to adapt large brains to themselves and to their bodies.

Greenough's work also gives a Darwinian explanation for how the adult brain is able to learn new skills, form new memories, and adapt to new environments. According to this theory, experience-dependent learning involves both addition and elimination of synapses. Addition involves growth of new synapses in response to the animal's attempt to control aspects of a new, complex environment. Although the brain does appear to know what part of itself has to be involved in this construction project, it need not (and most likely could not) know which particular individual connections to make. By forming a large variety and number of new connections, the brain can select the combinations that work best, in the same way that the immature, developing brain retains useful connections from its initial oversupply. The long-term result is an overall addition to the number of synapses.

But the actual selection process that fine-tunes the connections is a subtractive one in which useful connections are selectively retained and less useful ones eliminated. Although clear evidence exists for synaptic increase in learning, as I write this we still have no such evidence in mature learning for overproduction of synapses that are pruned away. However, evidence has been found for overproduction of dendrites in mature rats during readaptation of the brain after injury, suggesting that overproduction of synapses may be involved as well (Jones & Schallert 1992, 1994; Schallert & Jones 1993). These findings fit very nicely with the subtractive synapse findings on brain maturation and provide an elegant solution to the puzzle of how the brain could know exactly which new synaptic connections to establish to enable it to acquire new knowledge, skills, and memories.

Several years ago only a relatively small number of neuroscientists subscribed to the view that the adult brain develops and learns through a Darwinian process of cumulative neural variation and selection. Today, however, such a view is starting to be considered mainstream, although much debate remains (see Quartz & Sejnowski 1997 and following commentaries and response). Neuroscientist William Calvin has referred to the brain as a "Darwin machine" that follows the plan of making lots of random variants by brute bashing about, then selecting the good ones (Calvin 1987; see also Calvin 1996a, b). Gerald Edelman, who shared a Nobel prize in 1972 for his research on the chemical structure of antibodies in the immune system, has written several books describing aspects of his neuronal group selection theory of brain development and learning that he refers to as "neural Darwinism" (Edelman 1987, 1988, 1989, 1992).

Research is underway to find physical evidence for overproduction and elimination of newly formed synapses in the adult mammalian brain as the mechanism underlying learning. New imaging techniques such as magnetic resonance imaging are also being used to gain insights into the functioning of the human brain, the universe's most complex known object. Finding clear evidence for Darwinian processes in its structural modification and functioning would place the brain alongside the immune system as a second striking example of how the process of cumulative variation and selection during the lifetime of an organism makes it possible to adapt to new and changing environments.

The Complementarity of Among- and Within-Organism Selection

The discovery of within-organism Darwinian processes involving cumulative variation and selection offers some clear answers and suggests others to a number of vexing problems concerning the functioning of the immune system, the processes involved in human thought and creativity, and the development and modification of the brain. Since these phenomena all require the adaptation of one system to another, we should not be too surprised to learn that Darwinian processes are involved. In effect, through the process of among-organism variation and selection, mechanisms of within-organism variation and selection have evolved to solve the uncertain futures problem that all organisms face.

But this does not mean that all physiological and neural functioning involves variation and selection of some kind. We should be grateful that the human heart does not have to learn to pump blood by within-organism trial and error elimination. And although processes of neural Darwinism may be involved in the development of the human auditory system, once developed, it appears to be able to analyze the sounds of human speech directly and quickly with remarkable accuracy with few if any errors from guessing. The among-organism variation and selection of human evolution (along with, in the case of the auditory system, some fine-tuning involving selective neuronal and synaptic elimination) may have provided us with some systems that are able to function quite well without current variation and selection. But other systems that face continual challenges and new environments, such as other aspects of the mammalian nervous and immune systems, must rely on variation and selection to adapt to these new circumstances.

A clearer understanding of the roles of among-organism and within-organism selection can be achieved by considering figure 9.2, which is a simplified illustration of what is hypothesized to be the relative importance of the two processes for three different types of adaptations.[2] To the extreme left we have what are usually considered inborn instincts, such as a spider weaving a web or a newly hatched gosling following the first large moving object it sees (Konrad Lorenz's imprinting, mentioned in chapter 7). Such behaviors are adaptations that may be entirely due (or nearly so) to among-organism selection of biological evolution.

In the middle of figure 9.2 we have adaptive behavior that is not innate but acquired during the individual's lifetime. One obvious example is a rat in a Skinner box learning to push a lever to obtain bits of food. Here we have what appears to be within-organism selection of behaviors emitted by the rat. But better examples for our present purposes are the types of learning studied by Köhler (1925) in apes, such as learning to stack two or more boxes to reach a suspended banana, or use a stick to pull in a banana placed outside the cage. Such learning often appears insightful; that is, after what appears to be a period of incubation, the apes proceed directly to the solution with no overt variation and selection of behaviors. Thanks to Donald Campbell, we can understand such learning as the result of

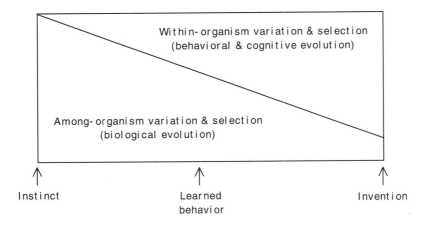

Figure 9.2
Complementarity of among-organism and within-organism variation and selection for three different types of adaptations

within-organism variation and selection involving the generation, evaluation, and selection of thought trials that substitute for overt behaviors.

Note, however, that among-organism evolution still plays an essential part in such learned behavior, as it is responsible for the ape having the necessary equipment (eyes, hands, arms, legs, brain) and motivation (a taste for bananas) for solving the problem. But among-organism (biological) selection is clearly not sufficient since, unlike instincts, what emerges is a new behavior that could not have been naturally selected in the ape's evolutionary past. Such acquired behavior also requires within-organism (cognitive or behavioral) variation and selection.

A useful way of conceptualizing the relative importance of among-organism variation and selection in learning is the degree to which it provides constraints for the blind variations of within-organism variation and selection. For example, young children readily learn the meanings of words spoken to them by their caretakers (as rapidly as one word per waking hour). Although biological evolution cannot in itself provide the child the meanings of these words (in the way that it may provide the meaning of a scream), it appears to set rather narrow (and very useful) limits on the possibilities that a child is willing to entertain. So whereas a child may have little difficulty in learning the meanings of *hand*, *arm*, and *forearm* (the latter referring to both the hand and arm up to around the elbow), she would not expect a single word to refer to both shoulder and hand, or to both knee and foot, or to both red and blue. Such constraints, the results of among-organism evolution, have the effect of usefully constraining or guiding the necessary within-organism variation and selection that must take place to acquire language.

Now we move to the extreme right of figure 9.2. Here we find certain forms of behavioral and/or cognitive adaptations that appear to rely primarily on within-organism variation and selection. Of course, among-organism variation and selection must still play a role since biological brains and limbs are involved (which is why in figure 9.2 the line separating among-organism from within-organism selection never makes it all the way to the lower right corner). But at this end there are fewer useful biological constraints on within-organism variations. Human invention is an example of such an adaptation, since there are apparently few useful biological constraints for the variations that must be considered for inventing steam engines, light bulbs, transistors, or nuclear fusion reactors.

A second important distinction exists between prior and current variation and selection. Obviously, from the viewpoint of the living organism, among-organism variation and selection of biological evolution is prior, but within-organism variation and selection can be seen as either prior or current. An ape confronted for the first time with boxes and a suspended banana must engage in some form of current behavioral and/or cognitive variation and selection to create a solution for reaching the banana. But the ape who solved the task yesterday requires little or no current variation and selection of behavioral or thought trials since the knowledge gained from that experience remain to guide the ape today. Such prior variation and selection can be of use even if the task is modified so that the boxes are different (such as being open on one end) or a desired object other than a banana (such as a favorite toy) is suspended out of reach. In other words, prior within-organism variation and selection results in knowledge that can be used to constrain current variation and selection for similar types of tasks.

Figure 9.3 indicates the complementary role of prior and current variation and selection for different types of behaviors or abilities. At

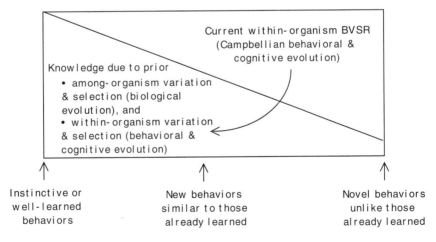

Figure 9.3
Complementarity of prior and current variation and selection for three different types of behaviors

the left end we find both instinctive (for example, bird nest building) and well-learned behaviors (as in a pianist's playing a familiar piece). For such behaviors, no current variation and selection may be necessary. For instincts, among-organism variation and selection supplies the necessary knowledge. For well-learned noninstinctive behaviors, it is a combination of among-organism variation and selection and prior within-organism variation and selection that provides the knowledge necessary for the new behavior or ability.

Moving toward the middle of figure 9.3 we find behaviors and abilities similar but not identical to acquired ones. Prior within-organism variation and selection provides some of the knowledge necessary for these behaviors, but it is not sufficient, thereby making additional current variation and selection necessary. Having created one successful musical composition or invention, one may find creating the next one quite a bit easier. But some additional current variation and selection will be necessary if the next work is not to be just a copy or imitation of the previous one.

Toward the right of figure 9.3 we find novel behaviors unlike those already learned. To learn such behaviors or develop new abilities, current variation and selection must play a major role since little has been learned to constrain or guide new variations that must be generated and tested. The arrow between "current within-organism variation and selection" and "prior within-organism variation and selection" indicates the transformation of current variation and selection to knowledge that may be used to constrain future within-organism variation and selection. This perspective on the complementary role of biological natural selection (that is, among-organism variation and selection) and continuing evolutionary processes (that is, within-organism variation and selection) suggests the universality of the Darwinian process of variation and selection as responsible for all instances of adaptation, indeed, for all knowledge processes broadly conceived (see Cziko 1995; Dennett 1995). If an animal appears to be born already knowing when and how to perform complex behaviors, such as finding food, defending itself, and mating, that knowledge is the result of the among-organism variation and selection of biological evolution. If, however, new behaviors are learned as a result of environmental demands (such as a seal learning to balance a ball on its nose to obtain food from its trainer, or a physicist developing a new superconductive material), this new learning or knowledge must also rely on a form of variation and selection, but now it is occurring within the organism.

This extension of Darwinian thinking to within-organism processes provides a major conceptual advance for many fields of inquiry, but it is not complete. For among-organism variation and selection, the environment (including other organisms) provides the selective filter to winnow the fit from the less fit. But what provides the selective filter for the within-organism selection of thoughts and ideas and new behaviors? Although biological evolution has no purpose in mind, the within-organism evolution of thoughts, ideas, and behaviors *is* purposeful. So to complete our understanding of how new knowledge and skills evolve within organisms, we have to pay heed once again to Bernard's lesson and combine it with this within-organism extension of Darwin's.

IV

Bernard and Darwin
Meet Behavioral Science:
Implications and Applications

10

Understanding Adaptive Behavior and Thought as Purposeful Evolution: Combining Bernard and Darwin

It is wonderful what the principle of selection by man, that is the picking out of individuals with any desired quality, and breeding from them, and again picking out, can do. Even breeders have been astounded at their own results. . . . Man, by his power of accumulating variations, adapts living beings to his wants—may be said to make the wool of one sheep good for carpets, of another for cloth, &c.
—Charles Darwin (from an 1858 letter to American biologist Asa Gray; reprinted in Bajema 1983, pp. 191–192)

Three Lessons of Biology for Behavioral Science

A major theme of this book as elaborated in the preceding chapters can be summarized by extracting a few important lessons about what biology has taught us about the what, why, and how of animate behavior.

The lesson inspired by Claude Bernard and introduced in chapter 4 is that the functioning of physiological systems can be understood as the means by which an organism controls its internal environment. But since physiological control is achieved by internal processes normally hidden from view, this lesson is more relevant to physiology and medicine than it is to behavioral science.

Instead, it is the *extended* Bernardian lesson that makes sense of observable behavior, grounded on Bernard's basic insight, further developed in the mid-twentieth century by cyberneticians, and systematized into a unified working theory of animate behavior by William T. Powers and his associates. Presented in chapters 5 and 6, the extended Bernardian lesson informs us that a living organism acts to control aspects of its external environment. And since an organism can know its environment only through its perceptual systems (including vision, hearing, touch, and other sensory modalities), animate behavior can be understood as the *control of perception*. The extended Bernardian lesson is concerned with the proximate (here and now) causes of behavior, and when augmented by perceptual control theory it establishes working models of behavior that are both physical and purposeful.

But controlling a perception requires the existence of an *intended* perception, that is, a goal, standard, or reference level with which to compare perception. This is where the basic Darwinian lesson becomes relevant. Chapters 7 and 8 informed us that the goals an organism pursues are not chosen at random. Neither are they determined in any direct, one-way causal manner by the organism's current environment. Instead, an organism's basic goals were selected during its evolutionary past for the effects they had on survival and reproductive success. It is not just a lucky coincidence that a male robin does all it can to maximize its distance from hawks while minimizing its distance from earthworms and female robins, since previous robins that didn't do likewise left few if any descendants. Human behavior is much more complex than that of other animals. But there are nonetheless good Darwinian reasons why men are much more inclined than women toward casual sex with a variety of partners, and why fast-food restaurants are able to attract millions of paying customers with their offerings of quick and conveniently packaged sugar, fat, and salt. Where the extended Bernardian lesson is concerned with the proximate causes of behavior, the basic Darwinian lesson has to do with the ultimate, evolutionary causes of behavior.

The third lesson of biology for behavioral science is the extended Darwinian lesson, presented in chapter 9. The basic Darwinian lesson draws its explanatory power from the cumulative variation and selection of organisms over long periods of phylogenetic time, resulting in the evolution of adaptive structures and behaviors. In contrast, the extended Darwinian lesson points out processes of cumulative variation and selection occurring *within* organisms over the much shorter span of their lives. Although the best currently understood example of cumulative within-organism variation and selection is the functioning of the mammalian immune system, growing evidence suggests that the brain also employs cumulative variation and selection to arrive at creative thoughts, innovative behaviors, and problem solutions.

How Evolution Can Be Purposeful

All three lessons (extended Bernardian, basic Darwinian, and extended Darwinian) are essential for making sense of animate behavior. But by combining the extended Bernardian and extended Darwinian lessons we gain special insight into why and how the goals of an organism change during its lifetime and how an organism is able adapt its perceptual-behavioral systems to achieve these new goals.

Last month a teenage boy was spending several hours a week in the gym trying to get in shape for the upcoming football season; today he no longer pumps iron but spends hours with his guitar. Last year a middle-aged housewife was content to remain at home performing domestic tasks, but now works long days selling real estate and has developed impressive computing, financial, and interpersonal skills that she did not have before. These changes in goals and abilities, resulting from the process we referred to as reorganization, require a directed, purposeful Darwinian process involving the cumulative variation and selection of lower-level goals to achieve higher-level ones. This combined lesson includes aspects of Bernard's and Darwin's insights and involves proximate and ultimate causes of behavior.

But to refer to a Darwinian process as "purposeful" or "directed" might seem to indicate a basic misunderstanding of the process itself. After all, Darwin proposed his theory of evolution by natural selection to explain how species could change over time and new ones appear without the involvement of a supernatural designer or preordained cosmic plan. This is why Richard Dawkins (1986, p. 5) described biological evolution as a blind watchmaker:

All appearances to the contrary, the only watchmaker in nature is the blind forces of physics, albeit deployed in a very special way. A true watchmaker has foresight: he designs his cogs and springs, and plans their interconnections, with a future purpose in his mind's eye. Natural selection, the blind, unconscious, automatic process which Darwin discovered, and which we now know is the explanation for the existence and apparently purposeful form of all life, has no purpose in mind. It has no mind and no mind's eye. It does not plan for the future. It has no vision, no foresight, no sight at all. If it can be said to play the role of watchmaker in nature, it is the *blind* watchmaker.

Biological evolution may have no goal or ultimate purpose and in this sense it *is* blind. But this does not mean that cumulative variation and selection cannot be used by organisms in purposeful ways. It could even be argued (as some do) that natural selection was (and still is) God's way of creating and modifying life on our planet. A truly omniscient God would be able to foresee the organisms that would evolve from such a process even if we (and Richard Dawkins) cannot, making the emergence of our species part of the God's overall plan. Still, the great strength of Darwin's theory (and what makes it a scientific theory) is that it provides an explanation for life in all its diverse forms without requiring the involvement of any such supernatural designer or the occurrence of miracles.

But it doesn't require a god to use the Darwinian process in a purposeful way. In fact, even one of the simplest forms of life is able to do so. *Escherichia coli* is a bacterium that lives in a liquid environment (such as the contents of your stomach) and can either swim in a more or less straight line or tumble randomly in one spot. If it senses that it is getting closer to food it will continue on its straight course. But if it finds that it is not getting closer to food, it will stop, tumble a while, and head off in a new, randomly generated direction. If the new heading brings the bacterium closer to food it will continue on this course; but it will stop and tumble again if the direction turns out to be no better than the previous one. Although this method of locomotion may initially appear quite crude, it turns out to be a remarkably adept and virtually foolproof way for the bacterium to get where it needs to go (see Koshland 1980, pp. 14–15). The reader can see just how effective it can be by trying out the *E. coli* program for either IBM-compatible or Macintosh personal computers available on the Web at *www.uiuc.edu/ph/www/g-cziko/twd/*.

E. coli's method of locomotion is of particular interest as an example of one form of purposeful evolution. What evolves in this sense is not a new organism but rather a sequence of swimming directions that is effective in leading the bacterium to food. When the heading is not taking it closer to a food source, it has no clue which way to turn since it has no sense of vision or other means of determining the location of food at a distance. So it simply varies its orientation randomly and tries a new heading. Although it has no guarantee that the new direction will be any better than the previous one, if it isn't better the bacterium can try yet another one and another, until eventually it is able to home in on a meal. So by randomly varying its direction, quickly eliminating those that do not take it closer to food and selecting those that do, *E. coli* is able to use a simple yet effective process to accomplish its goal. This is a form of purposeful behavior that combines Bernardian (control) and Darwinian (cumulative variation and selection) processes.

Not to be outdone by the lowly bacteria tumbling in our tummies, humans have also made use of various forms of purposeful evolution. One of the first was breeding plants and animals. Ever since the development of agriculture, humans have been selecting plants and animals with desirable characteristics for propagating more plants and animals. Since breeders usually have no idea what genes are responsible for the characteristics they desire in crops and livestock, all they can do is select and breed those plants or animals that are in some way better than others. Natural selection may have no purpose, but artificial selection of plants and animals involves a purposeful selector.

The last decade of the twentieth century has seen the development of some very promising high-tech forms of purposeful evolution. Computer scientists have developed a technique called *genetic programming* in which pairs of randomly generated computer programs "mate" with each other, and their resulting "offspring" (programs that resemble but are not identical to their parents) are either selected for another round of mating or eliminated according to how close they come to fulfilling the criteria of the human programmer (see Koza 1992, 1994).

In chemistry, techniques referred to as *directed molecular evolution* (Joyce 1992) and *combinatorial chemistry* (Hall 1997; Plunkett & Ellman 1997) have been developed in which a multitude of different molecules are generated and screened for desired properties, such as their ability to bind to other molecules or be biologically active in medicinally useful ways. Thus new drugs can be created using a form of purposeful variation and selection without having to know the structure of the compound or why it behaves the way it does (see Cziko 1995, chapters 13 & 14, for additional information on these and other forms of purposeful evolution).

In each of these cases, a type of directed or purposeful evolution is used to achieve a goal that cannot be achieved with already acquired knowledge. This requires a search using blind variation and selection, as you would have to do if you wanted to open a lock and possessed a large set of keys but didn't know which one fit the lock. Opening the lock is your goal, but since you don't know which key will work, you have no choice but to proceed by the trial-and-error-elimination method of the evolutionary process. Even if you are able to eliminate certain keys that are obviously too large, too small, or of the wrong shape, you will still have to employ blind variation and selection among the remaining keys. Although I refer to this process as a form of guided or purposeful evolution, it is important to recognize that the variations (trials) generated are not guided (although they may be usefully constrained). Rather, the process is purposeful insofar as a reference level serves as a selection criterion for which certain variations (trials) are retained and others are eliminated.

As we understand the normal process of biological evolution, there is no reference level, no selection by a purposeful agent. Rather, organisms that are more successful in surviving and reproducing come to dominate their populations while those that are less successful are eventually eliminated. Darwin referred to this as *natural* selection to contrast it with the *artificial* selection made by agriculturists in selecting plants and animals for breeding. But whereas artificial selection is purposeful (believe it or not, someone really did want to produce those grotesque goldfish you can see at any pet shop, with the swollen bodies and puffy sacks for eyes, and went through a lot of trouble to do so), natural selection is not, although it resulted in the evolution of purposeful behavior, such as artificial selection performed by humans. Still, artificial (purposeful) and natural (nonpurposeful) selection are similar in that the same processes of cumulative blind variation and selection (either by a purposeful agent or by inanimate physical processes) combine to generate entities that are adapted to some selection criteria (faster wild antelopes as lions and other predators eliminate slower ones; more productive domestic dairy cows as farmers purposefully breed animals that produce the most milk).

Problems of Learning

This concept of purposeful evolution based on the combination of Bernardian and Darwinian processes provides a key for understanding how it is that organisms change their behavior over time in adaptive ways, what is usually referred to as learning.

What does a theory of adaptive behavioral change have to explain? First, it must explain how an organism can come to perform an adaptive behavior that it could not do previously. This could be as simple as a rat learning to push a lever to obtain food in a Skinner box, or as complicated as a college student learning to solve differential equations. It may involve long hours of practice and gradually improving performance, such as learning to play a musical instrument or speak a foreign language. Or it may appear quite suddenly with no previous observable behavior or practice, as as when someone suddenly comes up with a new idea for an invention. We will refer to this as the new knowledge problem.

Second, we must account for how it is that new behaviors can remain adaptive under changing environmental conditions. We saw in chapter 6 that these changing conditions and the new disturbances they impose mean that learning cannot be the acquisition of invariant motor responses to stimuli. Instead, an organism's actions must continually vary to bring about desired results. No matter how many times you may have driven your car from home to your place of work, you cannot make the trip using the same pattern of arm and leg movements that you used on any previous trip. Continually changing traffic, weather, and road conditions would make any such fixed pattern of actions ineffective in getting to work (not to mention dangerous if not fatal). This behavioral flexibility in the achievement of goals is not limited to humans but is characteristic of all animate behavior (recall from chapter 7 the varied behaviors undertaken by the burying beetle to bury small animal corpses on which to lay its eggs). We will refer to this as the behavioral flexibility problem.

There are two general approaches to dealing with the new knowledge problem as it relates to learning. The first is to appeal to innate knowledge as the source of what appears to be new knowledge. For example, during the first four years of life a human child makes amazing progress in acquiring the language of its caretakers. This involves learning the sounds of the language (phonology), its grammatical structure (syntax), and the meanings of words and phrases (semantics). The most widely accepted account of this remarkable feat (although one that is contested by many, including yours truly) is that this knowledge is essentially innate, or "hardwired" into the child's brain. This innatist approach to the problem as it applies to humans essentially denies that new knowledge is actually acquired or created by an individual, so what looks like the acquisition of new knowledge is actually the growth or maturation of old knowledge. This is essentially the position taken by the influential linguist Noam Chomsky, to whom we return in chapter 11, where we examine more closely his decidedly un-Darwinian view of innate knowledge.

The other approach is to recognize that the acquisition of genuinely new knowledge is possible and that real learning does take place. Some attempts to solve the new knowledge problem, as noted in chapter 9, made explicit use of variation and selection, but to date they appear at best incomplete and at worst misguided and misleading. Among them is Skinner's theory of operant conditioning.

As discussed in chapters 3 and 7, that theory had at least three major flaws. First, it considered animate behavior as caused by the environment instead of the means by which aspects of the environment are controlled by the behaving organism. Second, all learning involved overt responses that were varied and then selected (or not) depending on whether or not the responses were followed by a reinforcing event (such as the presentation of food). The theory thus had no room for learning based on mental or internal processes that were not accompanied by overt behavior. Third, Skinner denied that internal purposes had a real role in behavior. He therefore could not account for how organisms were able to vary their behavior to achieve repeatable effects on their environment. He did recognize the power of variation and selection to account for new knowledge as reflected in new adaptive forms of behavior. But his inability to see behavior as purposeful, and his obsession with overt behavior to the exclusion of cognitive processes, made his attempt to incorporate within-organism Darwinism into a theory of learning a rather resounding (if nonetheless quite influential) failure.

Among incomplete Darwinian approaches to learning are theories of cognitive and neural variation and selection we have seen in the previous chapter. These attempts to apply Darwinian thinking to the new knowledge problem recognize that truly new, adaptive forms of knowledge (cognitive, perceptual, and behavioral) must rely on some process of cumulative variation and selection. Cognitive theories describe the variation and selection of ideas or thought patterns, and neural theories attempt to account for adaptive changes in the structure of the brain that are believed to underlie all forms of learning. But these theories are incomplete not only because of current limitations to our knowledge of the structure and functioning of the brain, but also because they fail to account for the purposeful nature of these Darwinian-based changes. Since all such adaptive changes allow the organism to control some aspect of its environment that it could not control before (or at least not as efficiently or precisely), such changes have to be understood as purposeful rather than as effects directly caused by environmental factors. In other words, these theories respect the extended Darwinian lesson, but they do not take into account the extended Bernardian lesson.

Moving on, it turns out that none of the major learning theories or their variations successfully deals with the behavioral flexibility problem. This is because they all embrace simple one-way causality from stimulus to response or (as more fashionable these days) from stimulus to cognitive computation to response. But any theory that posits behavior as an end product (output or response) that is elicited by an input (stimulus or perception) with or without intervening cognitive processes is inherently incapable of accounting for the continuous variations in behavior that we observe in the service of achieving goals in the face of continually changing disturbances. Thus a theory that attempts to explain learning as acquisition of a repertoire of responses must fail.

But by combining the insights of Bernard and Darwin we can arrive at an account of learning that solves both the behavioral flexibility and new knowledge problems.

With respect to the behavioral flexibility problem, chapter 6 showed how perceptual control theory gives us a working model for how organisms are able constantly to vary their behavior to achieve goals despite disturbances. An experienced driver can keep his car on the road and in the proper lane while maintaining a relatively constant speed, in spite of varying wind, road cambers, curves, and hills. He must constantly vary his behavior with respect to the steering wheel and accelerator pedal (and perhaps brake pedal) to achieve these effects, and he is able to do this because he has developed, through experience, the necessary perceptual control systems.

Now imagine that a teenager, having learned to drive during the summer, encounters winter driving conditions for the first time. These conditions present new disturbances for which his skills are inadequate. The first time on snow, he will likely accelerate, brake, and make turns too abruptly, resulting in skidding and (one hopes temporary) loss of control of the car. To maintain control of his vehicle in these new conditions, he must adapt his existing control systems, that is, reorganize them in ways so that he will be able to drive safely on winter roads.

Our driver can reorganize his currently existing network of driving-related control systems in a number of ways. The first involves resetting one or more reference levels. For example, under dry conditions negotiating a street corner at 15 mph may be quite safe. But this speed could be dangerous or even impossible to maintain safely while turning on a snow- or ice-covered street. Assuming that the driver's higher-level goal is to negotiate the turn successfully, he will have to reset his lower-level reference level to a lower speed. But since he doesn't actually know what speed is possible to maintain while turning on snow, this resetting will necessarily involve some degree of trial and error (variation and selection).

Another way that control systems can be modified is by reorganizing perceptual functions. This can occur in one of at least two ways. Trying out various combinations of lower-order perceptions can create new higher-level ones. For example, our driver will have to learn to recognize conditions that require reduced speed while turning. During warm weather he may have paid attention only to whether large objects (such as a person or another vehicle) lay before him in the road; now he must become perceptive to indications of the presence of snow or ice on the road surface. The second way to change one's perceptual function is to make it more or less sensitive to certain aspects of the environment. This is technically known as the *gain* of the perceptual function. The driver may have to learn to develop greater sensitivity to the beginning of the car's skid to take prompt corrective actions.

The third major way in which the reorganization of control systems can take place involves modification of their output functions. First it must to be recalled that outputs of an internal control system are not motor commands resulting in a specific action or muscle twitch. Instead, they serve as reference levels for lower-order control systems, and the particular action that results will depend on both this specified reference level and current environmental conditions. Like perceptual input functions, output functions vary with respect to their gain, so that a given error signal (that is, the discrepancy between a reference level and perceptual signal; see chapter 6) may result in output signals of different strengths. In our driving example, we might expect that certain output gains would have to be reduced to avoid too-quick steering, accelerating, or braking behaviors that could cause the car to skid on snow or ice.

Output functions may also change with respect to the particular lower-level reference signals they influence. Consider someone who has always driven a car with an automatic transmission but who now wants to drive one with a manual stick shift. Previously, accelerating from standing to highway cruising speed simply required depressing the accelerator with the right foot and waiting for the desired speed to be attained. Now it requires accomplishing additional lower-level goals involving the left foot and right hand as they operate the clutch and change gears until cruising speed is reached.

This account of learning as the reorganization of perceptual control systems leads to an interesting concept of learning. All traditional learning theories see learning as a modification of one-way cause-effect (stimulus-response or stimulus-computation-response) associations. Recall from chapter 3 that Pavlov understood learning as the association of new stimuli with old responses, as when his dog learned to salivate to the sound of a bell after the bell had preceded several times the introduction of food into the animal's mouth. Skinner (and Thorndike before him) was interested in how new responses to old stimuli were acquired, as when a rat learns to press a lever to obtain food. In marked contrast to both Pavlov and Skinner's stimulus-response theories of learning (and contrasting as well to stimulus-computation-response learning theories of current cognitive science), perceptual control theory sees learning as involving modification of *perceptual* associations, not stimulus-response associations.

To explore this idea, consider a chef who wants to develop a new shrimp entrée to serve at his restaurant. He has a definite goal in mind of what he is trying to achieve in terms of taste, appearance, and consistency (these are the higher-level perceptual goals), but he doesn't yet know what combination of lower-level goals (that is, perceptions) will lead to his higher-level goals. How many shallots should he mince (should the amount fill four or six tablespoons?)? How long to sauté (how much time should be seen to elapse on the timer?) and at what temperature (how high should the flame be under the pan?)? How well should the shrimp be cooked before adding the wine (offering little resistance to a probing fork or a bit more?)? His cooking experience may well suggest answers to many of these questions. But if he is developing a new dish, the chef is going to have to spend some time experimenting to find the right combination of lower-level perceptions that leads to the desired higher-level perception of a new culinary masterpiece. From this perspective, learning involves discovering new relationships among perceptions (and, of course, being able control them against disturbances), *not* the association of new stimuli with old responses (as in Pavlovian classical or respondent conditioning) or the association of new responses to old stimuli (as in Skinner's operant conditioning).

This culinary experimentation is, of course, an instance of Darwinian variation and selection. Since the chef does not yet know what combination of lower-level perceptions will lead to his desired dish, he will have to use some cumulative trial and error elimination to find out. Four tablespoons of shallots made the dish too bland when first tried, and six made it too spicy on the second attempt. So try five tablespoons and see what happens. Or perhaps stay with six and add a bit more wine. This process of within-organism variation and selection provides an answer to how new knowledge is possible. It does not involve variation and selection of specific overt responses as Skinner believed, but rather the variation and selection of controlled lower-level perceptions, eliminating those that do not lead to the desired higher-level goal and retaining those that do.

In further contrast to Skinner's theory, variation and selection of lower-level perceptions in the service of higher-level ones need not involve overt behavior, at least not with humans and some other primates. Instead, we can use our mental models of how our physical and social worlds work to try out combinations of lower-level reference perceptions and imagine their effects on higher-level ones. So if I am having a dinner party and inviting ten guests—some of whom get along well together while some others don't—I can imagine different seating plans (variations) before the guests arrive and eliminate potentially troublesome arrangements (those that put suspected antagonists within striking distance of each other) until I come up with a plan that seems best (selection). This process is an instance of Donald Campbell's vicarious variation and selection described in chapter 9.

A good deal of what we call thinking—at least thinking that involves problem solving, invention, and creativity—may actually be vicarious variation and selection of perceptual control systems. Such a concept lets us understand how cognitive processes involved in thinking can be purposeful even when they are not accompanied by concurrent purposeful behavior. And if thinking alone cannot generate solutions, we can assist it with other forms of substitute variation and selection: writing down our ideas on paper, using computers to run simulations of candidate solutions, or discussing the problem (proposing solutions, eliminating bad ones, and keeping the best) with other individuals.

A New Conception of Learning

By combining the extended Bernardian lesson (that organisms vary their behavior to control their perceptions) and the extended Darwinian lesson (that organisms make use of variation and selection to gain control of aspects of their environment) we arrive at a new conception of learning. Learning is no longer the association of new stimuli to old responses, or acquisition of new responses to old stimuli, but rather acquisition of new means of perceptual control by reorganizing existing perceptual control systems by within-organism variation and selection. In much the same way that *E. coli* randomly changes its direction when it senses that it is not moving closer to food, all learning requires an organism to make some change to its current organization of perceptual control systems when there is some chronic error between perception and reference level. And whereas previous learning experiences may usefully constrain the variations that are tried (an automobile mechanic is not likely to change the air pressure in a car's tires to see if doing so will make it start), acquisition of new knowledge requires at least some blind variation to explore and discover new useful relationships between combinations of perceptual variables.

The knowledge gained by such a process is discovering what combinations of lower-level perceptions are successful in bringing about desired higher-level perceptions controlling these lower-level perceptions against disturbances. A chef does not measure a cup a water by holding a container under an open faucet for a fixed amount of time, as this would lead to varying amounts of water due to the fluctuating pressure of the water supply line. Instead, he keeps the container under the faucet until the water level reaches the one-cup mark, no matter how long it may take. By successfully controlling this and other lower-level perceptual variables, he is able to prepare the entrée he has in mind, that is, match his higher-level reference perception. By extending this form of purposeful evolution to the mental realm when no overt behavior is involved, we obtain a new framework for understanding cognitive processes. Cognition is no longer seen as planning responses to certain stimuli, but rather as Darwinian reorganization of Bernardian perceptual control systems to control new aspects of the environment.

This view can be used to develop a general framework of knowledge and its acquisition. Within such a framework are three principal types of knowledge. First is the biologically based knowledge that we and all other organisms are essentially born with. This may be all the knowledge that a single-cell organism will ever have and it is reflected both in its structure and instinctive behavior. The way we see colors (or how we see at all) is a form of this knowledge and it cannot be changed, although certain experiences are necessary for it to develop, such as growing up and interacting in a world with visible light. This knowledge is derived from the cumulative among-organism selection of the fittest, as originally proposed by Darwin.

Second is the knowledge that some organisms acquire during their lifetimes. It results from the interaction of one's biological endowment with one's particular experiences, and it is limited in important ways by one's biologically provided knowledge. Humans can learn only certain types of languages. We cannot learn to make visual distinctions between two ultraviolet patterns the way bees can. Rats fail to learn certain tasks requiring visual discrimination, but can learn similar tasks involving their keen sense of smell. Such knowledge is similar to biologically based knowledge in that it also depends on variation and selection. But it is different in two key respects: it involves the within-organism variation and selection of modifications to perceptual control systems, and it is driven by the organism's internal goals. So unlike biological evolution, the knowledge that an organism acquires during its lifetime results from a purposeful form of continuing variation and selection.

Finally, some organisms, especially, humans, seem to acquire knowledge from others. But this is actually a special case of the second form since it is acquired as the result of one's individual experiences interacting with biological knowledge. We may be able to make use of the trial-and-error experience of others by observing their (successful and unsuccessful) behavior, or talking with them or reading their books. But we cannot simply absorb this knowledge in the way that a blank computer diskette can receive the information stored on another. Instead, it could be reasonably argued that the knowledge we derive from others' experiences also requires some degree of within-organism variation and selection (see Cziko 1995, chapter 10). I may observe how an expert skier moves his skis and holds his body as he descends the slope. He may even give me instructions and sell me his book and video on skiing. But although this information may facilitate my development as a skier, it cannot replace the need for me to reorganize my perceptual control systems, eliminate those modifications that leave me sitting in the snow, and retain those that keep my posterior above my skis.

The view of learning provided by combining the extended Bernardian and extended Darwinian lessons has important implications for all forms of education and training, a topic to which we will return in the final chapter.

11

Behavioral Science and the Cause-Effect Trap

The cognitive and biological sciences have discovered a lot about vision and motor control, but these discoveries are limited to mechanisms. No one even thinks of asking why a person looks at a sunset or reaches for a banana, and how such decisions are made. The same is true of language. A modern generative grammar seeks to determine the mechanisms that underlie the fact that the sentence I am now producing has the form and meaning it does, but has nothing to say about how I chose to form it, or why.

—Noam Chomsky (1996, pp. 9–10)

The scientific investigation of animate behavior began just about 120 years ago, using the founding of Wilhelm Wundt's psychological laboratory in 1879 as its date of birth. That is a short period of time compared with the other well-established sciences such as chemistry, physics, and even biology. Yet the science of animate behavior is arguably more complex than these older sciences. So it should not be too surprising that behavioral science has not had significant breakthroughs comparable with those of other sciences, such as the periodic table in chemistry, quantum theory in physics, or cracking the genetic code in biology.

But just such a breakthrough may now be within view as a small but growing group of behavioral scientists have started to explore the behavioral implications of Darwin, and a still smaller but also growing group has begun to take into consideration the implications of Bernard for understanding behavior. Indeed, for the first time we now have within our grasp a fundamental materialist understanding of the what, how, and why of animate behavior.

To a reader not well acquainted with the academic and professional literature in psychology and cognitive science, the synthesis provided here might well appear reasonable and uncontroversial. Of course a living organism controls aspects of its physical surroundings. If it did not, it would not be able to survive and reproduce in an uncaring and often hostile world. Clearly, its behavior is purposeful, whether or not the organism itself is consciously aware of its purposes. Its evolutionary past provides important clues as to what aspects of its environment it controls, and why and how it does so. And even the use of purposeful within-organism variation and selection by living organisms to solve problems for which biological evolution could not have prepared them in advance might seem a reasonable hypothesis, especially when growing evidence such as that reported in chapter 9 is considered. But, as noted throughout the previous chapters, this Bernardian and Darwinian view of behavior is not widely accepted among behavioral scientists for whom the one-way cause-effect perspective continues to dominate theory and research.

We will see in this chapter just how pervasive and dominant this simple cause-effect perspective remains. This will be accomplished by surveying several of this century's most cited and influential behavioral scientists and theorists and showing how their theories of behavior are in one way or another fundamentally incompatible with insights that originated with Bernard and Darwin. We will see that each of these individuals has either ignored or rejected one of the three lessons that biology has for behavioral science that were described at the beginning of the previous chapter, namely, the basic Darwinian, extended Darwinian, and extended Bernardian lessons.

Rejecting the Three Lessons: From Piaget to Pinker

Piaget's Disdain of Darwin

With the possible exception of Sigmund Freud, no twentieth-century European psychologist is better known and has had more impact on psychology than Jean Piaget (1896–1980). Prolific in research and writing from the age of ten until shortly before his death (with more than thirty books published as author or co-author), Piaget began his career as a biologist specializing in mollusks, like the snails inhabiting the lakes of his native Switzerland. But a job in Paris administering intelligence tests to children sparked a life-long interest in the development of human mental abilities and knowledge. He called this study "genetic epistemology," with *genetic* referring not to the genome but rather to a concept of the development of thought as internally guided cognitive growth.

Piaget employed a mélange of in-depth questioning and ingenious experiments to probe the perceptual and thought processes of young children, discovering that they are different not only in degree from that of adults, but in kind. He also concluded that each child goes through an invariant series of cognitive stages, each stage requiring a major overhaul of the preceding one. For example, from the perspective of a young infant an object exists only if it can be presently seen, felt, heard, or smelled. At this age, removing a desired object from the child's senses usually results in the infant abandoning all efforts to find and obtain it. But the child soon develops "object permanence," so that she is now able to seek and find objects that were hidden while she was watching. From a Piagetian perspective, the child is like a little scientist who is constantly developing and testing new theories about the world, rejecting old theories when a new one is discovered that is better at making sense of the world and meeting her needs.

It might be expected that Piaget's early training as a biologist, combined with his interest in the development of human cognitive abilities, would lead him to embrace the basic and extended Darwinian lessons of biology for psychology. Au contraire, his disdain of Darwinian ideas was such that he rejected natural selection as accounting for biological evolution. In the year that he received his *doctorat* in natural sciences he wrote (1918/1976, p. 40):

But natural selection cannot explain evolution. . . . The heredity of acquired traits is an experimental fact. . . . Hachet Souplet, by training cats, formed habits that were transmitted to later generations. . . . We can then decide in favor of Lamarckism without any qualms, without excluding natural selection as a secondary or accidental factor.

Fifty-eight years later, when Lamarckian evolution had been thoroughly discounted and evolution by Darwinian natural selection had become the central pillar of biology, Piaget remained unimpressed (1976; quoted in Vidal, Buscaglia, & Vonèche 1983, p. 87):

Either chance and selection can explain everything or else behavior is the motor of evolution. The choice is between an alarming waste in the shape of multitudinous and fruitless trials preceding any success no matter how modest, and a dynamics with an internal logic deriving from those general characteristics of organization and self-regulation peculiar to all living beings.

And yet while he rejected Darwin's theory of evolution, he did, if unwittingly, make use of Darwinian ideas. For example, in discussing instinctive behavior, the following passage is one that could have been written today by an ethologist, sociobiologist, evolutionary psychologist, or behavioral ecologist (1967/1976, p. 844):

Instinct is always at the service of the three fundamental needs of food, protection against enemies, and reproduction. If, with migration or various modes of social organization, instinct seems to pursue secondary ends, they are only secondary as being interests grafted onto the three main ones and still dependent upon them, so that in the last resort they are subordinated to the survival of the species and, as far as possible of the individual.

The major themes of Piaget's theory of cognitive development can also be understood from a Darwinian perspective. He stated that the two major ways in which children (as well as adults) interact with their world are through assimilation and accommodation. Assimilation refers to incorporation of sensory experience into a preexisting thought structure called a schema. For example, a child having seen sparrows and robins and able to recognize them as members of the category *bird* would likely include the first blackbird she sees in this same category. She might also attempt to assimilate the first observed butterfly into her bird schema since it shares certain similarities with other members of this category. However, calling a butterfly a bird would likely result in a correction by an adult or older child, "That's not a bird, it's a butterfly!" This would lead to accommodation of the child's thought so that butterflies and birds would be treated as different concepts, each with its own label and distinguishing characteristics. Assimilation thus is a process that involves the adjustment of perceptions to fit already developed knowledge, whereas accommodation involves modification of previously existing knowledge to fit new perceptions better.

But a parent cannot simply transmit the meanings of new words to a child. Instead, the child can only know that some sort of error has been made and that, according to her parent, the current object in view is not a bird but a butterfly. The parent's remark does not tell the child *why* it is a butterfly and not a bird. Is it because it is yellow and the other flying creatures she has seen are brown and black (but then what of canaries?)? Is it because it stops to sip nectar from flowers, while the other flying animals do not (but then what of hummingbirds?)? Or is it because the child has only seen birds in the afternoon, and it is now morning (but then what of the bird that gets the worm?)? Clearly, the child must make some sort of guess as to how to modify her bird schema and create a new butterfly one. This guess may well be initially wrong, but by continuing to generate and test additional hypotheses, she will eventually come to the notions of bird and butterfly that are shared by the adults of her speech community. Such necessary cumulative variation and selection (or trial and error elimination) is, of course, a form of within-organism selection, even if Piaget did not recognize it as such.

But why should a child even bother to change her way of thinking or using language to bring it closer in line with how others around her think and speak? Why should it bother her if what she calls a bird others call a butterfly? Why should she care if, when a ball of clay is rolled and stretched into a skinny sausage, she sees the sausage as containing more clay than it did as a ball because it is longer? Surely, she must have certain basic developmental goals selected by evolution because of their usefulness for living in a physical environment that includes other humans. One of these is to use words the same way others use them so that she can both understand and be understood. Another is to have a consistent, noncontradictory understanding of the environment.

Piaget referred to this process of keeping mental schemas and perceptions consistent with each other as equilibration. Equilibration is a form of cognitive regulation or control in which the competing processes of assimilation and accommodation are used to achieve the goal of cognitive *coherence*. As he explained (1958/1976, p. 833):

> . . . it must be stressed that the equilibration process which thus constitutes an intrinsic characteristic corresponds, in living beings, to specific needs, tendencies, or functions and not merely to an automatic balance independent of the activities of the subject. Thus, in the case of higher cognitive functions, there exists a tendency to equilibrium which manifests the need for coherence.

We see therefore that for Piaget, human cognitive development is driven by a basic human need for cognitive coherence, not by external environmental factors in the form of stimuli or rewards. He also recognized the circular nature of the causality required by his theory (1975/1976, pp. 840–841):

In biological or cognitive equilibrium . . . we have a system in which all parts are interdependent. It is a system which could be represented in the form of a cycle. *A* has its influence on *B*, which has its influence on *C*, which has its influence on *D*, which again influences *A*. It is a cycle of iterations among the different elements. It also has a special feature of being open to influences from the outside.

But Piaget did not seem to have an accurate extended Bernardian understanding of animate behavior, stating that "It is true, of course, that stimuli give rise to responses" (1970/1972, p. 5), explaining that (1970/1972, pp. 5–6):

The stimulus unleashes the response, and the possibility of response is necessary for the sensitivity to the stimulus. The relationship can also be described as circular which again poses the problem of equilibrium, an equilibrium between external information serving as the stimulus and the subject's schemes or internal structure of his activities.

Although Piaget used the word circular to describe the relationship between stimulus and response, he nonetheless appeared to be saying that stimuli lead to responses as mediated by the individual's internal cognitive structure. He did not recognize that it is not a stimulus that leads to response but rather the difference between the perceived stimulus (perception) and intended stimulus (reference level). Elsewhere, he referred to the process of self-regulation as providing "internal reinforcements" for behavior (quoted in Evans 1973, p. 67), further evidence for his misunderstanding of the nature of self-regulating feedback-control systems that do not "reward" specific actions but rather vary actions to control their perceptual inputs.

Despite Piaget's disdain of selectionist mechanisms and incomplete understanding of feedback-control systems, he does appear to have recognized to some degree the importance and power of combining Bernard with Darwin to derive a mechanism capable of a form of directed or purposeful evolution in changing old knowledge to fit new perceptions (that is, accommodation). This is indicated by his statement ". . . accommodation is carried out by gropings, and these are a prime example of feedbacks in which an action is corrected in terms of its results" (1967/1977, p. 847).

It is not surprising that a biologist turned developmental psychologist would find biological ideas of use in his psychological research and theorizing, and Piaget did just that. What is surprising is that while he drew on the lessons of Bernard and Darwin, he did so without recognizing their full importance.

His view of cognitive growth appears to recognize the goal-directed nature of development that can only be accounted for by a form of circular causality. But although his theory of cognitive development can certainly be seen from extended Bernardian and extended Darwinian perspectives, he never provided explicit working models as to how such development is goal-directed. Neither did he discuss the concept of an internally specified reference level and how it operates to maintain what he called cognitive equilibrium. He often pointed out how young children behave in a groping manner when learning skills and modifying their mental schemas to control aspects of their environment, but he provided no evidence of having understood animate behavior as the control of perception, or of having recognized the necessity of within-organism Darwinian selection for cognitive development.

Piaget was able to take some important preliminary steps leading out of the cause-effect trap, but he did not come close to escaping it completely.

Skinner's Skewed Selectionism

B. F. Skinner, introduced in chapter 3 and discussed further in chapter 7, remains one of the best-known psychologists of the twentieth century, and he certainly ranks as the most influential American psychologist of all time. His theory of radical behaviorism is no longer in vogue among psychologists and cognitive scientists, but his theory of behavior and how it is modified continues to be highly influential, especially among applied psychologists who attempt to change or otherwise control the behavior of other animals or people.

Skinner, unlike Piaget, had no qualms about accepting evolution by natural selection as the process responsible for life in all its varied forms. Nonetheless, he did not look to evolutionary theory for clues concerning animal and human behavior, and in this respect he rejected the basic Darwinian lesson. For him, evolution provided animals and humans with a general learning mechanism, namely, operant conditioning, by which behaviors were selected (or eliminated) as a result of their consequences for the organism. Thus an animal could be taught to do just about anything that was physically possible if reinforcement for the desired behavior was appropriately applied. That Skinner was not particularly concerned about behavioral differences among species, or even those between humans and animals, is indicated by the fact that he "conducted most of his research on animals and wrote most of his books about people" (Kohn 1993, p. 6). But we recognized in chapter 7, in discussing the phenomenon of instinctive drift, that different species clearly behave differently, and that an organism's evolutionary past plays an important role in influencing behavior and determining how and the extent to which the organism's behavior can be modified.

Although Skinner ignored the basic Darwinian lesson with respect to species-specific behavior, he was nonetheless keenly interested in extending the lesson to account for his theory of operant conditioning that involved spontaneous generation of behavior and its selection (or elimination) as determined by its consequences. But his exclusive concern with observable behavior led him astray. Since he denied the importance of internal mental events in accounting for behavior, he could not apply the extended Darwinian lesson to the variation and selection of mental processes or thought trials (Campbell's vicarious or substitute selection processes described in chapter 9).

As for the extended Bernardian lesson—animate behavior is the purposeful control of perception—Skinner rejected it outright. Chapter 3 described how he denied the central role of purpose in animate behavior, believing instead that "motives and purposes are at best the effects of reinforcements" (1974, p. 56). In other words, in keeping with the one-way cause-effect perspective, purposes were somehow caused by the environment rather than being generated from within the organism as a reference level or a standard for a perception. In keeping with his view that behavior is caused by environmental factors, he went so far as to even deny that he himself had feelings of personal involvement and purpose in his own work. He commented that after finishing his book *Beyond Freedom and Dignity*, "I had the very strange feeling that I hadn't even written the book. . . . [It] just naturally came out of my behavior not because of anything called a 'me' or an 'I' inside" (quoted in Kohn, 1993, p. 7).

Further evidence that he did not appreciate the importance of the extended Bernardian lesson is indicated by his serious misunderstanding of the operation of control systems, as shown in his discussion of the behavior of a "homing device" (1974, p. 56):

> Goals and purposes are confused in speaking of purpose in a homing device. A missile reaches its target when its course is appropriately controlled, in part by information coming from the target during its flight. Such a device is sometimes said to "have purpose built into it," but the feedback used in guidance (the heart of cybernetics) is not reinforcement, and the missile has no purpose in the present sense."

This statement may provide an important insight into Skinner's way of thinking about behavior, control, reinforcement, and purpose. By stating that "a missile reaches its target when its course is appropriately controlled, in part by information coming from the target during its flight," he sees the missile as an object being controlled by external factors, including the "information from the target," which is analogous to perceptual input in living organisms. He shows no recognition that the missile is actually varying its course as necessary to *control* its perception (or sensing) of the target. He then rejects the notion that such a control system "has purpose built into it," using the curiously circular reasoning that the negative feedback used by the system "is not reinforcement," and since purpose is always the result of reinforcement, the missile can have no purpose! Succumbing to the behavioral illusion of believing the missile's behavior is caused by environmental disturbances, he could not appreciate that such a homing device does in fact display purposeful behavior in varying its actions as necessary to reach its goal. This is exactly what it was designed to do, and in this respect the heat- (and therefore target-) seeking missile engages in purposeful behavior just like that of James's air-seeking frog and Shakespeare's Juliet-seeking Romeo.

Skinner's influence on behavioral science remains considerable. He was the principal influence in promoting a version of the behavioral illusion that can be described as the reinforcement illusion—the belief that an organism's behavior is controlled by environmental reinforcement. Although he is gone and his brand of behaviorism is not nearly as popular as it once was, the reinforcement illusion remains as one of the most influential and pernicious ideas from behavioral science, giving testament to the continued legacy of one-way cause-effect thinking as applied to animate behavior (see Kohn 1993).

Chomsky's Baseless Biologizing

Noam Chomsky not only revolutionized the study of language but also had a major impact on the cognitive and behavioral sciences. In his 1959 review of Skinner's book *Verbal Behavior*, he pointed out that just about every sentence a person produces is a novel combination of words that neither the speaker nor anyone else has ever uttered before. Therefore, language behavior cannot, as Skinner proposed, be the result of a fixed repertoire of utterances that were somehow reinforced in the past. Instead, language competence must be the result of a set of mental instructions or rules that permit the speaker to produce (and understand) an infinite number of novel sentences using the finite resources of the human brain. His convincing argument for a cognitive theory of human language helped to make it respectable once again to go beyond observable behavior and consider the types of mental knowledge and processes involved. For this achievement he is considered to be one of the founders of the cognitive revolution in psychology.

Chomsky also maintained that human language competence is essentially innate because every normal child rapidly develops competence in his native language without requiring formal instruction. Given the apparently large gap between what a child hears (the "poverty of the stimulus") and what he eventually comes to know about his language, such knowledge ("universal grammar") must be innate. The child uses experience only to guide him in deciding which variety of language is used in his environment.

Such an innatist view might lead one to expect Chomsky to accept a Darwinian account of the evolution of human language. But instead he has remained quite unimpressed by Darwinian accounts of evolution of any kind, saying (1988, p. 23):

evolutionary theory appears to have very little to say about speciation, or about any kind of innovation. It can explain how you get a different distribution of qualities that are already present, but it does not say much about how new qualities emerge.

This is quite a remarkable statement, since it shows that one of the most influential intellectuals of our time appears blind to the basic Darwinian lesson of how, through the evolutionary process of cumulative variation and selection, innovations of all types are generated, tested, selected, and refined.

But there is probably a good (for Chomsky) reason why he rejects a Darwinian account of human language. Recall the "poverty of the stimulus" view that a child's language knowledge must be innate since there is no way that a child could attain complete knowledge of his language based solely on what he hears spoken. But the very notion of a stimulus implies a one-way cause-effect view of learning in which what the child hears somehow transmits knowledge of the language. This is made quite clear when he states (1997, p. 13):

Evidently each language is a result of the interplay of two factors. One of them is whatever the genetically determined initial state is, and the second is the course of experience. We can rephrase that observation without changing anything by thinking of the initial state of the language faculty as a kind of device which operates on experience and turns it into the language that is attained, which we can think of as being just a state of the language faculty. Looked at that way, which just rephrases the observation, the initial state of the language faculty you can think of as kind of an input/output device, the kind one knows how to study: an input/output device where the input is the course of experience, and the output is the language obtained, that is, the state of the language faculty obtained.

If Chomsky were to recognize that language is an adaptive human ability and that the only reasonable nonmiraculous explanation for its emergence is a Darwinian one, he would have to confront the possibility that a process of learning involving within-organism variation and selection (the extended Darwinian lesson) might make it possible for the child to acquire language in a creative, evolutionary manner without the need for an innate universal grammar. So from this perspective it is not surprising that he rejects both the basic and extended Darwinian lessons. But it does put him in the rather odd position of advocating an innate biological basis for human language while rejecting the only understood process by which it could have evolved.

What about the extended Bernardian lesson? Whereas Chomsky indicated in his review of Skinner (1959, p. 554) that he believes people's wants, likes, and wishes have an influence on behavior, he has provided no theory to explain how these factors operate. In fact, he has always insisted that the study of the structure of human language (syntax) has little to do with the meaning (semantics) and communicative use of language. In all of his prolific writing about language that revolutionized the field of linguistics, he never recognized human language as an important form of purposeful behavior or one of the most powerful tools our species has developed for controlling our environment. He has not only restricted his own linguistic research to investigation of the formal structural properties of language (syntax), but as shown in the opening quotation of this chapter, he believes that explanations for questions concerning the why of human behavior are simply outside the realms of science.

Chomsky should then be surprised to learn that at least some behavioral scientists *are* asking why (and how and what) questions concerning animal and human behavior and answering such questions using Darwinian- and Bernardian-inspired explanations. It cannot be denied that Chomsky has made important contributions to our understanding of the structural aspects of language. But the next revolution in the science of human language will have to await someone of his intellectual powers who recognizes the evolutionary (Darwinian) nature of language's origin and acquisition, the purposeful (Bernardian) nature of its use, and the control-system mechanisms that account for the latter.

Dennett's Dangerous Darwinism

Daniel Dennett, director of the Center for Cognitive Studies at Tufts University near Boston, may well be the most widely read philosopher alive today. His 1991 book *Consciousness Explained* sold over 200,000 copies, an amazing number for a book written by a philosopher about the nature of human consciousness and related puzzling phenomena of the human mind. This was followed in 1995 by *Darwin's Dangerous Idea*, in which the theory of natural selection was explained, defended, and applied to a wide range of phenomena, many of them outside the bounds of biological evolution.

Dennett finds Darwin's theory to be not only dangerous since it demolishes many of our traditional beliefs about the origin and meaning of life, but also fascinating and extremely useful for explaining instances of apparent design. Darwin's idea is a "universal solvent, capable of cutting right to the heart of everything in sight" (1995, p. 521).

Dennett also recognizes that our evolutionary past played an important role in shaping the types of behaviors and mental characteristics that we share as a species, although he is cautious about attributing to evolution what is more likely the result of cultural and other environmental influences. He clearly has learned the basic Darwinian lesson that biology has to offer behavioral and cognitive science.

But Dennett goes further with this dangerous idea than most cognitive scientists, behavioral scientists, and philosophers would care or dare to go by seeing in Darwinian natural selection a model for the actual operation of the human brain. He refers to humans as "Popperian creatures" (1995, p. 375) since we can generate varied thoughts and hypothesis and test them mentally using within-organism selection. He might just as well have used the descriptor "Campbellian creatures" since his view of cognitive problem solving is similar to that of Donald T. Campbell, who (as discussed in chapter 9) considered human creative thought and problem solving to involve variation and selective retention. (It is curious that Dennett makes no reference to Campbell's important works that describe human thought as a Darwinian process.) So Dennett is clearly mindful of the extended Darwinian lesson and remains perhaps the best-known living philosopher to appreciate the importance and power of within-organism cognitive selection.

Dennett appears to have learned at least a part of the extended Bernardian lesson, too. He realizes that there is something special about systems that act as "agents" having goals they pursue and achieve by their actions. He refers to these as "intentional systems" and defines them thus (1996, p. 34):

Intentional systems are, by definition, all and only those entities whose behavior is predictable/explicable from the intentional stance. Self-replicating macromolecules, thermostats, amoebas, plants, rats, bats, people, and chess-playing computers are all intentional systems—some much more interesting than others.

But this smacks of circularity since it defines an intentional system as one whose behavior appears to be intentional! Better would be to define an intentional system as one whose actions serve to control some aspect of its environment, varying its behavior as necessary in the face of disturbances. But it does not appear that Dennett fully appreciates that an intentional system (what we have been calling a control system) uses circular causality to control its inputs by varying its behavior, and that consequently the purposeful (intentional) behavior of living organisms can be understood as the control of perception.

So although he appears to have some appreciation of the extended Bernardian lesson, Dennett makes no mention of its most important modern applications, such as those provided by William Powers (see chapter 6). Neither in *Darwin's Dangerous Idea* nor in *Kinds of Mind* (1996) does he make explicit mention of Bernard, cybernetics, feedback control, control theory, or perceptual control theory to account for the purposeful behavior of his intentional agents.

Nonetheless, among all the individuals reviewed in this chapter, Dennett comes closest to fully recognizing the lessons of biology for behavioral and cognitive science. The basic and extended Darwinian lessons he has both learned well and taught to many others through his lectures and his writings. And he at least partly appreciates the extended Bernardian lesson. When he fully appreciates it, Dennett will see that Bernard's big idea ranks with Darwin's dangerous one in importance for understanding the behavior of living organisms.

Picking on Pinker

Steven Pinker, director of the Center for Cognitive Neuroscience at the Massachusetts Institute of Technology, is one of today's most influential and popular cognitive scientists (for an informative profile of Pinker, see Hayashi 1999). His first book for general readers, *The Language Instinct* (1994), offered a scientific yet entertaining account of the wonders of human language and became a best seller. In its sequel with the bold title *How the Mind Works* (1997), he attempted to describe the workings of the human mind as physical processes occurring within the brain, a brain whose design can be understood only by taking into account its evolutionary past.

It is clear from *How the Mind Works* that Pinker has embraced the basic Darwinian lesson that our fundamental goals, preferences, and mental abilities—including human language—were shaped by natural selection. In this respect he differs from his MIT colleague Chomsky who, we noted, rejects the basic Darwinian lesson as it applies to human language. His paper written with Paul Bloom, "Natural language and natural selection" (1990), is a thorough and convincing argument for a Darwinian view.

In chapters 5 through 8 of *How the Mind Works,* Pinker moves beyond language matters and tackles many issues in evolutionary psychology using his characteristically engaging and entertaining style. That a recent book about the mind by a leading cognitive scientist should devote so many pages to evolution and its role in shaping human cognition and behavior is a hopeful sign that the basic Darwinian lesson will finally be accepted by many mainstream behavioral and cognitive scientists. But what about the other lessons—the extended Darwinian and extended Bernardian lessons—that biology has to offer these fields of study?

Being such a knowledgeable and influential proponent of the basic Darwinian lesson, we might well expect Pinker to embrace or at least give fair consideration to the extended Darwinian lesson. After all, if the process of cumulative variation and selection among organisms can produce such marvelously adapted creatures (such as ourselves) and organs (such as our eyes and brains), we might expect a similar process to be used within organisms to adapt to changing conditions for which biological evolution could not have prepared them.

Surprisingly, Pinker completely ignores the considerable theorizing and research on selectionist processes within the brain as summarized in chapter 9, and this despite numerous references throughout his book to Dennett, who is an important proponent of the extended Darwinian lesson. Instead, Pinker appears quite hostile to the notion that some form of cumulative variation and selection might be employed by human brains in the form of the variation and selection of synapses or ideas, or that cultural evolution (as in the development within societies of traditions, technology, or science) could also involve Darwinian processes.

For example, he dismisses the perspective offered by psychologists Elizabeth Bates and Brian MacWhinney, who "view the selectional processes operating during evolution and the selectional processes operating during [learning] as part of one seamless natural fabric" (quoted in Pinker 1997, p. 206). "The implication," Pinker commented, "is that there is no need for specialized mental machinery" (1997, p. 206). But why does the existence of Darwinian mental processes imply no need for specialized mental machinery? The types of variations produced, the mechanism by which they are produced, and the criteria and mechanisms for selection and retention would most certainly be different (and involve different parts, or modules, of the brain) for different types of learning, such as learning how to ice skate versus learning vocabulary in a foreign language. We know that our immune system uses variation and selection of lymphocyte cells to produce new antibodies, but this does not mean that selectionist brain processes must also employ lymphocytes! Pinker should be relieved to know that the extended Darwinian lesson is not incompatible with the modular view of the mind-brain that he and many other cognitive scientists embrace.

He concludes his chapter 4 with another argument against the extended Darwinian lesson, using the example of the stomach (1997, p. 210):

> The stomach is firmly grounded in biology, but it does not randomly secrete variants of acids and enzymes, retain the ones that break down food a bit, let them sexually recombine and reproduce, and so on for hundreds of thousands of meals. Natural selection already went through such trial and error in designing the stomach, and now the stomach is an efficient chemical processor, releasing the right acids and enzymes on cue.

But despite Pinker's straw-man argument, the extended Darwinian lesson does not tell us that all within-organism processes have to be Darwinian, only those that result in new solutions to new problems that our evolutionary ancestors did not confront (such as writing symphonies, breaking the genetic code, or ice skating). Through among-organism selection, biological evolution may have discovered some very useful processes, such as the production of digestive enzymes or the ability to see colors, that may be completely non-Darwinian in their current operation (see figure 9.3). But this does not mean that there are no within-organism Darwinian processes whatsoever. The obvious counterexample to Pinker's digestion example is once again the human immune system since it functions almost exactly as Pinker says the stomach does not, producing each day millions of new antigens by genetic recombination and mutation, selecting the ones that work best, and using them to generate still more novel antibodies over many generations. This within-organism Darwinian process allows the immune system to come up with adaptive solutions to the new problems posed by viruses and bacteria never encountered before. So whereas some mental processes may well be comparable with digestion in their directness, others are undoubtedly much more similar to antibody production, namely, those that we use to create new solutions to new problems. Pinker rightly exposes as a non sequitur the belief that the products of evolution have to look like evolution. But he counters with a non sequitur of his own that since *some* products of evolution do not look like evolution then *none* of them do.

But perhaps he is actually somewhat less hostile than even he realizes to the extended Darwinian lesson. In his discussion of creative geniuses such as Mozart, Einstein, and van Gogh, he made the following observations (1997, p. 361).

Geniuses are wonks.

[Geniuses] are either discriminating or lucky in their choice of problems. (The unlucky ones, however talented, aren't remembered as geniuses).

They work day and night and leave us with many works of subgenius.

Their interludes away from a problem are helpful . . . because they are exhausted and need the rest (and possibly so they can forget blind alleys).

The epiphany is not a masterstroke but a tweaking of an earlier attempt.

They revise endlessly, gradually closing in on their ideal.

Here Pinker is trying to get across the idea that geniuses are really not that different from more ordinary people like (probably) you and me. In doing so, he must emphasize the errorful, gradual, and groping nature of their achievements, coming quite close to what could be considered a selectionist, extended Darwinian account of creativity, not unlike that considered in chapter 9.

Turning to the extended Bernardian lesson, it is interesting that in chapter 2 of his book, Pinker uses the same passage from William James quoted in chapter 3 of this book, about Romeo wanting to put his lips on those of Juliet and his circumventing all obstacles to do so. He follows this quotation with the statement that "intelligence . . . is the ability to attain goals in the face of obstacles" (1997, p. 62). This certainly appears to be preparing the stage for the extended Bernardian lesson.

But nowhere in his book does he describe a model that can account for the very type of purposeful behavior that he takes as an indispensable indication of intelligence. He makes no mention of feedback control, cybernetics, Wiener, or control systems. No discussion of how a mechanical system (which he adamantly insists the brain is) can be designed to possess a goal and continuously act on the world so that its perceptions match the internally specified reference level that contitutes the goal. No explanation of how an organism's purposeful behavior serves to control perception. Pinker's ignorance, avoidance, or rejection of such concepts pushes him perilously close to embracing a dualist mind-body philosophy (1997, p. 315):

Goals and values are one of the vocabularies in which we mentally couch our experiences. They cannot be built out of simpler concepts from our physical knowledge in the way "momentum" can be built out of mass and velocity or "power" can be built out of energy and time. They are primitive or irreducible, and higher-level concepts are defined in terms of them.

It's enough to make one wonder if Pinker ever used a thermostat or drove a car with cruise control.

One of the major themes in *How the Mind Works* is that the brain is a computing device, orders of magnitude more complex than any electronic computer yet created, but a computing device nonetheless. So how does the brain get involved in behavior? According to Pinker, not by using the means at its disposal (such as muscles attached to bones) to manage its environment by controlling the perceptions provided by its sensory systems, but rather by using inputs to control its outputs, the interpretation of behavior based on one-way causality. This is especially clear in the most detailed example he provides of behavior (1997, pp. 11–12):

Controlling an arm presents a new challenge. Grab the shade of an architect's lamp and move it along a straight diagonal path from near you, low on the left, to far from you, high on the right. Look at the rods and hinges as the lamp moves. Though the shade proceeds along a straight line, each rod swings through a complicated arc, swooping rapidly at times, remaining almost stationary at other times, sometime reversing from a bending to a straightening motion. Now imagine having to do it in reverse: without looking at the shade, you must choreograph the sequence of twists around each joint that would send the shade along a straight path. The trigonometry is frightfully complicated. But your arm is an architect's lamp, and your brain effortlessly solves the equations everytime you point. And if you have ever held an architect's lamp by its clamp, you will appreciate that the problem is even harder than what I have described. The lamp flails under its weight as if it had a mind of its own; so would your arm if your brain did not compensate for its weight, solving a near-intractable physics problem.

Pinker's later mention of inverse kinematics and inverse dynamics (1997, p. 31) makes it clear that he views the brain's role in behavior as specifying outputs in the form of joint angles and muscle forces based on sensory inputs. But he might have had second thoughts about his analysis if he had paused to consider how the angles of the architect's lamp were computed. Of course, they were not computed at all, their resulting angles and velocities being determined automatically by simply moving the lamp to where you wanted it to be! This is basically how a control system analysis would account for how you are able to move your hand to where you want it to be, automatically compensating for the combined weight of hand and arm. And this is exactly what Powers's "Arm 1" demonstration does (described in chapter 6), using interconnected control systems to permit a robot to point to a target anywhere in reachable space (and even allowing the user to turn gravity on and off to see how the system so quickly and easily compensates). Pinker and others who may be skeptical that such seemingly complex behavior can be generated without having to solve a "near-intractable physics problem" required by the input-output Newtonian analysis of the behavior have only to download the program at *www.uiuc.edu/ph/www/g-cziko/twd* and run it on an IBM-compatible personal computer (even a slow, outdated 286 machine with no math coprocessor will suffice). Or simpler still, he can attempt to touch with his finger a small faintly glowing object in an otherwise completely darkened room (so that he cannot see his finger). He will then realize that without continuous visual feedback provided by seeing the target, his finger, and the space between them, the act of reaching for an object cannot be reliably performed.

But although he does not heed the extended Bernardian lesson, Pinker at least recognizes the importance of desires and beliefs (the latter we can understand as higher-level perceptions) in understanding human behavior (1997, pp. 63–64):

In our daily lives we all predict and explain other people's behavior from what we think they know and what we think they want. Beliefs and desires are the explanatory tools of our own intuitive psychology, and intuitive psychology is still the most useful and complete science of behavior there is. . . . It is not that common sense should have any more authority in psychology than it does in physics or astronomy. But this part of common sense has so much power and precision in predicting, controlling, and explaining everyday behavior, compared to any alternative ever entertained, that the odds are high that it will be incorporated in some form into our best scientific theories. . . . No science of mind or brain is likely to do better. That does not mean that the intuitive psychology of beliefs and desires is itself science, but it suggests that scientific psychology will have to explain how a hunk of matter, such as a human being, can have beliefs and desires and how the beliefs and desires work so well.

This is, of course, exactly what modern developments of the extended Bernardian lesson provide in the form of perceptual control theory and its working models of behavior as described in chapter 6. Pinker clearly understands the need, but it appears that the allure of the cause-effect trap is such that even a mind as keen as his fails to see the Bernardian-inspired materialist solution to the puzzle of purposeful behavior that he is seeking.

Finally, he has made some comments concerning the combination of the extended Bernardian and extended Darwinian lessons, that is, how by combining within an organism both Bernardian and Darwinian processes, a very useful form of directed or purposeful evolution can emerge. Here his words indicate a belief that biological evolution cannot be purposeful, as well as a failure to recognize the distinction between among-organism (basic Darwinian) and within-organism (extended Darwinian) selection.

Pinker correctly points out that "felt need," such as a giraffe's "need" for a long neck, has no role in the among-organism selection of biological evolution and that to believe otherwise would be Lamarckian (1997, pp. 206, 207):

They [needs] are met only when mutations appear that are capable of building an organ that meets the need, when the organism finds itself in an environment in which meeting the need translates into more surviving babies, and in which that selection pressure persists over thousands of generations. Otherwise the need goes unmet. Swimmers do not grow webbed fingers; Eskimos do not grow fur.

True enough. But swimmers might well begin to evolve webbed fingers (and Eskimos fur) if some human had the bizarre desire and means to breed swimmers and Eskimos for these characteristics in the way that farmers have been breeding animals and plants for hundreds if not thousands of years to meet their needs to produce more food for less cost and labor.

Pinker then moves on to within-organism selection (1997, p. 207):

I have studied three-dimensional mirror-images for twenty years, and though I know mathematically that you can convert a left shoe into a right shoe by turning it around in the fourth dimension, I have been unable to grow a 4-D mental space in which to visualize the flip.

He seems to be concluding here that since he cannot achieve a certain mental ability, *no* mental abilities can arise as the result of the needs of the owner of a human brain. Not only is his logic obviously faulty, but the reader has only once again to refer to chapter 9 to see how within-organism selection of antibodies, ideas, images, and synapses can meet new needs when embedded in a control system that contains an internal goal, a means to try out new actions on its environment, and a way to compare the continuing consequences of its actions with its goal.

How the Mind Works is well worth reading. In addition to Pinker's engaging treatment of the basic Darwinian lesson, his discussion of both the potential and problems of connectionism as a model of brain functioning (see his section "Connectoplasm" in chapter 2) should be of considerable interest to cognitive scientists and others interested in the inner workings of the human brain.

But the book falls far short of its ambitious title by ignoring or rejecting the extended Darwinian and Bernardian lessons and their combination. As a result Pinker neither accounts for how the mind is able to use behavior to satisfy its desires nor explains its remarkably adaptive ability to come up with creative solutions to problems. With this impoverished view of the mind as an input-output computing device, it is perhaps not surprising that Pinker's final message is a rather negative one, doubting that the human mind will ever be able to truly understand itself. In this respect he may be right. But the extended Bernardian and Darwinian lessons provide renewed hope. Given the strong desire (that many humans have) to understand the puzzle of our own minds, plus a remarkable Darwinian computational engine (that all humans have in the form of a human brain) capable of generating and testing many possible solutions to this puzzle, it may just be a matter of time—perhaps just another generation or two—before such understanding is ours. After all, as Dennett has observed (1995, p. 377), "we today—every one of us—can *easily* understand many ideas that were simply unthinkable *by the geniuses* in our grandparents' generation!"

The Cause-Effect Trap

I cannot pretend to have done justice to the important work of these five influential behavioral scientists by my cursory summaries and interpretations of their theories about human behavior. I hope nonetheless to have shown that none of them completely embraces all three of biology's lessons

Table 11.1
Acceptance of Bernardian and Darwinian lessons for animate behavior

Behavioral Scientist	Basic Darwinian Lesson	Extended Darwinian Lesson	Extended Bernardian Lesson	Score
Piaget	No	No	Partly	0.5
Skinner	No	Partly	No	0.5
Chomsky	No	No	No	0.0
Dennett	Yes	Yes	Partly	2.5
Pinker	Yes	No	No	1.0

for behavioral science. Table 11.1 provides a summary of the extent to which each man gave evidence of understanding the basic Darwinian, extended Darwinian, and extended Bernardian lessons. In addition, I could not resist (although I probably should have) assigning each one an overall score based on their demonstrated appreciation of biology's three lessons for behavior. Dennett comes closest to having learned all the lessons (scoring 2.5 out of 3), but Chomsky, considered by many to be the most important intellectual figure of the second half of the twentieth century, winds up with a big fat zero since he appears to have learned not a single one!

William T. Powers, whose perceptual control theory was discussed in chapter 6, comes closer than Dennett in appreciating the three lessons, but he has reservations about the basic Darwinian lesson. This is at least partly due to his belief that Darwin's theory of evolution by natural selection is incomplete, since organisms may have means of controlling their rate of mutation in response to environmental stresses (Powers 1995). So while I chide him for having only partly accepted the basic Darwinian lesson, it could turn out that his view of evolution as a feedback-control process is actually more complete and accurate than current Darwinian theory (see Rutherford & Lindquist 1998 for evidence consistent with Powers's view of evolution).

It therefore appears that Powers and perhaps some others influenced by him are the only behavioral scientists who have been able to free themselves completely from the one-way cause-effect trap. While they constitute only a tiny minority of today's behavioral scientists, I hope that this book will encourage others to join them.[1]

I conclude this chapter with a list of quotations from other influential scholars and scientists from the second half of the twentieth century to provide evidence that it is not only the five prominent individuals discussed above who have ignored or rejected biology's three lessons for behavioral science and therefore remain in the cause-effect trap.

The typical problem of higher behavior arises when there is a delay between stimulus and response. What bridges the S-R gap? In everyday language, "thinking" does it: the stimulus gives rise to thoughts or ideas that continue during the delay period, and then cause the response. (Donald Hebb 1972, p. 84)

It is possible to step back and treat the mind as one big monster response function from the total environment over the total past of the organism to future actions . . . (Allen Newell 1990, p. 44)

If the external environment is represented in the brain with high-dimensional coding vectors; and if the brain's "intended" bodily behavior is represented in its motor nerves with high-dimensional coding vectors; then what intelligence requires is some appropriate or well-tuned *transformation* of sensory vectors into motor vectors! (Paul M. Churchland 1995, p. 93)

Behavior is not randomly emitted; it is elicited by information which is gleaned from the organism's external environment, and, proprioceptively, from its internal states. . . . *the mind is a description of the operation of a brain that maps information input onto behavioral output.* (Leda Cosmides & John Tooby 1987, p. 283)

Learning must be a matter of finding the right connection strengths so that the right patterns of activation will be produced under the right circumstances. (James L. McClelland, David Rumelhart, & Geoffrey E. Hinton 1986, p. 32)

12

Applying the Lessons of Bernard and Darwin to Behavioral Theory, Research, and Practice

. . . any system based on the control of behavior through the use of rewards (or, of course, punishments) contains the seeds of its own destruction. There may be a temporary period, lasting even for many generations, during which some exciting new system concept so appeals to people that they will struggle to live within its principles, but if those principles include incentives, which is to say arbitrary deprivation or withholding at the whim of human beings, inexorable reorganization will destroy the system from within: nature intervenes with the message, "No! That feels bad. Change!"
—William T. Powers (1973, p. 269)

Having reached this final chapter, it is time to summarize what we have learned from the lessons of Bernard and Darwin about the what, how, and why of animate behavior, and to consider the application of these lessons to behavioral theory, research, and behavior-related issues and problems.

The What of Behavior

The question of the what of animate behavior might not at first appear to be particularly interesting, at least not for the purpose of applying Bernard's and Darwin's lessons and for distinguishing the behavior of living organisms from that of inanimate objects and systems. A falcon's dive to seize a sparrow in midflight can be objectively described in terms of acceleration and trajectory in much the same way that a stone falling to earth can be described adequately without applying Bernard's or Darwin's lessons. But closer examination reveals an important difference between raptor and rock: the falcon, by varying the configuration of its outstretched wings, continually adjusts its path so as to strike its evading prey, whereas the falling stone can do nothing but follow the path of least resistance to the earth's surface. So although the actions of living organisms can be described from the viewpoint of an objective observer, such a description misses the most striking characteristic of animate behavior: its orientation toward some goal or purpose. Such goals and purposes, whether they be conscious or not, are revealed by disturbing the suspected desired outcome and seeing if the organism takes action to compensate for the disturbance.

The answer to the question, "What is animate behavior?," that is provided by Bernard's extended lesson can be no better expressed than by referring to the title of Powers's 1973 book and responding that animate behavior is best understood as the *control of perception*. That is, by varying its behavior an organism maintains control over certain important aspects of its environment. This does not mean that an organism can control all aspects of its environment, or that the control that is achieved is always perfect. It does mean, however, that all living organisms use behavior as a means to control what they can. Or as William James observed a century ago (1890, p. 7), "the fixed end, the varying means!"

This answer to the question of the what of behavior means that a satisfactory account of observed animate behavior must specify the particular perception that the organism is controlling. Answering this question requires a methodology that is very different from standard methods used in behavioral sciences, whereby behavior is seen not as the control of perception but rather as being controlled by or caused by perception. This latter Newtonian perspective attempts to establish a one-way causal link between stimulus and response (with or without mediating cognitive processes) using statistical methods to uncover relationships between independent and dependent variables.

In contrast, a Bernardian approach applies what Powers refers to as "the test of the controlled variable," or more simply just "the test." A summary of this approach as applied to people was provided by Runkel (1990, pp. 14, 15):

1 Select a variable that you think the person might be maintaining at some level. In other words, guess at an input quantity. (Examples: light intensity, sensation of skin temperature, admiration in another person's voice.)

2 Predict what would happen if the person is *not* maintaining the variable at a preferred level.

3 Apply various amounts and directions of disturbance directly to the variable.

4 Measure the actual effects of the disturbances.

5 If the effects are what you predicted under the assumption that the person is *not* acting to control the variable, stop here. The person is indeed not acting to control it; you guessed wrong.

6 If an actual effect is markedly smaller than the predicted effect, look for what opposition to the disturbance that, by its own varying, can counterbalance variations in the input quantity. That may be caused by the person's output. You may have found the feedback function.

7 Look for the way by which the person can sense the variable. If you can find no way by which the person could sense the variable, the input quantity, stop. People cannot control what they cannot sense.

8 If you find a means of sensing, block it so that the person cannot now sense the variable. If the disturbance continues to be opposed, you have not found the right sensor. If you cannot find a sensor, stop. Make another guess at an input quantity.

9 If all of the preceding steps are passed, you have found the input quantity, the variable that the person is controlling.

Working computer demonstrations of this method are provided by Powers's "Demo 1" (DOS program) and Marken's "Test of the Controlled Variable" (Java program), available at *www.uiuc.edu/ph/www/g-cziko/twd*. What is most remarkable about the test for determining the variable that is being controlled by behavior is lack of an apparent relationship (as in a near-zero correlation coefficient) between the controlled variable and behavior. It must be recognized that this refers to lack of a systematic *one-way* relationship between stimulus and response. But this is just what is to be expected from understanding the circular causality characteristic of both living and artificial control systems, in which perception and behavior reciprocally and simultaneously influence each other to maintain some perception close to a goal or standard (reference level).

Use of the test for analyzing animate behavior contrasts with all other research methods of behavioral science. Whether behaviorist or cognitive, traditional methods attempt to establish causes (independent variables) for aspects of behavior (dependent variables) as objectively defined from the viewpoint of the researcher. This approach has two serious weaknesses. First, it is not focused on determining the perceptual variables being controlled by the behaving organism. At best it may discover disturbances that appear to cause behavior, but by ignoring perceptual variables that the organism is actually controlling, such an analysis is incomplete at best and misleading at worst. For example, imagine driving west on a straight road with winds gusting out of the north. A traditional one-way cause-effect analysis of your steering behavior will find that the gusts of wind (independent variable) cause you to turn the steering wheel to the right. Your act of turning the steering wheel can be measured objectively to the nearest millimeter if desired and correlated with wind speed and direction. But this analysis completely misses the fact that you are varying the angle of the steering wheel *to maintain your perception of keeping the car centered in its lane.*

This crucial knowledge of the variable you are controlling by varying your behavior allows us to make predictions as to what will happen if other factors act to disturb the position of the car. For example, if the road begins to slope to the right as it changes from a four-lane highway to a two-lane road with a high crown, knowledge of the controlled variable permits us to predict correctly that you will now turn the steering wheel to the left to maintain the car's position. In contrast, knowing only that there is a correlation between wind speed and steering behavior provides no clues at all as to what will happen when other disturbances to the car's position are encountered.

The second weakness of the traditional cause-effect analysis of animate behavior is that it cannot distinguish between the goals of behavior and its incidental, unintended side effects. If behavior is described objectively from the viewpoint of the impartial observer, there can be no significant difference between reaching for the salt and knocking over a glass of wine into the lap of your dining companion. Something must have caused you to reach for the salt, and something must have caused you to knock over the wine. A one-way cause-effect analysis provides no way to distinguish between the two behaviors, despite the fact that your apologies (and your companion's consequent forgiveness) indicate that an important difference does exist between intentions and accidents (a distinction also made in courts of law). In contrast, using Bernard's extended lesson to focus on the intended consequences of behavior makes a clear and important contrast between perceptions being controlled by behavior (such as the appearance of these letters on my computer screen as I type) and incidental, uncontrolled consequences of behavior (such as the clicking sounds made by the computer's keys as I type that are disturbing my wife trying to sleep in the next room).

The How of Behavior

The next question to consider concerns the how of behavior. For example, how is it that wanting some fresh bread results in the appearance of a steaming loaf in the kitchen a few hours later?

The extended Bernardian lesson, as developed by Powers, provides a clear non-Newtonian answer: we are able to achieve goals by setting and accomplishing prerequisite subgoals. The recipe for bread lists water, flour, sugar, salt, and yeast as ingredients. If these are not readily available, a trip to the grocery store is in order. Once obtained, the ingredients must be measured (four cups of flour, two cups of water, a tablespoon of sugar, one teaspoon each of yeast and salt), combined in a certain way (mixed and kneaded until a certain consistency is reached), and baked in the oven at a certain temperature until the crust is golden brown. Actually, many more subgoals are involved than can be conveniently listed here, all of which must be achieved in order to bake a loaf of bread, and with each one likely requiring its own subgoals (subsubgoals?).

In addition, each subgoal must be attained despite the inevitable real-world disturbances that will be encountered. We considered the disturbance of not having all the necessary ingredients on hand, and how that led to a visit to the grocery store. But many other disturbances are also likely to be encountered (such as variations in water pressure while measuring the water, or an oven that must be set at 475° Fahrenheit to reach 425°), and the only way to ensure that they will be successfully countered is by implementing a control system for each subgoal. It is this hierarchy of goals and the setting of lower-level reference levels by higher-level control systems that provide an accurate and useful answer to the how of behavior (introduced in chapter 6 and illustrated in figure 6.3). A useful working model of such a hierarchy of goals and subgoals is Marken's "Spreadsheet Model of a Hierarchy of Control Systems" (1990) for both Macintosh and IBM-compatible personal computers that is available at *www.uiuc.edu/ph/www/g-cziko/twd*.

Traditional cause-effect psychologists have a very different answer to how questions, believing that behavior is able to achieve what it does by generating necessary outputs. Pinker's example of reaching for an object, described in chapter 11, is a good example of this approach, which requires exceedingly complex computations of behavior as output based on inverse kinematics and inverse dynamics. But such computations are not only unnecessary, they are also incapable of producing animate behavior that remains functional despite continuous and unpredictable disturbances. An industrial robot that picks up automobile parts from a conveyor belt and places them in a box by repeating the same sequence of fixed actions over and over again can be effective in a disturbance- and surprise-free environment. But it will fail if the conveyor belt changes speed, or the spacing between the parts changes, or the receiving box is moved a few inches. For humans, it is only by seeing both one's hand and the desired object that one is able to reduce the distance between them to zero and grasp the object. Such behavior remains successful despite disturbances such as muscle fatigue, bulky clothing, or someone attempting to deflect your hand from the desired object. Computed behavioral outputs are simply incapable of achieving such goals in a real world subject to disturbances, and can be useful only in the tightly controlled, disturbance-free environment of a manufacturing plant or a computer simulation.

Questions concerning the how of behavior can be continued to levels of explanation beyond the domain of behavioral science as we ask for what could be considered to be more and more reductionist explanations. One of the answers to how you open a book involves understanding how specific reference levels are generated and sent to the control systems that govern the muscles of your arms and hands. How these reference levels are actually generated and transmitted by your nervous system to the appropriate lower-level control systems brings us to the domain of neuroscience. How the resulting error signals cause muscular contractions involves molecular biology and eventually chemistry and physics. So integration of knowledge from all these disciplines is necessary to answer all the many how questions we can formulate.

The how question is also relevant to the question of learning. How is it that we are able to do something today (such as hitting a tennis ball or playing a musical piece) that we could not do yesterday? A traditional approach sees such learning as the acquisition of new responses; a Bernardian approach sees it as the purposeful, goal-driven, within-organism evolution of new perceptual, reference, and/or motor functions (see chapter 10).

The Why of Behavior

Answering questions about the how of animate behavior leads us down the hierarchy of control systems to lower levels of control. But questions about the why of behavior are addressed by going up the hierarchy to higher levels of control.

Returning to our bread-baking example, we pick up the action as you begin to move your hand toward the kitchen faucet. Why are you changing the position of your arm and hand? Clearly, to turn on the water. Why turn on the water? To put sixteen ounces of it in your measuring cup. Why collect two cups of water? To add to the flour and other dry ingredients to make dough. Why make this dough? To bake a loaf of bread. The answer to each successive why question specifies the higher-level goal for which the current goal is a necessary subgoal.

So far, the answers to these why questions are rather obvious. Even so, they demonstrate how the answers to repeated why questions lead us to higher and higher levels of perception and control. But at a certain point things become more difficult. Why bake a loaf of bread? Perhaps you are hungry and just want something to eat. Or maybe you plan to share the bread with your family at your next meal. Or it could be you intend to give the loaf to a friend who has been sick. We cannot know the answer without further investigation. If your bread making ceased after receiving a phone call informing you that no one would be home for dinner tonight, that would suggest it was for the family to enjoy. If you made your bread despite the call, this would be consistent with the explanation that you intended to eat it yourself or give it to someone.

But in any case, continued why questions (such as why do you want to share a loaf of bread with your family, or give it to a friend, or eat it yourself?) eventually require a shift in perspective from what we have been calling the proximate explanations of behavior involving continuing processes of perceptual control to ultimate explanations involving the natural selection of organisms with adapted goals (discussed in chapters 8 and 9). The ultimate reason why we eat food rich in carbohydrates such as bread is because those who did so in the past were more successful in surviving and left more offspring (including us) than their contemporaries who did not eat such food. And there are good reasons why goals related to providing food for family and helping friends were also favored by evolution.

Humans evolved to prefer bread, whereas dung flies (having a quite different evolutionary history) prefer cow poop. But not all humans eat bread (although none eat cow poop). To answer the question of why an individual eats bread and not rice or potatoes or pasta, we must consider environmental factors, both physical and sociocultural. That all human beings eat foods containing carbohydrates is a universal characteristic of our species. Marriage, caring for children, and male sexual jealousy also appear to be universal features of humankind. But the particular foods we eat (as well as how we prepare them and with whom we eat them) vary widely from culture to culture, depending on what foods are available and what we have learned from others about their preparation and consumption. Similarly, a man's response to a mate's sexual infidelity will be influenced by local culture, with possible outcomes ranging from complete forgiveness to murder.

Universal human goals and desires interact with local conditions resulting in the quite varied proximate behavioral goals we see across human societies. A bride in India provides a dowry to her husband's family, whereas in Africa it is expected that the man make a generous contribution to his future in-laws. These behaviors may seem quite distinct, but they are in fact two different culturally adaptive solutions to the universal human concern of obtaining a high-quality mate and ensuring the survival and reproductive success of one's children.

Do all behaviors have ultimate evolutionary reasons? There is currently much debate about this. Ethologists, sociobiologists, and evolutionary psychologists tend to believe that such explanations exist for all behavior, and they point to the impressive success this approach has in making sense of animal behavior. Other behavioral scientists do not agree, particularly those who emphasize the importance of physical and cultural environments.

But if, as evolutionary psychologists are quick to point out, environmental factors do play an important role in influencing human behavior, this itself can be considered an adaptive trait that has an evolutionary origin. Humans' unmatched ability to engage in forms of within-organism purposeful evolution (see chapter 10) to modify goals and behaviors has made us the most widespread and adaptable species on the planet. This ability is so well developed that we are capable of behaviors that may even seem to be at odds with the basic concerns of survival and reproduction.

For example, we can vow, as Catholic priests and nuns do, to abstain from sexual activity and reproduction. We can, despite our long evolutionary history as omnivores, refrain from eating meat. We can endure great hardships and persecution, including torture and death, for our religious and political beliefs. We can even (which I suppose is the ultimate paradox) make a conscious effort to learn about the evolutionary origins of our desires, preferences, and consequent behaviors and decide to lead an austere life in opposition to the predilections of our selfish genes. Such flexibility can make it very difficult to apply an evolutionary perspective to all forms of human behavior. But priests, nuns, vegetarians, and religious martyrs are the exceptions rather than the rule, and I have no doubt that the general "rules" of human behavior will continue to make more sense as we continue to investigate them from an evolutionary perspective.

These Bernardian and Darwinian answers to why questions contrast sharply with answers provided by behavioral scientists using behaviorist and cognitive approaches. Skinner was not concerned with the evolutionary past of organisms whose behavior he studied, and he believed in spite of considerable evidence to the contrary (see Breland & Breland 1961) that under the proper conditions (contingencies of reinforcement) any organism could learn to perform just about any type of behavior that was physically possible. For him and other behaviorists, organisms do what they do for the simple reason that they were reinforced for such behaviors in the past.

Although cognitive scientists put less emphasis on reinforcement and more on mental processes, they also have traditionally shown little interest in adopting an evolutionary perspective to answer why questions. Exceptions, of course, are the relatively small group of cognitive psychologists who refer to themselves as evolutionary psychologists. But whereas evolutionary psychologists such as Tooby and Cosmides have learned the basic Darwinian lesson, they have not yet accepted the extended Darwinian and extended Bernardian lessons. For them, ultimate explanations for behavior are to be found in the evolutionary past of an organism. But proximate explanations are still cast in perceptual-input-causes-behavioral-output terms as used by all other cognitive scientists, rather than in behavioral-output-controls-perceptual-input terms as is consistent with the extended Bernardian lesson.

Applying the Bernardian and Darwinian Lessons

A biologically inspired approach to the what, how, and why of behavior has important implications for theory and research in behavioral science. But what does it mean for practice? Can this new approach, which takes heed of Bernard's and Darwin's lessons, provide new and effective solutions to the many serious issues and problems involving human behavior?

Skinner's Cause-Effect Approach

It was not so long ago that the application of a "truly scientific and objective approach" promised to solve such problems. By judicious application of operant conditioning techniques involving the establishment of proper contingencies of reinforcement and/or punishment as described by Skinner and his adherents, it was believed that one human could control another's behavior. In fact, this notion seems to have become the institutional policy in all societies where those in power provide rewards in the form of money and other benefits to motivate workers while meting out punishment in the form of imprisonment and hard labor to reform criminals.

It is generally accepted as common knowledge that this policy can work, but it has some serious problems. In his book *Punished by Rewards* (1993), Alfie Kohn described many disappointments encountered by those applying Skinnerian principles in a wide range of settings including the workplace, home, and school. After reviewing hundreds of such studies, Kohn concluded that attempts to control people by rewarding them for desired behaviors is not effective for a number of reasons. First, the quality of one's work suffers when emphasis is put on incentives such as money and grades. Second, the effect of reinforcement rarely generalizes to other settings (a child who is enticed to read a certain number of books over the summer to earn a pizza cannot be expected to continue reading books when no pizza is offered). Third, providing rewards for completing a task can turn what was previously an enjoyable activity pursued for its own sake into one that is perceived as disagreeable (as in the case of a child who used to read for pleasure, but now sees reading as inherently unpleasant work to be done only for a reward).

Although punishment was never actually advocated by Skinner, as it points out only what should not be done rather than what should be done, it remains a common means for controlling behavior in all societies despite considerable evidence that it is ineffective and counterproductive in the long term. Punishment may result in initial compliance to cease the offending behavior, but it also leads to resentment in the one punished and to devising ways to continue the behavior while avoiding punishment or retaliating against the punisher. Decades of research have shown consistently that children subjected to physical punishment turn out to be more aggressive and violent than other children and are more likely to use physical punishment on their own children (see Kohn 1973, p. 167). As to the effectiveness of punishment as institutionalized in the American penal system, James Gilligan (1996, p. 95) observed:

The murder rate in the United States is from five to twenty times higher than it is in any other industrialized democracy, even though we imprison proportionately five to twenty times more people than any other country on earth except Russia; and despite (or because of) the fact that we are the only Western democracy that still practices capital punishment (another respect in which we are like Russia).

The ineffectiveness of Skinnerian methods of behavior modification should come as no surprise to one who has carefully examined the basic premises of behaviorism. According to principles of operant conditioning, the probability of certain behaviors is increased by providing a reinforcement after the behavior is completed. Reinforcement is seen as strengthening the connection between the stimulus preceding the behavior and the behavior itself. So according to reinforcement theory, if a child is given a treat after reading a book, this should increase the frequency of future book reading *even if the student knows that no treat will be given the next time a book is read.*

It may well be that providing rewards will expose an otherwise reluctant child to the intrinsic pleasures of reading and thus be successful in encouraging the child to continue to read. But you can be sure that a child who does not find reading enjoyable and does it only to obtain extrinsic rewards will not continue to read books if he or she knows that rewards are no longer in the offing. And, as already noted, a child who initially found joy in reading may well come to consider it a disagreeable task when offered extrinsic rewards.

It is not the provision of *past* rewards and punishment that influences behavior, but rather anticipation of *future* rewards and punishment. Public hangings can be quite effective in getting the population to think twice about performing acts that are punishable at the end of a rope (it is, of course, completely effective in preventing such actions in the future by the punished individual). Promises of future rewards can also increase the likelihood of certain activities (which is how most religions operate to modify the behavior of their adherents, not to mention the threat of hell as future punishment). The reason why rewards and punishment often appear to be effective in modifying or controlling another person's behavior is not because their application in the past controls current behavior. Instead, humans vary their present behavior to obtain (or avoid) that which they want to obtain (or avoid). That is, rewards do not control behavior. Rather, behaviors are used to control rewards.

Another aspect of trying to use rewards to control behavior is often overlooked and may actually go a long way toward explaining why it is ineffective in the long term. For me to use reinforcement in an attempt to control your behavior, I must be able to control the resource that will serve as the reinforcement and make sure that you are in a state of *deprivation*. That is, I must make sure that you have less of the reinforcement than you want. I cannot use food as reinforcement if you are able to obtain all the food you want from other sources. Whereas such an arrangement may work well for a rat or pigeon that cannot question the fairness of such a situation, you as an intelligent adult human being will almost certainly find such a situation unfair if not intolerable. As Powers (1973, p. 268) noted:

Food rewards *will* cause modification of behavior, but how do you set up the conditions that give you sole control of the food supply? That is the step which Skinner and those who admire his methods have completely overlooked. That is the step that leads directly to violence.

This action of the would-be controllee against the would-be controller was recognized by Skinner who referred to it as "countercontrol," although it is seldom if ever mentioned now by advocates of his approach. In fact, anyone attempting to use Skinner's technique on another intelligent human being makes himself or herself susceptible to countercontrol. For example, a father may tell his teenage son that he must improve his high school grades to earn the right to use the family car. The teenager can then engage in countercontrol by making it known that if he can't use the car whenever he wants, he will simply not study at all! This is only one form that countercontrol can take, as more violent outcomes are also possible.

Bernard's Biological Approach

If reward and punishment fail to solve the problems caused by human behavior, why do those with political, military, and economic power persist in using them? One reason is that, as mentioned, the promise of reward and the threat of punishment can modify others' behavior, at least until ways are found to defeat the system (as in escaping from the situation or using violence to overcome the reinforcer-punisher). Another reason is the assumption of a one-way cause-effect view in which reinforcement causes desired behaviors and punishment eliminates undesirable ones.

In contrast, applying the extended Bernardian lesson leads to a very different approach. It differs from a cause-effect behaviorist approach in at least two main respects. This is due to Bernardian (as further developed by Powers) recognition that perceptions (such as the perception of stimuli as reward or punishment) do not control behavior. Rather, individuals vary their behavior as necessary to control their perceptions and thereby obtain desired outcomes and avoid unwanted ones.

A school discipline process based on Powers's perceptual control theory suggests that application of the extended Bernardian lesson can be quite effective in bringing about desired changes in behavior. The Responsible Thinking Process, developed by Edward E. Ford, was first implemented in Clarendon Elementary School in Phoenix, Arizona (1994, 1996). Ford, a social worker and counselor who discovered the work of Powers in 1981, conceived an approach to school discipline based on the Bernardian lesson that human beings act to control aspects of their environment.

No extrinsic reward or punishment (or promises or threats of them) are used, and teachers are not held responsible for the behavior of their students. Instead, students engaging in disruptive behavior are asked a series of questions by the teacher designed to have students reflect on their behavior and its consequences if continued. Students who need help learning how to behave responsibly (that is, in a way that does not disturb the learning activities of the classroom) go to a "responsible thinking classroom" where a full-time teacher-counselor helps them develop a plan for change to submit to the classroom teacher for approval.

From this all-too-brief description of Ford's process (for more information see *www.respthink.com*), it may seem that it is just another way of using rewards and punishment to control students' behavior, with reward being the privilege to remain in the regular classroom and punishment being sent to the responsible thinking classroom. But this is not an accurate assessment, since the student is always in control of his or her own situation in accordance with the rules that have been accepted by the school's students and teachers concerning acceptable behavior.

Nowadays it is almost always the case that a teacher responds to a disruptive student with the threat of punishment (if the disrupting behavior continues) or the promise of a reward (if the disrupting behavior stops). In contrast, teachers in Ford's process do not use threats, bribes, or commands in such situations. Instead, they ask a series of questions like the following: "What were you doing?" "What are the rules?" "What happens when you break the rules?" "Is that what you want to happen?" "Is what you are doing getting you want you want?" "Do you want to work at solving your problem?"

At no time is a student told what to do or not to do, or asked to explain his or her behavior. But the rules of the school are enforced in a clear and consistent way, and the student has the choice of following them and participating fully in school activities or being excluded from them until he or she comes up with a satisfactory plan to change the disruptive behavior.

Although easy to describe, the Responsible Thinking Process is not so easy to implement for the simple reason that it goes against the belief commonly held by teachers that they are responsible for the behavior of their students and that rewards and punishment can be used to control students' behavior. Ford found that it takes a serious, determined effort on the part of teachers to cease threatening and bribing their students, and he devotes considerable time and effort to help them change their reaction.

But once achieved, the results, as I personally witnessed in an elementary school near Chicago, are quite amazing. That is why in just a few years the Responsible Thinking Process has spread to more than forty schools in the United States and Australia.

Ford's work in public schools and other institutions (he has also worked in juvenile detention centers) is a clear demonstration of the potential of a Bernardian approach to behavior to solve behavior-related problems. Contingencies of reinforcement or punishment, or their associated bribes and threats, are not necessary. There is no risk of escalating control and countercontrol. Most important, it removes from teachers the onus of attempting to control students' behavior and allows them to devote their energies to teaching. As one sixth-grade teacher remarked, "We've waited for a program to come along that allows me to teach! We have finally found it!" (quotation on the back cover of Ford 1994).

Darwin's Biological Approach

If the application of Bernard's extended lesson to animate behavior has been effective as applied to education, what about applications of the basic and extended Darwinian lessons?

It is not easy to find applications to education of Darwin's basic lesson. The notion that our evolutionary past had a role in shaping the human mind and thereby influences our abilities, emotions, goals, desires, and fears does not appear to be popular among educators. This is particularly so in the United States, where the fact of biological evolution itself is not popular (and is often attacked by religious fundamentalists), and where the role of the current environment, not one's evolutionary past, is usually considered the determining factor in shaping cognitive skills and personalities. But at least some attempts have been made to use Darwin's basic lesson to change schools to optimize learning and to understand difficulties children have in learning certain concepts.

An example of the former is Gary Bernhard's book *Primates in the Classroom* (1988). Bernhard drew primarily on studies of the world's remaining hunter-gatherer groups (including the Semang of Malaysia, Mbuti Pygmies of the Congo's Ituri forest, !Kung of the Kahalari Desert, Aborigines of Australia, and Eskimos of Canada's Arctic) to understand how learning naturally occurs in groups that live in environments similar to the one in which our species evolved; that is, before the development of agriculture and industry. Bernhard (1988, pp. 178–179) pointed out many similarities among these groups and described their implications for education, stating that

> Learning by discovery in a democratic social context is one of the characteristics of our species, and we are kidding ourselves if we think that a longer school year, more rigorous basic-skills instruction, higher academic standards, and all of the other suggestions that have come out of studies such as A Nation at Risk will solve the "education problem" in this country. An evolutionary perspective also makes it clear that, in order for children to learn naturally, they need to have consistent yet varied adult models. Thus we are equally foolish if we believe children will be well served in an environment in which the only adults around are trying to get out of the children's way. Finally, an evolutionary way of looking at education issues is grounded in the need that all humans have to belong to a group and to be acknowledged as individuals by the other members of the group. It is thus hardly surprising that the more removed children are from their conception of who is in the "band," the greater their distress.

Some will question Bernhard's method of applying what has been observed in hunter-gatherer groups to urban children in modern schools, but many innovative changes taking place in education are consistent with his Darwinian perspective. Such progressive approaches typically give students more responsibility for their own learning, integrate many types of knowledge and skills in pursuing projects of interest to the students, employ adults not as authoritarian transmitters of information but rather as facilitators and role models, and have multiage classrooms in which children and teachers remain together for several years. All these, and many other progressive changes in education, are compatible with how human children appear to learn best "naturally."[1]

But many skills that we expect children to learn did not exist in the evolutionary past. Reading and writing are considered basic to all formal education, yet they are relatively recent cultural inventions that had no role in our evolution as a species. Mathematics is another branch of knowledge unknown to our early human forebears but occupies an important role in education. What might the basic Darwinian lesson have to say about learning in these areas?

Psychologist David Geary studied children's learning of various subjects and observed an important distinction between what he calls "biologically primary" and "biologically secondary" cognitive abilities. The former appear to have evolved largely by means of natural or sexual selection, whereas "biologically secondary cognitive abilities reflect the co-optation of primary abilities for purposes other than the original evolution-based function and appear to develop only in specific cultural contexts" (Geary 1995, p. 24).

A good example of this distinction is the contrast between oral language ability (listening and speaking) and literacy skills (ability to read and write language). Normal children require no special instruction to learn to speak and understand language. As long as they are exposed to a spoken language in interaction with older individuals, they will acquire this ability with little apparent effort and no formal instruction. Human evolution obviously shaped our species to excel at the acquisition and use of language (see Cziko 1995, chapter 11; Pinker and Bloom 1990).

But no evolutionary pressure existed for learning to read and write or understanding mathematics, as these skills are relatively modern cultural inventions. Accordingly, they take special concentrated effort to acquire. Geary concluded that learning secondary biological abilities must involve extensive practice, and since this may not be particularly enjoyable, ways must be found to encourage children to undertake it.

Considerable controversy exists among educators about how this should be done and what should be practiced (as in the phonics versus whole-language approaches to reading). Nonetheless, Geary's evolutionary analysis of biologically primary and biologically secondary cognitive abilities creates a useful framework for understanding the success and difficulties our children experience in school and shows one way that the basic Darwinian lesson can be applied.

What about applications of the extended Darwinian lesson? We saw in chapter 9 how within-organism variation and selection functions within the mammalian immune and nervous systems, and how the process permits these systems to adapt to new circumstances in the form of immune responses and learning new behaviors and abilities. Can this lesson be applied in practical settings? It turns out that does have important behavioral applications in at least the field of education, despite the fact that educators have for the most part ignored it.

An important exception is Henry Perkinson, a philosopher and historian of education. He observed important connections among the extended Darwinian lesson, the philosophy of Karl Popper, and major developments in educational theory and practice, notably those motivated by the work of Piaget, Skinner, Maria Montessori, A. S. Neill (of *Summerhill* fame), and Carl Rogers (Perkinson 1984). The approaches to educational theory and practice advocated by these five influential individuals certainly have important differences. But what they all have in common is rejection of the traditional cause-effect notion of education as the transmission of knowledge from teacher to student, and appreciation of education as a process of change that involves continuous modification of previous knowledge by trial and error elimination.

This essentially Darwinian approach can be summarized by the title of Perkinson's book: education involves learning from our mistakes. This means that it is facilitated by an environment in which learners are free to try out their knowledge and skills without fear of making mistakes. But it also means that the environment must provide critical feedback permitting students to discover the inadequacies of their knowledge and skills so that they can continually improve. This approach rejects the view of students as passive recipients of knowledge and sees them instead as active creators of their own knowledge. It is consistent not only with the essential core of the educational theories of Piaget, Skinner, Neill, Montessori, and Rogers, but with other progressive changes occurring in education, even if reformers are unable or unwilling to recognize the Darwinian roots of these changes (see Cziko 1995, chapter 12, for a more thorough Darwinian discussion of education).

Toward a Unified Theory of Behavior

Applying the lessons of Bernard and Darwin to the what, how, and why of behavior provides the building blocks for a unified theory of behavior drawing on biology, psychology, physiology, and ultimately physics. The concerns and contents of such a theory should be obvious from the preceding chapters. But it will be useful to conclude this book with an outline of such a theory and a consideration of its limitations.

The basic Darwinian lesson informs us that our evolutionary past provided us and all animals with certain basic preferences. We prefer certain foods, odors, and tastes and are repulsed by others. We prefer environments that are not too hot and not too cold. We look for certain characteristics in mates, which differ depending on our sex. We do what we can to assist the well-being of our children, close relatives, and other individuals from whom we can expect such assistance in return. We prefer the company of family members and others who are most like us, and are wary of others whom we perceive as physically, racially, or culturally different. But these preferences, naturally selected for their past survival and reproductive consequences, are not necessarily advantageous in these respects in the modern environment we inhabit.

The extended Bernardian lesson provides an explanation for how such preferences, existing as reference levels within feedback-control systems, influence our behavior, and how we are able to purposefully vary our behavior to make our perceptions match these reference levels. The extended Bernardian lesson, in its cybernetic formulation as perceptual control theory, shows how goals, desires, intentions, likes, and dislikes are emergent properties of thoroughly materialistic systems, having no need for spirits, souls, or other supernatural entities or processes.

But we humans have many goals and preferences that cannot be traced back to our evolutionary past. Thus we need the extended Darwinian lesson to explain how new goals can evolve in the service of more basic ones. An Eskimo spears seals and whales to make a living. A farmer in Illinois plants hundreds of acres of corn and soybeans for his livelihood. A musician in Paris supports herself by producing certain sounds with her flute. Such behaviors require preferences and control systems that cannot be provided by our evolutionary past, but they can be created by within-organism variation and selection as a process of purposeful evolution.

I have no doubt that a biologically inspired view of behavior that uses the insights of Bernard and Darwin is far superior to the one-way cause-effect approach currently embraced by mainstream behavioral scientists. But I also recognize that this new approach has certain inherent limitations of its own concerning our understanding, prediction, and control of animate behavior.

First, our search for the ultimate, evolutionary accounts for behavior are hampered by unavailability of fossil records of behavior (although certain extremely rare fossil finds, such as that of a dinosaur apparently guarding her eggs and newly hatched offspring, do provide some behavioral evidence). So whereas we can provide all sorts of evolutionary accounts of the emergence of our preferences and abilities (such as language), we cannot know for sure which if any of these comes close to what actually took place.

Also, compared with other species, our behavior is remarkably diverse, reflecting our varied physical and cultural environments. Pandas eat only bamboo shoots, and robins always make a nest of a certain shape in which to lay eggs; but we humans engage in a wide variety of tasks to accomplish whatever basic goals evolution has provided us. This diversity makes it especially difficult to find universal human behavioral characteristics. Nonetheless, a Darwinian approach offers clues as to what fundamental universals may exist. Furthermore, recognition of the hierarchical nature of human perceptual control systems is a way of recognizing similarity in the underlying goals of human behavior in spite of their apparent superficial diversity.

Considering first the extended Bernardian lesson that organisms act to control their perceptions, we must recognize that the actual behavior implemented by an organism has to compensate for disturbances that are encountered. To the extent that these disturbances are unpredictable, the organism's behaviors will also be unpredictable. For example, even if I know that you are driving down a straight road to travel from your home in Eastville to a friend's home in Westville, I cannot know in advance how you will move the steering wheel, since I cannot predict the wind, traffic, and road conditions you will encounter. Nonetheless, knowledge of your goal (that is, the perceptual variable that you are controlling) will allow me to predict the outcome of your behavior (arriving in Westville), even if the precise actions you make while driving remain unpredictable.

The extended Darwinian lesson of within-organism variation and selection also poses challenges to understanding and predicting behavior. Through reorganization, organisms acquire control over new variables in new situations. Since this process has an essential random component in the generation of variation (mathematicians refer to it as a *stochastic* process), it is in principle impossible to know exactly what type of reorganization will take place. A boy who is deprived of attention at home will look for it elsewhere. Whether he will attain it by excelling in academics, sports, or by committing a violent crime will be determined by the results of control system reorganization, whose outcome is by its very nature impossible to predict.

All of these are important limitations to a unified theory of behavior based on the Bernardian and Darwinian lessons. But this biologically inspired framework allows us to ask many new, interesting questions about behavior, and conceive of a methodology for answering them that avoids the push-pull straightjacket of cause-effect behavioral science, taking into account our evolutionary past and present (the latter in the form of within-organism variation and selection).

We have no guarantee that applying the lessons of Bernard and Darwin will ultimately allow us to answer all the important and interesting questions about animal and human behavior. Nor can we be certain that they will lead us to solutions for the major behavior-based problems our species is facing, such as failing schools, violence, pollution, overpopulation, spread of disease, and the growing division of the world's population into haves and have-nots.

What is clear is that the currently accepted one-way cause-effect model, successful in explaining much of the workings of the inanimate world, cannot account for the purposeful, goal-directed behavior by which living organisms control important aspects of their environment. It is also clear that attempts to modify human behavior based on the push-pull approach inherited from Newton have failed both as a theoretical account for animate behavior and as an applied tool for behavior change.

Major revolutions have taken place in the fields of astronomy, geology, physics, and biology, with important consequences for our understanding of the universe and our ability to predict and control important aspects of our environment. It is not unreasonable to expect that the consequences of a major revolution in the much younger discipline of behavioral science may have consequences as great as or greater than those of these earlier revolutions.

When the lessons of Bernard and Darwin become widely understood by behavioral scientists, the life, behavioral, and physical sciences will have achieved an integration that future scientists will find so obvious, satisfying, and useful that they will have difficulty understanding why, after Bernard's and Darwin's revolutionary breakthroughs in the nineteenth century, it was not until the twenty-first century that their lessons were widely learned and applied.

Notes

Chapter 1

1. *The American Heritage Dictionary* (1992) defines materialism as "the theory that physical matter is the only reality and that everything, including thought, feeling, mind, and will, can be explained in terms of matter and physical phenomena." "Physical phenomena" include forms of energy such as electricity and magnetism.

Chapter 5

1. This paragraph and the preceding one were written with the assistance of William T. Powers.

Chapter 6

1. Some of the better-known participants were social scientist Gregory Bateson, engineer Julian Bigelow, sociologist Paul Lazarsfeld, social psychologist Kurt Lewin, neurophysiologist Rafael Lorente de Nó, anthropologist Margaret Mead, neuropsychiatrist Warren McCulloch, mathematician Walter Pitts, physiologist Arturo Rosenblueth, information theorist Claude Shannon, electrical engineer Heinz von Foerster, mathematician John von Neumann, and, of course, cybernetician Norbert Wiener.

2. Apparently after rheostat, a device that resists the flow of electricity and whose resistance can be varied by mechanical means.

3. Figure 6.4 was provided by Bryan Thalhammer.

4. Another approach to modeling hierarchical networks of control systems is by Marken (1990), who created a three-level control hierarchy in the form of a computer spreadsheet that can be obtained from *www.uiuc.edu/ph/www/g-cziko/twd*.

5. Gather, a program for IBM-compatible personal computers, is also available from *www.uiuc.edu/www/ph/g-cziko/twd*.

6. Additional control system simulations of social behavior have been developed by Bourbon (1990).

Chapter 7

1. Although Lamarck did not see God as directly involved in the creation of currently existing forms of life, he nonetheless referred to God as "the supreme author of all things" (quoted in Burkhardt 1977, p. 185).

2. See Weiner (1994) for a fascinating account of the work of Peter and Rosemary Grant on the evolution of Darwin's finches on the Galápagos Islands.

3. Unfortunately, Weismann's research did nothing to dissuade Soviet biologist Trofim Denisovich Lysenko (1889–1976) from his doomed attempt to increase the productivity of Soviet agriculture based on Lamarckian principles. Stalin's receptivity to and imposition of Lysenko's Lamarckian beliefs crippled the development of Soviet biology and genetics until the 1960s (see Medvedev 1969, and Joravsky 1970, for accounts of the life and times of Lysenko).

4. It is the case that certain environmental factors (such as radiation and chemical substances known as *mutagens*) can increase mutation rates in organisms and thereby cause an increase in behavioral variation. However, these variations are like those that arise spontaneously in their being unrelated to the environmental factors that caused them and completely blind to the adaptive needs of the organism.

5. Since evolutionary theory recognizes all organisms as having descended from a common ancestor, all organisms are in this sense related to each other. I use the word "unrelated" in its more common definition of applying to two organisms with no close kin relationship and who are therefore unlikely to share a new or relatively uncommon gene.

6. This account of web building is taken primarily from Dawkins (1996, chapter 2) and Hoagland and Dodson (1995, pp. 140–141).

Chapter 8

1. Since Darwin's time, adaptive explanations have been provided for some human racial differences. For example, sunlight is an important factor in human health since skin exposed to sunlight permits the production of vitamin D, a vital nutrient. But because overexposure to the sun has damaging effects and may lead to skin cancer, the color of human skin is an adaptation to the intensity of sunlight. Tropical races have dark skin for protection against the sun's harmful effects, and temperate and Arctic races have light skin to allow more of the available solar radiation to enter the skin to be used for synthesis of vitamin D.

2. See Behe (1996) for a modern version of the same misguided argument.

3. See Buss (1999) for a valuable recent compilation of these findings. See also Johnston (1999) for a fascinating evolutionary account of human emotions.

Chapter 9

1. See Cziko (1995, pp. 186–187) and Dennett (1995, pp. 384–393) for two critiques of Chomsky's anti-Darwinian views.

2. Both figures 9.2 and 9.3 give a simple quantitative portrayal of the two complementary entities in question; however, their interaction is undoubtedly much more complex.

Chapter 11

1. For more information about these behavioral scientists and their work, see the Website of the Control Systems Group at *www.ed.uiuc.edu/csg*.

Chapter 12

1. For an example of a school consistent with such principles, see the video *A Learner-Centered School* about Williston Central School in Vermont (Burrello 1995).

References

Adler, T. (1997, January 4). Animals' fancies: Why members of some species prefer their own sex. *Science News, 151,* 8–9.

Alcock, J. (1993). *Animal behavior: An evolutionary approach* (5th ed.). Sunderland, MA: Sinauer Associates.

Alexander, R. D. (1979). *Darwinism and human affairs.* Seattle: University of Washington Press.

Allman, W. F. (1994). *The stone age present.* New York: Simon & Schuster.

Aquinas, T. (1914). *The "Summa Theologica" of St. Thomas Aquinas* (Part II). London: W. & T. Washbourne. (Original work written 1265–1273)

Aristotle. (1952). *Physics* (*Great books of the Western world,* Vol. 8, pp. 257–355). Chicago: Encylopaedia Britannica.

Bagemihl, B. (1999). *Biological exuberance: Animal homosexuality and biological diversity.* New York: St. Martin's Press.

Bain, A. (1868). *The senses and the intellect* (3rd ed.). London: Longmans, Green.

Bajema, C. J. (Ed.). (1983). *Natural selection theory.* Stroudsburg, PA: Hutchinson Ross.

Baylies, M. K., Bargiello, A., Jackson, F. R., & Young, M. W. (1987). Changes in abundance or structure of the *per* gene product can alter periodicity of the *Drosophila* clock. *Nature, 326,* 390–392.

Beach, F. A. (1955). The descent of instinct. *Psychological Review, 62,* 401–410.

Beckner, M. O. (1967). Vitalism. In P. Edwards (Ed.), *The encyclopedia of philosophy* (Vol. 8, pp. 253–256). New York: Macmillan.

Behe, M. J. (1996). *Darwin's black box: The biochemical challenge to evolution.* New York: Free Press.

Benzer, S. (1973, December). Genetic dissection of behavior. *Scientific American, 229,* 24–37.

Bernard, C. (1927). *An introduction to the study of experimental medicine* (H. C. Green, Trans.). New York: Macmillan. (Originally published 1865)

Bernhard, J. G. (1988). *Primates in the classroom: An evolutionary perspective on children's education*. Amherst, MA: University of Massachusetts Press.

Bizzi, E., Mussa-Invaldi, F. A., & Giszter, S. (1991). Computations underlying the execution of movement: A biological perspective. *Science, 253*, 287–291.

Blumenthal, A. L. (1988). A reappraisal of Wilhelm Wundt. In L. T. Benjamin, Jr. (Ed.), *A history of psychology: Original sources and contemporary research* (pp. 195–204). New York: McGraw-Hill.

Boakes, R. (1984). *From Darwin to behaviourism: Psychology and the minds of animals*. Cambridge: Cambridge University Press.

Bode, H. W. (1960). Feedback—The history of an idea. In R. Bellman & R. Kalaba (Eds.), *Mathematical trends in control theory* (pp. 106–123). New York: Dover.

Bourbon, W. T. (1990). Invitation to the dance: Explaining variance when control systems interact. *American Behavioral Scientist, 34*(1), 95–105.

Breland, K., & Breland, M. (1961). The misbehavior of organisms. *American Psychologist, 16*, 681–684.

Brown, D. E. (1991). *Human universals*. Philadelphia: Temple University Press.

Brown, J. L. (1974). Alternative routes to sociality in jays—With a theory for the evolution of altruism and communal breeding. *American Zoologist, 14*, 61–78.

Burkhardt, R. W., Jr. (1977). *The spirit of the system: Lamarck and evolutionary biology*. Cambridge: Harvard University Press.

Burrello, L. C. (Executive Producer). (1995). *A learner-centered school* [video]. (Available from Phi Delta Kappa, P.O. Box 789, 408 N. Union Street, Bloomington, IN 47402-0789.)

Buss, D. M. (1989). Sex differences in mate preferences: Evolutionary hypotheses tested in 37 different cultures. *Behavioral and Brain Sciences, 12*, 1–49.

Buss, D. M. (1999). *Evolutionary psychology: The new science of the mind*. Boston: Allyn & Bacon.

Calvin, W. H. (1987). The brain as a Darwin machine. *Nature, 330*, 33–34.

Calvin, W. H. (1990). *The cerebral symphony: Seashore reflections on the nature of consciousness*. New York: Bantam.

Calvin, W. H. (1996a). *The cerebral code: Thinking a thought in the mosaics of the mind*. Cambridge: MIT Press.

Calvin, W. H. (1996b). *How brains think: Evolving intelligence, then and now*. New York: Basic Books.

Campbell, D. T. (1960). Blind variation and selective retention in creative thought as in other knowledge processes. *Psychological Review, 67*, 380–400.

Campbell, D. T. (1974). Evolutionary epistemology. In P. A. Schilpp (Ed.), *The philosophy of Karl Popper* (Vol. 1, pp. 413–463). La Salle, IL: Open Court.

Campbell, D. T., & Stanley, J. C. (1966). *Experimental and quasi-experimental designs for research*. Chicago: Rand McNally.

Campbell, K. (1967). Materialism. In P. Edwards (Ed.), *The encyclopedia of philosophy* (Vol. 5, pp. 179–188). New York: Macmillan.

Cannon, W. B. (1939). *The wisdom of the body* (rev. ed.). New York: Norton.

Changeux, J.-P. (1985). *Neuronal man: The biology of mind.* New York: Oxford University Press.

Chomsky, N. (1959). A review of B. F. Skinner's *Verbal behavior. Language, 35*(1), 26–58. (Reprinted in Fodor, J. A., & Katz, J. J. (Eds.). (1964). *The structure of language: Readings in the philosophy of language* (pp. 547–578). Englewood Cliffs, NJ: Prentice-Hall)

Chomsky, N. (1988). *Noam Chomsky on the generative enterprise: A discussion with Riny Huybregts and Henk van Riemsdijk.* Dordrecht, The Netherlands: Foris Publications.

Chomsky, N. (1996). *Powers and prospects.* Boston: South End Press.

Chomsky, N. (1997). *Language and mind* (transcript of video). Los Angeles: Into the Classroom Media.

Churchland, P. M. (1995). *The engine of reason, the seat of the soul: A philosophical journey into the brain.* Cambridge: MIT Press.

Cook, T. D., & Campbell, D. T. (1979). *Quasi-experimentation: Design and analysis issues for field settings.* Boston: Houghton-Mifflin.

Cosmides, L., & Tooby, J. (1987). From evolution to behavior: Evolutionary psychology as the missing link. In J. Dupré (Ed.), *The latest on the best: Essays on evolution and optimality* (pp. 277–306). Cambridge: MIT Press.

Cziko, G. (1995). *Without miracles: Universal selection theory and the second Darwinian revolution.* Cambridge: MIT Press.

Daly, M., & Wilson, M. (1985). Child abuse and other risks of not living with both parents. *Ethology and Sociobiology, 6,* 197–210.

Daly, M., & Wilson, M. (1988). *Homocide.* Chicago: Aldine de Gruyter.

Darwin, C. (1874). *The descent of man and selection in relation to sex* (2nd ed.). New York: Thomas Y. Crowell.

Darwin, C. (1952). *The descent of man and selection in relation to sex.* (*Great books of the Western world*, Vol. 49, pp. 253–639). Chicago: Encyclopaedia Britannica. (Originally published 1871)

Darwin, C. (1955). *The expression of the emotions in man and animals.* New York: Philosophical Library. (Originally published 1872)

Darwin, C. (1975). *Charles Darwin's natural selection, being the second part of his big species book written from 1856–1858.* (Edited by Paul Barrett, 2 vols.). Cambridge: Cambridge University Press.

Dawkins, R. (1976). *The selfish gene.* Oxford: Oxford University Press.

Dawkins, R. (1986). *The blind watchmaker.* New York: Norton.

Dawkins, R. (1996). *Climbing mount improbable.* New York: Norton.

Deacon, T. W. (1997). *The symbolic species: The co-evolution of language and the brain*. New York: Norton.

Dennett, D. C. (1991). *Consciousness explained*. Boston: Little, Brown.

Dennett, D. C. (1995). *Darwin's dangerous idea: Evolution and the meanings of life*. New York: Simon & Schuster.

Dennett, D. C. (1996). *Kinds of minds: Towards an understanding of consciousness*. New York: Basic Books.

Depew, D. J., & Weber, B. H. (1995). *Darwinism evolving*. Cambridge: MIT Press.

Eccles, J. C. (1989). *Evolution of the brain: Creation of the self*. London: Routledge.

Edelman, G. M. (1987). *Neural Darwinism: The theory of neuronal group selection*. New York: Basic Books.

Edelman, G. M. (1988). *Topobiology: An introduction to molecular embryology*. New York: Basic Books.

Edelman, G. M. (1989). *Remembering the present: A biological theory of consciousness*. New York: Basic Books.

Edelman, G. M. (1992). *Bright air, brilliant fire: On the matter of the mind*. New York: Basic Books.

Edwards, P. (1967). Panpsychism. In P. Edwards (Ed.), *The encyclopedia of philosophy* (Vol. 6, pp. 22–31). New York: Macmillan.

Ehrlich, P. (1900, July 24). Croonian lecture: On immunity with special reference to cell life. *Proceedings of the Royal Society of London, 66*(432), 424–448.

Ellis, L. (1996). A discipline in peril: Sociology's future hinges on curing its biophobia. *American Sociologist, 27*, 21–41.

Emlen, S. T., Demong, N. J., & Emlen, J. (1989). Experimental induction of infanticide in female wattled jacanas. *Auk, 106*, 1–7.

Evans, R. I. (1973). *Jean Piaget: The man and his ideas*. New York: Dutton.

Eysenck, H. J. (1993). Creativity and personality: Suggestions for a theory. *Psychological Inquiry, 4*, 147–178.

Eysenck, H. J. (1994). Creativity and personality: Word associations, origence, and psychoticism. *Creativity Research Journal, 7*, 209–216.

Eysenck, H. J. (1995). *Genius: The natural history of creativity*. Cambridge: Cambridge University Press.

Finke, R. A., Ward, T. B., & Smith, S. M. (1992). *Creative cognition: Theory, research, and applications*. Cambridge: MIT Press.

Ford, E. E. (1994). *Discipline for home and school: Teaching children to respect the rights of others through responsible thinking based on perceptual control theory*. Scottsdale, AZ: Brandt.

Ford, E. E. (1996). *Discipline for home and school: Book 2: Program standards for schools*. Scottsdale, AZ: Brandt.

Fruton, J. S. (1975). Claude Bernard the scientist. In E. D. Robin (Ed.), *Claude Bernard and the internal environment: A memorial symposium* (pp. 35–41). New York: Marcel Dekker.

Garcia, J., & Koelling, R. A. (1966). Relation of cue to consequence in avoidance learning. *Psychonomic Science, 4,* 123–124.

Garcia, J., McGowan, B. K., Erwin, F. R., & Koelling, R. A. (1968). Cues: Their effectiveness as a function of the reinforcer. *Science, 160,* 794–795.

Gardner, H. (1987). *The mind's new science: A history of the cognitive revolution* (paperback ed.). New York: Basic Books.

Gaulin, S. J. C., & Boster, J. S. (1990). Dowry as female competition. *American Anthropologist, 92,* 994–1005.

Geary, D. C. (1995). Reflections on evolution and culture in children's cognition: Implications for mathematical development and instruction. *American Psychologist, 58*(1), 24–37.

Giddens, A. (1991). *Introduction to sociology.* New York: Norton.

Gilligan, J. G. (1996). *Violence: Our deadly epidemic and its causes.* New York: Putnam.

Greenough, W. T., & Black, J. E. (1992). Induction of brain structure by experience: Substrates for cognitive development. In M. Gunnar & C. Nelson (Eds.), *Developmental behavioral neurosciences,* Vol. 24: *Minnesota symposia on child development* (pp. 155–200). Hillsdale, NJ: Erlbaum.

Haldane, J. B. S. (1955). Population genetics. *New Biology, 18,* 34–51.

Hall, S. E. (1997). The future of combinatorial chemistry as a drug discovery paradigm. *Pharmaceutical Research, 14*(9), 1104–1112.

Hamburger, V. (1975). Cell death in the development of the lateral motor column of the chick embryo. *Journal of Comparative Neurology, 160,* 535–546.

Hamilton, W. D. (1963). The evolution of altruistic behavior. *American Naturalist, 97,* 354–356.

Hamilton, W. D. (1964). The genetical evolution of social behavior (Parts 1 & 2). *Journal of Theoretical Biology, 7,* 1–54.

Hamilton, W. D. (1971). The genetical evolution of social behavior, I. In G. C. Williams (Ed.), *Group selection* (pp. 23–43). Chicago: Aldine. (Reprinted from *Journal of Theoretical Biology,* 1964, 7, 1–16)

Harrison, C. J. O. (1969). Helpers at the nest in Australian passerine birds. *Emu, 69,* 30–40.

Hayashi, A. M. (1999, February). Pinker and the brain. *Scientific American, 280*(2), 32–33.

Hebb, D. O. (1949). *The organization of behavior: A neuropsychological theory.* New York: Wiley.

Hebb, D. O. (1953). Heredity and environment in mammalian behavior. *British Journal of Animal Behaviour, 1,* 43–47.

Hebb, D. O. (1972). *Textbook of psychology* (3rd ed.). Philadelphia: Saunders.

Herrnstein, R. J., & Murray, C. (1994). *The bell curve: Intelligence and class structure in American life*. New York: Free Press.

Hoagland, M., & Dodson, B. (1995). *The way life works*. New York: Times Books.

Hrdy, S. (1977). *The langurs of Abu*. Cambridge: Harvard University Press.

Huttenlocher, P. R., & Dabholkar, A. S. (1997). Regional differences in synaptogenesis in human cerebral cortex. *Journal of Comparative Neurology, 367*, 167–178.

James, W. (1880, October). Great men, great thoughts, and the environment. *Atlantic Monthly, 66* (276), 441–459.

James, W. (1890). *The principles of psychology* (Vol. 1). New York: Holt.

Jaynes, J. (1973). Animate motion in the 17th century. In M. Henle, J. Jaynes, & J. J. Sullivan (Eds.), *Historical conceptions of psychology*. New York: Springer.

Johnston, V. (1999). *Why we feel: The origin and function of human feelings*. Reading, MA: Perseus Books.

Jones, T. A., & Schallert, T. (1992). Overgrowth and pruning of dendrites in adult rats recovering from neocortical damage. *Brain Research, 581*, 156–160.

Jones, T. A., & Schallert, T. (1994). Use-dependent growth of pyramidal neurons after neocortical damage. *Journal of Neuroscience, 14*, 2140–2152.

Joravsky, D. (1970). *The Lysenko affair*. Cambridge: Harvard University Press.

Joyce, G. F. (1992, December). Directed molecular evolution. *Scientific American, 267*(6), 90–97.

Kant, I. (1952). *Critique of judgement*. (*Great books of the Western world*, Vol. 42, pp. 461–613). Chicago: Encyclopaedia Britannica. (Originally published 1790)

Kantovorich, A. (1993). *Scientific discovery: Logic and tinkering*. Albany: State University of New York Press.

Kelsen, H. (1946). *Society and nature: A sociological inquiry*. London: Kegan Paul.

Kenrick, D. T., & Keefe, R. C. (1992). Age preferences in mates reflect sex differences in reproductive strategies. *Behavioral and Brain Sciences, 15*, 75–133.

Kerferd, G. B. (1967). Aristotle. In P. Edwards (Ed.), *The encyclopedia of philosophy* (Vol. 1, pp. 151–162). New York: Macmillan.

Kihlstrom, J. F. (1987). The cognitive unconscious. *Science, 237*, 1445–1452.

Köhler, W. (1925). *The mentality of the apes* (2nd rev. ed., E. Winter, Trans.). New York: Harcourt, Brace.

Kohn, A. (1993). *Punished by rewards*. Boston: Houghton Mifflin.

Koshland, D. E., Jr. (1980). *Bacterial chemotaxis as a model behavioral system*. New York: Raven Press.

Koza, J. R. (1992). *Genetic programming: On the programming of computers by means of natural selection*. Cambridge: MIT Press.

Koza, J. R. (1994). *Genetic programming, II: Automatic discovery of reusable programs.* Cambridge: MIT Press.

Laplace, P. S. de. (1902). *A philosophical essay on probabilities* (F. W. Truscott & F. L. Emory, Trans.). New York: Wiley. (Originally published 1814)

Lewontin, R. C., Rose, S., & Kamin, L. J. (1984). *Not in our genes: Biology, ideology, and human nature.* New York: Pantheon.

Lorenz, K. (1981). *The foundations of ethology.* New York: Simon & Schuster.

Løvtrup, S. (1987). *Darwinism: The refutation of a myth.* London: Croom Helm.

Marken, R. S. (1990). Spreadsheet analysis of a hierarchical control system model of behavior. *Behavior Research Methods, Instruments, & Computers, 22,* 349–359. (Reprinted in Marken 1992, pp. 133–156)

Marken, R. S. (1992). *Mind readings: Experimental studies of purpose.* New Canaan, CT: Benchmark.

Mayr, O. (1970). *The origins of feedback control.* Cambridge: MIT Press.

McClelland, J. L., Rumelhart, D. E., & Hinton, G. E. (1986). The appeal of parallel distributed processing. In D. E. Rumelhart, J. L. McClelland, & the PDP Research Group (Eds.), *Parallel distributed processing: Explorations in the microstructure of cognition, Vol. 1: Foundations* (pp. 3–44). Cambridge: MIT Press.

McCracken, G. F. (1984). Communal nursing in Mexican free-tailed bat maternity colonies. *Science, 223,* 1090–1091.

McFarland, D. (1993). *Animal behaviour* (2nd ed.). Harlow, Essex: Longman.

McPhail, C., Powers, W. T., & Tucker, C. T. (1992). Simulating individual and collective action in temporary gatherings. *Social Science Computer Review, 10*(1), 1–28.

Mednick, S. A. (1962). The associative basis of the creative process. *Psychological Review, 69,* 220–232.

Medvedev, Z. A. (1969). *The rise and fall of T. D. Lysenko* (L. G. Lawrence, Trans.). New York: Columbia University Press.

Miller, G. A., Galanter, E., & Pribram, K. (1960). *Plans and the structure of behavior.* New York: Holt, Rinehart & Winston.

Mrosovsky, N. (1990). *Rheostasis: The physiology of change.* New York: Oxford University Press.

Murdock, G. P. (1967). *Ethnographic atlas.* Pittsburgh: Pittsburgh University Press.

Newell, A. (1990). *Unified theories of cognition.* Cambridge: Harvard University Press.

Nietzsche, F. (1967). *The will to power* (W. Kaufman & R. J. Hollingdale, Trans.). New York: Random House. (Originally published 1901)

Packer, C. (1977). Reciprocal altruism in *Papio anubis. Nature, 265,* 441–443.

Paley, W. (1813). *Natural theology* (14th ed.). London: S. Hamilton.

Perkinson, H. J. (1984). *Learning from our mistakes: A reinterpretation of twentieth-century educational theory.* Westport, CT: Greenwood Press.

Peters, R. S., & Mace, C. A. (1967). Psychology. In P. Edwards (Ed.), *The encyclopedia of philosophy* (Vol. 7, pp. 1–27). New York: Macmillan.

Piaget, J. (1972). *The principles of genetic epistemology* (W. Mays, Trans.). London: Routledge & Kegan Paul. (Originally published 1970)

Piaget, J. (1976). Biology and war. In H. E. Gruber & J. J. Vonèche (Eds.), *The essential Piaget* (pp. 38–41). New York: Basic Books. (Originally published 1918)

Piaget, J. (1976). Equilibration processes in the psychobiological development of the child. In H. E. Gruber & J. J. Vonèche (Eds.), *The essential Piaget* (pp. 832–837). New York: Basic Books. (Originally published 1958)

Piaget, J. (1976). Problems of equilibration. In H. E. Gruber & J. J. Vonèche (Eds.), *The essential Piaget* (pp. 838–841). New York: Basic Books. (Originally published 1975)

Piaget, J. (1976). The various forms of knowledge seen as differentiated organs of the regulation of functional exchanges with the external world. In H. E. Gruber & J. J. Vonèche (Eds.), *The essential Piaget* (pp. 842–859). New York: Basic Books. (Originally published 1967)

Pinker, S. (1994). *The language instinct.* New York: Morrow.

Pinker, S. (1997). *How the mind works.* New York: Norton.

Pinker, S., & Bloom, P. (1990). Natural language and natural selection. *Brain and Behavioral Sciences, 13,* 707–784.

Plotkin, H. (1994). *Darwin machines and the nature of knowledge.* Cambridge: Harvard University Press.

Plunkett, M. J., & Ellman, J. A. (1997, March). Combinatorial chemistry and new drugs. *Scientific American, 276*(4), 68–73.

Popkin, R. H. (1967). La Mettrie, J. O. de. In P. Edwards (Ed.), *The encyclopedia of philosophy* (Vol. 4, pp. 379–382). New York: Macmillan.

Powers, W. T. (1973). *Behavior: The control of perception.* Chicago: Aldine.

Powers, W. T. (1989). *Living control systems.* Gravel Switch, KY: Control Systems Group.

Powers, W. T. (1991, February). Skinner's mistake. *Control Systems Group Newsletter,* pp. 7–14.

Powers, W. T. (1995). The origins of purpose: The first metasystem transitions. *World Futures, 45,* 125–137.

Powers, W. T. (1999). A model of kinesthetically and visually controlled arm movement. *International Journal of Human-Computer Studies, 50*(6), 463–479.

Powers, W. T., Clark, R. K., & McFarland, R. L. (1960). A general feedback theory of human behavior (Parts 1 & 2). *Perceptual and Motor Skills, 11,* 71–88, 309–323. (Reprinted in Powers 1989, pp. 1–45)

Proctor, R. A. (1993). Computer stimulated associations. *Creativity Research Journal, 6*, 391–400.

Pusey, A. E., & Packer, C. (1992). Infanticide in lions. In S. Parmigiani, F. vom Saal, & B. Svare (Eds.), *Infanticide and parental care.* London: Harwood Academic Press.

Quartz, S. R., & Sejnowski, T. F. (1997). The neural basis of cognitive development: A constructivist manifesto. *Behavioral and Brain Sciences, 20*, 537–596.

Rahn, H. (1979). Acid-base balance and the *milieu intérieur.* In E. D. Robin (Ed.), *Claude Bernard and the internal environment: A memorial symposium* (pp. 179–190). New York: Marcel Dekker.

Reeve, H. K., Westneat, D. F., Noon, W. A., Sherman, P. W., & Aquadro, C. F. (1990). DNA "fingerprinting" reveals high levels of inbreeding in colonies of the eusocial naked mole-rat. *Proceedings of the National Academy of Sciences, 87*, 2496–2500.

Revusky, S. H., & Garcia, J. (1970). Learned associations over long delays. In G. H. Bower (Ed.), *Psychology of learning and motivation* (Vol. 4, pp. 1–83). New York: Academic Press.

Richards, R. J. (1987). *Darwin and the emergence of evolutionary theories of mind and behavior.* Chicago: University of Chicago Press.

Robertson, R. J., & Powers, W. T. (1990). *Introduction to modern psychology: The control-theory view.* Gravel Switch, KY: Control Systems Group.

Robin, E. D. (1979). Limits of the internal environment. In E. D. Robin (Ed.), *Claude Bernard and the internal environment: A memorial symposium* (pp. 257–267). New York: Marcel Dekker.

Rodgers, W., & Rozin, P. (1966). Novel food preferences in thiamine-deficient rats. *Journal of Comparative Physiological Psychology, 61*, 1–4.

Rosenblueth, A., Wiener, N., & Bigelow, J. (1943). Behavior, purpose, and teleology. *Philosophy of Science, 10*, 18–24.

Rosenblueth, A., & Wiener, N. (1950). Purposeful behavior and non-purposeful behavior. *Philosophy of Science, 17*, 318–326.

Runkel, P. J. (1990). *Casting nets and testing specimens: Two grand methods of psychology.* New York: Praeger.

Russell, E. S. (1945). *The directiveness of organic activities.* London: Cambridge University Press.

Rutherford, S. L., & Lindquist, S. (1998). Hsp90 as a capacitor for morphological evolution. *Nature, 396*, 336–342.

Schallert, T., & Jones, T. A. (1993). "Exuberant" neuronal growth after brain damage in adult rats: The essential role of behavioral experience. *Journal of Neurotransplantation and Plasticity, 4*(3), 193–198.

Searle, J. R. (1992). *The rediscovery of the mind.* Cambridge: MIT Press.

Sevenster, P. (1968). Motivation and learning in sticklebacks. In D. Ingle (Ed.), *The central nervous system and fish behavior* (pp. 233–245). Chicago: University of Chicago Press.

Sevenster, P. (1973). Incompatibility of response and reward. In R. A. Hinde & J. Stevenson-Hinde (Eds.), *Constraints on learning: Limitations and predispositions*. London: Academic Press.

Siegler, R. S. (1989). Mechanisms of cognitive development. *Annual Review of Psychology, 40,* 353–379.

Siegler, R. S. (1996). *Emerging minds: The process of change in children's thinking.* New York: Oxford University Press.

Silverman, I., & Eals, M. (1992). Sex differences in spatial abilities: Evolutionary theory and data. In J. H. Barkow, L. Cosmides, & J. Tooby (Eds.), *The adapted mind: Evolutionary psychology and the generation of culture* (pp. 533–549). New York: Oxford University Press.

Simonton, D. K. (1979). Multiple discovery and invention: Zeitgeist, genius, or chance? *Journal of Personality and Social Psychology, 37,* 1603–1616.

Simonton, D. K. (1985). Intelligence and personal influence in groups: Four non-linear models. *Psychological Review, 92,* 532–547.

Simonton, D. K. (1987). Multiples, chance, genius, creativity, and zeitgeist. In D. N. Jackson & J. P. Rushton (Eds.), *Scientific excellence: Origins and assessment* (pp. 98–128). Beverly Hills, CA: Sage.

Simonton, D. K. (1997). Creative productivity: A predictive and explanatory model of career trajectories and landmarks. *Psychological Review, 104*(1), 66–89.

Simonton, D. K. (1999a). Creativity as blind variation and selective retention: Is the creative process Darwinian? *Psychological Inquiry, 10,* 309–328.

Simonton, D. K. (1999b). *Origins of genius: Darwinian perspectives on creativity.* Oxford: Oxford University Press.

Singh, D. (1993). Adaptive significance of female physical attractiveness: Role of waist-to-hip ratio. *Journal of Personality and Social Psychology, 65,* 293–307.

Singh, D. (1997, June 7). *In search of the most alluring female waist-to-hip ratio: Quantifying female physical attractiveness.* Presented at the annual meeting of the Human Behavior and Evolution Society, Tucson, AZ.

Skinner, B. F. (1948). *Walden two.* London: Collier-Macmillan.

Skinner, B. F. (1953). *Science and human behavior.* New York: Free Press.

Skinner, B. F. (1954). Behaviorism at fifty. In T. W. Wann (Ed.). *Behaviorism and phenomenology: Contrasting bases for modern psychology* (pp. 79–97). Chicago: University of Chicago Press.

Skinner, B. F. (1958). Reinforcement today. *American Psychologist, 13,* 94–99.

Skinner, B. F. (1971). *Beyond freedom and dignity.* New York: Knopf.

Skinner, B. F. (1974). *About behaviorism.* New York: Knopf.

Slater, P. J. B. (1985). *An introduction to ethology*. Cambridge: Cambridge University Press.

Staddon, J. E. R. (1983). *Adaptive behavior and learning*. Cambridge: Cambridge University Press.

Symons, D. (1979). *The evolution of human sexuality*. New York: Oxford University Press.

Thornhill, R. (1976). Sexual selection and nuptial feeding behavior in *Bittacus apicalis* (Insecta: Mecoptera). *American Naturalist, 110,* 529–548.

Tolman, E. C. (1932). *Purposive behavior in animals and men*. New York: Century.

Tolman, E. C. (1959). Principles of purposive behavior. In S. Koch (Ed.), *Psychology: A study of a science* (Vol. 2, pp. 92–157). New York: McGraw-Hill.

Trivers, R. L. (1971). The evolution of reciprocal altruism. *Quarterly Review of Biology, 46*(4), 35–57.

Trivers, R. L. (1972). Parental investment and sexual selection. In B. Campbell (Ed.), *Sexual selection and the descent of man*. Chicago: Aldine.

Tylor, Sir E. B. (1958). *Religion in primitive culture*. New York: Harper & Brothers. (Originally published 1871)

Vidal, F., Buscaglia, M., & Vonèche, J. J. (1983). Darwinism and developmental psychology. *Journal of the History of the Behavioral Sciences, 19,* 81–94.

Vining, D. R., Jr. (1986). Social vs. reproductive success. *Behavioral and Brain Sciences, 9,* 167–186.

Waddington, C. H. (1962). *The nature of life*. New York: Atheneum.

Watson, J. B. (1913). Psychology as the behaviorist views it. *Psychological Review, 20,* 158–177.

Weiner, J. (1994). *The beak of the finch: A story of evolution in our time*. New York: Knopf.

Wiener, N. (1961). *Cybernetics: Or control and communication in the animal and the machine*. Cambridge: MIT Press.

Williams, G. C. (1966). *Adaptation and natural selection: A critique of some current evolutionary thought*. Princeton, NJ: Princeton University Press.

Wilson, E. O. (1975). *Sociobiology: The new synthesis*. Cambridge: Belknap Press of Harvard University Press.

Wilson, E. O. (1978). *On human nature*. Cambridge: Harvard University Press.

Wright, R. (1994). *The moral animal: Evolutionary psychology and everyday life*. New York: Pantheon.

Wundt, W. (1912). *An introduction to psychology* (R. Pinter, Trans.). New York: Macmillan.

Index